The Munchausen Complex
Socialization of Violence and Abuse

The Munchausen Complex
Socialization of Violence and Abuse

Dr. Richard L. Matteoli

First Conquer Thyself:

Nemean Press

P.O. Box 8427
Monterey, CA   93943-8427
USA

Matteoli, Richard L.
The Munchausen Complex: Socialization of Violence and Abuse
ISBN 978-0-578-06206-8

Cover image: Cheryl Leff

Cover, design, formatting and editing by Patricia Robinett
Author Suport Coop
PO Box 256; Eugene, Oregon   97440
Phone 541-484-0731

This book is a mandated report to the social body.

ACKNOWLEDGMENTS

If I can stop one heart from breaking,
I shall not live in vain;
If I can ease one life from aching,
Or cool one pain,
Or help one fainting robin
Unto his nest again,
I shall not live in vain.

Emily Dickinson

I thank Marcella Cloos, RDA, for insisting I write this mandated report. I am grateful for Dr. Lynn and Linda Schiveley's research, Rob Robert's correspondences, input from Drs. Frank Parker, James Musser, John Keitel, Joseph Cullo and Scott Faivre. I appreciate the suggestions of Charles R. Brown, and Jeanette Parker, RDA.

Thanks to Geoffrey Falk of cirp.org, Marilyn Milos of nocirc.org, Hugh Young of circumstitions.com, Robert Burney of Joy2MeU.com, Lloyd deMause of psychohistory.com, Drs. Sami Aldeeb Abu-Sahleih, David Chamberlain and Leonard Glick.

My research includes two Internet mailing lists owned and hosted by Gary Burlingame: one for men restoring their prepuces (foreskins) and the other for those interested in Intactivism (the advocacy of eliminating genital alterations of minors of either sex). Also, CatholicsAgainstCircumcision. org and JewsAgainstCircumcision.org are good resources.

Special thanks to Sigismond for helping with the concepts of Transgenerational Munchausen and Munchausen's Collective Transmission from Social Transference, and to John Geisheker and David Stevens for helping develop the concept of Collective Munchausen in Social Agency.

Thanks to Pete Stavrianoudakis and Crystal Haworth for providing the legal references in the Appendix.

LEGAL CONCEPTS
GOVERNING AN INDIVIDUAL'S RIGHTS

Peter S. Stavrianoudakis, Juris Doctor

It must be conceded that a state is not constrained in the exercise of its "police powers" to ignore experience which marks a class of victims nor is it prevented by the "equal protection of the laws" from confining its restrictions to cases where the need is deemed clearest.

Female Genital Mutilation, as counterpart to circumcision, has laid the gauntlet, by seeking through the proper channels to protect a class of citizens who, to date, have had no voice.

Prescribing a select path for males can be accomplished should the proponents save as limited by constitutional provisions safeguarding individual rights, so that a state may choose means to protect itself and its citizens against criminal or pseudo- criminal violations of its laws and with due regard to the comparative gravity of the criminal offense and whether their consequences are more or less injurious are matters for its determination.

The rational basis equal protection test is not appropriate for the constitutional evaluation of all criminal classification systems. .

Within constitutional limits, the legislature with sufficient power to define crime is absolute and command of equal protection leaves to lawmaker much leeway to affect separate groups divergently.

However, should Congressional power wane or exhibit signs of political atrophy, individual States may validly call upon its "police powers" into play and isolate a class of victims, seeking to rectify any perceived wrongs.

THE CALIFORNIA
CHILD ABUSE & NEGLECT REPORTING LAW

WHY MUST YOU REPORT?

The primary intent of the reporting law is to *protect the child*.

WHAT IS CHILD ABUSE?

The Penal Code (P.C.) defines child abuse as: "a physical injury which is inflicted by other than accidental means on a child by another person."

(a). A *physical injury* inflicted by other than accidental means on a child. (P.C. 11165.6).

(b). *Willful cruelty or unjustified punishment,* including inflicting or permitting unjustifiable physical pain or mental suffering, or the endangerment of the child's person or health. (P.C. 11165.3). "Mental Suffering" in and of itself not required to be reported. However, it may be reported. (P.C. 11165.4).

(d). Unlawful *corporal punishment or injury,* willfully inflicted, resulting in a traumatic condition. (P.C. 11165.4).

(e). *Neglect* of a child, whether "severe" or "general," must also be reported if the perpetrator is a person responsible for the child's welfare. It includes acts or omissions harming, or threatening to harm the child's health or welfare. (P.C. 11165.2).

WHO REPORTS?

Legally mandated reporters include "child care custodians," "health practitioners," "employees of a child protective agency," and "commercial film and photographic print processors."

State of California
Department of Social Services
Office of Child Abuse Prevention

Perhaps the sentiments contained in the following pages
are not yet sufficiently fashionable to procure them general favor.
A long habit of not thinking a thing wrong
gives it a superficial appearance of being right
and raises at first a formidable outcry in defense of custom.
Time makes more converts than reason.

Thomas Paine

CONTENTS

INTRODUCTION

Hearts know more than books can ever tell

This mandated report is academic tough love, not an *apologia* that clarifies a belief or position without guilt or regret, but rather an *apology* which acknowledges guilt, regret, offense and failure. The purpose of this report is to initiate genuine introspection and honest, open public discourse that will effect important social changes for the benefit of future generations.

A *mandated report* is required to be filed by health care, legal, social service and educational professionals who suspect child abuse, as well as by developers of film. This document is a mandated report covering the socialization of a particular form of abuse — a genital blood ritual euphemistically referred to as *circumcision*. Once the subject is thoroughly explored, as it is in this report, divorced from cultural programming and assumptions, it rapidly becomes clear that circumcision is indeed a form of child abuse and violation. It is also true that *many deaths occur due to genital rituals performed on both sexes — around the world and here in the USA.*

As socialized beings, we are often unaware why we think what we think and why we do what we do. Exploring beneath the surface, we may discover we are not who we imagine we are. Are our subtle perversions and aberrations so different from those of the ancients, or other cultures we label primitive?

Female Genital Mutilation (FGM) is a term Americans use when criticizing the genital cutting of women in foreign cultures, yet the people in those cultures prefer us to call it *circumcision*. And in America we use the word *circumcision* to refer to the genital cutting of males. Yet even some Americans are beginning to call male circumcision *genital reduction*, *genital modification*, *genital alteration* or even *genital mutilation*. The word *mutilate* means *to cut up, destroy, or alter radically*. Calling genital cutting an atrocity is a challenge and we must begin to look objectively at ourselves.

Some books are to be tasted, others to be swallowed; and some few, to be chewed and digested.
Sir Francis Bacon

Investigation is implied in our mandate.
Anakin Skywalker
Attack of the Clones

How am I going to make a report about this? If I say exactly what happened, they'll say I'm mad at headquarters.
Major de Boujolais
Beau Geste

They, they, they.
A good conspiracy
can't be proven...
I'm only paranoid
because they want me
dead.
Jerry Fletcher
Conspiracy Theory

This text is an introductory study and does not presume to be inclusive. The hope is that those who follow will expand understanding and create greater legal and social protection for present and future generations.

This study is interdisciplinary. For the sociologist, socialized child abuse involves individual behavior coupled with a developed social norm. Psychologists may begin to form connections between circumcision and many unfortunate human attitudes and behaviors. For the religious who think of genital blood ritual as obedience to a deity's demand, this report will raise some important questions and suggest a new direction. For the medical profession, may this study be an omen to end morally and ethically questionable behavior. Legislators and the judiciary need to consider the logic and fairness of guaranteeing equal protection under the law for both males and females. For the criminologist, may this report inspire investigation into the possibility that some criminal behavior may be the result of socialized child abuse; they may wish to encourage protective action and advocate prevention. May this mandated report give the legal profession the imperative to prosecute all impropriety. And may its victims begin to heal with this understanding.

The seeking of
one thing will find
another.
Irish Proverb

James Monteleone in his text *Recognition of Child Abuse for the Mandated Reporter* stated:[1]

> Child abuse involves every segment of society and crosses all social, ethnic, religious, and professional lines. The definition of child abuse can range from a narrow focus, limited to intentional inflicted injury, to a broad scope, covering any act that adversely affects the developmental potential of a child. Included in the definition are neglect (acts of omission) and physical, psychological, or sexual injury (acts of commission) by a parent or caretaker. *Intent is not considered in reporting abuse; protection of the child is paramount.* [Emphasis added.]

I was sitting here
eating a muffin and
drinking my coffee
when replaying the
incident in my head,
when I had what
alcoholics refer to
as "A Moment of
Clarity."
Jules
Pulp Fiction

Richard Dawkins in *The Selfish Gene* introduced the concept of *meme*.[2] A *gene* is the vehicle used by nature to pass down physical, as well as some psychological, characteristics. The *meme*, on the other hand is a social, psychological tool often used by humans to pass down cultural identity via imitation. Memes can include customs, language, music, dietary habits, catch phrases, fads, fashion and humor. *Circumcision is a meme*.[3]

If it bleeds,
we can kill it.
Dutch
Predator

Circumcision creates identification for group cohesion and is meant to be transmitted to successive generations for cultural continuity. Collective transmission is a process observable in the book of Genesis:

1. The mythic Abraham initiated circumcision with self-circumcision.
2. He passed it to the next generation by circumcising his children.
3. The circumcision circle was then extended by cutting all people under Abraham's control, including slaves and servants.
4. Collective transmission was fully established when it became the unspoken, unquestionable code of conduct throughout the land.

Most Bible scholars are unaware that the mythic depiction of Abraham is a much later expanded version of the metaphoric Abraham. After the Hebrews' exile in Babylon around 500 BCE (many centuries after Abraham's death), circumcision was added to the original history of the Jewish people. Circumcision as a blood ritual is a non-Jerusalemic acculturation mainly borrowed through influences derived from Egyptian and Midianite pagan cultures.

Conditioning is a form of learning that occurs in both human beings and lower animals when a neural connection is made between two or more positive, negative or neutral stimuli. Fear conditioning, with the use of a negative stimulus such as an electric shock, creates avoidance. Thus fear is a tool employed by parents and group leaders to instill desired behavior. The threat of social ostracism for objecting to cultural practices is a form of fear conditioning. Fear conditioning with physical abuse affects brain development. How fear conditioning (also called "fear by osmosis") becomes culturally-transmitted is demonstrated by *The Parable of the Five Monkeys*:[4]

Start with a cage containing five monkeys. Inside the cage, hang a banana on a string and place a set of stairs under it. Before long, a monkey will go to the stairs and start to climb towards the banana. As soon as he touches the stairs, spray all of the monkeys with cold water.

After a while, another monkey makes an attempt with the same result — all the other monkeys are sprayed with cold water. Pretty soon, when another monkey tries to climb the stairs, the other monkeys will try to prevent it. Now, put away the cold water. Remove one monkey from the cage and replace with a new one. The new monkey sees the banana and wants to climb the stairs. To his surprise and horror, all the other monkeys attack him. After another attempt and attack, he knows that if he tries to climb the stairs, he will be assaulted. Next, remove another of the original five monkeys and replace it with a new one. The newcomer goes to the stairs and is attacked. The previous newcomer takes part in the punishment with enthusiasm! Likewise, replace a third original monkey with a new one, then a fourth, and then a fifth. Every time the newest monkey takes to the stairs, he is attacked. Most of the monkeys that are beating him have no idea why they were not permitted

No aspect of human life seethes with so many unexorcised demons as does sex. No human activity is so hexed by superstition, so haunted by residual tribal lore, and so harassed by socially induced fear.
Harvey Cox

How many ages hence shall our lofty scene be acted over in states unborn and accents yet unknown?
Cassius
Julius Caesar

You had the bodies. They were all locked up... You knew then, and you did nothing.
Jules Levinson
Independence Day

to climb the stairs or why they are participating in the beating of the newest monkey.

After replacing all the original monkeys, none of the remaining monkeys have ever been sprayed with cold water. Nevertheless, no monkey ever again approaches the stairs to try for the banana. Why not? Because as far as they know *that's the way it's always been done around here*.

We have relieved our own pain by inflicting it on others.
Philip Caputo
A Rumor of War

Fashions change. Rituals change. Laws change. We can change our fear-based, conditioned behavior. *Modus vivendi* is an arrangement between conflicting parties to live peacefully as they work toward a new way of living.

PSYCHOLOGICAL CONDITIONS

The following are psychological conditions from the Diagnostic and Statistical Manual of Mental Disorders (DSM-IV), that lead people to perpetrate Munchausen behavior, as well as conditions created in its victims:

Our technology has exceeded our humanity.
Sotascope
Sentinel

DSM-IV
Acute Stress Disorder
Acute Stress Reaction
Adjustment Disorders
Antisocial Personality Disorder
Body Dysmorphic Disorder
Borderline Personality Disorder
Conduct Disorder
Conversion Disorder
Culture-Bound Syndrome
Defensive Functioning
Delusional Disorder
Depersonalization Disorder
Depressive Disorders
Dissociative Disorder
Factitious Disorders —
    including Munchausen behaviors
Gender Identity Disorder
Histrionic Disorder
Hypersomnia Due To …
Insomnia Related To …
Narcissistic Personality Disorder
Nightmare Disorder
Obsessive-Compulsive Disorder
Oppositional Defiant Disorder
Orgasmic Disorders

Pain Disorders
Paranoid Personality Disorder
    Obsessional PPD
    Paranoid Erotomania
Paraphilias
Personality Change Due To …
Post-traumatic Stress Disorder
Problems Related to Abuse or Neglect
Reactive Attachment Disorder
Schizoid Personality Disorder
Schizophrenia
Schizotypical Personality Disorder
Sexual Aversion Disorder
Sexual Arousal Disorder
Sexual Dysfunction Due To …
Sexual Masochism
Sexual Sadism
Shared Psychotic Disorder
Sleep Terror Disorder
Social Phobia

NON DSM-IV
Child Sexual Abuse Accommodation
Compassion Fatigue
Dacryphilia
Diffusion of Responsibility
Direct and Indirect Incest

I wasn't strong enough to save you.
Anakin Skywalker
Attack of the Clones

Disability Fetishism
Dorian Gray Syndrome
Emotional Incest
Genitally focused anxiety disorder
Piquerism
Rape Trauma Syndrome
Societal Stockholm Syndrome
Stigmatic-eligibilic (paradox)
Body Integrity Identity Disorder:
    Acrotomophilia
    Apotemnophilia
    Teratophilia
Stockholm Syndrome
Transformation Fetishism
    PROPOSED
Attenuated Homicide
Attenuated Filicide
Attenuated Infanticide
Attenuated Neonaticide
Clitoral Enhancement
Cultural Post-traumatic Attachment

Cultural Repetition Compulsion
Isisic Disorder
Induced Acrotophilia
Induced Teratophilia
Malignant Hero Syndrome
Munchausen Complex
    Agency
    Social Agency
    Collective Transmission
    For Profit
    Collective Profit
    Social Transference
    Transgenerational
Psychosexual Homicide
Societal Child Sexual Abuse
    Accommodation
Societal Post-traumatic Attachment
Societal Repetition Compulsion
Societal Sexual Harassment
Societal Stalking

We are only interested in friendship. Why do you attack us?
Zarkov
Why not?
Ming the Merciless
Flash Gordon

I'm going to track this thing down until we're eyeball to eyeball — then I'm going to kill it.
Alamo Joe
Werewolf

A BRIEF INTRODUCTION TO CIRCUMCISION AS A MANIFESTATION OF MUNCHAUSEN SYNDROME

Thousands of years ago circumcision, an insidious form of ancient pagan violence, began to infiltrate what has now become the Judeo-Christian-Islamic world. It became part of us individually and socially and we became part of it. People born outside our system shake their heads and wonder how it ever happened. How did this form of sexual molestation spread into the fabric of our lives until it became nearly synonymous with *conscientious parenting*?

Circumcision is a remnant of full human sacrifice. Since full human sacrifice eventually became frowned on, the Judeo-Christian-Islamic religions adopted, practiced and maintained circumcision as a scaled down human sacrifice, a *mock death ritual*.[5] Then a little over a century ago the opportunistic medical industry muddied the waters further as it entered the fray, claiming circumcision was a correction for the *sin* of masturbation. Routine Infant Circumcision (RIC) was hailed as a cure-all and by the last half of the 20th century (RIC) became nearly universal in the USA.

Perhaps I can find new ways to motivate them.
Darth Vader
Return of the Jedi

The only way to break the bonds of this deeply entrenched, socialized child abuse is through education. The will world change when parents and professionals see things differently and determine to protect and respect the children in their care from sharp knives and millennia of ignorance.

Circumcision is an intentional genital wounding, a violent injury for the sake of religious and social identity. As with other forms of sexual abuse, the topic of circumcision is taboo. Some ways adults enforce their values on children, like ear piercing, seem to be innocuous and others are quite destructive but the bottom line in all abuse is the same: adults have overwhelmed a child and intentionally hurt his or her body. They have taught the child that he or she is powerless. Without healing, some degree of lifelong PTSD results. Circumcision is not just an accidental wounding. It is a psychosexual crime with a perpetrator and victim. The unfortunate outcome of abuse is that this generation's victim becomes the next generation's perpetrator.

Portions of this report will undoubtedly stir the emotions. Child abuse is a tough subject and disturbing to think about. It is difficult to read or write about circumcision. Difficulty increases when contradicting socialization. When a superstition or ritual like circumcision permeates most, if not all, of society it becomes a secret, silent, *unspoken* cultural given. This creates an atmosphere of censorship within individuals themselves, their interpersonal, familial, community and professional relationships and in societal systems such as religion, medicine and the law. No one dares to question it.

Rituals most often employ *specialized agents* within the social body who are thought to possess extraordinary and sometimes mystic knowledge. In primitive societies the specialized agents were usually *shamans* and *elder wise women,* or what our modern thought perceives as the *witch doctor* and *witch.* As societies secularized, professions replaced shamanism. Medicine has colluded with religion and usurped circumcision's primitive origins. The witch doctor and witch are now replaced by physicians, nurses and Catholic nuns. Within the Munchausen Complex, circumcision is a crime with a victim. James Monteleone in his text *Recognition of Child Abuse for the Mandated Reporter* (see page vii in this book) stated:[6]

> Sexual abuse is a form of child abuse and must be reported to state child protective services. If the perpetrator is not a caregiver, the sexual activity is sexual assault and may not fall into the category of behaviors reportable to state protective services, but must be reported to a local law enforcement sex

crimes unit. The sex crimes unit deals with perpetrators of sex crimes who have no role in the child's care but are usually known to the victim or the victim's family. The sex offender often pursues this practice as a career and will abuse many children over the course of time.

According to John Douglas of the FBI, serial sexual predators are *narcissists*. *Narcissism* is beyond healthy self-esteem. Narcissists live in patterns of grandiosity in fantasy and/or behavior. They need admiration and lack empathy. The condition begins in early childhood and possesses various predictable elements such as an exaggerated sense of self-importance, fantasies of unlimited power, beauty, and beliefs that they are special with entitlements. Narcissists are interpersonally exploitive and are unwilling or unable to recognize the feelings and needs of others. Also, narcissists are often envious of others and believe others are envious of them.

Narcissism has a genetic component that parallels the personality trait of aggression. Psychoanalyst Karen Horney developed the NPA Personality theory where: N = Narcissism; P = Perfectionism; and, A = Aggression.[7] Variability occurs because each parent possesses a genotype, so individuals may possess a single factor from one parent or have two of a trait from both parents. A person who has one of each has *npa*, while another may have *nnpa*, or *nppa*, and so on. Also, gene expressivity is a factor regarding how strong of an influence the gene manifests itself.

In *Malignant Self Love — Narcissism Revisited* Shmuel (Sam) Vaknin wrote:[8]

> The narcissist is an actor in a melodrama, yet forced to remain behind the scenes. The scene takes center stage instead. The narcissist does not cater at all to his own needs. Contrary to his reputation, the narcissist does not "love" himself in any sense of the word. He feeds off other people who hurl back at him an image that he projects to them. This is their sole function in his world: to reflect, to admire, to applaud, to detest — in a word, to assure him that he exists. Otherwise, they have no right to tax his time, energy, or emotions — so he feels. The narcissist's ego is weak and lacks clear borders. Many of the ego functions are projected. The superego is sadistic and punishing. The id is unrestrained. Primary objects in the narcissist's childhood were badly idealized and destroyed… He becomes unscrupulous, never bothered by the constant use he makes of his milieu (surroundings), is indifferent to the consequences of his actions, the damage and the pain that he inflicts on others and even the social condemnation and sanctions that he often has to

Violent offenders usually begin where they feel most comfortable and at home.
John Douglas
Journey into Darkness

We all began as something else. Was hard for me to accept too.
Purifier
The Chronicles of Riddick

Who are you kidding? You have no feelings to hurt.
Roger
North by Northeast

endure. The narcissist does not suffer from a faulty sense of causation. He is not oblivious to the likely outcomes of his actions and to the price he may have to pay. But he doesn't care.

The narcissist lives in a world of all or nothing, of a constant "to be or not to be"... Thus, every minor disagreement with a source of narcissistic supply — another person — is interpreted as a threat to the narcissist's very self-definition... The narcissist has to condition his human environment to refrain from expressing criticism and disapproval of him or of his actions and decisions... The narcissist — wittingly or not — utilizes people to buttress his self image and sense of self-worth. As long and in as much as they are instrumental in achieving these goals — he holds them in high regard, they are valuable to him. He sees them only through his lens... The narcissist also takes forms hermetic or exclusive, cult-like, social circles, which share his delusions (Pathological Narcissistic Space). The function of these social cohorts is to serve as a psychological entourage and to provide "objective" proof of the narcissist's self-importance and grandeur. The narcissist convinces himself — by first convincing others — that he is in the process of making significant achievements... The narcissist represses the knowledge that it all rests on falsities.

The narcissist derives his Narcissistic Supply from Primary and Secondary sources. But this supply is used by the narcissistic much the same as one uses perishable goods. He uses the supply to substitute for certain ego functions. At first, he uses his False Self with the aim of obtaining Primary Narcissistic supply source by demonstrating his superiority and uniqueness. This he does by putting on his intellect and knowledge. Once this phase is over the narcissist believes that his excellence is established, securing a constant flow of Narcissistic Supply and narcissistic accumulation. His False Self is satisfied and exits the scene. It will not reappear unless the supply is threatened.

Child Sexual Abuse Accommodation Syndrome (CSAAS) was introduced by psychiatrist Roland Summit in 1983.[9] The Syndrome explains inconsistent and variable behaviors in child abuse victims. CSAAS occurs as a coping mechanism in many abused children where five (but not necessarily all) reactions may occur:

1. secrecy
2. helplessness
3. entrapment and accommodation
4. delayed, unconvincing disclosure
5. retraction of the disclosure

All reactions of the child with CSAAS apply to circumcision. The actions and defenses of adults perpetrating circumcision apply as well. Child abuse is often familial and generational. CSAAS is the child's reaction. *Societal Child Sexual Abuse Accommodation Syndrome* (SCSAAS) occurs when the abuse is a socially sanctioned event. This societal syndrome has become endemic in Judaism, Islam, and American Christianity.

With circumcision *secrecy* does not always appear to be a direct factor, as some circumcisions are public events. Yet secrecy is inherent in the denial that circumcision is an act of sexual abuse. Manipulation is present on several layers. Parents are not fully informed in either religious or medical circumcisions, for if they were they would never consent. The secretive assault is a shock to the victim, whether an infant, child or teen, as he is not fully informed, for if he was, he would never consent. Older children are tricked into circumcision by making light of the pain and shaming them for resisting or by having them circumcised when they are under anesthesia for another surgery. African boys and girls and Muslim boys are promised festivities, gold, gifts, special foods, adult status and future marriage. There is always a threat of negative consequences for those who refuse to comply.

When a victim or spectator cannot question, prevent or stop abuse, the result is *learned helplessness*. Children cannot protect themselves from adults and powerful social forces — but neither can concerned adults protect the child or themselves from this huge social bulldozer — they have all been *entrapped*. *Learned helplessness* is re-experienced and reinforced with each violent act witnessed. Victims and observers alike are forbidden to publicly question this socially sanctioned blood ritual. To disclose would destroy the family and endanger the social system, so in the case of circumcision *accommodation* becomes a perceived social virtue and the group is bonded in blood, guilt and shame.

If and when a victim finally breaks the silence barrier and discloses the abuse, the fact that the *disclosure* was *delayed* raises a question: Why did the child not disclose the abuse earlier? People are less convinced.

When disclosure occurs, the tendency is for abusers to deny, threaten and punish and the child will often *retract* his complaint in response. The child is plagued with deep inner fears that his actions actually decide the fate of the family — or group — and that cannot happen. After all, his very survival depends on the adults around him.[10,11]

History is a nightmare from which I am trying to awake.
James Joyce

Serial killers play a most dangerous game. The more we understand the way they play, the more we can stack the odds against them.
John Douglas
Mind Hunter

Meditate on this I will.
Yoda
Attack of the Clones

Stockholm Syndrome (SS) or loyalty to one's captors, is a rare condition, but *Societal Stockholm Syndrome* (SSS) is common among battered women, due to society's failure to protect them and SSS has been used successfully in court cases. Circumcision produces a similar form of *Societal Stockholm Syndrome* and intergenerational actions and reactions may be perceived as a *Societal Child Sexual Abuse Accommodation Syndrome*.

THE LIE

What is called *circumcision* today has little resemblance to the original ritual. There is a significant difference between circumcision past and present. The ancients differentiated between the *foreskin* and *prepuce*. The prepuce is the skin that covers the glans penis. In Greek, the word is *posthe*. The foreskin is only the skin that extends beyond the glans penis. The Greek word for the foreskin is *akroposthion*.[12] This verbal distinction also applies to the words used to describe the *foreskin* in the Torah.

Two Hebrew words were used for circumcision: *namal* and *muwl*. *Namal* only cuts the overhang foreskin. *Muwl* means to blunt an edge shorter.[13] It was only after the death of Jesus, around 140 AD, that circumcision took an official dramatic twist. Many Jewish men would pull on their remaining prepuce to lengthen it, because although in Greece nudity was allowed, to show the glans was considered an obscenity. After that time, a new tribal standard was established -- all preputial tissue was cut away and the full glans penis was exposed so Jewish men could no longer escape their heritage. Even then, the sensitive frenum was not removed in traditional Jewish ritual circumcision.

REMEMBER

And please remember, to repeat, James Monteleone in his text *Recognition of Child Abuse for the Mandated Reporter* stated:[14]

Sexual abuse is a form of child abuse and must be reported to state child protective services. If the perpetrator is not a caregiver, the sexual activity is sexual assault and may not fall into the category of behaviors reportable to state protective services, but must be reported to a local law enforcement sex crimes unit. The sex crimes unit deals with perpetrators of sex crimes who have no role in the child's care but are usually known to the victim or the victim's family. The sex offender often pursues this practice as a career and will abuse many children over the course of time.

KARL FREIDRICH VON MUNCHAUSEN

The German Baron who told tall tales

This book owes its name to *Baron Karl Freidrich von Munchausen,* an 18th century German baron who served in the German army and later was assigned with the Russians during two Turkish Wars against the Ottoman Empire.

After retiring in 1760, it was his habit to entertain others with extraordinary stories about his military and hunting experiences.

Rudolph Raspe created a myth around his friend Munchausen by publishing a book containing his fables, though not all the stories were the baron's.

Connecting the Munchausen name to *Munchausen Syndrome* indicates that, like the Baron's extraordinary stories, the claims of those exhibiting Munchausen behavior are not true — they are fabricated and exaggerated.

Similar to Baron von Munchausen's bold and dashing tales of adventure, the stories of those perpetrating Munchausen behavior can have serious, disastrous and even deadly effects on others.

US TWO

A. A. Milne

Wherever I am, there's always Pooh,
There's always Pooh and me.
Whatever I want to do, he wants to do.
"Where are you going to-day?" says Pooh:
"Well, that's very odd 'Cos I was too.
Let's go together," says Pooh, says he,
"Let's go together," says Pooh.

"What's twice eleven?" I said to Pooh.
("Twice what?" Said Pooh to me.)
"I think it ought to be twenty-two."
"Just what I think myself," said Pooh.
"It wasn't an easy sum to do,
But that's what it is," said Pooh, said he.
"That's what it is," said Pooh.

"Let's look for dragons," I said to Pooh.
"Yes, let's," said Pooh to me.
We crossed the river and found a few –
"Yes, those are dragons all right," said Pooh.
"As soon as I saw their beaks I knew.
That's what they are," said Pooh, said he.
"That's what they are," said Pooh.

"Let's frighten the dragons," I said to Pooh.
"That's right," said Pooh to me.
"I'm not afraid," I said to Pooh.
And I held his paw and I shouted "Shoo!
Silly old dragons!" — And off they flew.
"I wasn't afraid," said Pooh, said he.
"I'm never afraid to with you."

So wherever I am, there's always Pooh.
There's always Pooh and me.
"What would I do?" I said to Pooh,
"If it wasn't for you," and Pooh said: "True,
It isn't much fun for one, but two
Can stick together," says Pooh, says he.
"That's how it is," says Pooh.

MUNCHAUSEN

Both the petal and the thorn belong to the rose

When someone calls for attention by harming themselves, it is called *Munchausen Syndrome* in honor of Baron Karl Freidrich von Munchausen who fictionalized his military and hunting exploits. When one person harms another (usually someone under their care, such as an infant, child or elder) and subsequently gains attention by becoming involved in their victim's medical treatment, it is called *Munchausen Syndrome by Proxy*. This section of our mandated report explains *Munchausen Syndrome* and *Munchausen by Proxy* and how they spread throughout the family and the social body.

MUNCHAUSEN SYNDROME (MS)

In 1951, Sir Richard Asher, an English physician, introduced the term *Munchausen Syndrome*.[1] *Munchausen Syndrome* is a mental disorder in which a person fabricates signs and symptoms of illness for attention and sympathy. Munchausen perpetrators are not hypochondriacs who actually think they are ill. A Munchausen patient knows their condition is false. It is not unusual for some of them to actually poison themselves with medications, toxic substances or bodily wastes. They do not always clearly understand that their motivation is to obtain the attention and sympathy of others.

People with *Munchausen Syndrome* often exhibit an extensive knowledge of hospitals and medical terminology. They are eager to agree to tests, operations or other procedures. After treatment, their conditions typically become more severe. Signs and symptoms mysteriously change when treatment should have been successful. Symptoms usually exist only when the patient is alone.

When confronted by someone who realizes they are fabricating, they have been known to immediately remove themselves from care and go elsewhere. Thus, they have a history of treatment in numerous locations and often bear

You'd think at a certain point all these atypical somethings would amount to a typical something.
Dr. Sayer
Awakenings

What a vivid imagination.
Indiana Jones
Indiana Jones and the Temple of Doom

multiple surgical scars. Munchausen individuals are reluctant to have health care providers meet with their family members. People with *Munchausen Syndrome* have problems with self-esteem. According to the American Psychiatric Association *Munchausen Syndrome* is a form of *Factitious Disorder.*[2] *The Merck Manual* states:

> Commonly, there is an early history of emotional and physical abuse. Patients appear to have problems with their identity, intense feelings, inadequate impulse control, a deficient sense of reality, brief psychotic episodes and unstable interpersonal relationships. Their need to be taken care of conflicts with their inability to trust authority figures, whom they manipulate and continually provoke or test. Feelings of guilt and expiation are obvious.

MUNCHAUSEN SYNDROME BY PROXY (MSBP)

In 1977, Roy Meadow, an English pediatrician, introduced *Munchausen Syndrome by Proxy* (MSBP).[3] MSBP occurs when the person seeking attention causes harm by manufacturing injury, illness or disease in another person. The perpetrator's payoff is the attention gained from his or her involvement in their victim's treatment. This way they become an alter-patient without personally suffering injury. Most often MSBP involves a parent or caretaker harming a child in their care. The child is the means to an end.

The *DSM-IV* defines MSBP as a form of *Factitious Disorder.*[4] *MSBP is a crime with a victim.*

Munchausen Syndrome by Proxy perpetrators are indifferent to the well-being of their victims who are usually infants or toddlers. But older children, adults and the elderly may also be victimized. Children may become permanently deformed. Often there is a history of sibling death. Common victim symptoms are diarrhea, vomiting, seizures and respiratory failure. As with practitioners of *Munchausen Syndrome* who leave when confronted, the proxy perpetrator will take the victim under their care elsewhere. MSBP perpetrators are usually — but not always — mothers.

Health care providers, attorneys, social servants and even the courts are reluctant to believe that a mother would intentionally inflict harm on a child. Often professionals are so busy trying to find a proper diagnosis that they overlook the larger picture. Stopping the abusive behavior is difficult even when the perpetrator undergoes long-term therapy. Notification to Child Protective Services and arrest are often necessary to stop perpetrator behavior.

There are three types of *Munchausen Syndrome by Proxy* perpetrators: 1) help seekers, 2) doctor addicts and 3) active inducers.[5,6]

HELP SEEKERS are mothers who seek medical attention for their children in order to communicate their own anxiety, exhaustion, depression or frank inability to care for the child. Case examples of help seekers include homes studded with domestic violence, marital discord, unwanted pregnancies or single parenthood.

DOCTOR ADDICTS are obsessed with obtaining medical treatment for nonexistent illnesses in their children. The falsifications of doctor addicts consist of inaccurate reporting of history and symptoms. Such mothers believe their children are ill, refuse to accept medical evidence to the contrary and then develop their own treatment for the children. The children usually are older than six years and the [caretakers] are suspicious, antagonistic and paranoid. These mothers tend to be distrustful and angry.

ACTIVE INDUCERS induce illness in children by dramatic methods. These mothers are anxious, depressed and employ extreme degrees of denial, dissociation of affect and paranoid projection. Secondary gain for these mothers includes a controlling relationship with the treating physician and acknowledgment from medical staff as outstanding caretakers.

In another manifestation of MSBP, a perpetrators will induce a condition in order to heroically "save" the victim thereby showing they are a concerned caretaker. Sometimes health care providers — including nurses of both sexes — do this. Their actions are considered a type of *Munchausen Syndrome by Proxy*. This phenomenon may very well be a distinct category of Munchausen that should be researched and redefined as *Munchausen Malignant Hero Syndrome*.

Diagnosing *Munchausen Syndrome by Proxy* is difficult and may be over-diagnosed. Support groups are available for those falsely accused of *Munchausen Syndrome by Proxy*. It is always possible that a caretaker has legitimate concerns about his or her child's health that are not being adequately addressed. Some people wrongly prosecuted for *Munchausen Syndrome by Proxy* have had children with undiagnosed genetic defects.

MUNCHAUSEN COMPLEX

Munchausen Syndrome and *Munchausen Syndrome by Proxy* are conditions involving harm to self or another. When Munchausen behaviors enter the

There may be times when we are powerless to prevent injustice, but there must never be a time when we fail to protest.
Elie Wiesel

Through them I will be invincible! My power will be absolute.
Kane
Dr. Who

We have to make them see it's for their own good.
Dr. Brodeus
Miss Evers Boys

greater picture of the social arena, together they form a *Munchausen Complex* and the following designations are hereby proposed:

MUNCHAUSEN SYNDROME IN SOCIAL TRANSFERENCE

You can't see the wind; you can only see the rustling in the wind.
Eric
7th Heaven

When abusive Munchausen behavior manifests in a social context and becomes commonplace and acceptable, a social identity shift occurs through *social transference*. *Transference* is defined as the displacement of one's unresolved conflicts, dependencies and aggressions onto a substitute object. With male circumcision, the object is a specific part of the genitals, the prepuce.

> MUNCHAUSEN SYNDROME IN SOCIAL TRANSFERENCE is the identity transference of the self into a social group that practices forms of Munchausen behavior.

TRANSGENERATIONAL MUNCHAUSEN SYNDROME

The individual is not a killer, but the group is and by identifying with it the individual is transformed into a killer.
Arthur Koestler

Transgenerational Munchausen Syndrome is the passing of *Munchausen Syndrome by Proxy* abuses to successive generations. The purpose is to feed the need for belonging through *attachment seeking*.[7] Transgenerational Munchausen practices are not fully acculturated.

> TRANSGENERATIONAL MUNCHAUSEN SYNDROME is Munchausen generational abuse in family and social groups and a step toward acculturation.

MUNCHAUSEN SYNDROME IN COLLECTIVE TRANSMISSION

Munchausen Syndrome in Collective Transmission extends transgenerational abuses into a community, society or culture. Actions become social *mores* -- customs and conventions. *Mores* embody the fundamental collective views of a group. They are accepted without question and they give power to those who perform social ritual. By ostensibly honoring the social body's ritual honors the individual as part of the group. Group identity gives security through social cohesion and conformity.

Parenting has individual significance and social consequences.
Cornell West

Collective Munchausen can involve physical beautification or signify grieving. As with other forms of Munchausen, Collective Munchausen includes wounding.[8] The wounding is usually, though not always, performed by one member of the group onto another.[9]

A multi-layered example of Munchausen Syndrome, that forms the basic

Munchausen Complex is the Genesis myth of Abraham's circumcision.

1. First, Abraham cut his own foreskin, which is an example of *Munchausen Syndrome*.

2. Second, when Abraham circumcised his son Ishmael (who was not ill) he passed unnecessary physical damage to his son who was under his care. The circumcision of Ishmael is an example of *Munchausen Syndrome by Proxy* under the category of *Active Inducer*.

3. Third, Abraham circumcised the members of his household, servants and slaves. This could be thought of as *Transgenerational Munchausen Syndrome*.

4. And now that this genital blood ritual has been widely practiced in the Abrahamic tradition (Judaism, American and Coptic Christianity and Islam) for many successive generations it is an example of *Munchausen Syndrome in Collective Transmission*.

A more recent example is Queen Victoria of England who was convinced that members of European royalty were descendants of the lost tribes of Israel. She introduced circumcision into the British royal family and within decades circumcision spread throughout English-speaking countries.

> MUNCHAUSEN SYNDROME IN COLLECTIVE TRANSMISSION is the transmission of destructive behavior, harmful ritual, condition or simulation of disease taken to clinical significance whether to a person or another person or group of persons. The act involves the transference of an alleged identity into interpersonal, family, community, societal or cultural relationships. The act often operates by deliberate transmission from one generation to subsequent generations of unresolved conflicts, dependencies and aggressions onto an objectified substitute body part of heirs and associates.

SELF-WOUNDING & DENIAL

Munchausen's self-socialization involves a person acting against his own or someone else's body for social acceptance. These acts glorify pain and deny pleasure. They are often dedicated to a deity or another they imagine will be pleased with their behavior.

Self-wounding such as cutting, is often due to an inability to cope with overwhelming feelings and is also a trait of *Borderline Personality Disorder*. Incest, rape and physical abuse may eventually lead victims to self-harm. Self-

What we do in life echoes in eternity.
Maximus
Gladiator

History fades into fable; fact becomes clouded with doubt and controversy; the statue falls from the pedestal. Columns, arches, pyramids, what are they but heaps of sand; and their epitaphs, but characters written in the dust.
Washington Irving

Loyalty to petrified opinions never yet broke a chain or freed a human soul.
Mark Twain

wounding is observable in lower animals that experience social deprivation. In humans, self-wounding is most common in those who have been denied healthy self-assertion and adequate self-determination. Self-wounders create physical pain hoping to temporarily distract themselves from painful thoughts, memories and emotions. Often self-wounders report euphoria -- a result of naturally produced opiates and beta-endorphins.[10]

Self-wounding is thought to be an attempt to establish autonomy and affirmation for the disempowered. Body mortification mediates guilt and inner conflict. Pain is romanticized and glorified to lend meaning to the vacuum of a perceived impoverished existence.

Asceticism involves severe self-discipline and abstention from natural bodily needs and pleasures; fasting is one form, celibacy is another. Religious methods used in hopes of reaching the higher self are *prayer and fasting*. St. Simeon the Elder practiced his own form of *asceticism* by spending the entire period of Lent standing and neither eating or drinking.[11] When acted out in front of others, asceticism can be used to glorify the ascetic and his society. Asceticism may also serve to establish an interpersonal hierarchy.

WOUNDING FOR SOCIAL PURPOSES

Wounding can be performed by the persons themselves onto their own bodies, but most often the actions are performed by a *ritual expert,* such as a shaman or physician, onto another member of the community.

Some forms of *Munchausen Syndrome in Collective Transmission* may be minor, but other forms can become severe. Some become *Culture-Bound Syndromes*. Examples of wounding for the social purpose follow below and more can be found in the next chapter, *Genital Play*:

FLAGELLATION

Flagellation involves in part, the creation of a masochistic "sacred" pain. By denying pleasure and inflicting pain, the idea is that the self-flagellant will be able to mediate and control inner moral conflict. During the plague self-flagellation was used as both a penance and cure.

One of the first Catholic uses of social self-flagellation was introduced by Saint Peter Damian in the 11th century. Soon afterward, Saint Anthony of Padua initiated the Sect of the Flagellants. Often they would march to a church chanting and carrying banners, encircle it, strip to the waist and beat themselves

When combat trauma results in domestic violence and pathologic family life, there is an inter-generational transmission of trauma.
Jonathan Shay
Achilles in Vietnam

Society is frivolous and shreds its day into scraps, its conservations into ceremonies and escapes.
Ralph Waldo Emerson

I am ready to face the trials.
Obi-Wan Kenobi
The Phantom Menace

with whips. In 1261 Pope Alexander IV prohibited self-flagellation and in 1349 Pope Clement VI followed suit. Regardless of Papal edicts, however, local clergy endorsed the practice. Saint Theresa, who founded the Carmelites, practiced severe self-flagellation. One Carmelite nun, Caterina of Cardona, used chains and hooks.

Within two centuries the official prohibition was turned around and self-flagellation was officially accepted. In 1508 community flagellation was given a *Bull of Benefaction and Indulgence* by Pope Julian II and in 1536 Pope Paul III gave flagellation his blessing. This led to Spanish social whippings called the *Disciplina*.

When reality becomes unbearable, the mind must withdraw from it and create a world of artificial perfection.
Arthur Koestler

In 1928 Josemaria Escriva founded the *Opus Dei* (Latin for "work of God"). Members of the Opus Dei have a strict schedule of prayer and reading, often with self-mortifications that include self-flagellation while wearing a spiked leg band called a *cicile*.[12]

Self-flagellation is practiced during the 40-day festival celebrating Lent in the Philippines that ends with mock crucifixions on Easter Sunday. Self-flagellation is currently practiced in some convents and brotherhoods in Spain, Italy, Mexico, Latin America and the American state of New Mexico.

Most of our so-called reasoning consists in arguments for going on believing as we already do.
James Harvey Robinson

For Shia Muslims, the *Moharram* is an annual holy day of mourning within a ten-day festival. Self-flagellation is practiced using fists, whips and chains. *Moharram* commemorates the martyrdom of Hazrat Imam Hosein who was the Prophet Muhammad's grandson.[13]

Judaic flagellation preceded the Catholic practice. Dorothy Hayden, in *Masochism as a Spiritual Path*, stated:[14]

> Flagellation was part of the Jewish tradition 500 years after Christ; to lash one another with scourges after they had finished their prayers and confessed their sins.

PIERCING

You don't appreciate my enthusiasm.
Yves
Tango and Cash

Ear piercing is worldwide. Roman soldiers pierced their nipples. American Plains Indians practiced a *Vow to the Sun* ritual in which men threaded animal sinews through piercings between their muscles. They would then suspend themselves from ropes until they passed out.[15] Mayans pierced their tongues for virility and courage. Eskimos pierced the lower lip of infant girls. Ethiopians inserted large plates in their lips. And in India they skewered the tongue to maintain silence.

Piercing with object implantation may be a subcultural statement of self-empowerment to counter perceived interpersonal, familial and social control. Piercing is a present-day fetish in America. Common piercing sites include the genitals, navel, nipples, eyebrows, nose, cheeks, lips, tongue and as far back as the uvula. Complications of oral piercings include: local inflammation of the tongue and elsewhere, bacteremia, trauma to the gingiva (gums), tissue hyperplasia and/or tissue loss around the teeth, as well as cracked and fractured teeth.[16]

TATTOOING

The word *tattoo* is from the Tahitian word *tatau*, coupled with the Marquesian word *ta-tu*. The Polynesian islands had limited contact with one another so there was no uniform tribal marking and individual creativity was accepted but people were criticized if they were not tattooed.

Tattooing can indicate hierarchy. On one Marquesian island the chief's oldest son had to have an ancestry tattoo before he could succeed to the throne. Tattoos can indicate maturity level and increased social obligations. For example, a particular tattoo at the age of twelve indicated a young woman could make bread.

In Samoa the lower body was tattooed mainly for adornment, not as a rigid tribal indicator. The Maori of New Zealand covered their faces with tattoos. Every man decorated himself to his choosing while a woman would only tattoo her lips and chin.

In Europe tattooing can be traced back five millennia to the "Ice Man" in Italy whose tattoos correspond to acupuncture points.[17]

Red-haired Caucasian Celtic mummies dating from the same era have been found as far east as China. One mummy appears to be a priestess whose red forehead tattoo resembles the *tilak* worn by present day Hindu women in India[18] — a symbol of the spiritual *third eye*.[19]

2500-year-old Russian mummies have animal tattoos. Scandinavian and Northern Europeans were tattooed with family crests until the 8th Century when tattooing was prohibited by the Pope.

The Caddo Native Americans would cut a design into the skin and rub charcoal into the cuts. The design might extend from the forehead to the nose and all the way down to the chin. Drawings of animals were tattooed on men's bodies. Women accentuated the corners of their eyes with tattoos.

All actions are judged by the motives prompting them.
Mohammed

Ritualistic markings, very primitive.
Twitch Williams
Spawn

What we remember from childhood we remember forever — permanent ghosts, tamped, inked, imprinted, eternally seen.
Cynthia Ozick

Presently, social forms of tattooing are used by American gangs.

BRANDING

Reasons for *branding* include punishment and ownership (to keep track of slaves and animals), as well as tribal rites of passage. Most branding uses a hot object to burn a design into the skin. Dry ice is used for cold branding.

In the Jewish testament God branded Cain for killing Abel. The French government once branded criminals in an attempt to make them socially untouchable, but when Protestants were designated as criminals so many people were branded, branding lost all criminal significance. England branded criminals on different body parts to indicate the type of offense. A pickpocket, for instance, would be branded with an "S" on his cheek and might be sent to the American colonies to live as an indentured servant.

Branding is currently used by some African-American college fraternities. The Reverend Jesse Jackson and football superstar Emmit Smith are affiliates of such fraternities. It is said that rap musicians Treach and Me Phi Me are branded.

The Skull and Bones Society at Yale University — which boasts among its members several U.S. presidents, other high-ranking American federal officials and many corporate leaders — has been criticized for branding its initiates.[20]

SCARIFICATION

Scars signify success in initiation rites and can be tribal markings for beautification and social identification.

The Nubians in Sudan initiate pubescent girls into the sexual adult world by hooking their skin with thorns and slicing the tissue. The Bangwa in Cameroon scar the chest and stomach before marriage. After her first child, a Bangwa mother's back is scarred. Bangwa males mark their abdomen just to the right of their livers to ward off disease. Female Tiv in Nigeria scar the area around their navels to indicate lust and fertility. Tiv scar designs are gender specific and taboo for the opposite sex to wear.

Some Africans avoid raised scars (keloids) by cutting strips of skin away, creating smooth depressions.

Bloodletting is an important part of these ceremonies because practitioners believe bleeding releases evil.

Flaw?
Jake Giddes
Yes, it's sort of a birthmark.
Evelyn
The Two Jakes

The thought, the dream, the vision, always precedes the act.
O.S. Marden

He might have proved a useful adjunct, if not an ornament to society.
Charles Lamb
Captain Starkey

ORAL MODIFICATION

In Vietnam the Annamese blacken their teeth and the Moi chip the incisors down to the oral tissue before marriage. In other areas they chip both sides of the incisors leaving a pointed center. In Borneo the Iban blacken and file their teeth, plus they drill a hole in some teeth for ornamental studs. Filing the front teeth has been practiced in Africa. Members of Australian indigenous tribes remove one or two front teeth in a puberty ritual, usually with a sharp stick. In Uganda some remove the deciduous (baby) lower front teeth. Traumatically removing deciduous teeth sometimes leads to permanent tooth deformation. Some Chinese cut the frenum muscle attachment underneath the tongue thinking it will help them pronounce English words better.[21]

A well-documented example of acculturated tooth mutilation is in Samuel Fastlicht's *Tooth Mutilations and Dentistry in Pre-Columbian Mexico*. The origin of tooth mutilation in Mexico was meant to mimic the jaguar's dentition in the Jaguar animist religion. Two factors merged: magic-dominated medicine and adornment. There arose many variations. At first, they filed the incisal edges of the front teeth. Later, precious stones were inlaid into tooth surfaces. Then the custom included both tooth filing and inlaid stones. Eventually, tooth filing ceased but inlays retained — evidence that rituals do evolve over time.[22]

SKELETAL DEFORMATION

The ancient Chinese practiced *foot-binding* The feet of female children were tightly bound for up to eight years to restrict normal foot growth and development. Young males selected to be used for pedastry were also foot-bound.[23]

In Burma, some tribes use *neck coils* to depress women's shoulders. Starting at age five, each year another metal coil is added until the woman's neck appears to be about 15 inches long. Without the coil support she is unable to hold her head up.

Cranial plates do not fuse until after the first year of life. *Cranial deformation* has a long history, from the Neanderthals, Europe, Australia, Africa, Mesoamerica and North America. Currently, nylon stockings are used as cranial wrappings. Reasons for cranial deformation were and still are: beauty, health, intelligence and whim. *Teratophilia* is a term that indicates an attraction to people with deformaties.

TREPANATION

Trepanation entails drilling a hole to relieve pressure and pain. This procedure is used to relieve pressure over a dental abscess, under a bruised fingernail or in the skull. In ancient times, trepanation of the skull was used to remove a curse or evil spirits, cure diseases, madness or idiocy and give aid for headaches and epilepsy. Egyptians thought drilling a hole in the forehead would open the third eye.

FINGER AMPUTATIONS

Finger amputations have been depicted in Stone Age cave drawings. New Guinea girls of the Dani tribe sacrifice a finger joint at funerals. The finger is numbed by a blow with a rock and then cut off with a stone ax. Funerary finger amputations were common in the Pacific Islands. African Bushmen believed that cutting off parts of their fingers will cure illness. Hottentot finger amputations signified marriage and betrothal. A second finger was sacrificed if one wished to remarry.

AMPUTATION OF THE FLESH

Chief Sitting Bull knew he was too old to fight in the Sioux battle of the Little Bighorn, so he performed a special *Vow to the Sun* ceremony. His brother obliged him by cutting fifty pieces of flesh from each of Chief Sitting Bull's arms. Then Sitting Bull danced until he passed out at which time he had an accurate vision of the Sioux nation defeating Custer.

GENITAL PLAY

Genital play and ritual have strong connections to sexual identity and life in the social community. They deserve a chapter to themselves so you can read more about them in the next chapter. And now we turn to:

COLLECTIVE MUNCHAUSEN IN SOCIAL AGENCY

Agency relationships involve a person called an *agent* who acts for and represents another person called the *principal*. The agent acts through the authority transmitted to him by the principal. The fallacy for procedures such as circumcision performed on minors is that the doctor is not the agent of the parent (principal), but is actually the agent of the infant or child (principle and soon-to-be victim). Since the law does not allow nor acknowledge any

The utmost reverence due a child.
Juvenal

The ends justify the means.
Danny
The means is what you live with.
Nick
The Corrupter

It's true!
I chopped him up.
But I didn't kill him.
Seymour
Little Shop of Horrors

authority of agency to minors or to the mentally incompetent, the courts and law enforcement are the true agents of the infant or child when collusive abuse occurs.

At critical times the authorities always claim they have no authority or responsibility.
Anonymous

COLLECTIVE MUNCHAUSEN IN SOCIAL AGENCY is the relationship between the "principal" who is the person with a primary legal agency, usually a parent or caregiver and another person, the "agent" who accepts secondary agency, usually a doctor or shaman who creates an act of abuse within social group behavior.

MUNCHAUSEN SYNDROME FOR PROFIT

Usually Munchausen motives are attention, self-glorification and adulation from others. Yet financial gain is another motive. This may involve the collusion of a perpetrator with an expert, for example a complainant and an attorney. For *Munchausen Syndrome for Profit* to be successful the endeavor must be perceived to be socially acceptable.

The aristocracy created by business rarely settles in the midst of the manufacturing population which direct it; the object is not to govern that population, but to use it.
de Tocqueville

An example would be a case where an individual and his attorney have taken advantage of the California Disabilities Act. One such team took multiple landowners to court over minor infractions of parking space code. By intentionally cultivating poor health and exacerbating an existing medical condition, the individual presented an appearance of helplessness and persuaded the court to rule in his favor. Without knowledge of the *modus operandi*, such tactics are nearly impossible to prevent.

MUNCHAUSEN SYNDROME FOR PROFIT is 1) the fabrication of disease or exacerbation of an existing medical condition by a person, often with a specialized agent such as an attorney or special interest group, to gain sympathy from others and/or society for financial gain; as well as, 2) non-monetary gain including values associated, in part, power, prestige and employment security.

COLLECTIVE MUNCHAUSEN SYNDROME FOR PROFIT

For the merchant, even honesty is a financial speculation.
Baudelaire

An *Olay Regenerist* commercial euphemistically states: *Definitely, love the skin you're in*.

Munchausen can be performed in general society for the motive of financial gain. There are many ways to make money from circumcision. A few examples follow:

- The doctor charges a fee to amputate a baby's healthy prepuce.

- The hospital charges for use of its facilities, for the attending staff, for equipment, supplies and tending to the baby's wound. The parents of girls can go home the same day as the birth but parents of boys pay for an additional day in the hospital.

- The hospital sells the pristine prepuce to a tissue bank.

- The tissue bank sells the tissue to a pharmaceutical company.

- The pharmaceutical company makes a cosmetic base product which it sells to several different cosmetics manufacturers.

- The cosmetics manufacturers trademark products under fashionable, expensive labels.

- A doctor, store or salon sells the skin product to the public.

Besides *Olay*, *Organogenesis with Apligraf*, *Intercytex with Cosmoderm*, *Bare Minerals* and *Cosmoplast* have entered the market — along with others. You can identify which products use prepuce cells by the use of the term *pentapeptides*.

When Oprah Winfrey aired an episode featuring these products; neither hostess or participants seemed to mind that the products came from a baby's penis, as long as it made them prettier.[24]

Healthy baby penile skin is used to produce anti-aging cosmetics for the sake of someone else's social acceptance, self-glorification and to generate corporate profits.

Dr. Patricia Wexler of Olay's Tissue Nutrient Solution (TNS) reports some women admit placing vanity over morality with:

> When it comes to cosmetic matters, women have a "Don't ask, don't tell me, please!" policy.

COLLECTIVE MUNCHAUSEN SYNDROME FOR PROFIT refers to social activities that involve the abuse of a person or groups of persons for the motives of financial gain as well as other concepts of value including power, prestige and employment security.

I'm just a commodity to you, aren't I?
Jeffery
The Insider

How rude.
Jar Jar Binks
The Phantom Menace

Women will run the 21st Century.
Bella Abzug

GOVERNMENTAL MUNCHAUSEN

Governments and governmental agencies are not immune for Munchausen abuses. Within their organizations combinations of all forms of Munchausen behaviors may be discernible. Much of this behavior is through the savior persona of a Malignant Hero.

Governments may exhibit Munchausen uses in the methods of enacting a society's rules and regulations. Through negotiations between each politician in the ruling body, laws are often enacted favoring one group of people in contrast and detriment to other groups of people living in the society. This then extends to the administration of the social laws by a President, Prime Minister or other equivalent official. And the nation's top administrator may direct such rules and regulations to be enacted. And, in the end, then the Judicial system may accept such behavior as the law with all lower courts to be in compliance with their decisions.

Specific governmental agencies also become involved in Munchausen abuses in regard to the individuals and groups of individuals they are, as agents, to serve. Such behavior also includes how the agency is to behave, who to favor, who to deny, who to prosecute, who not to prosecute, who to administratively award and punish, as well as quite simply - who to ignore.

Quick and easy is not how you run a multi-million dollar business such as ours.
Yves
Tango and Cash

GENITAL PLAY

Some children do not survive adult entertainment

Genital play is a natural part of having a healthy human body. In the womb, the fetus touches its genitals. In childhood, genital play is for comfort and pleasure, not sexual stimulation because sex itself is a reproductive function and reproduction is years away. Eventually childhood exploration may evolve into self-pleasure or masturbation, which can give a child a small preview of what to expect in an adult sexual relationship. When the child has become an adult, he or she will turn to adult sexual relations for the purpose of reproduction.

Some adults use children for their own selfish pleasure. And as much as want to believe that they are not harming children by engaging them in sexual activities, it is not so. This has long been borne out by those children, who are now adults and recall being prematurely sexualized. A child feels powerless when confronted by adult sexual attention. He or she is outranked by adult authority, overpowered by adult size and strength and easily manipulated by adult wiles. The memories of childhood sexual abuse make grown men and women cry even 60 years later.

There is a great disturbance in the Force.
The Emperor
I have felt it.
Darth Vader
The Empire Strikes Back

Non-sexual genital play is part of adult life. Most forms are innocuous and some healthy, but others can become downright dangerous and abusive. This section of our mandated report discusses some fetishistic forms of genital play and how some have led to and become a part of, socialized abusive behavior.[1]

OBJECT IMPLANTATION

Men are more apt to believe what they least understand.
Montaigne

Sexual power and prestige are often motives for *object implantation*. In *Gender Pleasure: Exploration of Sex Gadgets, Penile Implants, and Related Beliefs in Thailand*,[2] the authors documented historical practices from the Far East when men inserted objects under the skin and/or through the penis, ostensibly for the purpose of satisfying their women. Jewels under the skin indicated wealth and position. The *Kama Sutra* mentions that in India the royal and wealthy would implant hollow gold beads under the skin with a grain of sand inside to produce a tinkling sound. Japanese men implanted pearls in the penis to create stimulating ridges to enhance feminine pleasure.

In the Philippines and Indonesia, pins and bars were inserted crosswise to hold a ring that encircled the penis. The *Ampallang* piercing goes through the glans side to side. The *Apadravya* piercing goes through the glans from top to bottom. And the *Magic Cross* combines both the Ampallang and the Apadravya. These types of piercings are also used on the penile shaft. The *Prince's Wand* is a urethral insert that is held in place by a piercing that goes through the urethra. Many women complained of painful intercourse from these implants. Penile infection was a frequent complication. To increase vaginal stimulation, some men cut the prepuce (foreskin) lengthwise into two or three strands so that an erection features raised flaps of skin.

Prince Albert, husband of Queen Victoria, is said to have had his penis pierced just behind the glans on the underside, as did other men in the British royal court. A ring was inserted that came out the urethral opening. From this ring, the penis was fastened downward, under their tight pants, giving the impression of a longer penis. In the West, the *Prince Albert piercing* is once again in style.

Enhanced sexual power is also the purpose of breast implants. Some topically applied cosmetics could be considered chemical implantations because they are designed to penetrate the skin. Collagen is injected to increase lip size and reduce wrinkles. Males have fat implantations to enlarge the girth of the penis. Inflatable penile implants are surgically inserted to counteract erectile dysfunction.

The clitoral hood, clitoris and both labia are also pierced for object implantation in the West. Pacific Island women would pierce and stretch their labia for beauty. In central Africa elongated labia made a woman more marriageable.

CHILD ABUSE THROUGH THE AGES

Most abuses that become socialized begin at home with a child as the target. Abuse is passed into succeeding generations. In *The Universality of Incest* Lloyd deMause discussed many examples of abusive genital play.[3] Following is this author's synopsis:

China used to have a system of adopting children for incestuous purposes. Their religion taught that the more partners a man acquired, the more life force he would have. Also, a girl might be adopted to be the family son's wife, and a boy might be adopted to be a daughter's husband. Boy and girl prostitution was widespread as well as use of slaves and servants. There was also a system for older men to marry young boys who were often castrated, and they had gods of pederasty. Foot binding of girls from all socioeconomic classes did not always include the large toe; it was left unbound for male sexual use. This penis-toe was used for anal stimulation of the male and for his sucking on it — both indicating his socialized childhood homosexual experiences. Boys adopted for sex were also foot bound.

Ancient Japan also used child prostitution of both sexes. Temple prostitution was common. Boys were used in pederasty by samurai and priests, and to some, the boys reached divine status. Royal incestuous marriage was encouraged for all ages. Incest was considered proper conduct. Some mothers masturbated their sons as if it was as common as toilet training. They thought it important that they gave him his first orgasm. It was not uncommon for sons to sleep with their mothers into their teens. The degree of incest varied to family sleeping habits with the mother, as well as the children sleeping together. Some in Japan considered Oedipus problems negated because, in essence, the father was rejected and he went elsewhere for sexual relations.

Some cultural practices, including parts of India, persisted from ancient Zoroastrianism. In India children of both sexes were masturbated by their mothers. After age five the children were used for sex by extended family members, and referred to as "little wives." Children partook of each other. Continued into adulthood, brothers shared wives. Uncle-niece and cross-cousin marriages were preferred. Children were prostituted by, and with, priestly authority by the Vedic Brahmins. Women were expected to kiss the genitals of the penis-god Siva's priests. The Indian epic *Mahabharata* states a 30-year-old man should marry a girl before she menstruates and a father who objects will go to hell. In these societies, adult intercourse was considered polluted. The Baiga of India practiced parent and grandparent incest marriage with children. The Muria, who lived in some relatively isolated forested areas of India, sent their children to sex dormitories after age five. Some children understood that they were being forced out of the family sleeping arrangements. Any sooner, the children would cry and begin bed-wetting. At first the new children massaged the older children before being introduced to intercourse. Older girls often gave instruction to the younger boys. Two types of dormitories existed. The first type is where a girl could not sleep with one particular boy longer than three days at a time. The other type used partners in marriage type relationships for certain periods of time. If she refused sex she was gang raped. Child marriage in India was said to protect the girl, but

Oops!
This is not good.
Anakin Skywalker
The Phantom Menace

There is a great deal of talk about loyalty from the bottom to the top. Loyalty from the top down is even more necessary and much less prevalent.
Gen. George S. Patton
War As I Knew It

Soon you will learn to appreciate me.
Jabba the Hutt
Return of the Jedi

child marriage only enhanced victimization. It was felt little girls have eight times the sex drive than boys, and their desire must be fed.

The Central Asian countries custom of *bacaboz* is where Muslim fathers trade sons for sex. And, Imams often have boys. Central Asia consists of the countries east of the Caspian Sea to China.

In the Egyptian oasis of Siwa mothers lend their sons to males, as well as masturbating their sons during the circumcision ritual. Elsewhere, family members masturbate male children to increase penis size and virility. For older boys, mutual masturbation, oral, and anal sex is common behavior. Circumcision is an unconscious effort to cleanse the boy of his molestation, after which he stops wearing his genitally accessible dress. Yet, he continues to share familial beds. In areas where mothers with children frequent the Hammam (Muslim public baths) all varieties of incest occur as well as homosexuality.

In Mexico older men commonly use post-pubertal boys for sex. In Puerto Rico some mothers and fathers masturbate their sons to show others his maleness. In Thailand and throughout eastern Asia seventy-five percent of males have had sex with child prostitutes. In northern Ghana and Togo, girls are given to priests in return for spiritual protection. And, Iran's Ayatollah Kohmeini decreed that a man could not have intercourse with a girl younger than nine years old, but he could engage in foreplay, rubbing, kissing and sodomy, but if a man had sex with a girl younger than nine, it was a minor infraction because she was not considered damaged. Similarly, statements concerning the use of children for sex from the Talmud (Hebrew/Jewish) are quoted below:[4]

- "At nine years a male attains sexual maturity... The sexual maturity of woman is reached at the age of three." (Sanhedrin 55)

- "It was asked, Do the features of virginity disappear and reappear again or is it possible that they cannot be completely destroyed until after the third year of her age? In what practical respect could this matter? — In one, for instance, where her husband had intercourse with her before the age of three and found blood, and when he had intercourse after the age of three he found no blood... Rabbi Hisda replied, Come and hear: if one was younger than this age, intercourse with her is like putting a finger in the eye; what need was there to state, like putting a finger in the eye' instead of merely saying: if one was younger than this age, intercourse with her is of no consequence'? Does not this then teach us that as the eye tears and tears again so do the features of virginity disappear and reappear again. Our Rabbis taught: It is related

Awful things happen in every apartment house.
Rosemary
Rosemary's Baby

The reason parents no longer lead their children in the right direction is that parents aren't going that way either.
Kim Hubbard

So long as the paperwork's clean, you boys can do as you like out there.
MacAfee
Mad Max

of Justinia the daughter of 'Aseverus son of Antonius that she once appeared before Rabbi 'Master', she said to him, 'at what age may a woman marry?'. 'At the age of three years and one day', he told her." (Niddah, 45)

- "A maiden aged three years and a day may be acquired in marriage by coition, and if her deceased husband's brother cohabited with her, she becomes his. The penalty of adultery may be incurred through her." (Sanhedrin, 69)

- "If a woman sported lewdly with her young son [a minor] and he committed the first stage of cohabitation with her... All agree that the connection of a boy aged nine years and a day is a real connection; whilst that of one less than eight years is not: their dispute refers only to one who is eight years old." (Sanhedrin, 69)

Christianity does not theologically or religiously condone or excuse child abuse, but it is understandable that opportunistic sexual predators will place themselves in situations where they have access to children. The history of child abuse among American Catholic priests is well-documented. Less publicized so far is sexual abuse by nuns.

In *The Emotional Life of Nations*,[5] deMause documents New Guinea and other Pacific Island's sexual habits. Summarizing:

Most people who study the cultural habits of New Guinea start their reports about how mothers consistently fondle their children's genitals when breastfeeding. Girl infants are given oral sex, and women pass their sons to one another so they can suck and hold the penis in their mouths. Mothers also stimulate themselves when nursing a child. Some mothers also use the child for sex by holding him over her and inducing penetration. It has been noted that the mothers become sadistic at times by pinching and pulling hard on the penis. Children spend a lot of time repeating their sexual experiences with dolls. Adult men eventuate to raping boys. And, as the boys become older they form rape gangs. For those who were cannibalistic, males would have sex with a dead woman and women would simulate as much as possible intercourse with a dead man, before they ate them.

In the Marquesas a girl's labia were stretched at bath time. For many Pacific Islanders, mothers also stretched the child's labia and the adult males orally tried to stretch the clitoris. The Ponape would also use the sting of ant to stimulate the clitoris.

It just sounds to me like you need to unplug, man.
Choi
The Matrix

No wonder it's so difficult to raise children properly — they are always imitating their parents.
Anonymous

Today is history. Today will be long remembered. Years from now the young will ask with wonder about this day. Today is history.
Goeth
Schindler's List

As societies become more complex, incestuous habits become more ritual-ized. deMause in *The History of Child Abuse* states Western childhood sexual contact is high. Briefly:[6]

We are our parent's future and our children's past, as well as our parent's past and our children's future, in a never-ending cycle of violence and abuse.

> Prior to prohibitions of masturbation in the west, adults would masturbate children and suck their breasts. Louis XIII as a child would have his penis and breasts sucked by all in the court. Later, Madame du Barry procured little girls for Louis XV. In England, Elizabeth I was used by her caretakers. Also, in 19th Century England when men were brought to court for raping a child, the men were let go because they were curing their venereal disease. Raping virgins, breaking the maiden's seal, was also thought to cure depression and impotence. Child sex was prescribed by British doctors, then doctors found the children of these men would also contract the same diseases.

NOTE: This 19th century British medical practice of *prescribing* sex with a child to cure illness has surfaced again in Africa, where it is rumored virgin rape will cure AIDS — this same medical system brought circumcision to English speaking countries as a punishment to stop the young of both sexes from masturbating.

This is turning out to be one hell of a day.
Finnegan
Deep Rising

Ancient Hawaiian women would assign *massagers* and *blowers* to their young children. For young girls they would gently massage the vulva with candlenut oil until the labia were prematurely separated. And for young boys the assigned blowers would gently blow air inside the prepuce to separate the prepuce from the glans. American health care providers recommend forced premature retraction of the male's prepuce which causes problems.

CHASTITY

Chastity was enforced by *infibulation* in ancient Troy, Greece, Rome, Egypt, Arabia, Western India, and parts of Asia where it existed until the 20th century. The term *infibulation* is a combination word. Its Latin root is derived from the word *fibula* that was a metal clasp similar to the safety-pin and used to close long flowing Roman robes. *Infibulate* means to fasten shut with a *fibula,* a tiny jewelry barbell, stud. The term *infibulation* with regard to one of the Female Genital Mutilation procedures is a Latin term.

What did I do to deserve this?
C3PO
Attack of the Clones

Male infibulation consists of piercing the prepuce and fastening it shut to make arousal painful and to prohibit intercourse and masturbation. Sexual activities of male slaves was controlled and when used for breeding the infibu-lation was reversed. Since it was thought that sex drained one's energy, Roman gladiators used infibulation to practice abstinence and thereby maintain their strength. Females also were infibulated; they had their labia pierced and closed. Both male and female infibulation was accomplished by using jewelry studs. These practices continue today mainly as fetishistic behavior.[7]

Chastity belts became common during the 15th century when knights went on crusades. In the 19th century in England and America many types of chastity belts were used on the young. Male contraptions were for the most part effective and became popular as anti-masturbating devices. Some "chastity" belts still allowed female masturbation and anal intercourse.

Today "chastity belts" are still worn to prevent intercourse and sometimes masturbation. As human ingenuity prevails and object use changes, some present-time female "chastity belts" feature vaginal plugs with a choice for different sizes and textures as well as anal plugs with variations for anal expansion.

GENITAL BLOOD RITUALS

Genital blood rituals have psychosexual connections to self-identity and to the way one fits into and lives in the social community. In primitive middle eastern and African societies, acculturated genital mutilation rituals are same-sex perpetrated — females mutilate females, and males mutilate males. Age levels for rituals differ from group to group.

BLOOD SACRIFICE

Mesoamerican Olmecs bled their penises. Later, Mayan males bled their prepuces making sure the drops of blood hit the grounds to fertilize the Mother Earth goddess. The fertilization of the goddess, common in the agricultural motif of Mayan art, is represented by Mayan men spreading corn. Most often women performed the ritual on the male. For the royal ceremony only the queen or his mother could bleed the king. Pain was necessary, for this genital male bleeding intended to mimic the travails of menstruation and child birth. Pain was accomplished by an instrument called a penis perforator.

Many penis perforators have been found with elaborately carved handles; some had feathers attached to them. The blades came from sting ray spines, sharks teeth, or jade. On the handle of the penis perforator were animal motifs: crocodiles or fish representing the feminine element, water. This blood sacrifice to the goddess was different than the Mayan blood sacrifice of cutting out the heart of a live victim. The heart blood sacrifice was for their male god.[8,9]

Deserve has nothing to do with this.
William Munny
Unforgiven

What's blood for, if not for shedding.
Candyman
Candyman

What the young one begs for, the grown-up throws away.
Russian Proverb

The names of *Ra* and *Re* for the same Egyptian god indicates the dual gender and circular mythology of Ra, the masculine and Re, the feminine.[10] When feminine Re began to bleed her/his penis, the shed blood fertilized the creation of the gods.[11]

The bosses will do terrible things to me.
Jar Jar Binks
The Phantom Menace

Australian folklore relates that since feminine blood was once considered supreme, inherent in the nature of menstruation and childbirth, long ago women held the power — but now men hold the power. How did that shift occur? To establish the importance of masculine blood, the males in the Australian indigenous tribes instituted a form of genital cutting called *subincision* that flayed the penis on the underside to make it resemble the vulva. The cutting made men bleed, hence they now had a form of "male menstruation". To sustain the shift of power from female to male required the male blood ritual to be repeated. This process of shifting blood power from the female to the male is called *incorporation*.[12]

You lost today kid; but, it doesn't mean you have to like it.
Roughrider
Indiana Jones and the Last Crusade

Circumcision as a genital blood ritual in the hands of the female was borrowed from the Arabian peninsula when Moses' pagan wife Zipporah circumcised their son in accordance with her Midianite tribe's Hathor-Horus mythology. After the circumcision, Zipporah told Moses that he was at last a "bridegroom of blood" to her. This story appears in the original history of the Hebrew people, *The Book of J*, which is thought to have been written when Solomon ruled. *The Book of J* is quite possibly the oldest written direct reference to circumcision in Judaism and this story clearly links the practice of genital cutting to a pagan goddess. This is an example of *comixio religionis*, a commingling, mixing or blending of religions.

After Solomon's death, the Hebrews split into Judah and Israel. Only the tribe of Benjamin with some elements of the tribes of Levi and Ephriam stayed with the tribe of Judah, whose descendants are the Jewish people. Abraham's mythic covenant of circumcision was added to *The Book of J* a full five centuries after his death.[13,14,15]

CANNIBALISM

Is it progress if a cannibal uses knife and fork?
Stanislaus Lec

A *cannibal* is an animal that feeds on the flesh of its own species. Slater claims *cannibalism* of circumcised tissue indicates possession of the individual. To balance the need of possession with the need for destruction, the Philippine Poro custom involved girls eating the boys circumcised tissue and boys eating the girls excised tissue. The possession makes each magically "bisexual", whereas before their circumcisions each was totally "monosexual".[17]

In the world of New Guinea cannibals, women ate the penis and men ate the vagina.[18] Even in the 21st century some South African Xhosas boys are instructed to eat their foreskins so a witch will not get it to cast spells.[19]

See Medicine chapter on "Infant Penile Tissue Marketing" for commercial uses of prepuce tissue that are related to: animals feeding on the flesh of their own species.

FEMALE GENITAL MUTILATION (FGM)

FGM was practiced in Ancient Egypt. Mummies have been found lacking clitorises and labia.[20] Pia Gallo has traced FGM back beyond five thousand years in certain areas of Africa.[21] Scholars categorize FGM according to the severity of the surgery. Cultures that perform African FGM are: some Muslim sects, the Falasha Ethiopian Jews and tribes that practice animism. FGM has been performed on unwilling minors by medical doctors in the UK, US and Canada.

VARIATION OF MUTILATIONS

In some African countries FGM is still regularly practiced. It is estimated that 15% are clitoridectomies and 85% are infibulations.[22] According to Heitman these are the three main categories of FGM:[23]

- *Sunna Circumcision (Traditional)* — the removal of the prepuce (retractable fold of skin, or hood) and/or the tip of the clitoris.

- *Clitoridectomy* — the removal of the entire clitoris (prepuce and glans) and sometimes including the removal of portions of the adjacent labia.

- *Infibulation (Pharonic)* — performing a clitoridectomy (with) removal of all or part of the labia minora and the labia majora. This is then stitched up allowing a small hole to remain open to allow for urine and menstrual blood to flow through.

Other procedures also exist, such as labial feathering, using corrosive chemicals, scraping, and cuttings. The World Health Organization presents the following typology:[24]

- *Type I* — prepuce excision, with or without excision of part or all of the clitoris

All a child's life depends on the ideal it has of its parents. Destroy that and everything goes.
E.M. Forester

I lost myself — today.
Daphne
The Substance of Things Hoped For

I'm looking for my daughter. I'm afraid she's been hurt.
Rose
We've lost all our children, our light.
Dalia
To find your daughter, you must face the darkness of hell.
Christabella
Silent Hill

- *Type II* — excision of the clitoris with partial or total excision of the labia minora

- *Type III* — excision of part or all of the external genitalia and stitching/narrowing of the vaginal opening (infibulation)

- *Type IV* — pricking, piercing or incising of the clitoris and/or labia; stretching of the clitoris and/or labia; cauterization by burning of the clitoris and surrounding tissue

- Scraping of corrosive substances or herbs into the vaginal orifice (angurya cuts) or cutting of the vagina (gishuri cuts)

- Introduction of corrosive substances or herbs into the vagina to cause bleeding or for the purpose of tightening or narrowing it.

RATIONALIZING FGM

In the ancient dualistic Egyptian philosophy, the male prepuce represented an element of softness and femininity and the clitoris represented an element of hard masculinity. Therefore, it was thought that to achieve 100% maleness or 100% femaleness, the incongruent anatomy must be removed. Adult male genitals were to contain nothing soft, wet and hidden and the adult female genitals were to contain nothing hard and protruding.[25]

Female genital rituals usually occur during childhood, in pubescence, or prior to marriage. Excuses used to justify FGM, similar to MGM excuses, include:[26-30]

- Only a small piece of the body is removed.
- The tissue is disgusting.
- The owner won't miss it.
- It is cleaner and healthier.
- It smells better.
- Everybody does it.
- It is good because doctors do it.
- There is beauty in the scar.
- An uncircumcised person will not find a sexual/marriage partner.

Excuses peculiar to females include:

- She won't get worms in her vagina.
- Mother's milk will be poisonous.
- Male impotency occurs when the penis touches the clitoris.
- She is tighter for the male's pleasure.

I was a daisy fresh girl and look what you've done to me.
Lolita
Lolita

It's my life they're messing with, you all.
Terry
Emmerdale Farm

It'll change your daughter from a beautiful child into an empty shell.
Evan
The Butterfly Effect

- Infibulation prevents the uterus from falling out.
- There is danger of hydrocephaly if the baby's head touches the clitoris during childbirth.

It is possible the idea of *uterine prolapse* represents an agricultural motif incorporated due to complications seen in sheep. Heitman listed other excuses for performing FGM:

- It reduces sexual desire and limits promiscuity.
- It enhances femininity.
- The female cannot conceive unless she is circumcised.
- Prevents a yellow face.
- Prevents nervousness.
- Prevents masturbation and lesbianism.
- If the clitoris touches a man, he will die.
- Older men may not be able to match her sex drive if she is not circumcised.

CONSEQUENCES OF FGM AND MGM

IMMEDIATE CONSEQUENCES
- severe pain
- shock
- urine retention
- hemorrhage
- ulcerations
- possible death
- highly elevated cortisol levels
- heart rate can increase and even double

LONG TERM CONSEQUENCES
- obstruction of vaginal opening
- repeated urinary and reproductive track infections
- incontinence
- cysts and abscesses
- amputation neuromas
- painful intercourse
- lack of tissue elasticity
- decreased fluids
- keloid scar formation
- psychological complications.

Except for the first long term consequences, these complications are similar for MGM.

Also, women suffering infibulation develop a short-stepped shuffling walk and recurring medical complications. Lightfoot-Klein documents denial of FGM complications in later life with the women's own words, such as:[31]

> Yes, I have suffered from chronic pelvic infections and terrible pain for years now. You say that all of this is the result of my circumcision? But I was circumcised over 30 years ago! How can something that was done for me when I was four years old have anything to do with my health now?

AMERICAN FGM

A 150-YEAR HISTORY

The introduction of FGM in America (and other English speaking countries) coincided with male circumcision in the last half of the 1800s. Both boys and girls were targeted. Reasons included religious concepts interlaced with a medical theory that disease was the result of masturbation. Out of that emerged a campaign to inhibit masturbation and sexuality in general. According to Patricia Robinett's book *The Rape of Innocence,* the medical insurance company Blue Cross/Blue Shield paid for clitoridectomies until 1977 and the FGM Bill outlawed "female genital mutilation" in America in 1996.

FEMALE CUTTING NOW

The US, Canada and UK doctors have practiced and still do practice their own forms of female genital cutting. Twenty-seven percent of American births are *Cesarean sections* -- far more commonly than the 5-10% the World Health Organization recommends. Doctors perform *episiotomies* at nearly every vaginal birth, slicing the *perineum* from vaginal opening to anus -- sometimes creating complications that take years to heal, if they ever do. Many American women have had *hysterectomies*, which remove some or all of the following: uterus, cervix and ovaries. In 2003, over 600,000 hysterectomies were performed in the United States -- 90% for benign conditions -- making hysterectomy the most commonly performed gynecological surgical procedure in the country.

One cosmetic surgeon's website claims that *labiaplasty* (labia reduction), *vaginoplasty* (tightening of the vagina) and *hoodectomy* (removal of the clitoral prepuce) are becoming as common today as tummy tucks and breast augmentation. Other forms of genital cutting in the US are *liposuction of the mons pubis* and *hymen repair* -- popular in some American subcultures where virginity has social and psychological significance for men. Hymen repair is also used in child prostitution rings where a significant amount of money is demanded and received for virgins.

Some have fondly dubbed *vaginoplasty* the *designer vagina*. Doctors have long winked and nodded at men after their wives have given birth saying they took an extra stitch for his sake -- to tighten the vagina and thereby increase the husband's pleasure.

It is rumored that girls involved in gymnastics have been encouraged to have clitoridectomies due to possible injuries.

African women have pointed out the irony (or hypocrisy) of the US campaign against their practice of genital cutting, while we perform so many forms of cutting here.

MALE GENITAL MUTILATION (MGM)

In the US, if a male is not cut as an infant, he still may be genitally altered as a child, adolescent or adult. *Male genital mutilation* or *circumcision* has typically been portrayed as a harmless little snip — it is not. Many deaths occur due to infection of the wound, loss of blood and other factors. Impartial, in-depth studies of the many and varied short- and long-range physiological and psychological effects of genital cutting need to be undertaken. No such studies have been performed to date. Circumcision is not "evidence-based" medicine. Instead it continues unquestioned simply because it was practiced by primitive tribes for thousands of years.

Before even one more circumcision is performed, it might be good to know why four times the number of men in the USA commit suicide than women. We would like to see an investigator explore whether suicide relates to circumcision status. Why? Because American women who were circumcised as children unanimously report lifelong suicidal ideation, including suicide attempts in childhood. Given that historically the circumcised nations were always warring -- and still the only three cultures that circumcise their young are at war in the Middle East -- we would also like to see if there is any relation between "tribal" or "national" violence and circumcision. And finally, since violent crime and childhood trauma have been connected by psychologists, we would like to know the circumcision status of inmates in US prisons.

Now why did I expect to be left alone today.
Hobert
Wasabi

The boy will not pass the Council's test. He is too old.
Obi-Wan Kenobi
The Phantom Menace

In one minute terrible things are going to happen to you.
Van Helsing
Saturday the 14th

RADICAL CUTTING

Originally the Jewish circumcision ritual entailed trimming the overhanging foreskin but as we mentioned in the introduction, that changed around 140 AD when Jewish boys stretched and grew their foreskins to participate in the nude Greek athletic games. To prevent future escape from tribal identification, a radical, new "improved" cut removed the entire prepuce. Today, routine infant medical circumcision means total prepuce removal. Some doctors pride themselves on removing the most sensitive remnant on the underside of the corona — the frenulum. This destroys nearly all pleasure for the male. Another form of male genital cutting is castration — removal of the testes.

Read again the rationalizations for FGM in the preceding section — most of the same excuses are used to justify MGM.

Psychological numbness is similar for men and women. Hanny Lightfoot-Klein documents male denial with the statement of a 35-year-old American man:[32] His words are remarkably similar to the words of the African woman quoted on page 38.

> I have lost nearly all interest in sex. You might say that I'm becoming impotent. I don't seem to have much sensation in my penis anymore, and it is difficult for me to reach orgasm. You say that this is the result of my circumcision? That doesn't make any sense. I was circumcised 35 years ago, when I was a little boy. How can that affect me in any way now?

WAR

In 1 Samuel 18:25, Saul demanded one hundred Philistine foreskins as the bride price for his daughter's hand in marriage. To prove his worthiness, David returned with two hundred foreskins.

In World War II many enlisted men were circumcised as a matter of course. Some were threatened with court martial if they refused to comply. After World War II, with so many returning newly circumcised GIs, routine infant circumcision became almost universal in the USA. The slick trick question, "You want your son to look like you, don't you?" was met with a nod. The post World War II baby boom was the first US generation that was widely circumcised. After that, Americans assumed the circumcised penis had always been part of their heritage.

Genital Play

41

CIRCUMCISION AS A "COMING OF AGE" RITUAL

Circumcision in primitive societies usually marked a coming of age or a warrior initiation. Since the Catholic Church has always officially considered circumcision to be a mortal sin -- both ritual circumcision and medical cutting in the absence of a legitimate health problem such as injury or disease -- the traditional Catholic passage into adulthood was and is *confirmation*.

AT BIRTH

American circumcision occurs on the day of birth or as soon as possible thereafter. Circumcision is considered to be "medical" -- neither religious or cultural. There is no ceremony and no celebration.

INFANCY

The Jewish blood ritual takes place on the eighth day. It is customary to have a celebration called a *bris*. This Jewish "mock death ritual" could be thought of as a *coming into life* ceremony. In contrast, the Jewish *Coming of Age* ceremony in the 12th year, the *bar mitzvah* does not require bloodletting.

CHILD & ADOLESCENT CIRCUMCISION

Male *child* and *adolescent circumcision* are similar to FGM in age range and social ceremony. Age is determined by cultural specifics and in this category, circumcision is seen as a *coming of age* ceremony.

In Islam, the *coming of age* ceremony is circumcision and it occurs anytime between age five and puberty. Here, circumcision represents leaving the mother.[33,34] A Muslim boy is initiated into adulthood with a lavish ceremony, promises of gifts, attention, feasting, music and dancing.

Adolescent circumcision is mainly practiced by tribal Africans who follow the path of animism and islanders who live south and west of mainland Asia. The Philippine's Tuli circumcision ritual consists of a partial dorsal slit. The prepuce is cut but no tissue is removed.[35,36]

In Turkey on his circumcision day, the boy is dressed like a prince. The boy's male sponsor masturbates him, since it is thought the cut is best performed with an erect penis. The boy keeps his bloodied circumcision robe as a wedding day present to his wife.

In Egypt, the mother often masturbates the son for his circumcision.[37]

In Canserver's study of adolescent male circumcision which concentrates on the Turkish tradition, he discusses the psychological effects on the boy.

Anonymous

If history has taught us anything, it's says you can kill anyone.
Michael Corleone
The Godfather: Part II

So long as I'm a little different don't you think — well maybe things could be the same again — only a little different, huh?
Jerry
The Awful Truth

The child perceives circumcision as an attack. Children who are given mis-information react more negatively.[38-41] Some boys feel totally destroyed in the feminine Life/Death/Life cycle described by Clarissa Pinkola Estes.[42] The ego weakens due to a perceived threat of castration. Directly afterward, some boys will express withdrawal, aggression and perhaps even a desire for retaliation. Tendency for withdrawal may increase each time he witnesses a circumcision. Repeated stimulation of his psychological trauma may develop into or deepen an existing tendency toward *Schizoid Personality Disorder*, a reluctance to engage with others.

Native Australian circumcision and body scarring precedes the subinci-sion that filets the under side of the penis to look like the vulva. After the circumcision follows a socially accepted gang rape.

ADULT CIRCUMCISION

There are no social glorification ceremonies to celebrate adult male circum-cision. Adult males are circumcised most often due to relationship demands, improper medicine or social pressures.

Some adult circumcisions have been forced. In Malaysia, the Philippines, Africa, and the Middle East including Lebanon and Yugoslavia both men and women, young and old were abducted, mutilated and released by misguided religious fanatics, who hoped to convert the victims to Islam. Some of the victims died.

AIDS is a recent excuse to promote universal adult circumcision in Africa. The campaign conveniently fails to include in their equation that if circumci-sion was truly a preventative, there would never have been an AIDS epidemic in the US, for most American men were circumcised as infants. Yet the USA leads the industrialized world both in numbers of males circumcised and inci-dence of HIV and AIDS. Who is to say, therefore, that circumcision might not be the very factor that increases one's susceptibility to the HIV virus?

Much of what is touted as circumcision "science" is based on supposition and old wives tales. Could medicine be promoting a false "cure" that harms more than it helps?

The campaigns to circumcise appear to be a carefully crafted public rela-tions projects replete with emotions, pathos, disgust, fear of rejection, fear of not belonging, false arguments, propaganda, persuasion, avoidance of the facts that connect USA circumcision to HIV, disregard of cultural sexual patterns

You must be made to understand what I can do to you.
Griffin
The Invisible Man

You were waving pompoms around this morning, and now you are a psychic hot line.
Scotty
Jeepers Creepers

A Prophesy that misread could have been.
Yoda
Revenge of the Sith

of Africans, faulty medical studies and the manipulation of statistics (see *Medicine* chapter and *Manipulation* chapter and study Eddie Bernays and his book *Propaganda*).

Unfortunately, the spread of HIV is a behavioral problem and medicine cannot control behavior. The hope circumcision proponents express is that less skin means less promiscuity. This argument merely reinforces the fact that behavior is the real issue underlying HIV transmission.

This elaborate campaign advocating universal circumcision in Africa is an example of *Munchausen Malignant Hero Syndrome* — fanning the fires of a much-dreaded problem and charging in to save the day with a remedy that has already miserably failed Americans.

SELF-CIRCUMCISION
ABRAHAM

The book of Genesis says that at God's command Abram circumcised himself. However, according to Dr. Leonard Glick and other Jewish scholars, this story is an example of historical myth-working to justify and lend Abraham's identity to a cultural movement. This myth was added around 500 BCE after Judah's return from Babylon, long after Abraham's demise.[43] This leads to a *Culture-Bound Syndrome*. In the shadow of this myth, many millions of men have been mutilated.

KOZO OKAMOTO

In May 1972, five Japanese Red Army terrorists attacked the Tel Aviv international airport and murdered 26 people. The only survivor was Kozo Okamoto. He was tried, convicted and sentenced to life in prison where he subsequently self-circumcised. It is unknown whether he was attempting to identify with his Israeli captors or the Muslim Palestinian cause for which the airport attack was carried out. This is what people call *Stockholm Syndrome*, identifying with one's captors.

FETISHISM

Some individuals who suffer from *Bodily Integrity Identity Disorder* (BIID) and *Body Dysmorphic Disorder* (BDD) seek adult circumcision.

Biology Professor Alfred Charles Kinsey for whom the Kinsey Institute for Research in Sex, Gender and Reproduction at Indiana University is named and the movie *Kinsey* was filmed, circumcised himself in a bathtub with a

We would be honored if you join us.
Darth Vader
The Empire Strikes Back

*Fun is fun.
Done is done.*
Alan
Riding the Bullet

Prepare to target the main generator.
General Veers
The Empire Strikes Back

pocketknife two years before his death at age 62. Kinsey earned himself the diagnosis of *masochist of the highest order*.

There are Internet groups and social clubs that openly advocate and support circumcision. Some groups advertise free circumcision and payment in exchange for an intact man's public circumcision. One man who contacted them out of curiosity was stalked for weeks thereafter.

According to Robinett, a Japanese urologist told the story of a quiet, serious kid who had walked into his clinic with the lower half of his body drenched in blood. The boy had tried to self-circumcise by stretching out the prepuce and hacking into it with a knife of the type usually used in handicrafts. *It wouldn't have been so bad*, said the doctor, *if this kid was the only one I had to treat after such an incident. But he was just one of several who'd done pretty much exactly the same thing.*

GENITAL AMPUTATION & SURGICAL ALTERATION

Although the Catholic church deemed circumcision to be a sin, they allowed castration so they could enjoy the music of the *castrati*. During the recent fighting since the breakup of Yugoslavia, some Muslims castrated the dead Serbians they killed.[44] Accidental medical genital organ amputations occur as well as genital amputations required after problems due to circumcision.[45] And the medical profession now trains doctors who specialize in sex-changes surgery for adults who think they were born into the wrong body. Women are especially susceptible to ads for cosmetic surgery.

CASTRATION

Castration is the removal of the testes to prevent the male from procreating. It is often imposed on captured prisoners of war and slaves. Castration has been used in *pederasty* by older adult males to keep boys from maturing so they can use them for homosexual purposes. Some countries that castrated for pederasty included Rome, Greece, China, Japan and various Islamic regions. In China, parents who volunteered their sons for castration kept the testicles in a jar. Castration was also used by the Catholic Church to create the *castrati* because a castrated male retains a child-like feminine voice.

Castration was practiced in ancient Mesopotamia and in other areas where priests of certain goddesses donated their testicles in fertility rituals. Priests of the Greek goddess Cybele were castrates.

He is as clumsy as he is stupid.
Darth Vader
The Empire Strikes Back

Once more the Sith will rule the Galaxy.
Supreme Chancellor Palpatine
Revenge of the Sith

To thy death art thou sped, Until God's word be said. In the white lily bloom, Brave boy, is thy tomb.
The Brothers Grimm

CONGENITAL ADRENAL HYPERPLASIA

Genital surgery used to be performed routinely in American hospitals shortly after birth for children afflicted with *Congenital Adrenal Hyperplasia* (CAH). Females with CAH are born with an enlarged clitoris and labia. A male might have a micropenis, underdeveloped and/or undescended testicles. Though treatment with the steroid cortisol is often successful, surgery (including clitoroplasty, clitoridectomy, and labioplasty) is also employed to make the genitals conform to social "norms."

CAH is ethnic specific, occurring in Jewish and Hispanic populations.[46] Because CAH occurs primarily in Jewish populations, the question is asked if it might be possible that generations of interbreeding could have been an original cause for circumcision.

As of the date this book was published, the Texas Department of Health's website advises,[47] "Girls born with CAH who have masculine external genitals *will need surgery* to reconstruct the clitoris and/or labia. This is usually performed between the ages of one and three." [Emphasis added.] Do they understand they are advocating female genital mutilation in the USA?

CIRCUMCISION & INVOLUNTARY SEX CHANGE

Male genital amputation has been required to correct a lost penis due to circumcision in more than one case, but the most famous may be that of identical twin, David Reimer. David and his brother were scheduled for circumcision when they were eight months old for "phimosis" due to concern about how the twins urinated. David's penis was damaged beyond repair by a cautery iron the doctor used. His brother's circumcision was cancelled and the condition cleared by itself; he never required circumcised.

Dr. John Money, a psychologist who had long promoted a theory that environmental factors alone were enough to determined gender identity, now had a perfect subject with an identical twin control. Money convinced the Reimer boys' parents that he could help their injured son become a girl. So David was castrated, renamed *Brenda*, surgically given female genitals and loaded up with hormones.

Money's theory failed miserably. David may have been one of the very few "girls" who has ever aspired to be a garbage collector. When David was finally told the truth about his male birth identity as a teen, he opted to stop taking hormones, had a double mastectomy, took a male name and lived the

*Pain, suffering, death
I feel something
terrible has happened.*
Yoda
Attack of the Clones

*You gotta get us outta
here. Something is
going to kill us soon.*
Bucky
Jeepers Creepers

*Life is worth living,
but only if we avoid
the amusements of
grown-up people.*
Robert Lynd

If I could live
my life over again,
I wouldn't.
John Smith

remainder of his life as a male. He married and adopted children but at age 38, he committed suicide. David's twin brother had already committed suicide earlier for reasons related to his brother's lifetime tragedy.[48]

GENDER REASSIGNMENT SURGERY

Not everyone is content with the body they were born into. Some simply dress like members of the opposite sex, which is easy for women to do but not so simple for men. Some are so unhappy with their physical gender that they go to great lengths to change their bodies with hormones and surgery. Gender reassignment is a speciality medical school students can elect. Psychiatric care may be required for many years after sex-reassignment surgery. The number of deaths in male-to-female transsexuals is five times the number expected due to increased suicides and deaths from unknown causes.[49]

1,500 years ago,
everybody 'knew'
that the earth was the
center of the universe.
500 years ago,
everybody 'knew'
that the earth was
flat. And 15 minutes
ago, you 'knew' that
humans were alone
on this planet.
Agent K
Men in Black

COSMETIC SURGERY

As we said before, many women in the USA choose to have breasts augmentation, tummy tucks, liposuction and many other "image enhancing" procedures. Female genital surgery is advertised freely on the Internet and in big cities for women who wish to have designer vaginas. Some female genital cosmetic surgery is not for vanity but to repair damage from cutting performed by medical doctors during hospital births.

FBI BEHAVIORAL SCIENCE UNIT

Educate . Respect . Protect

Howard Teton, a former California police officer, joined the Federal Bureau of Investigation (FBI) in 1962 and became an instructor at the National Police Academy in Washington, D.C. In 1972 the FBI formed the *Behavioral Science Unit* and Teton teamed with Patrick Mullany. Together they designed a method for analyzing violent crime scenes and connecting the evidence with the behavior of perpetrators. The approach is now commonly referred to as *criminal profiling*. In 1973, with Robert Ressler, they used their techniques to apprehend a previously unknown killer of seven-year-old Susan Jaeger.

In 1974 Robert Keppel used this ever-increasing knowledge to identify serial killer Ted Bundy and the Green River Killer. Later Richard Walter designed a system for grouping sex crimes and killings into four types:

- Power-assertive
- Power-reassurance
- Anger-retaliatory
- Anger-excitation – sadism

In 1978, when Howard Teton left the *Behavioral Science Unit*, Robert Ressler and John Douglas carried on his work of profiling. These men's efforts have established a solid relationship between law enforcement and psychology. Among the many disciplines that have emerged are *Forensic Psychology, Investigative Psychology* and *Criminal Investigative Analysis*.

With the continued expansion of knowledge the *Behavioral Science Unit* was reorganized into the *Behavioral Analysis Unit* (BAU) with specialized, interactive components including:

- CASMIRC – Child Abduction Serial Murder Investigative Resource Center
- NCAVC – The National Center for the Analysis of Violent Crime
- VICAP – Violent Criminal Apprehension Program

THE DUEL

Eugene Field

The gingham dog and the calico cat
Side by side on the table sat;
'Twas half past twelve, and (what do you think!)
Nor one nor t'other had slept a wink!
The old Dutch clock and the Chinese plate
Appeared to know as sure as fate
'Twas going to be a terrible spat.
(I wasn't there; I simply state
What was told to me by the Chinese plate.)

The gingham dog went, "Bow-wow-wow!"
And the calico cat replied, "Mee-ow!"
The air was littered, an hour or so,
With bits of gingham and calico,
While the old Dutch clock in the chimney place
Up with its hands before its face,
For it always dreaded a family row,
(Now mind: I'm only telling you
What the old Dutch clock declares is true.)

RITUAL

Rituals are adult games that should not be forced on children

Humans are a predator species. Many rituals, including circumcision are violent predations. Rituals are social enactments to control behavior. How do humans learn violence? Lion cubs have to be taught how to hunt. If we put an end to preventable trauma and abuse, what kind of world would we live in then? Would successive generations be more predatory or more peaceful?

Natural means not altered by mankind and *not made by humankind*. Normal merely means *usual, typical* or *standard; normal* is not synonymous with *healthy*. It is both "normal" and "natural" to have a physical body temperature around 98.6 degrees Fahrenheit, but when the social "norm" is a human contrivance, an alteration of a body part, then is "normal" synonymous with "healthy"?

How close or far apart are "natural" and "normal" and "healthy" when it comes to social behaviors? Do we have the objectivity we need to evaluate what is healthy socially? How influenced are we by our upbringing? Have we been programmed to think the way we do? How many of our assumptions are based on acculturation? We have learned much from our families, schools and societies. Can the human data base become unbiased? What do we know and what do we merely believe and accept? At what point do we turn an inquiring eye toward our ideas, beliefs and opinions? What happens when we challenge what we have learned from our elders? Do we even dare attempt introspection? How much are our decisions driven by social pressures, emotional blackmail, fear and guilt?

Could a people's and a culture's varied behaviors (such as circumcision, a blood ritual), teach: fear, distrust, learned helplessness, victim-consciousness, a self-defensive form of aggression, hostility and a "monkey-see-monkey-do" form of predation?

We are only interested in friendship. Why do you attack us?
Zarkov
Why not?
Ming the Merciless
Flash Gordon

Perhaps I can find new ways to motivate them.
Darth Vader
Return of the Jedi

PURPOSE OF RITUAL

Rituals are repeated acts performed with perceived symbolic value. They bond groups of people into a community, apart from other communities. They create an "us and them" mentality. Social rituals are usually part of religion or simple tradition. Ancient rituals were usually designed to ensure survival. In a more complex society, people adapt to the same contingencies in a more complicated way. Circumcision, a mock human sacrifice, is an social blood bonding ritual that evolved from full human sacrifice. Through circumcision a person "dies" to his or her individual nature and is "reborn" as a member of the group: the Life/Death/Life cycle.

ORDER

The ritual act attempts to magically provide order in an area of perceived chaos. Our primal fear is that the interests of nature are somehow opposed to those of humankind. For humans, forms of order seem to ensure success. Ritual is a method of ordering the hunt or the timing of a proper harvest. Seasonal horticultural festivals — spring fertility and fall harvest — are rituals that are tied to the cycles of the moon. Sun rituals also exist for the depth of winter's darkness and the height of summer's light. In it all is the implication that humanity and its survival are the ultimate good and not to be questioned.

Joseph Campbell suggests that human sacrifice may have evolved from horticultural ideologies that in turn originated as survival rituals.[1]

> Myth and rites referring to the mythological age, when the great mythological event took place that brought both death and reproduction into play and fixed the destiny of life-in-time through a chain reaction of significantly interlocked transformations, belong rather to the world system of planters than to the shamanistically dominated hunting sphere. Whenever such myths are found in a hunting society, acculturation from some horticultural or agricultural center can be supposed.

The circumcision myth says Sarah did not reproduce until Abraham was circumcised, tying circumcision to fertility and reproduction.

POWER, CONTROL & AUTHORITY

Those who advocate ritual think power over nature and other people is necessary for survival and that authority belongs to those who control both. In primitive cultures, circumcision serves as a test of membership and loyalty to the tribe. It establishes group cohesiveness through blood, fear and loathing for the purpose of bonding individuals together against perceived common external enemies. From Catherine Bell, Emeritus Professor of Religious Studies:[2]

> The orchestrated construction of power and authority in ritual, which is deeply evocative of the basic divisions of the social order, engage the social body in the objectification of oppositions and deployment of schemes that effectively reproduce the divisions of the social order... In this process such schemes become socially instinctive automatisms of the body and implicit strategies for shifting power relationships among symbols... Culture uses ritual to control by means of sets of assumptions about the way things are and should be.

DOMINATION & DESTRUCTION

Once leadership and social identity are firmly established, rituals pit one group competitively against another in activities such as sports or war.

Rituals also attempt to mediate the guilt of humanity's destruction — killing and taking from nature — against the perceived positive value of humanity's continuance. Prayers offered for animals killed in the hunt, or thanking god for a victory over enemies killed in war represent an attempt to assuage nature's anger and mitigate man's guilt. They communicate an implied hope of forgiveness for having taken life. The goal of ritual survival through domination. Bell illustrates with:[3]

> Ritual mastery is itself a capacity for, and relationship of, relative domination... Binary oppositions almost always involve asymmetrical relations of dominance and subordination by which they generate hierarchically organized relationships... Fairly standard understandings involve the positive notion of "influence" on the one hand and the negative notion of "force" on the other.

MANIPULATION

Through ritual, people address the properties of nature they desire to control. Symbolic gestures and objects are used to represent the desired quality of nature, or a portion of the actual natural object can be used. Sometimes the people dress and make images of themselves as if they are the object. Then, during the ritual, something is done to or with the object. What is done to and with the object explains man's intended manipulation of others and nature.

If I didn't mutilate the innocent, how could I make the guilty fear me?
Ugandan sub-chief of Karabenga
Tales of the African Frontier

I am just a simple man trying to make my way in the universe... They'll do their job well. I'll guarantee that.
Jango Fett
Attack of the Clones

He can be conditioned to behave the way we want.
Dr. Logan
Day of the Dead

Bell says:[4]

> Ritual practices never define anything except the terms of the expedient relationships that ritualization itself establishes among things, thereby manipulating the meaning of things by manipulating their relationships… What is distinctive about ritual is not what it says or symbolizes, but that first and foremost it does things: ritual is always a matter of "the performance of gestures and the manipulation of objects."

The hard fact is that violence breeds violence, and that, in turn, breeds insensitivity.
John Douglas
The Anatomy of Motive

RITUAL AS AN OUTLET FOR VIOLENCE

Some rituals are often violent social acts designed as outlets for violence. They mimic the violence considered necessary for controlling, directing, using and justifying social behavior. From Bell:[5]

> Hence, ritualization is central to culture as the means to dominate nature and the natural violence within human beings. Although ritual (= culture) is the necessary repression of this violence (= nature), culture is still dependent upon the energy of aggression as well as its restraint…

It's time for your rehabilitation.
Dr. Nordoff
Perversions of Science

SHIFTING THE ATTACK FROM NATURE TO HUMANITY

Originally, ritual was directed toward controlling nature. But once nature ceased to be seen as a threat because immediate survival issues were resolved through more advanced hunting techniques or an increase in agricultural sophistication, many rituals were abandoned. Emphasis then turned to creating internal tribal hierarchy and external exclusivity. Established leaders devised new rituals to maintain their positions of power. Some rituals changed and new ones were added, but all elements of ritual remained — power, control, and authority for domination.

I am altering the deal. Pray I don't alter it any further.
Darth Vader
The Empire Strikes Back

Circumcision requires parents to sacrifice the genitals of their child in a "mock-death ritual" to earn the parents good standing in the social body, the seal of approval of religious leaders or medical professionals as "devoted, responsible parents". If anthropologists looked at this mechanism from outside the system, such as in an ancient tribe it would be thought of as a "pledge of allegiance" or a "loyalty oath."

THE INEVITABILITY OF CHANGE

Dr. Joyce Brothers stated: *You can't make your kids not reinvent the wheel.*[6] Rituals have changed and will change, yet the message is still the same

— success for the unified group in whatever manner the members imagine will make success possible.

In the 1960's the Catholic Church allowed the Mass to be performed in the local language. Before that, the church required the use of ancient languages: Latin, Greek and Hebrew. The reason for the change was to increase attendance. This change in language strengthened the church. From Bell:[7-10]

> (Rituals) demonstrate that collective effervescences do not so much unite the community as strengthen the socially more dominant group through a "mobilization of bias."

Since circumcision is a "mock-death ritual" that supplanted full human sacrifice, we can only hope that with increased compassion and conscious awareness of the consequences, even genital sacrifice will not endure, but will change -- and it is changing. Some rabbis and parents already practice a new version of the naming celebration. The gentle *bris shalom* (welcoming) replaces the old *bris milah* (cutting).

CIRCUMCISION & GROUP IDENTITY

Ritual change is clear when observing puberty rites in neighboring cultures in the islands of Southeast Asia. The rites are basically the same, but with subtle differences among tribes. Each tribe considers its own puberty rites "normal" and "proper" and the other's variations "odd" and "improper". Though purpose and meaning of changes that developed in the puberty rites were surely obvious and meaningful to the participants at the time, they cannot be documented.

Circumcision gives group identity, thereby fulfilling the urge for belonging. Thus "belonging" itself establishes an "us and them" mentality and a bias against outsiders is established. Punishing nonconformity reinforces group identity and is allowed. In certain Muslim subcultures, a girl may be killed for just holding hands with a non-Muslim boy. Bell explains:[11]

> To approach cultural rituals as rooted in purely psychological conflicts is to see ritual as an oppression inherently necessary to society, which is defined in turn as the repression of the individual… Ritual structure is totally repressive; instead of channeling violence, the order of ritual completely denies it.

Unless we remember we cannot understand.
Edward Forester

With no memories they can have no past, no future, no will of their own. No purpose except to obey me.
Kane
Dr. Who

No woman can call herself free who does not own her own body.
Margaret Sanger

GENDER & MUTILATION PERPETRATION

Circumcision is usually same-sex perpetrated.[12] Women support and practice female circumcision (FGM), just as men support and practice male circumcision (MGM).[13,14] Maternal primacy can be observed in Egypt where the mother's educational status has been documented as the key factor in declining female mutilation statistics.[15]

However, in Judea when the Greeks outlawed circumcision, maternal maintenance of MGM went into gear. When men stopped circumcising, women took over and circumcised their sons.[16] Today in America, circumcision is declining but women are stepping into the role as rabbi mohels and doctors.[17] Dr. Bell supports the notion of ritual as an expression of competition and conflict between the sexes:[18]

> Ritual emerges as the means for a provisional synthesis of some form of original opposition… Such dispositions are, in turn, further differentiated into two kinds: moods and motivations.

INCREASED SEVERITY OF THE JEWISH CUT

Altering sacrificial ritual can change in either direction -- it can ease in severity or increase in harshness as a punishment. Originally, Jewish circumcision did not entail full glans exposure. Even though changes cannot be documented to an exact time or place, changes to the ritual have nonetheless taken place.

Bris milah, practiced at the time of Jesus, removed only the overhanging part of the prepuce that extended beyond the glans penis. What is practiced now is not *milah* but *peri'ah* which denudes the glans penis. *Peri'ah* was instituted after the Roman dispersion around 140 AD when Jewish men were erasing their tribal identification by pulling forward, stretching and lengthening the prepuce. Even though the severity of the ritual changed, the euphemism *circumcision* was retained. *The Oxford Dictionary of the Jewish Religion* states:[19]

> Many Hellenistic Jews, particularly those who participated in athletics at the gymnasium, had an operation performed to conceal the fact of their circumcision (1 Maccabees 1.15). Similar action was taken during the Hadrianic persecution, in which period a prohibition against circumcision was issued. It was probably in order to prevent the possibility of obliterating the traces of

circumcision that the rabbis added to the requirement of cutting the foreskin that of *peri'ah* (laying bare the glans).

Another layer was added to the *bris milah* around 500 AD, when sucking of the blood by the *mohel* (circumciser) after the cutting became part of the ritual.[20] As mentioned earlier, some Jewish parents today celebrate their children's birth without a genital cutting ritual — instead they hold a *brit shalom*, a welcoming celebration.

IDENTITY SHIFTS FROM INDIVIDUAL TO TRIBE

Through circumcision, individual identity is replaced with a group identity. Violent repression of the victim's individuality subdues the person and the experience is subconsciously ingrained. *Repression* goes deeper than conscious *suppression*. This occurs especially when the circumcision is performed preverbally, for the memory is stored in the more primitive parts of the brain. Since the infant victim cannot communicate, he or she then uses unconscious coping mechanisms: *sublimation* and *displacement*. He or she can also use *intellectualization* in *reaction formation* to make the harm seem good and virtuous, thereby increasing likelihood of passing on the same act in the future to future generations through *repetition compulsion*.[21] Bell explains:[22]

> Ultimately, the struggle between the individual psyche and society is never seen as simply out there in the social arena, but within each person as well. The formulation of ritual often appears to involve a distancing within actors of their private and social identities… Socialization cannot be anything less than the acquisition of schemes that can potentially restructure and renuance both self and society.

ALTERNATIVES TO RITUAL

Catherine Bell states there are only two alternatives to dissenters from social ritual. They appear to give a "no-win" situation for the weak of heart and mind. She writes:[23]

> The only real alternative to negotiated compliance is either total resistance or asocial self-exclusion.

Inherent in either alternative is a problem. In total resistance, he'll be accused of being *anti-social*. If he chooses asocial self-exclusion he will be diagnosed with a *Schizoid Personality Disorder*.

Remembrance wakes with all her busy train, swells at my breast, and turns the past to pain.
Oliver Goldsmith

Why is it that you want to shave him that way?
Jailer
It amuses me.
Dr. Nordoff
Perversions of Science

In the case of every horrible crime scene since the beginning of civilization, there is always that searing, fundamental question: What kind of a person could have done such a thing?
John Douglas
Mind Hunter

This does not mean an accepted personality disorder is not present, however the proper diagnosis would be: *Personality Change Due To ...* and then specify *Schizoid Personality Disorder Due To Circumcision Trauma*. The same is true for American circumcised females, as well as those females who were genitally altered because of *Congenital Adrenal Hyperplasia* (CAH).

RITUAL & PSYCHOLOGY

Ritual can be observed through the lens of psychology. For a very basic introductory understanding of ritual in psychology, we will briefly discuss five core theories of human behavior:

1. Sigmund Freud — personality
2. Carl Jung — psyche & archetypes
3. Abraham Maslow — motivation
4. Eric Berne — social communication
5. Kevin FitzMaurice — internal communication

SIGMUND FREUD — PERSONALITY

Sigmund Freud was the founder of contemporary psychology. Freud sectioned the individual personality into three parts: the *Id,* the *Ego and* the *Superego*.

ID: The *id* is the inheritance of the species, present from birth. It is the dark, inaccessible part of our personality. the hidden inner self, governed by the pleasure principle, completely unconscious, and the source of psychic energy derived from instinctual needs and drives. The id seeks to express impulses that the ego considers to be evil or excessively sexual.

EGO: The *ego* is the part that deals with reality, the negotiating, discerning self, partly conscious, and the portion of our personality that compares and contrasts ourself to others. It constantly struggles to defend itself from the external world, the libido of the id and the severity of the super-ego. The ego is never able fully to distinguish itself from the id, of which the ego is, in fact, a part. The ego works to repress the id or at least express it in a socially acceptable way.

SUPEREGO: The *superego* is the "conscience". It is what we have learned from our parents and society, our sense of "right" and "wrong." It tries to suppress the id and attempts to make the ego operate morally. It functions on a conscious level and in social settings. It psychologically rewards or punishes through a developed system of moral attitudes.

The child has been fully sexualized before the advent of Frued.
James Kincaid

We're doomed.
C3PO
Star Wars

The pills were ethical because they didn't interfere with a person's ability to reproduce, which would have been unnatural and immoral.
All the pills did was to take every bit of pleasure out of sex.
Kurt Vonnegut

CARL JUNG — PSYCHE & ARCHETYPES

Carl Jung divided the human psyche into four parts: *male* and *female*, with each possessing a *light* and *dark* side. Jung explained there is an element of the masculine in the feminine that he termed the *animus*. Also there is an element of the feminine in the masculine termed the *anima*. Jung's animus and anima appear to represent the eyes in the combined inseparable *yin* and *yang* symbol from the ancient Far East. Together the *yin* and *yang* combine into a circle. The elements are:

	Female	Male
Light	Yin	Yang
Dark	Animus (male)	Anima (female)

Contemporary application of the word *animus* to impropriety has become commonplace and can be problematic, for that is not how Jung intended the word to be used.

How we usually present ourselves to others in society, said Jung, is usually through our outward, light-side *persona*. What lies beneath the facade is a hidden dark-side *shadow*. "Evil" is perceived as the archetype shadow -- the "devil." Everyone possesses both elements and sometimes they are reversed. For example in the film *Star Wars* Darth Vader appears at first to be totally evil and dark, but we ultimately discover that he has an inner light side in his original personality as Anakin Skywalker.

The ancient Egyptians, Nubians and other African tribes believed that the clitoris was the masculine, hard, erectile tissue; and, the male foreskin was the feminine, soft, feeling part of the penis. They amputated the parts they thought threatened proper development. To eradicate any trace of hardness from the female, they cut off the clitoris; to eradicate any trace of softness from the male, they cut off the prepuce. Masculine involvement in circumcision belongs to the *dark anima*.

ABRAHAM MASLOW — MOTIVATION

Abraham Maslow developed the *hierarchy of needs*. Whereas Freud studied mentally ill patients, Maslow studied people who excelled. He found that people follow a certain predictable pattern consisting of five levels, from obtaining the mundane essentials of food, clothing and shelter, all the way to conscious contact with the sublime, which he called *self-actualization*. He

There's bigger things here besides me and you.
Spiderman
Spiderman2

Fascism is not defined by the number of its victims, but by the way it kills them.
Jean-Paul Sartre

Exactly how much motivation is your client looking for.
Jarred
Kiss Tomorrow Goodbye

observed that we move back and forth through these levels throughout our lives as circumstances demand. When the lower, physical necessities are met we are free to move to the next higher level and we may regress during challenging times.

Maslow's five levels are briefly explained below:[24]

PHYSIOLOGICAL

Physiological needs encompass the essentials: food, water, air, oxygen, nutrients, elimination of waste, activity, rest, sleep, to maintain a certain body temperature (98.6F), avoidance of pain, sex, etc. Without these things, life on planet earth ceases to exist.

SAFETY

After one's basic physical needs are met, next come safety and security concerns — a desire for stability, structure, limits, law and order.

LOVE & BELONGING

We have a need for closeness with affection: for friends, spouse and children. We need community.

ESTEEM

There are two forms of esteem. Self-esteem carries feelings of confidence, competence, achievement, mastery, independence, and freedom. The other is the esteem that comes from status, fame, glory, recognition, attention, reputation, appreciation, dignity — even dominance.

SELF-ACTUALIZATION

Maslow found that self-actualized people tended to have more peak experiences than the average person, a high in which they felt at one with life or nature or God, part of the infinite and the eternal. They were honest, able to discern the real and genuine. They were problem-centered, looking for solutions. They believed the means were often more important than the ends. They enjoyed solitude and were comfortable being alone. They enjoyed deep, personal relations with a few close friends and family members rather than shallow relationships with large numbers of people. They enjoyed autonomy and resisted enculturation (social pressure to be "well adjusted" or to "fit in"). They did not use humor at the expense of others. They accepted their own and others' foibles, yet they were strongly motivated to change negative qualities

Life is not a spectacle; it is a predicament.
Santayna

The motive of the crime is only known to the offender. It is his personal-cause homicide. It is not a crime of violence that comes up suddenly, passionately; it is a very methodological, organized crime.
Robert Ressler
I have Lived in the Monster

Your own presence should be motivation enough.
Professor Phipps
Higher Learning

in themselves. They were spontaneous and simple rather than pretentious or artificial, yet they tended to be conventional on the surface, where "nonconformists" tend to be the most dramatic. They had a sense of humility and respect towards others — "democratic values" — treasuring ethnic and individual variety. Maslow called their social interest, compassion and humanity *Gemeinschaftsgefühl*. Self-actualizers have a strong ethic and are spiritual but seldom conventionally religious in nature. They had a freshness of appreciation and wonder, which allowed them to be creative, inventive and original.

How does circumcision impair a person's life experience? Looking at circumcision from within the Maslow hierarchy, this is what we find:

PHYSIOLOGICAL
Cutting a child's genitals destroys their bodily integrity and inflicts traumatic levels of pain. Some report children lose interest in breastfeeding. Since cutting interferes with the primal suckling instinct, such a severe impact on a child's physiology could only indicate everlasting harm. Sex is an instinctual, physiological primary motivator, at the base of Maslow's pyramid. All subsequent behavior rests on this foundation and the foundation is shaky due to this unnecessary, early childhood sexual assault. Their body identity is insecure and the loss of essential genital skin detrimentally changes sexual function and therefore undermines sexual relationships in adulthood.

SAFETY
The child is infused with feelings of fear, dread, danger, threat, distrust, betrayal. Many people who were circumcised have sub-clinical PTSD and are fixated in an unconscious primary level of fear. Subsequently, they carry a life-long concern for their safety, which often appears as defensive quirks and oddities. They do not feel safe.

LOVE AND BELONGING
Circumcision is sold by promising beauty, love, belonging. Yet can anyone truly trust a group that wounds its members? Can anyone truly trust a family or social order that does not protect children? Trust has been shattered at a very fundamental level. One behavior that fits well is the psychological category *Schizoid Personality Disorder*, because they'd rather be alone and safe than to be around someone who might hurt them. If they can't trust their own loved ones, religious and medical authorities, then who can they trust? No one. When natural sexual function shifts due to loss of important genital skin, sexual bonding is impaired and family relationships are undermined.

In some cases non-violence requires more militancy than violence.
Cesar Chavez

I claim not to have controlled events, but confess plainly that events have controlled me.
Abraham Lincoln

It is in your nature to destroy yourselves.
The Terminator
Terminator 2: Judgement Day

ESTEEM

Even though a baby or child is celebrated as the star of the circumcision show — queen or king for a day — and he has a veneer of "I am special because I am the center of attention today," beyond that, s/he is still deeply wounded on the level of healthy esteem. A child always initially at least shoulders the blame for child abuse: "If I was really good, really worthy, no one would have hurt me in that way... If I was okay, no one would have cut my body." These children will be trying to prove for the rest of their lives that they are okay. They will never feel they are acceptable and may take the route of self-deprecation, or their insecurity might compel them to overcompensate by becoming pompous, disdainful and arrogant.

SELF ACTUALIZATION

Human awareness is either in the prison of the physical/mental/emotional plane or in what Maslow calls the *peak experience*. All beings long for that experience. Ritual attempts to make it happen.

Under the influence of drugs, sex, music, dance, repetition, near-death experiences and unbearable horror, the human mind short-circuits, there is a rush of adrenalin and endorphins giving a quick, temporarily peek at the transcendental realm. At a circumcision event child, parents, circumcisers and spectators -- all are pushed to their limits by cognitive dissonance. They achieve an adrenalin rush, a momentary "crack in the cosmic egg," a "high." But at whose expense? The baby may be stuck for life, not at the top of the pyramid, but at the bottom — in distrust and fear for his bodily survival. There has to be a better, safer, kinder, gentler way to achieve the "high" humans long for.

Performing ritual as a circuitous route to bliss indicates a form of *repetition compulsion* for both the individual and the society, so circumcision might be considered *societal repetition compulsion* as well as a *societal post-traumatic attachment*. This then leads to *Body Integrity Identity Disorder* where amputation becomes the norm and people in that culture not only want to be amputees, they are also sexually attracted to amputees -- a form of *Societally-Induced Body Dysmorphic Disorder*.

ERIC BERNE — SOCIAL COMMUNICATION

Eric Berne's *Transactional Analysis* (TA) discusses the types of *communication* essential in formulating ritual. He segments communication psychology into three negotiating *ego* elements, *Parent*, *Adult* and *Child*, abbreviated as PAC.[25] In the PAC structure, *Parent* and *Child* communication is mediated through the *Adult*. Berne's categories are similar but not identical to Freud's *id*, *ego* and *superego*.

> CHILD: The manner and intent of reaction is the same as it would be for a very little boy or girl.

> PARENT: To dominate and control children, parents assume certain postures, gestures, vocabulary, feelings, etc.

> ADULT: This is the mature, autonomous, objective state that appraises situations and states thought processes, perceived problems and conclusions in a non-prejudicial manner.

Communication often starts with an initial *transaction* between two individuals and ends with a dishonest *game*. From beginning to end, the sequence involves movement through the stages of *transaction*, *procedure*, *ritual*, *pastime* and *game*. Games may be played by individuals or groups.

Each step in the process builds on the previous step. So, for proper analysis and understanding of how circumcision is perpetuated, no step should be left out. Following are the stepwise concepts quoted from Berne's *Games People Play*.[26]

> TRANSACTION: The unit of social intercourse is called a transaction. If two or more people encounter each other in a social aggregation, sooner or later one of them will speak, or give some other indication of acknowledging the presence of others. This is called *transactional stimulus*. Another person will then say or do something which is in some way related to this stimulus, and that is called the *transactional response*. Simple transactional analysis is concerned with diagnosing which ego state implemented the transactional stimulus, and which one executed the transactional response. The simplest transactions are those in which both stimulus and response arise from the Adults of the parties concerned. The agent, estimating from the data before him that a scalpel is now the instrument of choice, holds out his hand. The respondent appraises this gesture correctly, estimates the forces and distances involved, and places the handle of the scalpel exactly where the surgeon expects it. Next in simplicity are Child-Parent transactions. The fevered child asks for a glass of water, and the nurturing mother brings it. Both these transactions are *complementary*; that is, the response is appropriate and expected and follows the natural order of healthy human relationships.

You're supposed to be stupid, so don't abuse the privilege.
Braddock
Blue Thunder

Had he been born in the Republic, we would have identified him earlier.
Qui-Gon Jinn
The Phantom Menace

And may we not say that the mind of the one who knows has knowledge, and that the mind of the other, who opines only, has opinion.
Socrates

PROCEDURE: A procedure is a series of simple complementary Adult transactions directed toward the manipulation of reality... Procedures are based on data processing and probability estimates concerning the *material* of reality, and reach their highest development in professional techniques... Two variables are used in evaluating procedures. A procedure is said to be *efficient* when the agent makes the best possible use of the data and experience available to him, regardless of any deficiencies that may exist in his knowledge. If the Parent or the Child interferes with the Adult's data processing, the procedure becomes *contaminated* and will be less efficient. The *effectiveness* of a procedure is judged by the actual results. The efficiency is a psychological criterion and effectiveness is a material one.

RITUAL: A ritual is a stereotyped series of simple complementary transactions programmed by external social forces. An informal ritual, such as social leave-taking, may be subject to considerable local variations in details, although the basic form remains the same. A formal ritual, such as a Roman Catholic mass, offers much less option... Many formal rituals started off as heavily contaminated though fairly efficient procedures, but as time passed and circumstances changed, they lost all procedural validity while still retaining their usefulness as acts of faith. Transactionally, they represent guilt-relieving or reward-seeking compliances with traditional Parental demands. They offer a safe, reassuring (apotropiac), and are often an enjoyable method of structuring time.

PASTIMES: This may be defined as a series of semi-ritualistic, simple, complementary transactions arranged around a single field of material, whose primary object is to structure an interval of time. The beginning and the end of the interval are typically signaled by procedures or rituals. The transactions are adaptively programmed so that each party will obtain the maximum gains or advantages during the interval. The better his adaptation, the more he will get out of it.

GAME: A game is an ongoing series of complementary ulterior transactions progressing to a well-defined, predictable outcome. Descriptively it is a recurring set of transactions, often repetitious, superficially plausible, with a snare, or "gimmick." Games are clearly differentiated from procedures, rituals, and pastimes by two chief characteristics: (1) their ulterior quality and (2) the payoff. Procedures may be successful, rituals effective, and pastimes profitable, but all of them are by definition candid, and the ending may be sensational, but it is not dramatic. Every game, on the other hand, is basically dishonest, and the outcome has a dramatic, as distinct from merely exciting, quality.

In the circumcision ritual, the infant *child* is not the only child in the interaction. The religious or medical authority figure or figures assume the role of *parent-adult* and all other grown-ups involved assume the role of *child-adult*. No *child* present at the ritual dares question the authority of the circumciser.

KEVIN FITZMAURICE — INTERNAL COMMUNICATION

FitzMaurice explains that the ego has only five actions with many variations:

1. Seek death and destruction
2. Cover death and destruction with darkness
3. Cover death and destruction with names of good
4. Cover calling evil good (#3) with darkness
5. Cover death and destruction with victim role

He explains these as ego responses to threat or disturbance from:

1. Pain, hurt, shame, loss of face, humiliation
2. Fear of ego pain
3. Anger, fighting
4. Anxiety, avoidance, fear, escapism, flight

THE TRIPARTITE NATURE OF EGO

Kevin FitzMaurice segments Freud's *ego* into three parts which he calls the *Tripartite Nature of Ego*.[27] These three parts each possess four aspects. FitzMaurice demonstrates that our thought processes are neutral, and the individual has the *choice* whether to act on his/her thoughts in ways that are socially responsible or criminal. Possible thought process around circumcision for some practitioners might be as follows:

SECRET SELF
Self-Images, Self-Concepts, Self-Constructs

1. I think I am a good person, but when I think about sex, I think about children, not adults. And I think about inflicting pain rather than giving pleasure.

2. I certainly don't want to think of myself as perverse or abusive.

3. I think that others think of me as a good person, a pillar of the community.

4. I certainly never would want others to think of me as perverse or abusive.

True signature is the aspect of the crime that emotionally fulfills the offender, and so remains relatively the same. Torture, for example, is almost always a signature.
John Douglas
The Anatomy of Motive

We don't live in the world of reality, we live in the world of how we perceive reality.
Byron Singer

My purpose is to entertain myself first and other people secondly.
John D. McDonald

SCRIPT SELF
Rules for secret and social selves — What, When, Where, How, and Why

*It's always
 more pleasant to
stone a martyr, no
matter how much we
admire him.*
John Barth

1. It is OK for me to find a way to touch children's genitals and inflict pain.

2. But I must always be perceived as a pillar of the community, so I don't want to get caught or break the law.

3. In a "service" capacity, I can legally exercise my compulsions.

4. Therefore, I will become a professional circumciser. I will be held in high esteem and get paid for touching children's genitals and inflicting pain.

SOCIAL SELF
Social-Images, Social-Concepts, Social-Constructs

*Washing one's hands
of the conflict between
the powerful and the
powerless means to
side with the
powerful,
not to be neutral.*
Paulo Freire

1. I think of myself as a model citizen, a good doctor or a holy man, a pillar of the community.

2. I will not think of myself as perverse or abusive.

3. Others think of me as an upstanding member of society, a good doctor or a holy man.

4. I won't even entertain the possibility that anyone could ever think of me as a child abuser or perpetrator.

CRIMINOLOGY

The psychological indicators of serial predation are similar to those of religious ritual

What does ritual have to do with criminology? In *Ritual Theory, Ritual Practice* Catherine Bell writes that ritual is motivated by five things: power, control, authority, manipulation and domination. The FBI agents who originated criminal profiling use the exact same five words to describe the motivation of criminal serial predators and to Bell's words, they add one more: selfishness.

Criminologist, Colin Evans connects the dots between criminology and the repetitive nature of genital mutilation ritual:[1]

> Serial killers are usually creatures of habit; they find a method of destruction that works and stick to it.

In this chapter we explore the stunning similarities between the practice of ritual and criminology. The books of retired FBI agents Robert Ressler, and John Douglas with Mark Olshaker are a good place to start researching sexual crimes. Recommended initial readings are: *I Have Lived in the Monster*, *Mind Hunter* and *Journey into Darkness*.

SEXUAL PREDATION

Objectification is the degradation of another person by perceiving him or her as an object as opposed to honoring him or her as a valuable human being. This is a form of *dissociation* or separating people from their fundamental humanity. *Dissociation* is integral to the perpetration of violence against others. Circumcision reduces the humanity of the child to his or her genitals. Circumcision is an intent focus and vicious attack on the child's genitals. *Circumcision is where sex and violence meet.*

Any empathy expressed by a predator for the victim is purely self-serving.[2]

Religious and sexual mania are closely related.
Chief Inspector London
Frenzy

Most of these guys have no burn-out point.
John Douglas
Mind Hunter

Sexual predation is pathologically directed by *objectifying* another person's healthy body and sexuality with intent to damage and harm. *Sexual predation* can be defined in this way:

> SEXUAL PREDATION: a pathologically directed activity, involving the objectification of another person from a perceived sexual nature, which often, though not necessarily, possesses the intent to do harm to another, whether physical and/or psychological, often including motivations of power, control, and authority using manipulation for domination from selfishness

To clarify the nature of socialized sexual crime, we will first discuss individual sexual crime. Connie Fletcher in *What Cops Know* wrote:[3]

> Rape is about anger, power, control, and the need to humiliate somebody. It's not sex driven. Many times, the rapist is also having consensual sex while he's going out raping... Usually, it's not the sex that excites them; it's the sense of power they get over the victim. With some rapists, they're not there for the sex. They're there to inflict pain.

GENDER, VIOLENCE & CRUELTY

Men tend to act out with violent, aggressive, physical action. Men's violent rage is quick, explosive, active and intense. Males tend to react quickly, suddenly, without thinking. Once it is over, it is usually over.

Women's cruelty on the other hand, is slow to develop, deep and predominately verbal. Once a cruel word has been spoken or a cruel act has been performed, brooding continues. Because women are physically smaller and weaker, they tend to internalize anger and brood on it before taking action. In many situations, women can be more dangerous because their internal anger lingers and sometimes never goes away. Knowledgeable female correctional officers often prefer to guard male inmates, regarding them as less dangerous than female inmates.[4]

MODUS OPERANDI & SIGNATURE

The *modus operandi* (MO) is the type of crime and the way it is carried out — the *procedure*. A criminal usually targets the prospective victim according to gender, race, age, physical type and availability.[5] MO includes weapons or instruments and the perpetrator's approach to the victim. MO can change and be refined over time to ensure perpetrator safety and security.

The perpetrator signs his work almost as an artist does. The *signature* is the violent criminal's "calling card" or his unique ritual which provides him psychological fulfillment.[6] The fantasy of violent crime is often present long before it is enacted. Crime scenes reveal peculiar characteristics or unusual offender input that identify the offender because his *signature* or ritual never changes, though it may evolve. Level of violence can be a factor in *signature*.[7] Dismemberment is a *signature* in lust murders.[8] Circumcision is, of course, a form of dismemberment.

Circumcision's particular MO may be culture-specific. Its Signature is genital wounding by dismemberment. Genital mutilation is a socialized form of child abuse and molestation.[9] Douglas and Olshaker wrote:[10]

> Modus Operandi — MO — is learned behavior. It's what the perpetrator does to commit the crime. It is dynamic — that is, it can change. Signature, a term I [Douglas] coined to distinguish it from MO, is what the perpetrator has to do to fulfill himself. It is static; it does not change.

THE MOTIVATIONAL CYCLE OF BETRAYAL

The motivational process of most sexual crimes is circular and similar to a serial offender's criminal ritual. It is a Cycle of Betrayal. The cycle begins with a feeling *betrayal* which the perpetrator tries to mediate by obtaining and exercising *power*. Performing a power-based action another person is to effect *control* over them. This gives the perpetrator a sense of *authority*. It also assumes a right to exercise influence over another person's life in

order to fill a lack in the perpetrator's own inner self. The active component is *manipulation*. *Domination* is established by a successful manipulation. The act is perpetrated out of *selfishness*. If unchallenged, rule is established with maintenance assured. With success another *betrayal* is then perpetrated.

The *cycle of betrayal* begins with a betrayal of a victim and ends with that victim's betrayal of another victim and may be thought of as *Signature's Desire*. Seventy-six percent of rapists were sexual abuse victims when young. A very high percentage of circumcisers were also circumcised.

It is by its promise of an occult sense of power that evil often attracts the weak.
Eric Hoffer

Serial killers get a sense of control from their killings.
Karen
The Ugly

Remember, most serial offenders are expert manipulators of other people.
Robert Ressler
I Have Lived in the Monster

TRANSFERENCE OF AGGRESSION

To be remembered after we are dead is poor recompense for being treated with contempt while we are alive.
William Hazlitt

Genital ritual is a psychosexual *transference* of aggression:

TRANSFERENCE: The deliberate displacement of one's unresolved conflicts, dependencies, and aggressions onto a substitute object

In domestic violence, women are more likely to use weapons such as guns, knives and baseball bats[11] attempting to compensate for their weaker physique. Sexually dysfunctional males compensate by using weapons, especially knives, as *penile enhancements*.[12] Knives are also associated with many goddesses. Since a woman has no penis, her choice to use a knife might be thought of as a *penile substitute* or *clitoral enhancement*.

If a victim's resentment is toward the father, aggression will most often be directed at males. If resentment is toward the mother, aggression will most often be directed at females.

Circumcision of either sex has been described as a *mock-death ceremony*.[13,14] The following concept of *representation* is derived from Douglas and Olshaker's *The Anatomy of Motive*:[15]

Attack him when he's unprepared, appear when you are not expected.
Sun Tzu
The Art of War

The victim is a *representation*. It is as if the American President represents the United States society, and the male child represents the masculine. The intellectual overlay, especially to the Organized type is a cause.

The cause used as an excuse is a convenient justification. It is transference in Reason Avoidance so not to confront and deal with reality. There is often a dissociation of the perpetrator's parental figure to the same sex of the victim. The violent act is from a deep seated inadequacy. To solve the problem of inadequacy the represented object must be defiled or eliminated. The male becomes an object and inferior.

Once the course of action is decided, the Organized offender is calm and the internal conflict of stress is mostly eliminated... The offenders who get close and personal to their victim actually do not get emotionally involved. This dissociation maintains distance. Thus, they feel comfortable in the situations they are able to control.

These are crimes of passion, not of profit.
Dr. Richmond
Psycho

There is no remorse or contrition. Everything is matter of fact. They know the difference between right and wrong. Changing wrong to right changes the standards.

This then makes the consequences non-consequential.

THREE APPROACHES

Serial rapists use one of three approaches to gain access to their victims.[16,17] They act within their favorite comfort zone: the *con*, *blitz* or *surprise*.[18] Violence never decreases over time; it only increases with success. All modes are *narcissistic*. Perpetrators believe it is their right to take from others.

This criminal behavior typing may help us understand the structure of *socialized* sexual predation. Notice that in the "con" category, a *narcissistic service personality* is assumed.

CON: The *con* is used to gain the victim's confidence. They act friendly and have a calm attitude. Often they wear uniforms. They are confident, organized, patient, and meticulous. The *con* approach increases over time as the serial predator becomes more confident and organized.

BLITZ: The *blitz* is brutally violent. Suddenness is not the defining factor. The blitz approach describes the attack itself. Total time with the act may vary. It is commonly used by the *anger retaliatory* type of predator.

SURPRISE: The victim is chosen and a trap is set. They usually attack from behind. Threats are made if the victim does not cooperate. This approach is often used by the *power reassurance* rapist.

PASSIVE INITIATION

Passive initiation is having another person commit an act without the initiator's direct involvement. *Delegation* is common with females and used by some males. Charles Manson himself, for instance, is not known to have killed.

Excuse is also used as a method of Passive Initiation. Ritual circumcision hides behind theology and religion using the excuse of a *deity demand*. Instead of *the devil made me do it*, religious circumcision says, *God made me do it*. In medicine, blame-shifting can go from doctor to parents, from parents to doctor, to the kids in the locker room, to the need for dad to have a son who matches him, to the *disease du jour*, to the need to make it easy for mom, etc.

VICTIMOLOGY

Victimology is the criminologist's study of victim traits, such as lifestyle, employment, background, likes and dislikes, financial troubles, alcohol or drug abuse, daily routines — and even whom the victim spoke to last. This

There are certain realities. I want us to have a clear understanding.
Han
Enter the Dragon

Cowboy Erwin up there is repressing a memory of a milking gone bad.
Laurence
Cupid

What arrogance to think you could ever understand my intentions.
Ivan
Face Off

information helps law enforcement officials understand why specific victims are targeted. It enables them to pinpoint persons who might be at risk. It also narrows the perpetrator's profile and helps them understand his motive. A *victimology* profile may help law enforcement personnel take proactive measures to draw out and apprehend the offender.

Victimology provides direction for use in interrogation techniques. For example, does the perpetrator feel remorse, does he feel he is on a mission, is he proud of his crime, or is he trying to get revenge? This will aid in obtaining a confession. It also helps to protect the public, making it possible to warn those who are most likely to be in danger. Knowing the victim profile also aids the criminologist understand what happened during the commission of the crime.[19]

OBSESSION — STALKING

Obsession entails *stalking* and *narcissistic* behavior. *Love obsession* is a term the FBI's John Douglas uses to refer to a variety of stalking situations.[20] Twenty to twenty-five percent of stalkers are within *love obsession* guidelines.[21] Stalkers want to control the object of their desire. Obsessive personalities are blindly focused on their target and do not lose interest.[22]

Circumcision is similar to *love obsession*. It is *societal stalking. Narcissists* are not in love with themselves; they are in love with their reflection. A *narcissist* with a mission feels he is chosen and is convinced that he has a right to perpetrate a cultural ritual like genital cutting onto others. He feels compelled to conform the victim to his own image. He disregards facts that contradict his mission — they are useless to him.[23] Self-perceived superiority and a sense of entitlement lead to aggression individually and socially.

SEXUAL SADISM

According to retired FBI criminal profiler Roy Hazelwood, the term *sadism* is overused in criminology, accounting for about ten percent of sexual crime. The definition of *sexual sadism* is sexual arousal gained from inflicting pain and suffering on others. Sexual sadists are among the most destructive of all predators. They are focused on the goal and process of inflicting pain and humiliation on the victim. They torture to inflict both physical pain and mental anguish. Sadism is highly symbolic and often hides behind the excuse of religion.

I will buy his secret in a bounty of pain.
Pinhead
Hellraiser IV: Bloodline

There are only three sins — causing pain, causing fear, and causing anguish. The rest is window dressing.
Roger Caras

Is it usual for the host to kill a guest?
The Doctor
In certain rarified circles.
Monarch
Dr. Who

The sadist's core fantasies are cemented by age sixteen. Sadists have no remorse or sympathy. The victim is depersonalized to object status. Killing is their apogee in obsessive control (and remember that circumcision is a "mock-death ceremony").

There are two types of sadism: *minor* and *major*. *Minor sadism* involves *partners who consent* to bondage, discipline, spanking, and submission to degrading acts. An example of *minor sadism* might be when genitally intact men have agreed to be tied down and circumcised in the center of a circle with masturbating men looking on.

Major sadism involves consenting partners or *non-consenting victims*. Some acts of *major sadism* include:

- *lust murder* — sexual arousal to the act of killing, often with dismemberment

- *vampirism* — sexual arousal from bloodletting and drinking blood

- *necrophilia* — arousal through sexual experience with a corpse

- *cannibalism*

Since circumcision involves a non-consenting child, it is clearly a form of sadistic, pathological group behavior. Adult participants, including parents of minors, medical and religious personnel, are required to prove themselves by negating their natural instincts to protect the child, so they can belong to the group. Genital blood ritual in the mock-death ritual of circumcision belongs in the *lust dismemberment* subcategory under *major sadism*.

PSYCHOPATHOLOGY

Douglas and Olshaker state:[24]

> When you've analyzed what should be the motive based on the crime scenario and that doesn't make sense, and you go through all the other "logical" ones and you can't make one of them fit reasonably, then you start looking into psychiatric territory. All crimes have a motive; all crimes make sense according to some logic, though that logic may be a strictly internal one with no relationship to any "objective" logic. In many instances, a hidden sexual motive emerges, a motive that originates in fantasy. Tragically, this motive of uncontrolled anger and the need for sexual domination doesn't always occur against strangers. Many sexual sadists are married or in ongoing relationships — totally self-involved narcissists.

*You were born
to be murdered.*
Calloway
The Third Man

*The vilest deeds
like poison weeds
Bloom well
in prison air;
It is only what is good
in Man
that wastes and
withers there:
Pale Anguish keeps
the heavy gate
And the Warden is
Despair.*
Oscar Wilde

*Psychopaths suffer no
qualm about the fate
of their victims, and
may even savor the
pain they inflict.*
Robert D. Hare

Psychopathology involves three characteristics: 1) egocentricity, 2) lack of empathy and 3) no remorse. Narcissistic psychopaths feel they have special entitlement. As with serial killers, they have a system of destruction and bring that destruction to others. This permits using and taking from others to enhance their status internally, monetarily and socially.

Psychopaths lie. When caught, they make up other lies. This can be seen in the various rationalizations for circumcision. They restructure the argument as needed. Circumcision has been touted as a remedy for many ailments and when disproved, they invent another excuse. The *service personality* appears to be humble, sensitive and profound, and they say publicly what would be expected. Yet behind the scenes they laugh, joke and brag about their deeds.

Psychopaths are not emotionally attached to other people; they do not see others as valuable. Instead, they are attached to impersonal objects such as knives, blood and human body tissue. Their object possesses magical powers and they use it almost like a magic wand. The genitals, which possess natural, pleasurable, reproductive powers are made subservient to the psychopath's will. The natural genitalia are defeated by the "magical power" of the knife. Psychopaths gravitate toward sexual sadism.[25] They will not change or stop. They are untreatable. Douglas and Olshaker wrote: [26]

> This is really nothing but elementary butchery. And we have long since learned that serial killers need nothing but will to commit whatever atrocities they want on a body... They are willing to have someone else die for their selfish purposes, and that is one of the definitions of sociopathic behavior... based on my research and experience, there is no possibility of rehabilitating this type of individual. If he is ever let out, he will kill again.

ORGANIZED & DISORGANIZED OFFENDERS

The two types of offenders are *organized* or *disorganized*.[27] Circumcision, whether religious or medical, fits within the organized category. Organized perpetrators are more controlled and controlling. From the FBI's Behavioral Science Unit (BSU) findings, the University of Dundee once posted a comparative synopsis on the Internet. In summary, it stated:[28]

ORGANIZED and DISORGANIZED can be separated by analysis of four criteria: 1) murderer's action during the offense, 2) victim characteristics, 3) use of vehicles in the crime, mobility and 4) types of evidence left at the crime scene.

ORGANIZED OFFENDER

PROFILE CHARACTERISTICS: Usually first born. Organized offenders come from a stable family with erratic discipline. They have a higher than average intelligence, are mature and sane.[29] They work below their abilities, but have skilled jobs. Often there is sporadic employment. Stressful events, including financial, employment, or relationship difficulties, precipitate criminal behavior. Organized offenders are socially adequate, live with a partner, or dominant female family member. They are sexually competent within the limits of normalcy. Anger elicits the crime yet they are calm, controlled, and relaxed during the act. Their fantasies are fixed. They take items as tokens from the victim and use them to relive the experience and they acquire documentation from the press. After the crime they may move elsewhere.

CRIME SCENE: The organized offender's crime scene shows order before, during, and after the act of violence. Their acts are carefully planned to avoid detection. Victims are victims of opportunity, yet for the most part the victims share common characteristics. There is careful planning and searching for the preferred type of victim. Selection may hinge on age, appearance, occupation, hairstyle or lifestyle. Being socially adept, they attempt to strike up a pseudo-relationship. They often use some type of impersonation to hide their true demeanor. They usually have a clean appearance and dress well. This is aimed to gain the victim's confidence. They lure their victims rather than forcibly abduct them. Sexual control is required, and when resistance ceases, violence increases. The outcome is largely predetermined. Control is obtained with various types of restraints. Weapons are sadistically used with elements of eroticism. These weapons are brought to, and taken away from, the crime scene. Death is tortured and methodical. They carefully avoid leaving evidence. Fantasy and ritual predominate. Obsessive-compulsive behavior is indicated in the crime scene. Victims may be posed.

DISORGANIZED OFFENDER

PROFILE CHARACTERISTICS: Disorganized offenders typically have below-average intelligence. They are usually later-born children in the family. There is harsh parental discipline. Their father's work history is unstable and an inconsistent life persists. They are confused and distressed, with recurring primal obsessions. They are socially inadequate and have probably never married. They often live alone or with a parent or parental figure. They are usually paranoid of others and live close to the crime scene. They act compulsively under stress. Sexual inadequacy precludes any involved or sustained relationship. They are usually heterosexual but ignorant of sex and have sexual aversions.

The only thing I could control was when, and how, and where it was going to happen.
Chuck
Cast Away

He plans with obsessive detail what props he'll bring and what knots he will tie.
Helen Hudson
Copycat

The killer had the ability to hide his mental disease from co-workers or other people around him, this suggested average or above-average intelligence.
Robert Cullen
Citizen X

All efforts of violence are powerless to weaken truth, and serve only to make it stronger.
Blaise Pascal

CRIME SCENE: The crime scene shows sudden action with no plan to avoid detection. The scene is in disarray indicating spontaneous, unplanned behavior. The victim may be someone the victim knows. The age and sex of the victim is not an indicator. Killing is immediate often using a blitz or surprise type of attack, giving immediate total control over the victim, which gives the perpetrator relief from his sense of inadequacy. With this type of attack the victim can never gain control. The victim is depersonalized with extreme bodily defacing. There is no verbal communication and restraints are not necessary. Sexual acts are sadistic. The victim is not posed. Usually the weapon is obtained at the scene and is left at the crime scene.

Organized killers are often *anal retentive personalities*, which is broadly defined as orderliness, stubbornness, a compulsion for control with an interest in collecting, possessing, and retaining objects and a tendency toward obsessive-compulsive disorder or obsessive-compulsive personality disorder.

The one means that wins the easiest victory over reason: terror and force.
Adolf Hitler

Disorganized killers are more often *anal expulsive personalities,* which is broadly defined as exhibiting cruelty, emotional outbursts, disorganization, self-confidence, (sometimes) artistic ability, generosity, rebelliousness and general carelessness.

PERSONALITY TYPES

This typology has four modalities: *visionary*, *mission-oriented*, *hedonistic*, and *power/control*.[30]

VISIONARY: The only killer with biogenic etiology, such as a brain tumor or brain damage. Etiology may be from auditory or visual delusions or hallucinations. They are often psychotic, paranoid schizophrenics. Often they justify their acts with theological explanations.

A technological advance and a social lag were responsible for the rise of the mercenary.
William Weir
Fatal Victories

MISSION-ORIENTED: Their goal is elimination of those deemed improper and they are correcting a perceived wrong. They are not delusional.

HEDONISTIC: These are the lust killers who kill for emotional and/or sexual pleasure. They are thrill-oriented, sadistic and kill in comfort. Main motivation is just the ability to kill — why not?

POWER/CONTROL: These predators seek total domination over the life of another. The victim is subject to the perpetrator's whim. Excitement is in power and control, through a perceived authority do so.

TRAUMA

There are two types of traumatic events. Type I may be a single short-term event such as rape, assault, or severe beating. This is the event of the circumcision. Type II, involves repeated, long-term exposure within chronic victimization.[31]

Though circumcision is a single event, it may be re-triggered with a negative psychological emotion from subsequent ritualistic community events. Even a mention of circumcision may create anxiety. The fact of circumcision is often observed during urination and sexual activities and can stir PTSD symptoms.

TYPES OF CHILD MALTREATMENT

The American government defines *child maltreatment* as:[32]

CHILD MALTREATMENT: The physical and mental injury, sexual abuse, negligent treatment, or maltreatment of a child under the age of 18 by a person who was responsible for the child's welfare under circumstances which indicate that the child's health or welfare is harmed or threatened.

The National Association of Counsel for Children defines four types of *child maltreatment.*[33]

PHYSICAL ABUSE: Non-accidental physical injury as a result of caretaker acts. Physical abuse frequently includes: shaking, slapping, punching, beating, kicking, biting and burning.

SEXUAL ABUSE: Involvement is with dependent developmentally immature children and adolescents in sexual activities which they do not fully comprehend, and to which they are unable to give informed consent. Sexual abuse includes touching, fondling and penetration.

NEGLECT: Failure of caretakers to provide for a child's fundamental needs. Although neglect can include children's necessary emotional needs, neglect typically concerns adequate food, housing, clothing, medical care and education.

EMOTIONAL–PSYCHOLOGICAL ABUSE: This is habitual verbal harassment of a child by disparagement, criticism, threat and ridicule. Emotional or psychological abuse includes behavior that threatens or intimidates a child. It includes threats, name calling, belittling and shaming.

There is not a man here that has a right to watch me beg for my life.
Morel
Pit Fighter

A form of sexual satisfaction called 'piquerism'... is sexual pleasure gained by stabbing, cutting, or slicing of another person.
Robert Keppel
Signature Killers

Why inflict pain on oneself, when so many others are ready to save us the trouble.
George Pacaud

SEXUAL ABUSE

Men are not hanged for stealing horses, but that horses may not be stolen.
George Saville

Abuse is defined by the dictionary as a corrupt act or custom and a wrongful use, which injures and damages; a deceptive improper use or treatment and can involve physical maltreatment. Monteleone's *Recognition of Child Abuse for the Mandated Reporter* states:[34]

> Sexual abuse occurs between a child and an adult or older child and is defined as sexual contact or interaction for sexual stimulation and gratification of the adult or older child, who is a parent or caretaker and responsible for the child's care. Sexual abuse is a form of child abuse and must be reported to state child protective services.

People who have no hope are easy to control, and whoever has the control has the power.
G'mork
The NeverEnding Story

Genital modifications performed on children are intentional sexual contacts that alter and damage the child's body and mind. DeMause considers circumcision incestuous.[35] Originally, in the strict Jewish rite of circumcision women were not allowed. Now, however, women observe from front-row seats. It has been reported that some mothers have even held their infants while the ritual occurs. And women are now becoming *mohels* — religious ritual circumcisers.

As we have stated before, and bears repeating, psychological indicators that drive both ritual and criminal behavior are power, control, and authority through manipulation for dominance out of selfishness. Hence, we can safely conclude that for some, circumcision may be a ritualistic sexual fetish.

It has been reported that in hospital circumcisions, some medical personnel have become sexually aroused. One nurse described seeing the newly-bared glans as a deep religious experience. This is a pedophilic indicator.

You brought your kids to the court room?
Fletcher
Sympathy.
Samantha
Well, it's working! I feel sorry for them already.
Fletcher
Liar Liar

Circumcision is an infant's first sexual experience and he is initiated by an adult wielding a knife. To put it into perspective: it is illegal to genitally cut any baby girl or female child in America. Some even call it a form of rape.

In blood ritual, the knife, or other instrument used to cut, represents the masculine penile function and the blood represents feminine power.

The Marquis de Sade theorized when you decrease one person's sexual pleasure, you increase it for the partner. Genital mutilations are meant to desensitize the sexual organs. Thus, the ritual of circumcision serves three sexual functions:

1. Arousal during the act itself
2. Sexual enhancement for the victim's partner
3. Permanent sexual desensitization throughout the victim's lifetime

Both male and female circumcision have been sold as methods of reducing pleasure for the circumcised party in hopes of increasing pleasure for the partner. But the gratification is mainly intended for another person or to qualify the child to obtain a hypothetical sexual partner in adulthood. Again we must ask, *at what cost to the child?*

THE CHILD MOLESTER

Child molesters believe they do no wrong and even imagine that they improve their victim's lives. Child molesters and serial killers share the same personality type. Their attack neutralizes their greatest threats first.[36] In the case of circumcision, the parent must be disarmed, usually with charm.

One method of classifying child molesters separates them into two groups: 1) situational and 2) preferential.

The *situational molester* has four subsets 1) regressed, 2) morally indiscriminate, 3) sexually indiscriminate and 4) inadequate.

Genital mutilators mainly fit the *situational child molester* subset *morally indiscriminate*, though the other three subsets cannot be totally excluded because social rituals like circumcision allow everyone to participate with their own particular quirk. Criteria for the *morally indiscriminate situational molester* are:[37]

- Motivation — Why not?
- Victim criteria — vulnerability and opportunity
- MO/method of operation — lure, force or manipulate

Another classification system divides child molester into *fixated* or *regressed*. Fixated closely represents infant and child genital mutilation of both sexes with emphasis on male genital mutilation. Regressed most closely represents adult genital mutilation to both sexes depending on culture and current power relations including improper medicine. Some relationship variables are:[38]

The killer's anger was the focus of the assault, and not sexual satisfaction.
Robert Keppel
Signature Killers

He really wants someone to think what he's doing is an art. I think we're looking for someone desperate for acceptance.
Helen Hudson
Copycat

It excites him. Most serial killers keep some sort of trophies from their victims.
Clarice Starling
Silence of the Lambs

FIXATED

- Primary sexual orientation is to children

- Persistent interests and compulsive behavior

- Male victims are primary targets

- *Identification*: offender identifies closely with the victim and equalizes behavior to the level of the child and/or adopts a pseudo-parental role

- Offense = maladaptive resolution of life development (maturation)

REGRESSED

- Primary sexual orientation is to same age

- Involvement may be more episodic and may wax and wane with stress

- Female victims are primary targets

- *Substitution*: Offender replaces conflictual adult relationships with behavior to the level of the child, pseudo-adult relationship

- Offense = maladaptive attempt to cope with specific stresses

RAPISTS

Genital mutilation is akin to rape.[39] There are six types of *rapists*. Briefly Michaud and Hazelwood classify them as follows:

1. Power reassurance rapist
2. Power assertive rapist
3. Angry retaliatory rapist
4. Anger excitation rapist
5. Opportunistic rapist
6. Gang rape

Actions and motivations of rapists, genital mutilators, and societies that perpetrate genital mutilation are comparable. Again, 76% of rapists were sexual victims as youngsters.[40] Briefly, Michaud and Hazelwood classify them as:[41] (Author comments are in *Notes:*)

POWER REASSURANCE RAPIST — COMPENSATORY: Stranger-to-stranger rape. Power is gained through sex. No other physical injury than the rape itself. He compliments the victim, often asking if he pleases her. He doubts his masculinity. It is as if his unhappy personal history somehow explains and mitigates the denigration and trauma he is inflicting on her. Crimes are ritualistic. *Note*: The psychology is to create a *willing* sacrifice through

You can't give back what you've taken from me.
Archer
Face Off

You've got a lot to learn about homicide. Why, morons have committed murders so shrewdly that it's taken a hundred trained police minds to catch them.
Lt. Doyle
Rear Window

Excess on occasion is exhilarating.
Somerset Maughm

an admission by the victim that she is being pleased. According to Joseph Campbell, the victim's *willingness* to be a sacrifice is essential in ritual.[42] Willingness may be expressed by an adult victim, but permission through transferred projection from a "willing" parent or adult caretaker on behalf of an infant or child is unacceptable.

POWER ASSERTIVE RAPIST — EXPLOITIVE: The victim is in the same age range as the perpetrator. The rapist has no doubts about his masculinity but assaults to reassure it. He often wants other males to see him as a man's man. He has a macho self-image. They are aggressive but not lethal. *Note*: This occurs when someone asks their sexual partner to be mutilated. By having the victim do this, the perpetrator's power in the relationship is forever established. They are still present even if the relationship ends. From this conquest, they will have a psychological token to relive when desired, just as a rapist who takes a souvenir.

ANGRY RETALIATORY RAPIST — DISPLACED: Victims of this type of assault frequently require hospitalization. Perpetrators are violent and impulsive in expressing control. Often they rip off the victim's clothes. The predator experiences sexual dysfunction. This is the most common form of date and spousal rape. *Note*: The circumcision corollary to this rape usually occurs right after birth. Mothers have been heard to say, "If I had to go through the pain of childbirth, then my son should go through the pain of circumcision." The hostile masculine element was exemplified by a mohel who stated during a circumcision he was performing, "Every time we circumcise a Jewish child, we are getting revenge upon the anti-Semites who wanted to crush us." This ritual expert's actions may very well indicate an identity conflict in the form of *Munchausen Syndrome in Social Transference*.

ANGER EXCITATION RAPIST — SADISTIC: This is the most dangerous rape. Hospitalization is usually required. Perpetrators are impulsive and opportunistic. Control is paramount. Perpetrators experience sexual dysfunction. These are the most methodical and well-planned rapes. Every detail is carefully planned, rehearsed, and acted out in detail. *Note*: Circumcision is carefully planned, rehearsed and acted out. A physician or mohel has a tool kit and bindings are used, such as the *Circumstraint* board. The anger in this case can be hidden envies, resentments and revenge for the perpetrator's own wounds. Their excitement comes from the power they derive when performing the act or adrenalin from the sense of guilt and fear of being found out.

We're dealing with a very organized killer. He's someone who plans his killings, they're not random spur of the moment things. He only kills who he wants to kill: low risk victims and low risk areas.
Ken O'Hara
Bloodmoon

Revenge, the expression of power, dominance, and the like are present in the killing acts, and so are a need to humiliate the victim sexually, and to degrade them, below even the status of objects.
Robert Ressler
I Have Lived in the Monster

Arriving at a goal is the starting point of another.
John Dewey

*Another improvement
was that we built
gas chambers to
accommodate
two thousand people
at a time.*
Rudolph Hess

OPPORTUNISTIC RAPIST: This form of rape occurs when the perpetrator is committing another act, such as a burglary. It is impulsive because the ability to commit the crime has unexpectedly presented itself. Minimal force is used and time with the victim is short. It is the only rape where sexual satisfaction is more important than power. Power has already been established from the crime of origin, such as burglary. The victim has already been bound rendering escape impossible and the rape is almost an afterthought. *Note*: This used to happen in hospitals when a physician saw an uncircumcised male infant and unilaterally made the decision to circumcise him. In the past this was treated with impunity in the doctor's favor by peer review committees. Due to recent lawsuits, physicians are beginning to understand the consequences of such preemptive action.

GANG RAPE: This is pathological behavior of three or more. Rapists make a game of it. Victims are always seriously injured. *Note*: Socialized genital mutilation ritual is an expression of gang rape where all participate in their own particular way: as cutter, assistant or observer. In Africa and Islamic countries, boys are circumcised en masse. Africans have week long "coming of age" rituals of which circumcision is one part. In 2005, in Morocco, when the son of the king was circumcised, 5,000 boys were circumcised in Casablanca and thousands more in other cities and towns. Gang mutilation has also occurred in some Far Eastern countries where Christians were kidnapped, circumcised and then released.

*The problem with the
serial killer is that
after the first killing,
however it was trig-
gered, that motiva-
tion can disappear,
and the killing itself
becomes the purpose,
because the killer
enjoys himself and
cannot stop.*
Dr. Stewart
Dead to Rights

FEMALE SERIAL KILLERS

Females are quiet killers. There are six motivational types of female serial killers.

1. Black Widow
2. Angel of Death
3. Sexual Predator
4. Revenge
5. For profit or crime
6. Team killer

*This could be the day
of days, but the timing
must be flawless.*
Dame Vaaco
*The Chronicles
of Riddick*

Kelleher and Kelleher in *Murder Most Rare: Female Serial Killer,*[43] discuss perpetrator types. Though discussing females, males are not excluded in these killer types. As you read the following, hold in your mind the concept of circumcision as a mock-death ceremony. (Author comments are in *Notes*:)

BLACK WIDOW: The *Black Widow* killer is careful, patient, deliberate, intelligent, organized, and methodical. Victims include children, spouses and relatives and rarely extend beyond the family. This killer type starts after age thirty. Victims have confidence and trust in her. She gets close and stays close. Over 90% of the time her method is extended poisoning, but she may also suffocate or strangle. She behaves as a concerned parent, spouse or relative. Motives can also include money in conjunction with psychotic fear of rejection. *Note:* The Black Widow's age most closely corresponds to the onset of menopause. The post-menopausal Wise Woman maintains both the light and dark aspects of the feminine power. And the ancient male sage is her masculine counterpart. The Black Widow most often attacks the family and often exhibits *Munchausen by Proxy*.

You're so adorable when you're going for the kill.
Sara
Laws of Attraction

ANGEL OF DEATH: The *Angel of Death* is subtle and hidden. She usually attacks those under her care. Her victims are the weakest and most infirm, with no ability for self defense. The excuse is euthanasia. Often, in *Munchausen by Proxy*, the *Angel of Death* creates a medical emergency and comes to the rescue, presenting herself as a savior. Tools and methodology are interwoven with her environment. Ego and domination are at the core of her motivation. She sets up control of life and death over her victims. In her mind, her victims have no right to survive in their present state of existence. *Note*: Medicine always looks for new diseases to justify circumcision.[44,45] Nurses, both male and female, who murder are also called *Angels of Death*. See *Malignant Hero Syndrome*.

I trusted you with my life.
President James Marshall
So will the next president.
Agent Gibbs
Air Force One

SEXUAL PREDATORS: There is only one American female *Sexual Predator* known to have committed this crime alone — that was Aileen Wuornos. She used a 22-caliber hand gun which could be said to represent an emotional sexual dysfunction and may have served as a penile substitute.[46] In this category the female usually participates as a facilitator for a male, a vicarious bystander, and/or possibly a *Passive Initiator*. *Note*: When males have refused to obey the social circumcision mandate, their female counterparts have been known to assume responsibility for enforcing the rite.[47] Similar to sexually inadequate males who use knives as penile enhancements to mutilate their female victims' vaginas, a gun or knife used for killing -- or the blade used in the mock-death ritual of circumcision -- may be thought of as a penile substitute or a form of clitoral enhancement when female perpetrators wield the weapon or verbally demand the cutting of a child through passive initiation. Whether a knife, handgun or verbal manipulation, the significance is in the

Are you gonna kill my baby?
Maddie
No.
Katherine
Why not?
Maddie
The Reaping

psychological use of the weapon. When considering circumcision as sexual predation, the category of female involvement in this form of sexual violence exponentially increases. Mothers and grandmothers have been known to passionately advocate for circumcision in opposition to the wishes of the father.

REVENGE: Revenge murders are crimes of passion and often connect to family discord. Methods used are similar to the Black Widow, but here profit is not the motive. Usually a triggering event occurs. Intense emotion is involved when revenge becomes serial killing. Secondary victims are persons close to the primary victim. Part of the emotion is a sense of abandonment. Her revenge killings are an attempt to regain a semblance of control in her life. *Note*: Revenge is also retaliation for perceived patriarchy where all males are guilty because one is guilty.[48] One female doctor freely admitted to a private encounter group that she loved to do circumcisions as they allowed her to "get even with men" This category also relates to parents of either sex who demand the circumcision of a child, making him a symbol and secondary victim of their revenge against a spouse or divorced partner.

CRIME FOR PROFIT: Unlike the Black Widow who kills relatives and those close to her for profit, this murderer kills victims *outside* the family unit *for profit*. Yet she, like the Black Widow, mainly uses poison. Location of activity is often similar to the Angel of Death. She may work in a nursing home, as a live-in caretaker or a health care practitioner. She is sane and she will meticulously seek out victims previously unknown to her. There is no emotional passion involved in her actions. Any familiarity with the victim is a means to an end. She is very organized, precise, patient, manipulative and mature. *Note*: Turning to murder (or mock-death ritual) to enhance income denotes fear of inadequacy. Since Africa societies prohibit women from education and working outside the home, older women turn to Female Genital Mutilation as a way of supporting themselves. Re-suturing women after childbirth is even more profitable than the initial girl child circumcision.

TEAM KILLERS: The more people in a team of killers, the more convoluted the crime. Weapon choice varies and they tend to torture victims. Dismemberments are common. Genital mutilations are dismemberments of sorts. Female members are usually the youngest of female serial killers. Average age is between 20 and 25. The more stable the interpersonal relationships among the members, the longer the activity continues. This category includes one third of the female serial killers. It has three subsets: male/ female teams. female teams and family teams:

MALE/FEMALE TEAMS: This two-person team is made of a single male and single female. The male is not always the dominate partner. The couple is sexually involved and their crimes are sexually brutal. Organization varies within each relationship. She is an equal predator.[49] *Note*: In the macro-social of *Munchausen's Collective Transmission*, matriarchal and patriarchal functions cannot exist without each other. Genital mutilations involve a tacit social agreement.

FEMALE TEAMS: Two or more females, most often two, with one dominant. Motives are similar to Angel of Death and Crime for Profit perpetrators. Killings are more quiet and subtle than male/female teams. *Note*: Similar to *Munchausen Syndrome in Collective Transmission* as it involves the social sisterhood in Female Genital Mutilations as well as Male Genital Mutilations.

FAMILY TEAMS: This grouping involves three or more family members with both sexes participating. It also includes people who band together into a quasi-familial relationship. Their actions are similar to the male/female team. Crimes are sexually violent. *Note*: The cultural setting again connects *Munchausen's Collective Transmission* to circumcision in mock-death ceremonies.

HOMICIDE OF CHILDREN

Three socialized forms of *child homicide* are: *neonaticide*, *infanticide* and *filicide*.[50,51] They correlate to the three age groups used in ritual circumcision. Alan Tuckman in *Psychiatry and the Law: Child Murder* stated:[52]

> Ancient civilizations considered children omens from the gods. Those born with deformities were routinely sacrificed. Asian cultures routinely killed female infants, Roman fathers had the right to murder their children, and Japanese fathers could also have their newborns killed to keep family size down. The slaying of children is an international phenomenon...
>
> In certain Eskimo tribes, Indian, and Chinese cultures there is evidence that female newborns are still killed.

Most child homicides are committed by women who have minimal social involvement with other adults. These women are usually isolated, constant caretakers, driven to be perfect mothers, overwhelmed and subsequently, depressed. And as for victim availability, mothers typically spend more time with children than fathers do.

Serial killers are inadequate types to begin with, and the ones who need partners to carry out their work are the most inadequate of all.
John Douglas
Mind Hunter

When I look at you I see nothing but trouble. I like trouble.
Yaz
Double Team

Why don't you want to go out and play with your friends?
Cameron
They're all dead.
Seth
The Reflecting Skin

Women who commit child murders often use the defense of psychosis[53] from postpartum depression. The defense is used as the excuse of being a trapped mother in a male-dominated society. This defense is often successful and results in a lighter sentence. *US News & World Report* explained:[54]

He was getting away with murder because no one was firing back.
Narrator
Target: Pearl Harbor

> Even when a mother's mental illness doesn't meet the legal definition of insanity, jurors and the public are whipsawed between horror at the act and sympathy for the troubled mother... In Great Britain, the law sanctions such leniency. There, a mother who kills her children within the first twelve months of life is unlikely to face jail, a legal nod to the fact that, as Duke obstetrician and psychiatrist Diana Dell puts it, the period right after birth is "the most biologically vulnerable time in a woman's life psychiatrically." Dell says postpartum depression affects at least ten percent of new mothers.

ATTENUATED & PSYCHOSEXUAL HOMICIDE

An *attenuation* is a substitute, a lessening of severity, a reduction of effect. Circumcision is a mock-death ceremony representing *attenuated homicide* and *psychosexual homicide*.

We are going to make her just like us.
Miss Frank
Twilight Zone

Perpetrators performing circumcision, as well as participants observing, fulfill themselves in the same manner as other serial sexual predators.

> ATTENUATED HOMICIDE is the psychological act of homicide lessened to not cause death and often performed in ritual, specifically circumcision.

> PSYCHOSEXUAL HOMICIDE is the killing, inhibiting or stunting of a part of the natural, normal and healthy psychological growth and development of a person during infancy, childhood, adolescence or adulthood

NEONATICIDE

Neonaticide is the killing of a newborn in the first day of life. It is almost exclusively perpetrated by the newborn's mothers. Neil Kay stated:[55]

In the war of ideas it is people who get killed.
Stanislaw Lec

> Although relatively uncommon, numerous cases of neonaticide have been reported. To date [May 2009], only two cases of paternal neonaticide have appeared in the literature.

Not to dispute Kay's report, but he does not take into consideration fathers or other males who may assist in the murder as the non-dominant participant.

That aside, *neonaticide* is most often perpetrated by young, poor, unmarried and socially isolated women who are not ready for parenthood. Many times they hide their pregnancies. There is total dissociation of the newborn as an individually distinct and different human being. The newborn is seen as an object, one of the mother's discardable body parts like clipped fingernails or cut hair. Women who kill neonates show no signs of psychopathy as those who kill older children.[56] This puts *neonaticide* in criminology rather than a biological abnormality or psychological condition.

In the English-speaking Christian population of America, the practice of routine medical neonatal circumcision occurs the day of or the day following birth. This represents an *attenuated neonaticide*.

INFANTICIDE

Infanticide is the killing of a child in the first year of life. Spartan parents would take an infant to a counsel which determined if the child had proper physical qualities. If not, the child would be placed on a stone and left to die from exposure. Child graveyards have been found in the Middle East and North Africa; one example is Carthage. Anthropologists studying Celtic mummies found in China theorize that female infanticide may have existed in the ancient past to serve deceased priestesses in death.[57]

Female infanticide was practiced in Medieval Europe, leading to limited numbers of available females, high bride prices and dowries. In an effort to stop the practice, one Pope issued an edict for parents to stop rolling over their children when they slept.[58] Exposure is still used to kill female infants.

Jewish culture circumcises its male children on the eighth day of life. Jewish female genital excisions at this age occur due to *congenital adrenal hyperplasia*. This represents an *attenuated infanticide*.

FILICIDE

Filicide is the killing of a child twelve months or older by the parent. These killings are more common than expected.[59] Psychosis results in a great number of filicides. Male filicide is often from explosive rage and anger where the child is used as a substitute object in transference from real resentment. Philip Resnick formulated five forensic filicide typologies.[60] A sixth has subsequently been added.

> ACCIDENTAL: Killing of a child in the course of a beating or other violent outburst toward a child.

The problem with genocide is that it always turns in on itself.
CDR Robert Harger, USN

Compulsory depopulation by infanticide, genocide or whatever means suggest themselves.
Philip Marlow
The Singing Detective

Trust in Allah, but tie your camel.
Arabian Proverb

ACUTELY PSYCHOTIC: Occurs when a child is killed by one under the influence of hallucination, epilepsy or delirium.

ALTRUISTIC: Killing of a child by parents who believe the family is doomed or in conjunction with their own suicide.

SPOUSAL REVENGE: The murder is committed in a deliberate attempt to torment the spouse

UNWANTED CHILD: The murder of a child simply because the child was not wanted by the murderer.

MERCY KILLING: Where there is intense suffering by the child, or to assist an impending death.

Accidental filicide may occur while committing harm under any Munchausen behavior. Psychotic, not neurotic, filicide may occur in conjunction with postpartum depression, or other forms of depression. The last four types are often expressed religiously. Mothers usually say they sent their children to a better place. Many of the children have disabilities. Others are just in the way. With non-judicial punishment, social inhibition is eliminated and these crimes increase.[61,62,63]

Maternal filicide reaches into fable. One fable is the *Legend of La Llorna*, meaning *Weeping Woman*.[64]

It is a tale of a young woman who fell in love with a handsome ranchero. But when he left her for another, she went mad and drowned their children in a river. The spirit of La Llorna, the tale goes, still roams the riverbanks, crying for her lost children.

African tribal Female Genital Mutilation and male circumcision occur in childhood and young adulthood. Islam circumcises males as young as age three and well into puberty. Some Islamic sects also circumcise females in this age category. In Ethiopia, Jewish women circumcise their young girls. American doctors in the 19th and 20th centuries circumcised females in early childhood and young adulthood and they still to this day target older males who escaped circumcision as newborns. All this represents *attenuated filicide*.

SOCIALIZED SEXUAL PREDATION

Research is necessary to understand more about group predation. Circumcision is the cause and also a result of *misandry*, the hatred or distrust of males — and *misogyny*, the hatred or distrust of females. The following definitions apply to both serial sexual predation and to circumcision.

> SOCIALIZED SEXUAL PREDATION: Any form of improper psychosexual conditioning which may also include physical alteration and/or sexual mutilation as a perceived culturally acceptable form of plastic surgery performed on the genitals of any human being.

> OVERBOUNDER: Improper individual or social domination of another using actions that transgress the autonomy, physical and psychological boundaries of another person.

What social team-predators crave with circumcision is to perpetrate their social structure and themselves in their social hierarchy by making circumcision the social norm ritual, regardless of how that ritual affects themselves or their victims. As in serial killing, the object of circumcision is power, control and authority through manipulation for domination out of selfishness. Douglas and Olshaker stated:[65]

> So let's get this straight and state it plainly: It is my belief, based on several decades of experience, study, and analysis, that the overwhelming majority of repeat sexual predators do what they do because they want to, because it gives them a satisfaction they do not achieve in any other aspect of their lives, and because it makes them feel good, regardless of the consequences to others. In that respect, the crime represents the ultimate in selfishness; the perpetrator doesn't care what happens to his victim as long as he gets what he wants. In fact, exercising this manipulation, domination, and control — and the infliction of pain and death are for him their ultimate expressions — are the critical factors in making him feel complete and fully alive.

Hey! Do you want to focus on the problem at hand.
Zeus
Die Hard: With A Vengeance

Is she dead, Master?
Ralphus
Not quite.
Oh yes!
Now we're getting the proper reaction.
Master Sardu
Blood Sucking Freaks

And soon I will become the hunted.
Selene
Underworld

DR. IGNATZ SEMMELWEIS

He died a broken man

Dr. Ignatz Semmelweis was in charge of two birthing wards in his hospital. The first ward was run by midwives and had no unusual complication rates. When a medical school teaching facility was added as a second ward, staggering infection and death rates occurred in that ward. Mothers were dying from childbed fever.

Dr. Semmelweis observed that physicians and students were moving directly from the morgue to the maternity ward. He surmised that they were carrying disease from the dead to the new mothers. Semmelweis suggested that the doctors should wash their hands before performing pelvic examinations. This simple suggestion encountered tremendous resistance. Doctors complained that even if his concept was correct, washing their hands would be too much work. Nor were the doctors eager to admit that they had caused so many deaths.

In 1861, Semmelweis wrote *The Etiology, Concept, and Prophylaxis of Childbed Fever,* which included over 50 pages of statistics documenting patient morbidity and mortality rates. At that time, the medical establishment had little appreciation for Semmelweis' premise because it would be another 30 years before Louis Pasteur proved the germ theory of disease. Consequently, they ridiculed him and removed him from both his hospital and medical school positions. He died a broken man.

Rejection of new ideas based on negative emotional reactions is now known as the Semmelweis Reflex.[1]

SEMMELWEIS REFLEX: The Semmelweis Reflex is the dismissal or rejecting out of hand any information, automatically, without thought, inspection, or experiment.

I SAW A CHAPEL ALL OF GOLD

William Blake

I saw a chapel all of gold
That none did dare to enter in,
And many weeping stood without,
Weeping morning, worshipping.

I saw a serpent rise between
The white pillars on the door,
And he forc'd and forc'd and forc'd
Down the gold hinges tore.

And along the pavement sweet,
Set with pearls and rubies bright,
All his shining length he drew,
Till upon the alter white.

Vomiting his poison out
On the bread and the wine.
So I turned into a sty,
And laid me down with the swine.

VIOLENT INITIATION

Ultimately, children judge parents

Genital rituals are a fusion of sex and violence. Circumcision involves a power struggle in an impossible imbalance of power between perpetrator and victim. It contains both aggressive and libidinal elements, and threatens a child's sexual integrity by amputating part of the genitalia. When helpless children are attacked, physical and psychological repercussions are inevitably welded into their beings.

If society assumes the right to genitally mutilate their children, those children have a right to be disturbed by it. The detrimental effects of circumcision are similar for both genders. Perpetrators appear to be blind to the suffering of their tiny victims.

Pathetic earthlings. Hurling your bodies out into the void, without the slightest inkling of who or what is out there.
Ming the Merciless
Flash Gordon

RAPE TRAUMA SYNDROME

Circumcision of either sex can create psychological symptoms and behavioral patterns similar to rape. Clinical significance varies with the individual, social and family environments, and age. For the most part symptoms remain subclinical. However, they may at any time become overt and pathological. Psychosocial behaviors related to circumcision act synergistically with other factors, conditions and predispositions.

In 1974, Burgess and Holstrom described *Rape Trauma Syndrome* (RTS), also called *Rape-Related Post-Traumatic Stress Disorder*. Rape victims' reactions range from passivity to violent defense. Shock and disbelief occur early and may look like passivity. The three phases of Burgess and Holstrom's RTS are:[1-8]

Though the physical attack was over, now enters a new phase. It is inflicted on the victim's soul.
Rape Expert
Sexual Violence: Our War Against Rape

1. Acute (initial) phase
2. Reorganization (long-term) phase
3. Integration (resolution) phase

The last two are latent responses regardless of how the person reacts during the assault.

ACUTE PHASE

The Dark Side has clouded their vision.
Count Dooku
Attack of the Clones

The *acute phase* starts directly after the assault and may last for weeks. Life is totally disrupted. Individuals experience two reactions to trauma: expressed and controlled. *Expressed reactions* are open, overt demonstrations of emotions. *Controlled reactions* are attempts to claim composure. Specific combinations of symptoms will vary according to the individual:

EXPRESSED REACTIONS

crying	laughing	joking
smiling	pacing	shaking
screaming	tenseness	restlessness
confusion	self-hatred	disorganization

CONTROLLED REACTIONS

Violence begets fear.
Jay Carney

fear	numbness	dehumanized
anxiety	depression	self blame
degradation	revenge	resentment
denial	moodiness	torment
humiliation	embarrassment	hate
guilt	anger	shame
withdrawal	ignominy	manipulated
abandonment	paranoia	betrayal
restlessness	dirty feeling	hostility
vengeance	weight change	loss of trust
dissociation	avoidances	sadness
neglected	disgrace	disfranchisement
difficulty concentrating		

PHYSICAL REACTIONS

It looks like a type of disorder that you rarely see anymore, except in primitive cultures.
Dr. Barringer
The Exorcist

bruises	eating disturbed	sleep disturbed
soreness	infections	stomach/headache
fatigue	hypervigilance	heart palpitations
diarrhea	nightmares	high blood pressure

REORGANIZATION PHASE

The *reorganization phase* is the time to find answers and resolution. This phase may last for months to years. Coping techniques include: minimization, dramatization, suppression, and explanation with:

- *Lifestyle changes*: residence, telephone number, friends
- *Phobias*: fear opposite sex, sex, crowds, being alone
- *Physical concerns*: scarring, STD's, other infections
- *Regain control*: increases family contact, self choice, work
- *Overcome insecurity*: self-defense courses
- *Sexual dysfunction*: flashbacks, feelings of disgust, vulnerability
- *Nightmares*: continue and change through resolution
- *Compound reactions*: money, school, alcohol, drugs

No day be so sacred
but that
the laugh of a child
will make it holier still.
Robert Ingersoll
Liberty of Man,
Woman and Child

INTEGRATION PHASE

In the *integration phase*, permanent changes are expected. Emotional illness commonly develops. Life now adapts. RTS symptoms change over time. Some symptoms last a lifetime. It is difficult for rape victims who smoke, to quit.

substance abuse	developments of reorganization
hyper-sexuality	hypo-sexuality
flashbacks	suicidal attempts
psychotherapy — 19%	

Suffering is the
coin of the realm.
Pinhead
Hellraiser IV:
Bloodline

MINOR'S AGE & MATURITY DIFFERENTIALS

As always, individual responses vary:

VERY YOUNG

nightmares	acting out sexually
bedwetting	attachment to perpetrators

PRE-TEENS

poor hygiene	excessive crying
withdrawal	layered dressing
sleep disorders	sexual knowledge

Pain is deeper
than all thought.
Elbert Hubbard

TEENAGERS

truancy	running away
promiscuity	pregnancy
decreased socialization	

SOCIETAL SECONDARY ASSAULTS

Victims of sexual assault may be further accosted by rude and disrespectful comments from and treatment by others:[9]

*Pain is such an
uncomfortable
feeling that even
a tiny amount of
it is enough to
ruin every enjoyment.*
Will Rogers

1. Get on with your life

2. Inappropriate remarks

3. Lack of confidentiality

4. Termination of employment due to legal absence or perceived inappropriate sick leave

5. Abandonment by the legal system

In the case of circumcision, people who speak up for the children or themselves can face retaliation from the social body. If they complain or even attempt to discuss the subject, due to the phenomenon of *Munchausen's Social Transference* and denial, their former way of life may be jeopardized. Professional relationships may also be negatively affected. Lives have been threatened.

*There is always mad
impatience for results,
without considering
the means.*
Ardant duPicq
Battle Studies

NEUROLOGICAL DEVELOPMENT

In 1987, Dr. J.K.S. Anand and P.R. Hickey, M.D. published their study on fetal and neonatal pain.[10] Until that time, physicians had been taught — and therefore believed — that the fetus or neonate could not experience pain because the nerves were not fully myelinated at birth. Consequently, anesthesia was not administered to children undergoing circumcision or even heart surgery.

Myelin is a fatty-protein layer covering nerves that aid impulse transmission. Because of this, early research concentrated on nociperception reflexes. However, nociceptive nerve ending density in an infant's body is more concentrated and therefore he is far more sensitive than an adult. In the womb, during gestation sensory nerves begin developing at the seventh week and cover the skin by the twentieth week. The complete nervous system is active prenatally. The fetus possesses specific opiate receptors which possibly ease the birthing process for the baby. The full-term baby is naturally biochemically prepared for birth. The level of endorphins and lipotropins in the natural neonate's body and umbilical cord is three to five times that of adults. These levels increase during a difficult birth to ease the baby's distress.

*None so deaf vas
those who will not
hear.*
English Proverb

Maria Fitzgerald, Professor of Developmental Neurobiology, reported that infants have a threefold different pain mechanism than adults:[11]

1. Infant spinal nerves are more excitable, so responses are greater and longer. Responses from a baby's spinal cord arrive in a different location than in the adult brain. The effect is that, compared to the adult, natural neurological pain-killing mechanisms are not present.

2. There is greater nerve overlap in the skin so receptive fields are larger. A baby's sensory mechanism is more sensitive and more susceptible to injury. Hypersensitivity lasts longer in the wound area.

3. Infant nerves register pressure and pain similarly, so adults who try to interpret neonate and infant pain response may find it difficult to distinguish between the two. In an attempt to distract the child from pain during circumcision some physicians give their tiny patient sugar[12] and in the Jewish ceremony, a cloth soaked in wine is put in the infant's mouth.

DENIAL OF INFANT & NEONATAL PAIN

Rabbi Maimonides clearly stated, *The bodily pain caused to that member is the real purpose of circumcision.* Yet the current historical myth that babies do not feel pain allowed circumcision to be performed without anesthesia of any kind. Ideas gleaned from David Chamberlain's presentation, *Babies Don't Feel Pain: A Century of Denial in Medicine* follow:[13]

Until recent studies, medicine dismissed infant and neonatal reaction to induced trauma as being random sounds, muscle spasms, gas, and fantasies. Responses were ignored. In the 16th century neonates and infants were considered pre-human. Early studies showed different water temperatures in tubes passed over the infant's legs, abdomen, or forehead gave different reactions as the water was made hotter or colder. Babies reacted more violently to cold water and their respiratory and circulatory changes were noted.[14,15]

In 1917 Mary Blanton wrote that defensive reactions were considered primitive reflexes.[16] Other studies were performed after birth in which the mother was given narcotics to ease birth pains and this was not considered.

Myrtle McGraw, in 1941, performed pinprick studies and decided defensive reactions did not extend beyond thalamus level.[17] This thinking pervaded well beyond 1974 with a study by E. C. Rich of pinpricks on the knee which

Without their death, their pain, without the sacrifice, we would be nothing
Tyler Durden
Fight Club

Pain, suffering, death I feel. Something terrible has happened.
Yoda
Attack of the Clones

Well, how's our little patient today?
Master Sardu
I won't dance.
Natasa
Blood Sucking Freaks

concluded grimaces and crying were only normal sub-level responses even after six stabbings.[18]

PHYSIOLOGICAL & BEHAVIORAL CHANGES

Anand's study also documented physiological and behavioral changes during circumcision without anesthesia. It is as if the brain lights up and gets scrambled. Yet, the fact remains that even if anesthesia is used, circumcision is an act of violence. The anesthesia excuse uses the same flawed logic that states if a date rape drug is given, then no rape occurs. Findings include:[19-22]

PHYSIOLOGICAL INDICATIONS

palmar sweating	heart rate	plasma amino acids
blood pressure	intracranial pressure	nitrogen excretion
plasma resin activity	plasma cortisol levels	protein breakdown
insulin suppression	catecholamine release	
aldosterone/corticosteroids	elevated glucagon	
total ketone increase	plasma and norepinephrine cortical shock	

BEHAVIORAL INDICATIONS

grimacing	surprise	chin quiver
diffuse movements	try to escape	tongue taut
altered sleep/wake	jerk	pull back
eyes squeeze shut	swing arms	
prolonged stress	acute urinary retention	
naso-labial bulge	crying — to gastric rupture	
lips purse	defensive leg movements to point of trauma	

Circumcised individuals have altered development. Richards compared gender differences between circumcised male infants to uncircumcised infants of both sexes.[23] Because America routinely circumcises its males, the study compared psychological and behavioral gender differences of Americans to Europeans. Summarizing:[24-37]

In the early 1970's the circumcision rate in the United States was over 80%, and rates in England were 0.41%. This difference directly correlates to different results in studying neonatal and infant studies between the United States and Europe. With sleep/wake cycles, behavior of sleep, and auditory responsiveness, there was a significant clinical deviation from normal with circumcised male infants. Other American neonatal and infant studies that did not take into consideration the male's circumcision status, reported gender differences in skin touch, electrical stimulation, visual and eating responses

The human race has a long history of hurting the ones we love — or should love.
John Douglas
Mind Hunter

Practice proves more than theory.
Abraham Lincoln

The first killer I ever studied had put bandages over the wounds of the people he stabbed once they were dead. Other killers have done the same thing.
Robert Ressler
I Have Lived in the Monster

including sweets between males and females. European studies do not show the same differences between the sexes. Extending beyond this neonate and infant comparative analysis, the study found that mothering also differed. American mothers treated their males different, and European mothers nurtured equally. Studies on animals induced with various traumas, indicate altered behavior and psychophysiology can continue long term. The animal studies inferred that it would be wise to study more effects on humans.

FETAL & NEONATAL MEMORY

In *Fetal Memory: Does it exist? What does it do?*, Dr. P. G. Hepper concludes that fetal and newborn memory indeed exist. He goes on to state that fetal memory, however, is not developed in the same way as adult memory. Research shows newborns acquire memory through habituation, conditioning, association, and imitation. Memory even precedes birth. Habituation studies have proved that if music is played before birth, the newborn will react to the same music. Females develop this response earlier, however no study was performed to differentiate the response of circumcised versus natural, intact baby boys. Reaction to familiar music increases alertness and decreases heart rate. In the womb, many responses develop prior to need, such as eye movement and suckling. Language may also begin to become acquired prior to birth.[38]

Milos and Macris contradicted circumcision pain myths. They observed:[39]

- Even with anesthesia, circumcision will hurt after pain relief wears off.

- Pain will be experienced during urination, defecation, and diaper change for at least ten days.

- If an infant seems to sleep through a circumcision the reason is a natural shutting down into a semi-comatose state due to the assault.

- That circumcision will be forgotten is an adult misperception.

Van der Kolk showed that memory of trauma depends on existing mental development. Memory and the way it is imprinted are both flexible. When severe trauma occurs, neurohormones are secreted and affect imprinting. The limbic system is the switchboard for survival emotions. Two limbic structures that transfer messages to other parts of the mind and body are the amygdala which evaluates the stimulus, and the septo-hippocampal system which records the memory. Intense amygdala stimulus decreases hippocampal function and

A memory is what is left when something happens and does not completely unhappen.
Edward de Bono

Every man's memory is his private literature
Aldous Huxley

Memories is all we really own.
Elias Lieberman

interferes with proper evaluation. Years later if the adult who has been traumatized as a child comes under stress, reaction to the original stimulus can be retriggered, but with distorted and unclear connection.[40]

Examples of remembered infant trauma follow:

4 to 6 months after traumatic event: Anna Taddio performed randomized trials on infants 4 to 6 months old. They measured pain responses for DPT and influenza immunizations. The variable was infant male circumcision status. All other histories to trauma were eliminated for the test groups. They found that even after half a year, circumcised infant males had an increased pain response which lasted longer than uncircumcised males. The mechanism for this comparable inability for circumcised males to handle pain is unknown and warrants further study.[41] They repeated the study with a larger number of infants with the same results.[42]

2 years or more after trauma: David Chamberlain, Ph.D. Psychologist discussed an event that happened with his granddaughter. When she was two years old she asked her parents *Why did they poke me with that thing? They hurted me*. What they surmised was she was talking about her neonatal heel stick. This is the common method for an initial blood test.

Chamberlain also reports that a 29-year-old woman under regression hypnosis described her neonatal pain. She described how cold the metal scales were, the eye drops that were administered stinging, and her crying because it all hurt.

In yet another case a little boy had hydrocephalus so shunts had been placed in his head. The child was paralyzed with curare, a drug that immobilizes but does not mediate pain. Even at ten years of age he would not allow anyone to touch his head and the sight of a hospital caused him to tremble, sweat, scream and vomit. Curare was commonly administered to neonates, infants and children under the age of 15 months. Previously it was thought that children could not feel pain so their crying was only a primal reaction to cold or separation from mother. Recent research indicates that crying is an infant's way of communicating messages about illness, malnutrition, malformations, and other problems.[43]

Jeane Rhodes studied children between ages five to nine. For her doctoral thesis she performed research on how yoga positions relate to prenatal and birth trauma. Her unexpected observation was that the seven circumcised boys in the study could not place their hips on the floor when doing the *cobra* position (lying on the abdomen and raising the head to create an arch in the back). The two uncircumcised boys in the group did it without a problem. She related this to a body-worker who said her circumcised adult clients are also more rigid in the pelvis.[44]

I believe that this neglected, wounded inner child of the past is the major source of human misery.
John Bradshaw

You know children are growing up when they start asking questions that have answers.
John J. Plomp

Nothing fixes a thing so intensely in the memory as the wish to forget it.
Montaigne

A adult woman reported to the author that she clearly remembered open-heart surgery when she was first born. No anesthesia was given to deaden the pain or her memory. Her grandfather was a heart surgeon and he performed the surgery.

Some men circumcised in infancy or childhood without their consent have described their present feelings in the language of violation, torture, mutilation and sexual assault.

BRAIN ALTERATION

Immerman and Mackey[45] cited animal research and postulated its importance to human circumcision. If an animal's digit is removed, the brain area that serves that limb will both structurally and functionally reorganize to compensate. The earlier the amputation the greater the neural change. On the cortical cellular level these changes occur randomly within each individual. With this, the cortical reorganization affects the thalamus which is the primary sensory switchboard.

They found that when stimulating the original severed nerves, there was no response. Nerve regeneration was incomplete and disorderly and left a "silent zone" within the brain. Silent zones can occur through sensory deprivation alone. Nerve reorganization also occurs in skin and peripheral nerves as well as the central cortical area.

That established, one may then presume that changes in the neural pattern of the sexual response from circumcision can also alter behavioral interactions and adult sexual relationships, regardless of whether anesthesia is used or not. Rabbi Moses Maimonides wrote:

> It is hard for a woman with whom an uncircumcised man has had sexual intercourse to separate from him. In my opinion this is the strongest of the reasons for circumcision.

We often wonder how many families ties have weakened or even broken due to circumcision-caused neurological amputation.[46-57] Immerman and Mackey also quote Maimonides on the subject of sexual desire:

> The bodily injury caused to that organ is exactly that which is desired; it does not interrupt any vital function, nor does it destroy the power of generation. Circumcision simply counteracts excessive lust; for there is no doubt that circumcision weakens the power of sexual excitement.

The best way to elevate the masses is to raise children properly.
Anonymous

Gravity swallowed remains but the star and all the planets disappeared they have. How can this be?
Yoda
If an item does not exist in our records, it does not exist.
Madame Jocasta
Because someone erased it from the archive memory.
Zett Jukassa
Attack of the Clones

Now, this isn't going to be easy for you, but I'm going to tell you things about yourself of which you have no memory.
Brian
Blakes 7

Anand and Scalzo postulated that N-methyl-Daspartate (NMDA), which maintains cell integrity and nerve receptor activity, is lowered by the physical trauma of infant circumcision. This causes cell fragmentation and phagocytosis by other cells in many areas of the immature brain. Yet, with even more severe traumatic events, NMDA is elevated. With excessive stimulation, glutamate is released from the central nervous system's neurons. Glutamate binds to metabatrophic and NMDA receptors leading to a phosphorylation thus altering gene regulation. This, in turn, causes toxic damage to the neonatal developing brain cells.

Eventual outcome in later life manifests as increased anxiety, altered pain response, stress disorders, hyperactivity, attention deficit, impaired social skills and self-destructive behavior. Animal studies show differences in how postnatal handling affects adult behavior and cognitive ability. Differences are many, partly due to minute genetic variation. Induced chemical changes have been shown to precipitate neuron migration compensating for other neuron deaths. The human brain has a critical window of development at the time before and after birth. Some of these chemical interactions affect later learning.[58]

Daniel Goleman wrote a New York Times article titled, *Early Violence Leaves Its Mark on the Brain: Adolescent violence is traced to abuse and neglect in childhood, early violence found to be etched in the brain,* in which he compared hamster studies and human behavior. Young hamsters subjected to violence, grow up violent. Their violence was directed at younger and smaller hamsters, while with hamsters of equal size, the violent hamsters would cower. This is seen in violent humans and correlates to abuse. A 20-year study shows a 50% increase in violent crime by abused children.[59,60]

Circumcision is a system of establishing social dominance through violence, also known as *bullying*.

Lawrence Barichello, in *The Sexual and Psychological Consequences of Infant Circumcision,*[61] spoke of a special structure lost from the penis during circumcision; Taylor called it the *Ridged Band*. This band of skin is located at the circumference of the foreskin and is attached by the frenum.[62-65] The ridged band contains specialized *Meissner corpuscles* which occur in bundles on other juncto-cutaneous body areas such as the vulva, clitoris, clitoral prepuce, lips, and perianal area, as well as on the fingertips and eyelid. He noted male and female genital cutting causes the same devastating losses in both sexes. Nerve pathways and corresponding portions of the brain are forever lost.

A thick cable of nerve cells connecting the right and left sides of the brain (corpus callosum) is smaller than normal in abused children, says Martin Teicher, associate professor of psychiatry at Harvard Medical School. He and his colleagues at McLean Hospital, a psychiatric facility affiliated with Harvard, compared brain scans from 51 patients and 97 healthy children. The researchers concluded that in boys neglect was associated with a significant reduction in the size of the corpus callosum. The corpus callosum was also abnormally small in girls who had been sexually abused.[66-67]

PSYCHOSEXUAL EFFECTS

Circumcision's psychological effects are diffuse, many, and varied. Research links it to *Post-Traumatic Stress Disorder*, *neurological alterations*, and *social conflict* in personal and interpersonal dynamics. Renowned Swiss psychoanalyst and author Alice Miller sees in this kind of cruelty the roots of social violence. Anne Pyterek postulates circumcision is the root of *misogyny* with:[68]

> How could they not grow up and stomp us under their boots after we allow such a hideous, agonizing torture to be inflicted on their freshly born little bodies?

Janov and Holden in separate studies indicate neonatal and infant pain may cause adult *neuroses* and *psychosomatic illnesses*.[69] Jim Bigelow observed that circumcision combines with self-image to the detriment of the circumcised individual on both the personal and psychosocial levels.[70] Falk made a list of psychological effects:[71]

- grieving loss of a body part
- effects on parent — bonding
- pain and perinatal trauma on the child
- decision factors of parents and doctors
- societal effects

Chamberlain in *Birth and the Origins of Violence* states that current studies of violent criminals show they have poorly functioning brains. Most dysfunction from violence centers in the brain's frontal portion. The underdeveloped brain cannot stop frustration and produces marginal self-control. Even children exposed to repeated ultrasounds have lowered birth weight and improperly constructed brain structure.[72]

The loss of a friend is like that of a limb; time may heal the anguish of the wound, but the loss cannot be repaired.
Robert Southey

We will hunt down those with blood on their hands.
Golda Meir

Truly wonderful the mind of a child is.
Yoda
Attack of the Clones

William H. Teicher of Harvard Medical School agrees:[73]

> We believe that a smaller corpus collosum leads to less integration of the two halves of the brain, and that this can result in dramatic shifts in mood and personality.

In Teicher's book *Wounds that Time won't Heal: The Neurobiology of Child Abuse* he reports that inflicting physical abuse on babies, "sets off a ripple of hormonal changes that wire the child's brain to cope with a malevolent world."

Van der Kolk observed the human response to trauma is universal. Traumatic memories are dissociated from other memories and stored outside other life experiences. This leads to self *dysregulation*, *aggression* against the self and others, *learning disabilities*, *dissociation*, *somatization* (the conversion of anxiety into physical symptoms), and *distorted perceptions* of the self and others. Long-term studies show many traumatized individuals suffer from subclinical *Post-Traumatic Stress*, which may manifest later during challenging times as difficulty in coping and controlling their lives. Interpersonal elements of *betrayal, mistrust, dependency,* and *helplessness*, interlaced with feelings of love and hate replay, especially during psychotherapy.[74]

Alice Miller has written extensively on the social effects of child maltreatment. A child's integrity is compromised when vital needs are frustrated by undue punishment, exploitation for parental wants, manipulation, neglect, or deceit. These victims become eternally impaired. Unable to express their anger in an appropriate manner, they suppress it and repress the traumatic memory. Affected dissociation causes destructive criminal acts. Destructive acts to the self include drug addiction, alcoholism, prostitution, psychic disorders, and suicide. Just like hamsters in a cage, a wheel of misplaced revenge is perpetrated on children by parents and caregivers for the violence that happened to them. Society usually protects parental rights at the expense of the child. The dependent child with no hope is bound to the parent in fear.[75]

Jacobson et al. correlated self-destructive behavior with birth traumas. They studied suicides, drug addiction, and alcoholism. Suicides by asphyxiation correlated to birth asphyxia. Violent suicides associated to mechanical birth trauma. Drug addiction correlated to opiates and barbiturates given mothers during labor. Trauma may be thought of as a type of imprinting.[76] Nonsuicidal siblings had fewer birth complications.[77] Collins related that there is a rise of schizophrenia in those who have suffered child abuse and trauma.[78]

In regression therapy, John Rhinehart, M.D., practicing psychiatrist and psychotherapist, found links from PTSD in middle aged men to childhood circumcision. In *somatic redecision* regression therapy, once somatic body language is achieved, the patient can reach deep into forgotten, unconscious matters from the distant past. Later-life symptoms which are not specific, but rather generalized to trauma including:[79-81]

We can only know as adults what we feel as children.
Leslie Fielder

powerlessness	victimization	shame
fear	vulnerability	shyness
prone to addiction	sense of defeat	
low self-esteem	rage reactions	
guarded in relationships	defensiveness	
permanently damaged	uncommunicative	
lack of trust	sexual callousness	
decreased tenderness	diminished maleness	

In a report of adult clinical cases Rhinehart concluded that a man circumcised as a child is more likely to react with terror, rage and/or dissociation when confronted with situations interpreted as threatening. As in any situation of post-traumatic stress, an event resembling any aspect of the original traumatic experience is more likely to provoke negative emotions such as panic, rage, violence, or dissociation.

The Panic Button is for emergencies only.
Wolfe
The Pacifier

Psychologist Ronald Goldman, Ph.D., explored the effects of circumcision on males who were cut at birth. He discovered:[82]

> The feelings reported generally include anger, sense of loss, shame, sense of having been victimized and violated, fear, distrust, grief, and jealousy of intact men.

Goldman also determined that the age at the time of circumcision trauma correlates with subsequent asocial and antisocial behavior. The more men learned and discovered what circumcision actually entailed, the more their feelings evolved and emerged. Masculinity is closely connected to a man's feelings about his penis, so circumcision often produces a negative body image. When a physical wound to the penis occurs, a psychic wound results. This wound affects motivation and lowers feelings of self-esteem. It manifests in behaviors which are considered normal male traits in circumcising cultures.

After all they are emotionally inexperienced... We create a cushion, a pillow for their emotions and consequently we can control them better.
Dr. Eldon James
Blade Runner

*We do not see with
our eyes, but with our
understandings and
our hearts.*
Hazlitt

Whatever the age of the male when circumcised, repressed feelings of *not being whole* are equivalent to a woman with a mastectomy. Resultant psychopathology may be deeply hidden and can manifest as personality quirks.[82] Circumcision can lead to *Body Dysmorphic Disorder* (BDD), in which the person is excessively concerned about and preoccupied by an imagined or minor defect in their physical features. BDD combines obsessive and compulsive aspects, linking it to the obsessive-compulsive spectrum of disorders.

PENILE INJURY ANXIETY

Freud's *Castration Anxiety* only goes part way. The author proposes that circumcision engenders *Penile Injury Anxiety*. This blood ritual of circumcision binds the group with a *(Cultural) Societal Post-Traumatic Attachment*. Circumcision causes forms of neurosis, psychosis and paranoia within the individual (commonly seen in the three cultures that circumcise their young: Americans, Jews and Muslims) and these psychosexual conditions then transfer into the social environment.

*There is nothing like
an amputated spirit.
There is not prosthetic
device for that.*
Frank Slade
Scent of a Woman

In some cultures the male cannot find a marriage partner unless he is circumcised (and where females are circumcised the same stigma applies). Due to group dynamics a pack identity is established through penile injury and traumatized members become a cohesive military unit and fight together, as in war. In ages past, circumcision was reserved for men who were going into battle. Now we do it to our children and our streets have become battlegrounds.

AN AMERICAN EPIDEMIC

*Science is
organized knowledge.
Wisdom is
organized life.*
Immanuel Kant

Most cultures do not allow males to be perceived as victims. Yet most cultures that circumcise boys still perceive mutilated females as victims. The following is paraphrased from Elaine Landau's *An American Epidemic* on the effects of child abuse.[83] Landau describes many unfortunate signs we see in our society from early childhood abuse, and relates to circumcision.

> Sympathy is given to young victims of abuse yet as these children grow, anti-social behavior clinically presents. In frustration, an attitude of deserving what has happened to them may develop.
>
> Adolescents, as well as adults, are unable to remove themselves from destructive relationships. The symptoms of abuse are many and varied, specific to the individual: physical, emotional and mental impairment; paralyzing fear or separation from the parent; impaired personal development; feelings of shame and guilt; bed-wetting; low self-esteem; hostility and other

disruptive anti-social behaviors; a sense of desperation or unresolved anger; involvement in gangs, drugs, prostitution and/or crime; a pathological uncertainty about self and the world; either a profound lack of empathy for others, or an exaggerated "search for love"; hopelessness; and suicidal and/or homicidal impulses. Silently suffering, victims of abuse are too ashamed and afraid to seek help. Hand in hand with physical abuse, emotional abuse is generational mirroring the parental child-rearing techniques.

Emotional scars are often untreated because they are sub-clinically *unseen*, yet they last a lifetime. It is important for victims of genital cutting to learn stress management, otherwise abuses will continue to be passed down from one generation to the other both individually and socially.

UNSEEN DISTURBED BEHAVIOR

Children are our most valuable resource.
Herbert Hoover

Unseen, unrecognized, disturbed behavior of circumcised individuals can be correlated to unseen disturbed cultural behavior in mutilating societies. Quoting Steven Lukes from *Political Ritual and Social Integration*:[84]

[Ritual] helps define as authoritative certain ways of seeing society: it serves to specify what in society is of specific significance, it draws people's attention to certain forms of relationships and activities — and at the same time, therefore, it deflects their attention from other forms, since every way of seeing is also a way of not seeing.

MEDICINE

The most noble part of the art of medicine is knowing when to do nothing

William Sears, author, professor, pediatrician and father of eight states:[1] *There are no significant medical benefits that make circumcision worth doing.*

Reasons and excuses for circumcision may sound convincing when presented with authority but they are, nonetheless, false. Although no medical organization in the world advocates routine infant circumcision, to this day most contemporary American medical texts still feature illustrations of the denuded penis rather than the natural intact penis with its protective prepuce and most boys are still genitally altered soon after birth.

Whenever a doctor cannot do good, he must be kept from doing harm.
Hippocrates

CLOAKED AUTHORITY

The genital alteration of minors is performed on healthy infants and is therefore beyond the standard of care for the treatment of disease. Consequently, through the combined cloaked authority of the medical smock and clerical robe working in unison, doctors have become socialized medico-religious ritual specialists replacing parental authority and even their own religious authority. Bell in *Ritual Theory, Ritual Practice* wrote:[2]

> As institutions of specialists take on the formulation of reality, there is a decreased need for personal or collective rituals to assume that function. Ultimately, when the strategies of ritualization are dominated by a special group, recognized as official experts, the definition of reality that they objectify works primarily to retain the status and authority of the experts themselves.
>
> Specific relations of domination and subordination are generated and orchestrated by the participants themselves simply by participating.
>
> It is this type of control that must be understood. These bodies of knowledge act simultaneously to secure a particular form of authority.

Once you give up your integrity, the rest is a piece of cake.
J. R. Ewing
Dallas

THE CLERIC-PHYSICIAN

Medicine has attempted to justify improper ritual. Genital alterations are often based on the *imago vivendi* (world view or way of life) of physicians and other health care providers, as well as their *imago Dei* (their religious perception of God). History shows that physicians were instrumental in weaving circumcision into the social fabric. Add religious assumptions to medicine and the outcome is doctors who are *cleric-physicians*.[3,4]

In the film *It's a Boy!*, Dr. Jenny Goodman, a Jewish Medical Doctor and Psychotherapist says: "None of us do it for medical reasons. We do it because we fear being cast out from the tribe. But after having done it, we comfort ourselves with these medical myths... If we could progress from sacrifice through castration to circumcision, then we can continue to progress all the way away from any kind of physical injury."

In Victorian England both sexes were subjected to genital alterations for the purpose of lessening sexual pleasure, which was at that time considered to be a sin. In England, Schwartz recorded:[5]

> Routine neonatal circumcision began in this country in the 1870's and was practiced on both boys and girls for the ensuing two decades.

Masturbation was one reason often cited to introduce circumcision into English-speaking countries[6] and it continues to this day.[7] Dacryphilia (is a form of paraphilia in which one is aroused by tears or sobbing) and/or piquerism (a paraphilia and form of sadomasochism in which one finds sexual gratification through penetration of another person, most commonly by stabbing or cutting the body with sharp objects) are terms that indicate deriving pleasure, including sexual pleasure, from another's pain and tears. In 1860 Dr. Athol Johnson wrote:[8]

> In cases of masturbation we must, I believe, break the habit by inducing such a condition of the parts as will cause too much local suffering to allow of the practice to be continued. For this purpose, if the prepuce is long, we may circumcise the male patient with present and probably with future advantages; the operation, too, should *not* be performed under chloroform, so that the pain experienced may be associated with the habit we wish to eradicate.

Christian elements influencing medicine included three main categories:

1. Female physicians (suffrage)
2. Seventh Day Adventists
3. Catholicism

FEMALE PHYSICIANS — SUFFRAGE

By the time the Inquisition ended in the early 1800s, women healers were conspicuously absent from the medical profession except in menial capacities. The first American all-female medical school opened in 1850. Feminine influence helped change overt patriarchal medical behavior and some gender feminists introduced social medical practices as well. In his translator's introduction to Ignatz Semmelweis' book on childbed fever, K. Codell Carter stated:[9]

> Women were gradually admitted to the medical profession. There was a revolution in therapeutics... Because physicians treat as well as describe and explain, medical theories are socially immanent in a way that the theories of physics or biology, for instance, are not. Consequently, one must expect that medical theory will intimately reflect and be reflected by the social role of the physician... changes in medical theory often correlate with social changes in the practice of medicine or in the organization of the profession.

SEVENTH DAY ADVENTISTS

In 1860 the *Seventh Day Adventists*, under the leadership of Ellen G. White, opened their first hospital. Their most prominent physician was Dr. John Harvey Kellogg. Kellogg ran a fashionable clinic called the "Sanitarium" in Battle Creek, Michigan. He believed that sex weakened one, so he focused on means of reducing the sex drive. He advocated circumcision for both men and women, a morning enema and cold baths. Dr. Kellogg invented the corn flake ostensibly for bowel regularity, yet it is said he had daily enemas and health advocates today say that, ironically, grain gluten creates bowel problems. In 1888, Kellogg published *Treatment for Self-Abuse and its Effects* stating:[10]

> A remedy for masturbation which is almost always successful in small boys is circumcision. The operation should be performed without administering anesthetic, as the pain attending the operation will have a salutary effect upon the mind, especially, if it is connected with the idea of punishment, as it may well be in some cases.
>
> The soreness which continues for several weeks interrupts the practice, and if it had not previously become too firmly fixed, it may be forgotten and not resumed. If any attempt is made to watch the child, he should be so

My son is in pain! Please, stop this!
Mrs. Lowe
He's fighting.
Dr. Sayer
He's losing.
Mrs. Lowe
Awakenings

It is not titles that honor men, but men that honor titles.
Eric Hobsbawn

It is better to deserves honors and not have them than to have them and not deserve them.
Mark Twain

carefully surrounded by vigilance that he cannot possibly transgress without detection. If he is only partially watched, he soon learns to elude observation, and thus the effect is only to make him cunning in his vice.

In females, the author has found the application of pure carbolic acid to the clitoris an excellent means of allying the abnormal excitement, and preventing the recurrence of the practice in those whose will-power has become so weakened that the patient is unable to exercise entire self-control.

A century later, in the 1950s, Seventh Day Adventist physician, Harold Shryock, was still advising clitoridectomy and circumcision:[11]

> There are teenage girls who, impelled by an unwholesome curiosity or by the example of unscrupulous girl friends, have fallen into the habit of manipulating these sensitive tissues as a means of excitement. This habit is spoken of as masturbation... There is an anatomical factor that sometimes causes irritation about the clitoris and thus encourages a manipulation of the delicate reproductive organs... Oftentimes the remedy for this situation consists of a minor surgical operation spoken of as circumcision. This operation is not hazardous and is much to be preferred to allowing the condition of irritation to continue.

CATHOLICISM

Jo Ann McNamara in *Sisters in Arms* wrote:[12]

> Unlike nuns of earlier centuries, nineteenth-century sisters could make space in a widening world to develop their own visions... Strengthened by their new prominence in the world at large, they were more articulate in expressing their own goals and convictions than they had in their established churches of the *ancien regime*... As the century progressed, these vocations were transformed into professions, professions created by women and stamped with a peculiarly feminine character that betrayed their religious origins.

Catholic nuns established a vast number of hospitals. In the early 1950's, under their pressure, the Pope eventually relented and allowed circumcision under the false premise of curing existing disease. Soon thereafter Catholic hospitals had lines of children lying on gurneys waiting in the halls to be circumcised under the premise of prophylactic care, not disease cure. Many of the children did not know what was going to happen to them.

One eight child in Canada was circumcised by priests in his when other students jokingly lied that he was masturbating resulting in a broken nose and wrist trying to fight them off.[13]

THE RELIGION CALLED "MEDICINE"

According to Dr. Robert Mendelsohn, medicine is a belief system, much like a religion. Its focus has moved from one disease theory to another throughout the centuries and you can rest assured it will continue to reinvent itself as needed. In his book *Confessions of a Medical Heretic*, Mendelsohn compares medicine to religion:[14,15]

- The hospital is the church
- Doctors are the priests
- Nurses are the nuns
- Medications are the sacraments
- X-rays and surgery are the rituals
- Questioning or disobedience equates to heresy

PROPER TERMINOLOGY

Proper terminology is important when discussing any subject. The words used will determine whether confusion or clarity will result. Many words have lost their original meanings and have assumed new meanings. The problem is further complicated by mistranslation when using biblical reference. Circumcision at the time of Jesus, and the Hebrew etymology of the word circumcision, referred only to removing the very tip of the prepuce. As we mentioned before, until 140 A.D. the glans penis was not exposed. Therefore, proper terms are:

FORESKIN: That naturally occurring portion of skin extending beyond the glans of the flaccid penis and clitoris, which constitutes the furthest extending portion of the prepuce

CIRCUMCISION: 1. The original ritual that removed only a portion of the normal and healthy foreskin; that is, the furthest extension of the penile prepuce as it extends beyond, and does not have direct contact with, the glans penis 2. Any form of female genital mutilation

PREPUCE: 1. That naturally occurring portion of skin that is in contact with and covers the glans penis and includes the extending foreskin 2. The complete clitoral hood that naturally covers the glans clitoris along with the extending portion of skin.

PREPUCECTOMY: the surgical and/or ritualistic removal of the complete male prepuce or the complete clitoral hood

Your scientists were so preoccupied with whether or not they could, they didn't stop to think if they should.
Dr. Malcom
Jurassic Park

Besides the noble art of getting things done, there is the noble art of leaving things undone.
Lin Yutang

There are some remedies worse than the disease.
Publius Syrus

MEDICAL ETHICS

Opinion, belief and conviction, no matter how sincerely expressed, do not constitute truth or correctness.[16,17] With the secularization of society, cleric-physicians have usurped the ritual of circumcision from the shaman and have justified it as a medical routine by manipulating statistics, whether they realize it or not.[18-20] Benjamin Disraeli said there are three kinds of lies: lies, damned lies and statistics[21] — in other words, the use of statistics goes beyond lying. Twisting statistics to justify genital reduction surgery on healthy, normal tissue is especially egregious and indicates malpractice (illegal, improper or negligent professional activity).[22]

MISLEADING WITH STATISTICS

Regarding the problem of statistics and the medical belief system, Carl Jung, in *The Undiscovered Self,* observed:[23]

> In this broad band of unconsciousness, which is immune to conscious criticism and control, we stand defenseless, open to all kinds of influences and psychic inflections. As with all dangers, we can guard against the risk of psychic inflection only when we know what is attacking us, and how, where and when the attack will come. Since self-knowledge is a matter of getting to know the individual facts, theories help very little in this respect. For the more a theory lays claim to universal validity, the less capable it is of doing justice to the individual facts. Any theory based on experience is necessarily *statistical*; that is to say, it formulates an *ideal average* which abolishes all exceptions at either end of the scale and replaces them by an abstract mean. This mean is quite valid, though it need not necessarily occur in reality....
>
> The statistical method shows the facts in the light of the ideal average but does not give us a picture of their empirical reality. While reflecting an indisputable aspect of reality, it can falsify the actual truth in a most misleading way. This is particularly true of theories which are based on statistics. The distinctive thing about real facts, however, is their individuality. Not to put too fine a point on it, one could say that the real picture consists of nothing but exceptions to the rule, and that, in consequence, absolute reality has predominately the character of irregularity.

DOUBLING

Dr. Robert Lifton used the word *doubling* in *The Nazi Doctors* for the psychological split that allowed Nazi doctors to commit atrocities in the concentration camps, while still behaving normally while at home. Lifton states:[24]

If you are curing a sickness *anything* is possible. The image of cure lends itself to the restorative myth of state violence and to the literal enactment of that myth... The key to understanding how Nazi doctors came to do the work of Auschwitz is the psychological principle I call *doubling*: the division of the self into two functioning wholes, so that a part-self acts as the entire self. An Auschwitz doctor could, through doubling, not only kill and contribute to killing but organize silently, on behalf of that evil project, an entire self-structure (or self-process) encompassing virtually all aspects of his behavior... In doubling, one part of the self "disavows" another part. What is repudiated is not reality itself — the individual Nazi doctor was aware of what he was doing via the Auschwitz self — but the meaning of that reality. The Nazi doctor knew that he selected, but did not interpret selections as murder. One level of disavowal, then, was the Auschwitz self's altering of the meaning of murder; and on another, the repudiation by the original self of *anything* done by the Auschwitz self.. Indeed, disavowal was the life blood of the Auschwitz self... Doubling can include elements considered characteristic of "psychopathic" character impairment;.. Doubling may well be an important psychological mechanism for individuals living within any criminal substructure.

Three aspects of doubling will be examined: 1) a medical ethicist, 2) ritual medical treatment, and 3) selective ethics.

MEDICAL ETHICIST

A former California Board of Medical Examiners medical ethicist, during a radio interview cited five reasons for circumcision:[25]

1. Women think it looks better.
2. It's easier for a man to get a marriage partner.[26]
3. It's from our Judaic culture.
4. It is cleaner.
5. There are fewer urinary tract infections.

When asked by a caller about the psychological damages of circumcision, the ethicist circumvented the question and its implications by referring to John Bobbitt whose penis had been amputated by his wife. The ethicist diverted the conversation and minimized the harm of unnecessary genital alteration by joking that men should be happy since circumcision is not penile amputation.

The first four of his reasons for circumcision are social attitudes. The fifth is improper medicine. His response to the caller's question was a *Lesser of Two Evils* logical fallacy and false argument, an attempt to persuade and justify by claiming that a larger wrong makes a lesser wrong, right.

The medicine increases the disease.
Virgil
The Aeneid

Somehow I'm confident it's not my rugged good looks to which I owe the honor of this visit.
Mullins
High Crimes

Egotism is that special "something" which enables a man who's in a rut to think he's in a groove.
Anonymous

RITUAL MEDICAL TREATMENT

Medical peer review has become a hollow, meaningless formality.[27] Medical practitioners enjoy impunity largely due to self-regulation. Circumcision (including clitoridectomy, clitoroplasty and labioplasty) are ritualistic surgeries[28] and U.S. federal and individual state laws prohibit Female Genital Mutilation on minors. Laws don't stop doctors from doing it and calling it by another name, such as *gender normalization surgery*.

Congenital Adrenal Hyperplasia causes enlarged external female genitalia and male micropenis. Doctors capitalize on parents' fear of embarrassment and projected social concerns and encourage them to allow surgery on infants and children, Perhaps it has not occurred to doctors to counsel parents to simply love and accept their children as they are and allow them to make their own decisions when they are adults. Many adults who were recipients of infant *gender normalization surgery* have loudly and publicly voiced their resentment of it. In *gender normalization surgery* the labia are reduced, the clitoris is either partially or totally ablated, and boys are sometimes turned into girls.

Other examples of opinion-based pediatric medicine — fashionable in the mid 20th century and nearly non-existent now — were tonsillectomies, appendectomies and the practice of irradiating infants' thymus glands. All three of those body parts are now recognized as important elements of the immune system. Everyone with the thymus irradiation treatment has had or will suffer a tumor — benign or malignant — if they live long enough. Malformations in growth and development have occurred due to it.

The term *iatrogenic* refers to harm caused to patients by medical treatment. The term used for somatic dysfunction is *pathophysiology*:

> IATROGENIC PATHOPHYSIOLOGY: disordered bodily processes that result from intervention by a physician or another acting as a health care provider. Specifically, genital mutilations

SELECTIVE ETHICS

Selective ethics is a form of hypocrisy. It means to extend different rules for different people or groups of people. In the case of circumcision in the USA, *selective ethics* clearly involves psychosexual power relations.

The following quotes were taken randomly from the book *Our Bodies, Ourselves*. These statements eloquently contradict human compassion and human rights standards.[29]

1. This practice, often referred to female genital mutilation, has been harmful to millions of girls and women.

2. If you have been circumcised, you may be at a higher risk of catching a STD from an infected partner... For further advice, talk to a gynecologist or to a support group that helps circumcised women with their physical and emotional needs.

3. As more women who have undergone circumcision live in the U.S., it is important that health care providers learn about this issue and approach it with sensitivity.

4. The idea that the state or the majority community can protect children from their own families is unacceptable to many and is probably unfeasible. The best way to prevent circumcision of girls in this country and elsewhere is to empower women to protect their own children... The important thing is to understand that any of us can be abused by her family or society.

5. Another form of violence against women is female circumcision, or female genital mutilation (FGM), which affects two million girls and women worldwide every year.

6. Although the practice is concentrated in parts of the African continent, global migration patterns have made it a significant health issue in other parts of the world as well. The enormous media exposure given to this issue in recent years has led to more open discussions in countries where it is taking place.

7. If you have a son, you may want to consider the pros and cons of circumcision. You have the right to make this and any other medical decision until such time as you relinquish that right.

THE COMMERCIALIZATION OF MEDICINE

When it comes to genital mutilation, medicine has betrayed its own values. When money becomes more important than people, a professional service becomes a business, an industry, an economic venture. Circumcisions are seen by many physicians as quick money compared to the nine months spent caring for an expectant mother.[30] Over a million infants are genitally altered annually at an average cost of more than $200 per procedure, which amounts to a large sum of money. Some midwives are now seeking permission to circumcise.[31]

Greed is a powerful ally. **Qui-Gon Jinn** *The Phantom Menace*

It is less of a problem to be poor, than to be dishonest. **Anishinabe Proverb**

I'm a businessman now. **Keaton** *The Usual Suspects*

Dr. Thomas Wiswell, a physician who advocates circumcision, stated frankly before his military retirement in 1987:[32]

> I have some good friends who are obstetricians outside the military, and they look at a foreskin and almost see $125 price tag on it. Each one is that much money. Heck, if I do ten a week, that's over $1,000 a week and they don't take that much time.

A retired OB/GYN told the author he never liked doing circumcisions but if he hadn't done them, "Someone else would get the money!" He looked shocked after he heard the stark, honest words from his own mouth.

How can health care workers who purport to serve compassionately go home at night, eat dinner as if nothing happened and laugh with their families after cutting unnecessarily on screaming babies? From Lifton in *The Nazi Doctors*:[33]

> In doubling, one part of the self "disavows" another part. What is repudiated is not reality itself — but the meaning of that reality... The SS doctor — deeply involved in the stark contradictions of the "schizophrenic condition"... lay in the idea of doing constructive medical work within a slaughterhouse.

INSURANCE COMPANIES & STATE AGENCIES

Beyond religion and medicine are insurance companies and state agencies that pay the fee, keeping the financial incentive alive for doctors, hospitals and parents. Most state assistance programs pay for circumcision from taxpayer monies.[34] Yet some states have ceased to pay for circumcision in order to channel the funds into legitimate medical needs and each year more states are following suit.

INFANT PENILE TISSUE MARKETING

Fetal tissue controversies are sidestepped by harvesting circumcised prepuces instead.[35] Once severed, the newborn's pristine prepuce, rich in stem cells and human growth factors, becomes property of the hospital and some hospitals sell the amputated tissue to the pharmaceutical industry for research and cosmetic products.[36] One prepuce is said to yield a football-field size piece of skin.

In 2006, the McGhan Medical Corporation applied to the FDA for approval of two formulas for foreskin-derived collagen, designed to be injected in lips and wrinkles for the purpose of making women look younger.[37]

Foreskin face creams are presently marketed using pentapeptides derived from preputial tissue. Skin Medica, the Coriell Institute for Medical Research, Organogenesis, Intercytex and Olay are just a few involved. Oprah Winfrey and Barbara Walters have publicly endorsed these products. Again, narcissism does not see the humanity of the male child in the equation.

LYING TO NEW PARENTS

In the 1960's and 1970's two San Francisco South Bay area hospitals are known to have blatantly lied to parents. Both Kaiser hospital[38] (home of the doctor who wrote the poem at the end of this chapter), and Palo Alto hospital (now affiliated with Stanford University's medical school),[39] were telling parents that it was *against the law* for them to take their sons home until they were circumcised.

Due to such obfuscation and improper behavior, the medical community may be questioned with regard to: agency, assault and battery, assault with intent to disfigure, cause, coercion, competence, consent, cruel and unusual punishment, due process, duty and its breach, endangerment, extortion and exaction, fraud, intent, *mens rea,* molestation, negligence, racketeering (see RICO Act), denial of religious freedom, right to privacy, sexual harassment, societal sexual harassment, *Societal Stockholm Syndrome*, *Societal Child Sexual Abuse Accommodation Syndrome* and tort.[40]

A prospective litigant may explore his or her own medical records and find it fruitful to investigate the professional relationships of those working in the office or hospital where the circumcision occurred. Medical records investigators should be aware of the practice of miscoding, because medical offices and hospitals are known to bill circumcisions as a completely different procedure. Currently, there is evidence that purposeful miscoding is happening in Canada's province of British Columbia.[41]

OVERDIAGNOSIS

Overdiagnosis approaches disinformation. Historically and to the present day, nearly every disease has been attributed to the genitals at one time or another. The natural, normal, healthy body and natural, normal, healthy sexuality have been blamed for all manners of disease. Among the diseases that have been unfairly blamed on the male prepuce are:[42-60]

They will all suffer this outrage.
Jabba the Hutt
Return of the Jedi

You just keep propositioning people until they say yes?
Lois
The Insider

It is reasonable to expect the doctor to recognize that science may not have all the answers to problems of health and healing.
Norman Cousins

Hip trouble due to weakened muscles; brain defects; nerve tension, derangements of the digestive organs, restlessness, irritability, chorea, convulsions, paralysis, nerve waste; phimosis, paraphimosis, redundancy, adhesions, papillomata, eschemia, edema, chancre and chancroid (both from syphilis), cicatrices (scars), inflammatory thickening, elephantitis, naevus, epithelioma, gangrene, tuberculosis, preputal calculi, hernia, dysurea, enuresis, impotence, and hystero-epilepsy. Circumcision has been claimed to increases male sexual pleasure (actually decreases); cause nervous exhaustion, dyspepsia, diarrhea, rectal prolapse; backwardness in studies, marasmus, muscular incoordination, epilepsy; dropsy, hydrocephalus; nervous pneumonia; rape and divorce. Circumcision has been blamed for meatal ulcer; heart disease, suicide; urinary tract infections; alcoholism, bed-wetting, gastritis, nymphomania (feminine preputal preference), kleptomania, truancy, baldness, poor eyesight, loss of memory, tabes dorsalis, vertigo, meningitis, laziness, melancholy, AIDS; penile, cervical and prostatic cancers (penile and cervical cancers have viral etiology), as well as Prune Belly (Eagle-Barrett) Syndrome.

The clitoris has been blamed for barrenness, falling breasts, nymphomania (feminine desire), uterine prolapse and miscarriage.

Phimosis is the inability to retract the prepuce. Paraphimosis is when the retracted prepuce cannot be returned forward. Overdiagnosis of both is indicated from a study conducted by the Finnish National Board of Health. It found that only 0.00023% of uncircumcised Finnish boys at age 15 suffer from phimosis or paraphimosis. This means 99.997% of children are in no danger of phimosis or paraphimosis. Neither phimosis or paraphimosis is a reason to circumcise infants or children.

MEDICINE & GENOCIDAL PURIFICATION

We have established that circumcision is a psychosexual mock-death ritual. The secular, commercial demand for it constitutes a genocide of sorts, the end of the natural body, the end of natural sex, the end of certain cultures, the end of a way of being for a majority of the world's population. Recommendations for universal circumcision are wrapped in dubious statistics. Circumcision studies should always be evaluated with the possibility of an investigator's biased point of view based on his own cultural background, personal narcissism, financial gain and other selfish interests. When a researcher has a pet theory, he can easily overlook facts that contradict his desired outcome.

Once upon a time a medical study claimed that the virus which caused cervical cancer hid under the skin of the prepuce. Why? Because Jewish women had less cervical cancer and so it was assumed that cervical cancer was caused by the presence of the prepuce This was reminiscent of an ancient Egyptian theory that semen caught in the folds of the prepuce decreased fertility.[61] The cervical cancer myth has lingered in the minds of the public, though it was disproved many years ago.

The conclusion drawn from the cervical cancer study was that *every* man should be circumcised to end cervical cancer. A demand for universal circumcision could be said to constitute a stamping out of non-circumcising civilizations, a cultural genocide of sorts.

Currently the United Nations and the World Health Organization are advocating the circumcision of all males in some regions of Africa based on flawed studies of HIV patterns and faulty evaluations of them. They propose to start first with the youngest, then circumcise adolescents and finally adult men.[62] We have to ask if their concern is for the health of the African people or — since the U.S.A. has "cut back" on circumcising — is the tissue harvesting industry desperate for a new source of skin for beauty products?

The push for universal African circumcision is based on crystal ball "predestined" studies that are skewed due to the following errors:

THE GEOGRAPHIC FALLACY

The country chosen for one HIV study was Kenya. In six of ten African countries in that region, there is a higher rate of HIV among circumcised males. Kenya is the only country in the area where HIV is more prevalent in intact men than circumcised men. It has been argued and clearly demonstrated that the study results were distorted by the choice of country.[63] Another African study was performed in Uganda where the statistics are similar to Kenya. Thus two distorted representatives of African populations were studied to support the desired conclusions of those conducting the studies.

THE DEMOGRAPHIC FALLACY

The circumcised men chosen for one HIV study were Muslims who have a strict sexual moral code. In contrast, the uncircumcised men chosen for the study were mainly transient non-Muslim long-distance truck drivers[64] who often seek the services of prostitutes. Behavior is the key element in the spread of sexually transmitted diseases, but it is rarely, if ever, considered or mentioned.

He achieves his conquest by applying specific mechanisms of control. This is usually a specific series of actions signature killers use to assume and exert control, and then a set of potent ritualisms that reinforce their thrill of control long after the crime has been committed.
Robert Keppel
Signature Killers

Where there's a will, there's a weapon.
Yuri
Lord of War

Nothing is more fatal to health than an overcare of it.
Benjamin Franklin

BEHAVIOR OVERSIGHTS

Behavior is the hallmark of both African studies:[65-67] The behaviors that have yet to be addressed and are overlooked by these researchers are:

MULTIPLE CONCURRENT PARTNERS

The phenomenon of multiple concurrent sexual partners is common in Southern African culture and promotes the spread of HIV/AIDS. Multiple concurrent partners are long-term relationships outside of marriage. These relationships are not casual and are known by the spouse. They occur mainly in the non-circumcising non-Muslim population. Some use this method of obtaining sex rather then to use the services of prostitutes. Again, we say the HIV/AIDS issue is an issue of behavior.[68,69]

DRY SEX

Dry sex is another behavior which is commonly practiced where African AIDS studies have taken place. African males do not like vaginal wetness and find it repulsive. Therefore, to dry the vagina African women apply shredded newspapers, cotton, salt, detergents, and even a baboon urine mixture obtained from local medicine men. This leads to chaffing and skin tears which spread STDs. The problem of HIV transmission is complicated by open sores caused by a high incidence of herpes infection. With tears and sores, washing the penis soon after intercourse in an attempt to avoid HIV only increases its transmission. Also, most men refuse to use condoms.[70-72] Behavior is the key element in HIV transmission.

ADVERSE EFFECTS OF CIRCUMCISION

Over 200 American infants die annually from unnecessary circumcisions.[73] It is claimed that circumcision has a 4% complication rate[74] but this is a conservative estimate because *iatrogenic* (doctor-caused) problems are typically only reported immediately after the procedure in the clinical setting. Outpatient care for infection or blood loss associated with circumcision is not attributed to the unnecessary cutting on the baby's healthy genital tissue.[75]

Complications following circumcision that do not always show up immediately include:[76-107]

> Shortened penis, skin bridges, deformation, coma, loss of penis; a permanently twisted, curved, or bowed penis during erection; bleeding and infection which have lead to death, gangrene leading to Fournier's syndrome,

Knowledge that is not used is abused.
Cree Proverb

Common sense is in medicine the master workman.
Peter Latham

Violence and technology — not good bedfellows.
Eddie
Lost World: Jurassic Park

osteomyelitis, and leg cyanosis due to compromised circulation. Nerve block complications have been reported. Accidental amputations from a portion of the glans penis to the entire penis are too common. Acute renal failure, tetanus, ruptured bladder and scrotal gangrene are known to have occurred. A predictable nine to ten percent of circumcised infants suffer meatal stenosis. Neither meatal ulcers nor meatal stenosis occur in intact (uncircumcised) infants and children. A lack of circulation to the glans due to severed nerves and blood vessels, plus the loss of its natural protective covering results in contraction and scaring of the opening to the urinary tract. When the meatus dries and hardens, it restricts the free flow of urine. Dermal and urethral fistulas are common. Amputation neuromas, sexual pain, erectile dysfunction. From all the focus on and pain to the genitals, it is only understandable that psychological conditions are likely to result.

The practice of medicine is a thinker's art; the practice of surgery, a plumber's.
Martin Fisher

Add to the 4% known complication rate in the clinic, a solid and predictable 9-10% meatal stenosis rate brings the number quickly to 13-14%. Meatal stenosis occurs *only* in circumcised boys due to loss of protection for the urinary opening. This problem requires medical attention and sometimes entails surgical repair. Pediatric urologists who sub-specialize in the repair of iatrogenically-caused problems resulting from botched circumcisions can expect to make $500,000 a year.[108] All this would be unnecessary if circumcision was not practiced. This includes new strains of MSRA infecctions.

They have not the sure direction of a weapon well in hand.
Ardant duPicq
Battle Studies

In areas where the African AIDS studies occurred, the circumcision complication rate far exceeded 4%. It was 35% in traditional tribal circumcisions and an embarrassing 18% in African health clinics where circumcisions were medically performed. But then, adults can complain whereas babies cannot.

And we can only guess the effect circumcision has on the penis in the long term. We do know that the demand for Viagra in the USA and the other two cultures that circumcise their young far outstrips the demand in other areas of the world where they do not circumcise.

ADVERSE EFFECTS OF PREMATURE RETRACTION

These doctors are savages.
Leo Getz
Lethal Weapon 3

Pathological phimosis is a condition where the foreskin cannot be fully retracted from the head of the penis. Occasionally a foreskin will need some medical attention, but most cases of genuine phimosis can be easily remedied by self-stretching. Phimosis can only be diagnosed accurately after the child is grown. No infant can be accurately diagnosed with phimosis because his genitals are immature and still developing.

"Non-retractability can be considered normal for males up to and includ-ing adolescence."[109] Yet American medical schools apparently train students to call the natural non-retractable condition of the penis, "phimosis" and doc-tors charge insurance companies and government health programs for routine infant circumcision on healthy baby boys, as if it is a valid treatment for a medical condition, which it is not.

The normal prepuce and glans are still fused at birth and to circumcise most boys, a blunt instrument is inserted between the foreskin and glans and the two are torn apart, much like a fingernail from the finger.

Retracting the prepuce and cleaning under it is as necessary (unnecessary) as retracting and washing under the eyelid. This intrusive process of foreskin retraction could be interpreted by the child as an assault because it is excru-ciatingly painful and therefore emotionally traumatic. That it is done at all is, at best, evidence of inadequate medical education about and experience with the natural, intact penis.[110] Premature prepuce retraction causes urinary tract infections (UTIs).[111]

Current medical estimates for retraction by age are unrealistically early. The American Academy of Pediatrics says that retraction at age five is normal, but forced retraction is always improper.[112] It is always inappropriate to recom-mend infant circumcision for phimosis. Genuine phimosis is rare, can only be diagnosed when the child is in teens or twenties and can be easily remedied at that time by the patient himself by gently stretching the skin.

The ridged band is too narrow to allow the glans out of its prepuce — this can also happen in females. But even in cases of genuine phimosis, if cutting is necessary only a small slit is required — not total ablation of the prepuce.

Some problems arising from circumcision do not even arise until adult-hood. It is known that adult circumcised men have more UTIs than adult intact men.[113]

FETISH/ABERRATION

An *aberration* is a deviation from the usual, normal, or right course. A *fetish* is an aberration involving sexual fantasies. Some males who perform the operation have reported erections observing and performing the surgery. One nurse waxed poetically, seeing a baby's glans penis exposed for the first time, as if it was an erotic experience for her.[114] In one Oregon hospital the nurses call circumcision *weenie whacking*.[115] Circumcision is an *aberration*.

Penile fetish with socialized medical aberration is exampled in Dorothy Marlow's *Textbook of Pediatric Nursing*[116] by advocating daily retraction for cleansing. And Dr. Mark Foley in *The Unkindest Cut*[117] stated that circumcision is a socially perverted libido outlet, perverted and a form of as well as circumcisions has origins in sadism within crypto-perversion.

UNNECESSARY SURGERY IS UNETHICAL & CRIMINAL

Dr. Janet Menage, supported by Dr. George Denniston, stated: *It is time that genital mutilation was banned completely and that the medical profession faced up to its collusion in the harming of patients.*[118-119] Dr. Eva Solomon is one example of a circumcision performed without parental or patient concent, whether accidental or not.[120] Van Lewis noted:[121]

> The American Academy of Pediatrics says there is no medical indication for circumcising healthy newborns. After carefully reviewing the last 40 years of medical research, it now says circumcising healthy males is medically unjustified and does not recommend it. The American Medical Association agrees, calling circumcision "non-therapeutic." The American College of Obstetrics and Gynecologists concurs.

Widespread medical circumcision has consistently been a result of dishonest claims, flawed statistics as with UTI's and social causations - and increases complication events.[122--150] Faulty correlations originally created a false demand but doctors never bothered to correct the error. Circumcision also does not prevent *sexually transmitted diseases* (STDs). Dr. Paul Fleiss, pediatrician, reports that circumcision increases STDs and UTIs because the prepuce has immunological functions which are lost to circumcision. Fleiss' study covers viral and bacterial infections, gonorrhea, nongonoccocal urethritis, human papilloma virus, herpes simplex virus type 2, and chlamydia (which increases coronary disease). Fleiss also mentions two Australian studies of wound infections by staphylococcus, proteus, pseudomonas, and tuberculosis.

Faulty correlations can have unanticipated, disastrous effects. African HIV diagnoses, for instance, are based not on blood tests, but weight loss, which could be caused by any number of things — including lack of food and water. Diagnosed with HIV, some tribal South Africans who believe that sex with a virgin will cure them of AIDS, sexually abuse children and even infants to ostensibly cure themselves of a disease which they do not actually have.

Fetishism is classified in psychiatric circles as a paraphilia, or disorder of sexual aim.
John Douglas
The Anatomy of Motive

Battlefield doctors decide who lives and who dies.
Johns
They kept calling it murder when I did it.
Riddick
Pitch Black

I thought we were friends.
Oz
That's what you get for trusting a contract killer.
Jimmy
The Whole 10 Yards

INFORMED CONSENT

*Once you are able
to kill mentally,
the physical part
will be easy.
The difficult part
is to learn
how to turn it off.*
L.T.
The Hunted

The vast majority of circumcisions are performed without truly informed parental consent. For an adult the Dorsal Slit is an alternative.[151] For decades in the USA infant circumcisions were performed without patient (child) consent and parental consent as well as given no knowledge of the surgery beforehand. This was due to forced social acceptability and lax precautions. A few lawsuits convinced doctors that they should at least have a signed consent form. See Legal chapter.

WHAT IS LOST

Gary Harryman's *Lost List* paints a devastating picture of what is lost due to circumcision.[152] The entire *ridged band* and most of the *frenum* (or *frenulum*) are lost. These two structures are similar in function to the string under the tongue and the lips; the frenum holds the prepuce forward and the ridged band seals the area from dirt and air. The *ridged band* and *frenum* contain specialized nerves and glands. At least ten to twenty thousand nerve endings are lost. For the most part, the nerve cells taken are:

*When you kill
with your hands
there is a reverence.*
Aaron
High Crimes

1. Meissner's corpuscles that sense fine touch, and are found elsewhere mainly on the fingertips and the eye's conjunctiva

2. Merkel cells that also sense touch

3. Vater-Pacinian corpuscles that sense deep pressure

4. Nociceptors that are defensive by sensing injury

Together these nerve structures also sense stretching and fine gradations of texture. Half the smooth muscle sheath called the *dartos facia* that senses temperature is lost. And, *proprioception*, knowing where your body is in space and motion, is diminished. Sensitivity is also diminished because the *glans* becomes calloused. Losing glandular materials eliminates all *natural lubrication*, *immunological functions*, and *pheremones* that heighten the female's sexual response.[153,154]

*That was my religious
period. I ain't sung a
hymn in 104 years.*
Jack Crabb
Little Big Man

In the young male, erections are due in large part to testosterone. In the mature male, erections depend more on sensation. Because sensation has been lost to circumcision, *erectile dysfunction* is common in circumcising cultures. Loss of the prepuce prematurely ages the penis up to thirty years. Erectile dysfunction drugs are used extensively in circumcising locations.

PREPUCE RESTORATION

Physicians are beginning to listen when patients ask about prepuce restoration. But, you must be aware that your doctor may refer you for a psychiatric evaluation. This was a common referral for women requesting breast implants. One psychiatrist dismisses patient complaints about circumcision as *garrulous,* which means: *foolish, trivial, frivolous conversation.*

> SEMMELWEIS REFLEX: The Semmelweis Reflex is the dismissal or rejecting out of hand any information, automatically, without thought, inspection, or experiment.

SURGICAL RESTORATION

Originally, prepuce restoration was thought to be strictly in the realm of medicine. However, it is now understood that surgery is unnecessary for prepuce restoration and can even reduce the remaining sensation to nothing. During surgical restoration, some doctors have "tidied up" and removed all remaining preputial tissue including the frenulum, which is for most men the only remnants of the prepuce left after circumcision. These men have lost almost all penile sensation. Use of skin grafts from other parts of the body can be disastrous, as the prepuce is very fine, thin, specialized skin with inner and outer, double-layer functions, much like the eyelid. No cutting of genital tissue is advised. If surgery is chosen, the book *Clinical Ethics* states:[155]

> 2.1.3 Stringency: The moral and legal obligation of disclosure also varies in terms of the situation. It becomes more stringent and demanding as the treatment moves from emergency through elective to experimental.

SKIN STRETCHING

Prepuce restoration involves stretching the remaining penile skin to achieve glans coverage. People have stretched skin in many ways throughout the ages. Doctors who work with a woman without a vagina (a condition called *congenital vaginal aplasia*) may stretch the opening she has, to create a vagina.[156] To date, many thousands of men have restored their foreskins by stretching their skin. Stretching to full skin coverage takes years, but men report that the effort it takes is worth the time and effort. Jim Bigelow's book *The Joy of Uncircumcising* includes examples of non-surgical techniques to restore glans coverage.[157]

If a technological feat is possible, man will do it.
Motoko
Ghost in a Shell

Dismembering sadistic killers are at the highest level of the deviancy scale.
Dr. Michael Stone
Most Evil

We all can't do good, but at least no harm.
Halsey
Brain Dead

AGENT OF THE PATIENT

A medical degree does not give American doctors a "right" to practice medicine. It is a privilege to practice medicine, granted by the respective State entity which is the functioning representative of the people. Therefore, the people allow physicians to practice pursuant to proper conduct.[158] A physician is an *agent* of the *patient*, and when treating a child, the child is their patient, not the parent. Like children, many adults under anesthesia have experienced unconsented genital mutilations.[159,160] Patient preference is:[161]

> PATIENT PREFERENCE: In all medical treatment, the preferences of the patient, based on the patient's own values and his or her personal assessment of the benefits and burdens, are ethically relevant. In every clinical case, the questions must be raised: what are the patient's goals? What does the patient want? The systematic review of this topic requires further questions: Has the patient been provided sufficient information? Does the patient comprehend? Is the patient consenting voluntarily? Has the patient been coerced?

Dr. Janet Menage explained *Constructive Displacement* as the psychological process that gives a physician the mental ability to cut on another person for that patient's benefit.[162] This is similar, yet different from, Lifton's *Doubling*.[163] The difference lies in the doctor's ethics and morality.[164]

Medicine has legal consequences for failure to inform.[165] Future suits by circumcised men will assert they did not require circumcision surgery as infants and children; the skin removed was healthy and in no need of treatment. Such cases have already been successful.[166] Also, women will start suing for various forms of female genital mutilation. Insurance companies would be wise to stop funding both the circumcision procedure and offering malpractice coverage for doctors who perform circumcisions. The book *Clinical Ethics* addresses medical paternalism with.[167]

> 2.05 PATERNALISM: One of the most common ethical issues raised by the principle of respect for autonomy is paternalism. The term refers to the practice of overriding or ignoring a person's preferences in order to benefit them or enhance their welfare. In essence, it consists in the judgement that beneficence takes priority over autonomy. Historically, the medical profession has endorsed paternalism. Today, while still common it is considered ethically suspect.

PATHOLOGICAL SCIENCE AND BIOETHICS

Pathological science is where "people are tricked into false results by subjective effects, wishful thinking or threshold interactions from pseudoscience, amateur science, deviant or fraudulent science, bad science, junk science, and popular science." Pathological science involves 1) observer-expectancy effect and 2) subject-expectancy effect.[168]

Bioethics committees have issued guidelines that medical intervention should be permissible only in cases of clinically verifiable disease, deformity, or injury.[169-170] Medicine has a cavalier attitude which approaches hubris. The following poem was published in a medical journal and some feel it is an excellent example of the sophomoric lack of dignity and disrespect for the patient that some doctors exhibit regarding the subject of circumcision:[171]

Like Alice, I try to believe three impossible things before breakfast.
The Doctor
Dr. Who

ODE TO THE CIRCUMCISED MALE

We have a new topic to heat up our passion –
The foreskin is currently top of the fashions.
If you're the new son of a Berkeley professor,
Your genital skin will be greater, not lesser.
For if you've been circ'ed or are Moslem or Jewish,
You're outside the mode; you are old-ish not new-ish.
You have broken the latest society's rules;
You may never get into the finest of schools.
Noncircumcised males are the "genital chic" –
If your foreskin is gone, you are now up a creek.
It's a great work of art like the statue of Venus,
If you're wearing a hat on the head of your penis.
When you gaze through a looking glass,
Don't rue that you suffered a rape of the phallus
Just hope that one day you can say with a smile
That your glans ain't passe; it will rise up in style.

Dismembering sadistic killers are at the highest level of the deviancy scale.
Dr. Michael Stone
Most Evil

FIRST, DO NO HARM

The Hippocratic Oath includes the promise "to abstain from doing harm" — from the Greek "ἐπὶ δηλήσει δὲ καὶ ἀδικίῃ εἴρξειν".

Once he had killed, that taboo was gone. He realized he could do it, enjoy it, and get away with it.
John Douglas
Mind Hunter

HIPPOCRATIC OATH[172]

I swear by Apollo the physician, by Aesculapius, Hygea, and Panacea, and I take to witness all the gods, all the goddesses, to keep according to my abilities and my judgment the following oath.

To consider dear to me as my parents him who taught me this art; to live in common with him and if necessary to share my goods with him; to look upon his children as my own brothers, to teach them this art if they so desire without fee or written promise; to impart to my sons and the sons of the master who taught me and the disciples who have enrolled themselves and have agreed to the rules of the profession, but to these alone, the precepts and the instruction. I will prescribe regimen for the good of my patients according to my ability and my judgment and *never do harm to anyone*. To please no one will I prescribe a deadly drug, nor give advise which will cause his death. Nor will I give a woman a pessary to procure abortion. But I will preserve the purity of my life and my art. I will not cut for stone, even for patients in whom the disease is manifest; I will leave this operation to be performed by practitioners (specialists in this art). In every house where I come I will only enter for the good of my patients, keeping myself far from all intentional ill-doing and all seduction, and especially from the pleasures of love with women or with men, be they free or slave. All that may come to my knowledge in the exercise of my profession or outside of my profession or in daily commerce with men, which ought not to be spread abroad, I will keep secret and will never reveal. If I keep this oath faithfully, may I enjoy my life and practice my art, respected by all men and in all times; but if I swerve from it or violate it, may the reverse be my lot.

Today's technology provides physicians the opportunity to wears protective gloves and clothing according to OSHA dictates and they use instruments of refinement. Other than that, is the physician who circumcises children all that different from an evolved medicine man?[173] He may just as well wear a sacred animal skin[174] and use a honed flint knife[175] or a feather-decorated tool[176] to manipulate the victim's genitals.

You medical people will have more lives to answer for in the other world than we generals.
Napoleon

By the way, the insurance company paid off.
Angelo
Prizzi's Honor

RABBI MOSES MAIMONAIDES

What is the real purpose of circumcision?

Moses Maimonides (born Moshe ben Maimon), rabbi, physician and philosopher, was born in Spain in 1135. When he was thirteen years old, the Almohades Dynasty conquered Spain and threatened the Jewish population with death or exile if they did not convert to Islam. After ten years spent avoiding persecution, the family moved to Morocco. Maimonides also lived in the Holy Land and eventually settled in Egypt. As a rabbi, Maimonides was the first to write a systematic code of Jewish law, the *Mishneh Torah*. He also wrote numerous medical texts and served as a leader of Cairo's Jewish community.

Long before the Marquis de Sade, 19th Century English and American medicine, and FBI analysis of serial sexual predators, Maimonides eloquently clarified the historical motivation underlying circumcision. In *The Guide of the Perplexed* he wrote:

> The bodily pain caused to that member is the real purpose of circumcision. None of the activities necessary for the preservation of the individual is harmed thereby, nor is procreation rendered impossible, but violent concupiscence and lust that goes beyond what is needed are diminished. The fact that circumcision weakens the faculty of sexual excitement and sometimes perhaps diminishes the pleasure is indubitable. For if at birth this member has been made to bleed and has had its covering taken away from it, it must be indubitably weakened. The Sages, may their memory be blessed, have explicitly stated: It is hard for a woman with whom an uncircumcised man has had sexual intercourse to separate from him...
>
> The perfection and perpetuation of this Law can only be achieved if circumcision is performed in childhood... The parents of the child that is just born take lightly matters concerning it, for up to that time the imaginative form that compels the parents to love it is not yet consolidated.

CITY BLOCK

Robert Louis Stevenson

What are you able to build with your blocks?
Castles and palaces, temples and docks,
Rain may keep raining, and others go roam,
But I can be happy and building at home.

Let the sofa be mountains, the carpet be sea,
There I'll establish a city for me:
A kirk and a mill and a palace beside,
And a harbour's well where my vessels may ride.

Great is the palace with pillar and wall,
A sort of a tower on top of it all,
And steps coming down in an orderly way
To where my toy vessels lie safe in the bay.

This one is sailing and that one is moored:
Hark to the song of the sailors on board!
And see, on the steps of my palace, the kings
Coming and going with presents and things!

Now I have done with it, down let it go!
And all in a moment the town is laid low.
Block upon block lying shattered and free,
What is there left of my town by the sea?

Yet as I saw it, I see it again,
The kirk and the palace, the ships and the men,
And as long as I live and where'er I may be,
I'll always remember my town by the sea.

TRANSGENERATION

Sometimes we choose to suffer alone; sometimes we choose to make others suffer with us

---

When individual habits grow into local and regional patterns of behavior, we call this level of transmission, *transgeneration*. At this stage, practices are not yet officially sanctioned in a culture or integrated into a country's social conscious so they do not have legal protection. However, covert legal sanction exists when an act is against the law and proscribed by religion, and there is failure to apply the law and prosecute the behavior.

Abuses of all types are a result of *repetition-compulsion*. Re-inflicting trauma on oneself or passing it on to another is an attempt to resolve the anxiety created by an initial trauma.[1] Battered girls, as women, often marry violent husbands, and adult children of alcoholics often marry drinkers. Goldman showed that a male circumciser is attempting to resolve his own circumcision by now playing the role of attacker.[2,3] Striking out at the young is transference of unresolved adult conflicts.[4] In this way children become social prey in an ongoing transgenerational cycle of violence and abuse.

Using a specialized agent transfers parental power to the social order, allowing the parent as well as society, non-responsibility through denial, deferral, deflection and deceit. However, circumcision demands explanation because it crosses physical boundaries.

The quest for perfection in the child stems from the parents concern about adult imperfection. From this parental perception, the *elect* transfer the general concept of human imperfection to the younger generation so that they may establish, maintain and enforce social mores.[5] Transgenerational transmission of unresolved conflicts may come from parental feelings including but not limited to: a miserable existence, insignificance, loneliness, abandonment, rejection, insecurity or a need to belong.[6] Attempts to resolve distress, where there is high dependence on others, involves a special anointing of self and society.

It's a hard world for little things.
Rachel Cooper
The Night of the Hunter

Repetition is reality, and it is the seriouness of life.
Kierkegaard

You must understand you are being groomed for a life of responsibility and wealth.
Cadwell
Richy Rich

Anointing includes special claims of authority, justification for physical punishment, identification in pain, inhibition of dissent, lack of accountability for the parent, a ritual agent, and the excuse of a social *right*.[7]

Ritual attempts to transform the initiate into society's vision of what is necessary for him or her to become an acceptable member in good standing. Mystical traditions in social ritual often rely on history, theology, and religious practice. Traditions often displace proper ethics allowing actions that would otherwise not occur. Ancient tribes used a specialized shamanic agent to perform rituals. Medical doctor as specialized agent attempts to prepare the infant to meet his circumcised father, future peers in the locker room, and eventually, a prospective spouse. Routine medical circumcision is a product of pagan magical thought and mythology.

Justification for child abuse stands on a rickety ethical framework that supplants *immorality* with a *transmorality*.[8] The damaged internal child lives on for a lifetime. Susan Forward, in *Toxic Parents*, wrote:[9]

> When you're young, our godlike parents are everything to us... With nothing and no one to judge them against, we assume them to be the perfect parents... The only way emotional assaults or physical abuse can make sense to the child is if he or she accepts responsibility for the toxic parent's behavior... No matter how toxic your parents may be, you still have to deify them... There are two central doctrines in this faith of godlike parents: 1) "I am bad and my parents are good." 2) "I am weak and my parents are good," these are powerful beliefs that can outlive your physical dependence on your parents. These beliefs keep the faith alive; they allow you to avoid facing the painful truth that your godlike parents actually betrayed you when you were most vulnerable... there are many parents whose negative patterns of behavior are consistent and dominant in a child's life. These are the parents who do harm... Many of the time-honored techniques that have been passed down from generation to generation are, quite simply, bad advice masquerading as wisdom.
>
> There are parents whose negative patterns of behavior are consistent and dominant in a child's life. These are the parents who do harm. As difficult as it may be to believe, battered children accept the blame for the crimes perpetrated against them just as surely as verbally abused children do. Sexual or physical abuse can be so traumatic that often a single occurrence is enough to cause tremendous emotional damage.
>
> *You are **not** responsible for what was done to you as a defenseless child! You **are** responsible for taking positive steps to do something about it now.*

What bothers you most? — That you don't have a life... or that I do?
Linda
Hollow Man

Mother is God in the eyes of a child.
Rose
Silent Hill

Heaven lieth at the feet of mothers.
Mohammed

POISONOUS PEDAGOGY

Pedagogy is the art and science of indoctrinating children.[10] Institutional pedagogy addresses psychosexuality and may reinforce abuse. Critical pedagogy teaches a person to consciously question domination in a positive manner. Abused children are denied questioning and dissent. Alice Miller defined *poisonous pedagogy* by these abusive parental assumptions:[11]

- Adults are the masters (not the servants) of the dependent child.

- They determine in godlike fashion what is right and what is wrong.

- The child is held responsible for parental anger.

- The parents must always be shielded.

- The child's life-affirming feelings pose a threat to autocratic adults.

- The child must be "broken" as soon as possible.

- All this must happen at a very early age, so the child "won't notice" and will therefore not be able to expose the adults.

EVOLUTION OF CHILDHOOD

The following is a brief outline of deMause's *Evolution of Childhood* which has six aspects of acculturated child-rearing practices. Summarizing:[12]

- *First: 1a*. Early Infanticidal Mode occurs mainly in small kinship groups. The mothers used their children as symbols of poison containment and the killing represented purification.

- *First: 1b*. Late Infanticidal Mode evolves as societies become more complex. The poison container theory was kept, and the earth mother goddess became the most common medium in child sacrifice. The excuse of satisfying the gods relates to the internalized parents.

- *Second* is the Abandoning Mode which sacrifices by exposure instead of actual killing. Reasons may include birth defects.

- *Third*, the Ambivalent Mode tolerates love-hate feelings and actions without connecting the differences between them.

- *Fourth* is the Intrusive Mode which establishes child abuse within the frame-working of discipline.

So long as little children are allowed to suffer, there is no true love in this world.
Isadora Duncan
Isadora: A Sensational Life

The child cannot develop a sense of the self, or objective self-awareness, alone.
Michael Lewis
Shame: The Exposed Self

Whatever happened to the good old days when kids was scared to death of their parents?
Archie Bunker
All in the Family

- The *fifth* is the Socializing Mode where the mother is perceived the perfect parent and the male the family provider and social enforcer.

- Lastly, the *sixth*, the Helping Mode removes conditions of violation.

CODEPENDENCY

Codependency is a maladaptive unhealthy mutual dependency with others. Children learn codependency as a coping mechanism in a seemingly inescapable environment of stress. Codependency involves distrust with avoidance of intimacy and feelings. People apply perfectionism to control others, and hide in perfectionism for their own safety.[13] Circumcision is an example of applied perfectionism that creates codependent relationships.

There are four roles a child will assume to cope and survive. They involve both passive and aggressive behaviors from competition, validation, and attention. Briefly, the four roles of the child are:[14]

- *Responsible child — Family Hero*: This child takes a parental role and is rigid, controlling, and judgmental.

- *Acting-out child — Scapegoat*: The family is ashamed of this child, but these children are the most emotionally honest. They are sensitive and caring.

- *Placater — Mascot*: They assume the responsibility for the family's mental health. They become kind, generous, and good listeners.

- *Adjuster — Lost Child*: These children attempt invisibility, daydream and fantasize. They have low self-esteem and are unable to feel.

Many factors are involved when people do well despite circumstances. Others bring tragedy to themselves and those they come in contact with. Freud and Hitler may have had codependent relationships with their mothers and attempted to become the *Responsible Child — Family Hero* for both self and society.

Freud was the oldest child and the eldest son. His father was not successful. He was his mother's prince. She regarded him so highly that when he complained about his sister's music lessons disturbing his concentration, the music lessons stopped. He was concerned about becoming successful, supporting his family and finding answers to questions.

Power — to make the multitudes run squealing in terror!
The Invisible Man
The Invisible Man

Your children will become what you are, so be what you want them to be.
David Bly

Wait, young man, you cannot escape your destiny by running away.
Prof. Buler
Nosferatu

Hitler suffered *severe* physical abuse from his father. After one beating he was left in a coma for days. Hitler was also his mother's prince. He moved in and took care of her when she was suffering a fatal illness. And he gave his part of the inheritance to his sister because she had a family.

ANXIETY

Anxiety is fear that occurs when reasonable concerns are addressed about one's sexuality.[15] It is possible that Freud's concern about his own circumcision may have been the factor that led him to leaving his sons intact, uncircumcised. Russian pathologists who claimed to have exhumed and examined Hitler's body found that Hitler had only one testicle. The cause is unknown but the most convincing story is from a medic who treated an injury to Hitler's groin in World War I; the absent testicle was collaborated by Hitler's World War I company commander during a wartime VD exam.

In the 1950s, psychoanalyst Margaret Little explained that, through transference, patterns of abuse become generational. Explaining how anxiety affects an individual, Little defined *psychotic anxiety* and *neurotic anxiety*:[16]

> *Psychotic anxiety* has to do with questions of survival or annihilation, the question of separation from something of which you are a part (or which is a part of you), and problems of identity.

> *Neurotic anxiety* has to do with separation from an object perceived as whole and separate from you, problems of sexual identity, loss of a part of one's body,

Little then immediately stressed the primacy of motherhood with:

> *I am starting with the pregnant mother — a very obvious thing.*

PARAPHILIA

Paraphilias are disorders possessing sexual fantasies with aberrant or deviant sexual behavior. Concentration may be on a non-consenting partner or child. Non-destructive play among consenting adults may not be considered pathologic. The following will briefly introduce,

* *Pedophilia*: the attraction to children under age thirteen

* *Infantophilia*: a subcategory of pedophilia with attraction toward those under age five

The process of advancement is interesting; it isn't that you get bigger to the world, the world gets smaller to fit you.
T.S. Eliot

I figured since I was taking all the punches, only fair that you share some of the anxiety.
Roy
Diggstown

Anxiety never successfully bridged any chasm.
Ruffini

- *Ephebophilia*: the attraction to pubescent individuals

- *Hebephilia*: the attraction to post pubescent adolescents

Holmes in *Profiling Violent Crimes* wrote:[17]

> There are adults who regard children as sex objects and as somehow deserving of exploitation as objects. For the person with such a mind-set, there is nothing wrong with sexually assaulting children. In fact, many child abusers apparently believe that children pursue adults for sex — an interesting rationalization that negates the adult's personal responsibility. From this perspective, the child is the cause, the prime mover; the molester is the victim.

Full prepuce male circumcision psychosexually makes the young male appear to be physically ready for sexual intercourse because glans exposure normally only occurs upon erection when the prepuce retracts.

PEDOPHILIA

Pedophilia is a category of child molestation that includes attraction to, and fantasies involving, children under thirteen that causes stress in the pedophile leading to social and occupational dysfunction. Pedophilia is also diagnosed when the victim is five or more years younger than a teenage and young adult perpetrator.

Pedophiles who molest children may be *situational*, with few victims, where the victim is vulnerable, or *preferential* in character, with many victims, whose purpose is taking pleasure in children.[18] Child molesters put themselves in proximity to victims.

America's Catholic priest child molestation cases have received a lot of attention because of the Catholic Church's rules on celibacy, but pedophilia among the Catholic religious is not unique unto that religion alone. Catholicism is high profile due to its hierarchy and openness but Judaism and Islam are less hierarchal in structure and therefore less accessible for public scrutiny and accountability. Judaism's cases of child molestation by rabbis in America appear to be as numerous as Catholic molestations, if not more numerous when considering percent population, though it remains less reported and spectacular.[19]

Dr. Sami Aldeeb reports instances in Islam where young males directly under the tutelage of local school Imams must suffer controlled homosexual attack. The parents are aware, but socially powerless in the face of religious power, control and authority. Without recourse, the parents must then mutely sanction their son's acceptance of the *seed of the imam* both physically and educationally.[20]

INFANTOPHILIA

Infantophilia is a subcategory of pedophilia. The adult's primary sexual attraction is to children age five and under. Being a new category, some argue the maximum age should be three or four. Infantophilia is primarily seen as starting with nursing mothers using their children beyond normal breastfeeding pleasure. The purpose is for orgasm with the child in preference to their male partners. Sexual acts include masturbating and giving oral sex to their infants and young children. Infantophilia sometimes becomes communal. This type of molestation may be suspected in groups with long nursing periods that have adult prohibitions to coitus.[21] Paraphilias often become sadistic,[22,23] and infantophilia is no exception.

EPHEBOPHILIA

Ephebophilia is when an adult is sexually attracted to people in puberty. It is colloquially called the Lolita syndrome. This is the timing of puberty rituals where the initiate enters adult sexual activity and expectations. Children are entering puberty sooner, partly due to increased dietary fat. During the American Civil War the average onset of menses was age fifteen. Presently, age eleven is common.

The usual female standard for puberty ritual is menses. Most often older adult women are group sponsors for the girl's ritual. The male standard varies with age and usually his ritual sponsor is a male relative other than the father.

HEBEPHILIA

Hebephilia is when an adult is sexually attracted to post-pubertal adolescents between ages fourteen and seventeen. Most probably before dietary changes of more fat being included since after the Civil War this was a common age of puberty rituals. Adolescents are now kept in childhood longer than any previous time in human history. This is partly due to an increased need for education before assuming adult duties and responsibilities.

After a while you learn the subtle difference between holding a hand and chaining the soul.
Policeman
Sexual Violence: Our War Against Rape

Let's face it, Le Chuck. You are an evil, foul smelling, vile, codependent villain and that's not what I'm looking for in a romantic relationship right now.
Elaine
The Curse of Monkey Island

Once you familiarize yourself with the chains of bondage you prepare your limbs to wear them.
Rudy
The Negotiator

INCEST

Spirituality is, theology explains, religion practices. Theology is expressed in mythological language. Religious practice takes a mythical story and develops it into a sacred contract. These sacred contracts based on myth-working do not always prohibit incest. Besides parental incest, other forms of incest that appear in mythology include sibling, cousin, and niece/uncle incest as discussed in the Genital Play chapter. Though niece/uncle marriage is illegal in America, a Jewish exception exists in the state of Rhode Island.[24]

When thinking of incest, a person first thinks of an adult male with a minor female relative.[25] One rarely thinks that boys might also be used sexually by mothers. It is rare for a male child or a grown man to talk about sexual abuse they have suffered at the hands of women, but one man, Robert Miller, recalled the details of mother-son sexual abuse while in treatment at the Veteran's Administration for PTSD and Miller's incredibly moving poetry has been published in *Collection of Tears*.[26] According to deMause in, *The Universality of Incest*, there are two types of incest — *direct* and *indirect*:[27]

> Two kinds will be considered: *direct incest*, overt sexual activity between family members other than spouses; and *indirect incest*, the providing of children by their parents to others in order for them to be sexually molested. There are two reasons why I believe indirect incest must be included in any definition of incestuous activity. First of all, arranging for children to have sex with other household members or neighbors is usually motivated by the incestuous wishes of the parent; and, in any case, it is usually perceived by the child to be similar to direct incest. Secondly, clinical studies show that contemporary sexual abuse involves a parent or guardian, who, if not the direct perpetrator, covertly brings about the incident in order to satisfy their own incestuous wishes.

Circumcision links to *societal indirect incest*. Circumcision in Islam signifies the boy leaving the mother to be with other women.[28,29] She is, in essence, giving her son to another female member of the social group. As for young ladies in groups that practice Female Genital Mutilation, circumcision allows them to marry. Female Genital Mutilation is practiced only by a minority in Islam. deMause references Kitahara's: *A Cross-Cultural Test of the Freudian Theory of Circumcision* that states:[30]

> Genital mutilation, which is always a punishment for growing up, is — rather a self-punishment for real maternal incest for which children blame

themselves. Genital mutilation rituals are cross-culturally correlated with exclusive mother infant skin-to-skin sleeping arrangements, where the father sleeps separate, so the mother is likely to use the child incestuously.

Excerpts from deMause's *The Universality of Incest* and paraphrasing including examples of incestuous habits that expand the Genital Play chapter:[31]

As an adult, the pedophile must have sex with children in order to maintain the illusion of being loved, while at the same time dominating the children as they themselves once experienced domination, repeating actively their own caretaker's sadism. The pedophile uses the child... for gratification and also as an object for sadistic aggression... the pedophile's sexual targets are interchangeable and an active pedophile often seduces hundreds of children in his or her life. Adults who molest children have extremely powerful punitive superegos and are often highly religious.

Originally, male analysts regarded accounts of incest as wishful fantasies. Some had the opinion that incest did not present a problem. They considered the Incest Taboo that is common in all societies to be functionally effective.

Female analysts better understood the seriousness of incest and reported accounts of their child patients. Many children were forced to handle their parent's genitals. Both mothers and fathers gave daughters to male family members and friends for sexual purposes.

Incest statistics are probably higher than reported because high probability populations have not been well surveyed. These include incarcerated criminals, prostitutes, institutionalized children, psychotics and those who refuse to be questioned.

Memories prior to age five are usually suppressed. And half of reported molestations, with a fifth of reported rapes, are committed by those under age eighteen. Incidence would likely be higher where many societies are just beyond the Infanticidal Child Rearing Mode and use children for emotional needs. Using children for sexual purposes is also common in the Far, Middle and Near East, though forbidden by the *Qu'ran* according to their age standards of when maturity begins.

These last five paragraphs are direct quotes:

As girls in the Middle East are considered worth less than boys, it has been reported that their incestuous use during childhood is even more prevalent. One report found that four out of five Middle Eastern women recalled having been forced into fellatio between the ages of 3 and 6 by older brothers and other relatives.

Men are what their mothers made them.
Ralph Waldo Emerson

Your parents must be proud. You hit the trailer park trifecta: racist, pedophile, and stupid.
C-Note
Prison Break

Once her anger found vent, she managed to keep it in check to conceal her acts of violence on the child.
Judith Spencer
Suffer the Child

'Arab women, of course, are often aware that their spouses prefer having sex with little boys and girls to having sex with them. Their retribution for the men's pedophilia comes when a girl is about age 6, when the women of the house grab her, pull her thighs apart and cut off her clitoris and sometimes her labia with a razor, thus usually ending her ability to feel sexual pleasure forever.

Clitoridectomy — like all genital mutilations of children — is, of course, an act of incest motivated by the perversions of the adults who perform the mutilation... Although we are not used to thinking of it in this way, in fact mothers who attack their daughters' genitals with knives are as incestuous as fathers who rape them.

Since genital mutilation is one of the most widespread child-rearing practices, its presence alone makes incest a universal practice — despite our habit of denying its sexual motivation by terming it a Rite of Passage or a Puberty Rite. Also, the sexual excitement of the adults attending the mutilation is overlooked, even when — as in Siwa — the mother masturbates the child prior to the mutilation, or when — as in Morocco — prostitutes regularly attend the mutilation in order to relive the sexual tensions generated, or when — as in Australia — the mutilation is followed by group rape.

The mutilation of children's genitals is such an important need in humans that whole religions and state systems have been founded upon the practice. Yet when scholars attempt to explain why almost everyone since the beginning of recorded history has massively assaulted the genitals of their children, they assiduously deny that it is a sexual perversion or that those who do it ever mean any harm to the children.

The maternal incestuous behavior with Female Genital Mutilation correlates to the masculine dominated incestuous social behaviors 19th Century British medicine that initiated, with the aid of American physicians, genital mutilation of both sexes. And, again, these British doctors *prescribed* child sex, best with a virgin, for men suffering illnesses as depression, impotence and venereal diseases.[32]

EMOTIONAL INCEST

Incest is prevalent in emotionally dishonest societies. Dishonesty makes it difficult for the child in later life to set proper boundaries. Incest produces an inability to achieve successful adult relationships.[33] *Emotional incest*[34] is a type of covert incest. Most do not recognize or admit victimization. Circumcision is a form of emotional blackmail.[35] Circumcision forces the child to live in systems of codependency. The parent uses the child for self worth and definition.

It permanently transfers power away from the child, regarding bodily integrity, to the parent and society in the generational cultural system of abusive control.[36]

Both Freud's and Hitler's possible codependent relationships with their mothers could have been from their mother's emotional incest. Freud was his own first patient which may have led him to discover the *Oedipus complex*, with its feminine counterpart, the *Electra complex*. Patricia Love in *The Emotional Incest Syndrome* stated:[37]

> To a large degree, our parents determined which parts of the self we were allowed to keep. Some of us were allowed to have needs, but not to be independent. We were catered to and indulged, but kept immature. Some of us were allowed a great deal of freedom, but not to have needs. We were allowed to wander at will around the neighborhood, but were not given enough comfort and reassurance. Some of us were allowed to develop our talents, but were asked to repress our needs and emotions. We grew up to be compulsive achievers to hide an inner sense of inadequacy. To a greater degree than other children, we were not allowed to be whole. In exchange for love and a position of privilege in the family hierarchy, we had to give up a large portion of the self.

Circumcision presents a physical *forever being*. Pathology continues with the child being subjugated to the role of being responsible for parental self-gratification, safety, security, and well being. And, when the child matures he or she now assumes parental prerogatives. *Emotional incest* may take many forms in a culture that accepts genital assaults on their children. deMause exemplifies this with the following commentary:[38]

> *If I blow myself up and become a martyr, I'll finally be loved by my mother.*

> That is what Palestinian terrorists say. They aren't looking for political change; they're looking for *love*. Love from Allah, yes — but really love from their parents. Palestinian mothers say they are raising martyrs, and pick which son should kill himself for her and never leave her. And as the terrorists strap their bombs on, they imagine they'll get the love they missed all their lives. How can mothers of martyrs say things like, "I was happy he blew himself up. Now he'll always be close to me."?

Reaction time is a factor in this, so please pay attention.
Mr. Holden
Is this supposed to be an empathy test?
Leon
Blade Runner

The cult gave a grotesque confirmation of the necessity for actions against the child.
Judith Spencer
Suffer the Child

Are you crazy?
Audrey
Yes, but I'm your mother.
Sara
Laws of Attraction

BREAST IRONING

In Cameroon breast ironing is practiced on pubescent and pre-pubescent girls.[39] The breasts are flattened to inhibit growth. About one quarter of the girls in Cameroon undergo this procedure. It is primarily performed by their mothers to make them unattractive, prevent rape, early marriage, coitus, and to obtain an education without hindrance. The mother massages the girl's breasts and uses warmed objects to iron them. Objects include grinding stones, coconut shells, bananas, ladles, and spatulas.[40]

Breast ironing is another representation of a punishment for growing up and possibly an act of maternal incest that appears to correlate to deMauses' discussion of Female Genital Mutilation.[41] It also indicates a retributive act of incest before the girl enters the adult world, and to keep the child close to the mother for an extended period of time. If the daughter obtains an education she will be better able to support the mother in her old age because the men are perceived by the mother as being unreliable — which may be the truth.

SHARING ADULTS

Paraphilia and incest do not become per-se fully *legalized*[42] by the secular, though they exist everywhere. Historically one of incest's main uses is in explaining relationships of the union of the opposite sexes through mythology where the society is structured. This is exampled by the twin deity mating's of Isis/Osiris and Zeus/Hera. Yet, as Lifton described in *The Nazi Doctors*, Doubling has the ability to reach into all facets of life.[43]

Adult sharing has reached legal acculturation in societies that allow other than *monogamy*. Most multiple marriage societies are *polygynous* where there are more than one wife. For some, having multiple wives is a sign of wealth. In more ancient times it may have arisen from distant small societies with a high male mortality rate to the recent American Mormon past.

The Kenyan custom of *joter* is wife inheritance: if a man dies the widow marries another in her husband's family.[44] Some men acquire more than one wife this way. Though it is called "wife inheritance" as a form of a wife prize from the death of a relative, it may also be considered a "husband prize" because he assumes the responsibility of supporting his new wife as well as her children. The purpose is clear, in the local economic situation *wife inheritance* or *husband prize* assures family continuance. This is not an unusual practice and assumes many forms. In feudal Japan a man would marry his daughter for sexual purposes if his wife died or became incapacitated.[45] *Polygynous* cultures appear to place a low value on women.

In Tibet a few practice *polyandry* where a woman has more than one husband. For the Tre-ba all brothers marry one wife. Tibet also has *polygynandry* which involves multiple members of each sex. The Tibetan examples are mainly successful arrangements for economic reasons, and many individuals will at some time try *monogamy*.[46] This also occurs in South America with the Kuikura in Brazil. Dahari brothers of India marry one woman and increase wives as wealth increases.

In another vein, to induce pregnancy the Pagan Gaddang of the Philippines exchange spouses; the husband's parents initiate the process only with the agreement of the barren wife.[47] The Chuckchee of Siberia make wife-lending contracts and the Quolla of Peru exchange spouses.[48]

Prohibiting prostitution may be an economic decision clothed in morality. Prostitution does not evenly divide the productive resources of its males. Prostitutes with no habits, as drug abuse, may do well with the income from six to seven reliable men. The current method of social taxation for mother-child units more evenly distribute resources, yet decreases and devastates the stability of marriage and society as well as the value of the individual male because the male has been replaced by society's governmental agencies.

Currently, the practice of multiple sexual partners is practiced in the parts of Southern Africa where the newest AIDS studies are being conducted. By not including multiple partners and other habits as dry sex in their studies, these studies must be considered suspect. African non-marriage multiple partner sexual partnerships are not in practicing Muslim polygynous households, but occur more in the non-Muslim portions of society. The African studies are contrasts of two internally distinct societies where *behavior*, not circumcision, is the determining factor in the spread of AIDS.

Marrying a man is like buying something you've been admiring for a long time in a shop window. You may love it when you get home, but it doesn't always go with everything else in the house.
Jean Kerr

A diplomat is one who can tell a man he's open-minded when he has a hole in his head.
Anonymous

SOCIALIZATION

The societal apocalyptic vision is forced upon the child

From our inner selves, reaching out and interacting with others, we develop social psychologies and ways to create cultural bonding. We establish social bodies with unique group identities: countries, schools, families, gangs. Celebrating diversity is good and fine, but of the some factors that knit us together into groups can also be used to separate us into hostile camps. Some of our bonding activities can border on abuse. We accept abusive behavior as normal within our groups, only because we have become inured to the inherent violence due to historically agreed-upon social, moral, and legal codes of conduct.

Social rituals are repetitious and ever-changing due to each generation's existing power relationships. Changes may result in explanations for the ritual, or the way the ritual is performed, but the ritual — however explained or performed — must always take place because it establishes the seat of social power, control and authority.

All societies integrate some violence and aggression into socially sanctioned outlets. Most notably are competitive sports. Strikingly, the apogee of cultural sports coincides with the apogee of the culture itself — before its downfall. Violence can also be experienced vicariously through film and theater. Some rituals themselves may be violent and create harm through Munchausen behavior. Rituals like circumcision create a *Cultural Post-Traumatic Attachment* that leads to a *Cultural Repetition Compulsion*.

Ritual in some cases is an extension of compassion from one person or group to another. Since the two most basic biological functions perceived as suffering and violent primal wounds are menstruation and childbirth, men attempt through ritual to empathize with women or to even outdo women's pain and suffer it in stoic manly silence. Suffering, even if self-inflicted, can

Some of the most successful relationships are based on lies and deceit. Since that's where they usually wind up anyway, it's a logical place to start.
Yuri
Lord of War

The cost of liberty is less than the price of repression.
W.E.B. Du Bois

be used to elicit sympathy or worn as a badge of courage. This may be why suffering enters ritual. Male initiation rites do not permit expressions of weakness. Joseph Campbell illustrated shared suffering in ritual during the Native American Plains Indians male ritual of *Vow to the Sun* where men would chant:[1] *We must suffer as women suffer.* Campbell explains that: *Man doesn't enter life except by woman, and so it is woman who brings us into this world of pairs of opposites and suffering.*

ACCULTURATION

Acculturation is the change in the original culture from contact with another culture or many cultures. This is different than *assimilation*, where different groups come together and form a new way of life. Acculturation deals with survival, resistance, modification, adaptation, and destruction of the old culture. *Diffusion* is adopting another culture's practice independent of population movement.[2]

CULTURAL APPROPRIATION

Cultural appropriation occurs when a culture adopts an introduced behavior. Circumcision is reaching into some Far East countries like Korea and it is moving into Mexico. This spread is mainly due to American influence. Cultural appropriation can lie apparently dormant for an extended period of time. Again, Victorian Era physicians would prescribe sex with a child (preferably a virgin) to cure venereal disease. Currently there is an epidemic of virgin rape in parts of past British held Africa where men believe the rape of a virgin will cure their AIDS. Virgin rape for curing other venereal diseases may have existed in Africa since the Victorian Era. And, virgin rape may have been one reason many Cameroon women have adopted breast ironing to disfigure their developing young girls thus making them unattractive. If so, this is female suffering in ritual because of male asocial violence. Again, all these mutilations are basically a punishment by adults for the child's "sin" of growing up, no matter which gender is involved or at what age the ritual takes place.

CULTURAL IMPERIALISM

Cultural imperialism is the phenomenon of an incoming group forcing a new practice in their adopted culture. Some immigrants from Africa are pressuring Italy to legally allow a lesser form of female genital abuse: pin-pricking the girl's clitoris to draw blood. The USA is also experiencing this pressure.

SOCIALIZATION

Socialization of the child into the existing culture is *enculturation*. Enculturation is established through *communal reinforcement* by repeating the values and norms of the society to the child regardless of the lack of evidence to support society's position. *Introjection* occurs when such behaviors become unconsciously accepted in the child's personality. Introjection is *internalization* of identification with parental figures and other aspects of the child's known world. Introjection is often accompanied with defense mechanisms for coping. Coping mechanisms are forms of denial, self-deception, and deferral and are, as well, essential in ritual.

> *It is not paranoia. The embedding is very subtle.*
> **David Levinson**
> *Independence Day*

GROUP DYNAMICS

Group dynamics involves behavior to current happenings. This behavior differs according to the individual's response to the local group. To achieve a new agreement the barriers of prejudices, expectations, ideology, theology, and control must be overcome. This can give rise to *social constructionism* which creates a perceived reality. The new reality birthed in social constructionism is an invention of the culture that eventually appears obvious and as natural knowledge. This then establishes a *consensus reality* that is the reality the group or culture wishes to believe.

> *So this is how liberty dies... With thunderous applause.*
> **Padme**
> *Revenge of the Sith*

PEER PRESSURE

Peer pressure then imposes the group norm on individuals and requires people to conform. Peer pressure works when *opinion leaders* prevail. Currently, this process is used to create the false demand for circumcision as a cure for AIDS. Many attempts to medically instill circumcision have been successful, but all have been proven false. The AIDS quest for circumcision is no exception.[3]

> *The Empire will compensate you if he dies.*
> **Darth Vader**
> *The Empire Strikes Back*

GROUPTHINK

Groupthink occurs when people intentionally go along with what they think is the group's opinion. Groupthink leads to improper and non-logical decisions. Groupthink uses the need for people to belong with others. Symptoms of groupthink include :

- illusion with invulnerability from unity
- unquestioned belief.
- group rationalization
- stereotyping of opponents
- self-censorship
- direct pressure to conform
- self-appointed guardians.

Groupthink creates *communal reinforcement* by repeating their assertions even if the assertions cannot be proven.

COMMUNAL BEHAVIOR

Community reinforces *collective behavior* by instilling fear. The basis of all medical claims for circumcision is fear. The medical community has fear when it does not have true knowledge of how to prevent a disease that is overwhelming it. And, medicine passes its fear to the general public. They try to whip up a state of *collective hysteria* to ignite an immediate social change.

STRUCTURATION

The overall method used is *structuration* which is repeating the position of leaders with implied special knowledge who are setting the rules for others to live by. These people are acting as the *social agent* in an effort to change people's behavior. This agency is also used by those countering circumcision hysteria.

INSTITUTIONALIZATION

The overall result of both sides is *institutionalization*: those who advocate circumcision want to continue and expand its use, while those who oppose circumcision want to instill the fact that cutting children's genitals is truly improper behavior.

SOCIAL NORM

Once circumcision is established as a *social norm* it becomes easily enforced. Violations of norms are punished, even if it is only through social shunning. Violators are thought to be eccentric and alternatives are not acknowledged.

MORES

Mores are strongly held norms and customs that (similar to social norms) increase the ability to isolate detractors from society.

FOLKWAY

The endpoint is a *folkway* and folkways are most strictly reinforced. Sometimes the *folkway* becomes the means of cultural identification and such is circumcision. Thus, you could say that the circumcised genitalia become a cultural totem in blood, flesh and mind.

MEME BONDING

The *meme*, introduced by Dawkins in his book *The Selfish Gene*, is the pathway of cultural practice and may be thought of as a *social gene*. Circumcision is a cultural practice and therefore circumcision is a *meme*. Knight explains that:[4]

> A successful *meme*, according to Dawkins, is a portion of cultural tradition — say, a tune, an idea or a catch-phrase which survives in the memories of generations of humans and is capable of evolution at a very rapid pace. Just as genes propagate themselves in the gene pool by leaping from cell to cell, so according to this view *memes* propagate themselves in the *meme* pool by being transmitted from brain to brain through a process which, in a broad sense, can be called *learning* or *imitation*.

For a social *meme* such as circumcision to be successful, societal matriarchal and patriarchal functions cannot exist in isolation; they must cooperate. Synergistically, the influence of each enhances and multiplies the effect that each would have working alone:

INTERARCHY is the functioning aspect of matriarchy and patriarchy in cooperative effort

SYNARCHY is the synergistic affect of matriarchy and patriarchy working together in interarchy

PSYCHOHISTORY

Lloyd deMause's book *Foundations of Psychohistory* documents generational abuse caused by:[5]

• the psychosexual unified group

I and the public know that what all schoolchildren learn, those to whom evil is done do evil in return.
W.H. Auden

Together we can rule the galaxy.
Darth Vader
Revenge of the Sith

The man who boasts about his ancestors of a century ago is not likely to become an ancestor they will boast about a century hence.
Anonymous

- the effects of the group's abuse on the individual and
- the individual's subsequent responses back to the group.

Summarizing and commenting on deMause, but not quoting:

Psychohistory is the science of historical motivation. It interprets history, using psychoanalytical methods, for causes of historical events. It is normal and healthy for a person and community to organize existence in a structured environment so that life may be better for all. Final outcomes are unique to each individual, community and culture. Sex is tied to social control.[6,7] Basic motivations are the same with serial predators and religious ritual: power, control and authority for domination, through manipulation out of selfishness.

Obtaining *macro-social* psychosexual cohesion in primitive society, the customs, mores and rituals are centered on the reciprocal social functions of the sexes. The macro-social is the entire social that includes all sub-groups. Each sub-group is a micro-social. The feminine function is procreation and taking care of offspring. The masculine function is to provide for the mother-child unit. This created two societies. The feminine is the internal central core. Mircea Eliade termed this the Concept of the Center.[8] The masculine is the external periphery, surrounding the center. Primitive social rituals for the female stress the moon and menstruation. The social structure, for cohesion, needs controlling and protecting feminine reproduction. Masculine penile rituals were often designed to mimic the trials and tribulations of the feminine, such as menstruation and birthing, thus creating empathy between men and women. Purely male rituals for the social purpose do not attack the penis — even though men's rituals often include odd behaviors such as object implantation (see *Genital Play* chapter).

Lloyd deMause explains what cults do to children. These are *micro-social* forms of abuse because the cults deMause refers to, here, are sub-groups within the entire social. He says the children are often kept in cages, boxes and coffins as womb symbols. They are beaten and tortured; made to eat feces and drink urine and blood; eat food off adult genitals; forced to cannibalize; and sometimes are disemboweled and dismembered while reaching orgasm.

In these sadistic activities, some perpetrators are acting in regression and fear of reality, attempting to relive their own past trauma and relieve the anxiety caused by that trauma. The ritual is a delusional attempt to absorb the child's essence — to reclaim the power the perpetrator felt they lost as a child under similar conditions. Their actions are a literal acting out of what happened to them.

Cult abuse includes penetration of infants vaginally, anally and orally.

Unlike grown-ups, children have little need to deceive themselves.
Goeth
Schindler's List

We think it is time that you recognized that you are masters in someone else's home. Despite the best intentions of the best of you, you must, in the nature of things, humiliate us to control us.
Gandhi
Gandhi

They just stared straight ahead with eyes that seemed to see nothing, and kept on following the man in front.
Fred Majdalany
The Monastery

One common cult ritual is the Sacrificial Rebirth Ritual that may include a genital modification. Children abused through sexual ritual are more psychologically symptomatic than those not sexually abused through ritual. Psychotherapists treating these children find themselves faced with death threats and vandalism — as do those opposing circumcision.

When infants and young children are abused in the preverbal state they are amnesic. Preverbal memories are stored in the amygdala where our deepest fears reside. When in touch with these night monsters, we do not act as our normal selves and the stored memories are, as deMause terms them, *alters*. Declarative memory starts around age three to four when memory is stored in the hippocampus. In social groups deMause termed the declarative memory as the basis of the a *social alter*.

Now quoting deMause:[9,10]

A group-fantasy, then, is produced by a collection of *social alters* as an agreement by groups of people to pool their traumas into a delusional social construction. Social alters have four main characteristics. They are:

(1) separate neural memory modules that are repositories for traumatic events and accompany feelings frozen in time;

(2) organized into dynamic structures containing a different set of goals, values and defenses than the main self that help prevent the traumas and resulting despair from overwhelming the one's life;

(3) split off by a senseless wall of denial, depersonalization, discontinuity of affect and disownership of responsibility that is maintained in collusion with others in society who have similar alters to deny; and

(4) communicated, elaborated and acted out in group-fantasies embedded in political, religious and social institutions.

SOCIAL PSYCHOLOGY

Social psychology is the branch of psychology that concentrates on any and all aspects of human behavior. It involves our relationships to other persons, groups, social institutions, and to society as a whole. Following are summaries of numerous articles with circumcision-relevant comments added:[11]

ASSOCIATION

Psychosocial growth and development imply *association* with other individuals. Much of a person's mental content comes from others including

There is no winning in this, only degrees of losing.
Gavin D'Amato
War of the Roses

The public will believe anything so long as it is not founded on the truth.
Edith Stillwell

You couldn't tell the parents from the kids until the old man lit up a cigar.
Archie Bunker
All in the Family

beliefs, standards, values and ideals. Customs are powerful. And institutions of power, control, and authority with their laws in government, religion, social mores and ceremony are somewhat static because *prestige* lies in *precedent*, which is to say, antiquity. Thus a person's experiences are connected in subordination to the group's leading principles. But, *leading principles* evolve over time through suggestive interaction and are not static, uniform, or final. Stasis, uniformity, and finality attach themselves to closed scientific systems like mathematics but the open system of the human mind does not restrict pursuits like language, literature or religion.

ACTS

Social *acts* or behavior, whether collective or individual, often have the purpose of influencing and controlling others. They are attempts to modify a group's behavior which essentially includes the behavior of each individual. *Acts* such as circumcision that modify objects, are *technical* acts. *Acts* that elicit pleasure or avoid pain are *hedonistic* acts. One motive of circumcision is to decrease the pleasure of the victim and increase pleasure of the uncircumcised partner. *Esthetic acts* are those that give meaning to an object. The genitals, in the case of circumcision, are the esthetic object. Beside the final outcome, that object part becomes the *social token*. Tokens are used in all rituals, and the prepuce or clitoris is a token in the power of the ritual agent, whether the ritual agent is an individual or culture.

PROGRESSION OF SOCIAL MOVEMENTS

The following three systems work in unison in the creation of social movements: social situation, social act and social tendency.

- A *social situation* usually starts with a idealized purpose. Advocates of that ideal work together to create a new social system. Examples can include governments, economic systems or religions.

- The *social act* puts the social purpose into effect.

- *Social tendency* evolves from the perception of the social act as the proper way to behave. Then it becomes static behavior until a new social situation enters to correct any problems created by the original social situation, act and tendency.

Mobilization toward a new social reality is generated when current social

---

Sidebar quotes:

Can you look me in the eye and guarantee me this is not some sort of flimflam.
Evelyn
The Mummy

Natural leaders are rarely encumbered with intelligence. Greed, egotism, animal cunning, and viciousness are the important attributes.
Egorian
Blakes 7

What is it about earth people that makes them think a futile gesture is a noble one?
Thurlough
Doctor Who

procedures are deemed improper and it is thought a new social order will provide an improved social experience. *Rebellion* and *changes* produced from mobilization create a new social tendency.

Circumcision of both men and women was first introduced in America to decrease genital sensitivity and thereby end masturbation, which at that time was considered to be the source of both mental and physical disease. With education, many people are turning away from the practice to create a new social tendency.

SOCIAL ORDER

Social order refers to a set of interlocking social structures, social institutions and social practices that conserve, maintain and enforce group defined "normal" ways of behaving and relating that are considered essential for control and order in the society. The *social order* is forced upon the individual. *Social sublimation* occurs with conformity to and psychological acceptance of the *social ideal*.

The impact of the social order on the individual person is ignored to a point. Reactions are minimized when changes are gradual or precede cognizance; reactions may vary from individual to individual. With *cognizance*, an individual may react positively if his expectations of the social ideal and value system are met, or negatively if the results do not meet his expectations. If he has a negative reaction, the social body will meet him with a corresponding negative reaction to maintain social stability.

This leads to *social repression* of the individual and his negative reaction is perceived as *anti-social behavior*. *Social defense* occurs if the negative originates from outside the social order. African circumcisers resist mightily American challenges to female genital mutilation. Even in the US, those people who actively oppose male circumcision have encountered death threats and vandalism to their property.

THE GENITALS AS A SOCIAL OBJECT

Making the genitals a *social object* targets the most private, intimate, sensual and vulnerable of a child's body. When the genitals are a *social object,* the child is objectified in the eyes of the social body (see *Criminology* chapter).

When the object is inaccessible or part of another's body whether in an individual or a group of the opposite sex, it involves *abstraction*. In the case of

I am exhausted from living up to your expectations.
Jareth
Labyrinth

What are your expectations from this prison?
Winter
The Last Castle

Each generation will bear the burden in turn.
Arthur
Merlin's Apprentice

circumcision, both the child and his parents are forced by social pressures to submit to an "ideal" of being socially submissive.

The altered, abstracted social object becomes a genital generalization that intimates inclusiveness of all social objects sharing the same characteristics, thereby indicating a uniform, conformed individual and society. The individual's body and genitalia are subordinate to the *social purpose* as merely a part of the social whole which assumes the right to take the social object and maintain its tribal identity.

COMIXIO RELIGIONIS

In the big picture, circumcision is an outcome of *comixio religionis*, since it originated in the pagan world. Both the Egyptian goddess Isis and the Midianite goddess Hathor had a moon god son named Horus. The "Lord" referred to by Moses' Midianite wife Zipporah was the pagan god of her tribe. Baal-Berith was the local Canaanite god in the area where Joshua circumcised the Israelites. *Baal-Berith* literally means *Lord of the Covenant*.[12]

In a much later revision in 550 BCE, the story of Abraham's circumcision first appeared, although he had been dead for centuries by that time. When the Jews returned from Babylon and started intermarrying with people who followed Hathor, this inspired Ezra's warning against intermarriage.

And even though neither the New Testament nor the Koran ask for circumcision, the mythic tale of Abraham and the fictitious circumcision "covenant" spread throughout Judaism, eventually infiltrating Christianity and Islam and establishing itself as the "norm".

OBJECT PERSON

An *object person* is someone who has been dehumanized due to an attribute or physical quality they possess (see *Victimology* section in the *Criminology* chapter). Body modifications or sacrifices are, for the most part, accepted by the *object person* if those social practices do not alter what the person sees as their social purpose. If the person objects, then psychological inner conflict occurs. The perpetrator — the ritual agent or parent — is likewise conflicted when the victim's doubt attempts to stop the perpetrator's desired action. This inhibits the original *social act* and the perpetrator must then resort to making claims and arguments in support of his *social ideal* as a counter moral force to inhibit the object person's moral protestations. Or, the perpetrating *social*

You talk about redefining my identity. I want a guarantee that I can still be myself.
Motoko
Ghost in a Shell

History is the sum total of all things that could have been avoided.
Konrad Adenauer

Cruelty hardens and degrades.
Robert Ingersoll

force[13] may impose repression.

Repression creates opposing *social values* that must eventually be resolved. *Moral standards* are a part of social values that are often upheld by manipulative arguments that do not allow comment.

REFLECTED SELF IMAGE

How does the victim of tribal ritual feel about himself or herself after he or she has been forced to submit to genital alteration practices? The inner, *reflected self image* of the person whose genitals have been cut is also altered due to the overwhelming power of *social forces*. The prevailing *social personality* has essentially told him he must submit or be shunned. But if the person removes himself from the overpowering social process and uses logical, objective thought, it will sometimes lead him to end the *social subjugation* (see *Ritual* chapter on *Alternatives*). When this happens the social body in identity crisis must necessarily take steps to maintain itself.

SOCIAL JUSTIFICATION

Covenants are religious contracts. The *Ten Commandments* are moral laws: the first four dealing with man's relationship to God and the last six explaining how to live peacefully with others. The bridge between the two groups of commandments is the fifth commandment: *Honor thy father and mother*. As Susan Forward wrote, *When we are young, our godlike parents are everything to us*.[14] The danger in this commandment is that it can be used to justify power, control and social pathology for a group's own sake — dominance.[15] Group dominance envelops and surrounds individuals and from there it can penetrate into other societies (see *Munchausen* chapter on *Munchausen in Collective Transmission*).

Henry Flynt wrote *Self-Justification in Human Relations*, and G. Herbert Mead wrote *The Social Self*. Summarizing both, with comments relating to our topic, circumcision:[16,17]

DEPENDENCY

Dependence also means that people are opportunities; they can be used both personally and socially, for one's selfish gratification and fulfillment. This leads to *conflict* when needs, wants, desires and perceptions among individuals or groups differ. And it drives people,

What maintains one vice, would bring up two children.
Benjamin Franklin

Their kind of chivalry. Respect and obligation. If you don't respect them, they feel obligated to beat you. Nothing personal.
Coates
To End All Wars

Imagination is the only weapon in the war against reality.
Jules De Gaultier

both individually and socially, to *impose* their conceptual way of life onto others. Reasons and excuses to perpetrate abuse are easy to justify through moral doctrines and codes such as commandments and covenants. When successful, social movements overwhelm individual choice, free will and human rights.

A baby is absolutely dependent on the solicitude of elders.
Henry Flynt

INJURY

Injuries and *wrongs*, when defined as crimes, mean such acts are culturally improper. In America *female genital mutilation* is considered improper and is a crime yet its counterpart, *male genital mutilation* is not. As Joseph Campbell said, *The sacrifice must be willing*. When the victim is willing, the wound is worn proudly. But the proponent of the sacrificial ritual of circumcision is delusional if he imagines circumcision entails a willing victim; it is a forced sacrifice.

INTERDEPENDENCE

We can enter a situation believing that it will reward us or that our actions can extract a reward from it.
Henry Flynt

Interdependence entails personal and societal responsibilities. We subsist through the monetary *reward* our *occupations* provide but occupations are more than simple jobs; they carry significant *responsibilities*. Ideally, medicine and religion are businesses that we would prefer to be service-oriented rather than selfish. Medical personnel and religious representatives would serve the community. The question we must always ask is whether the occupation's "service" or contribution to society is more beneficial, mischievous or harmful.

ABUSE

We can deliberately harm other people to gratify ourselves.
Henry Flynt

Abuse occurs when one party harms something or someone. Moral laws from every spiritual tradition — and medicine as well — instruct proponents to not harm others; we are told to be harmless. In addition to physical harm, harmlessness extends to psychological harm — including humiliation and insult to dignity — psychological harm is included in the definition of abuse.

Most social systems manage *vengeance* through a legal system. The rule of law requires *inverted self-regard*. This means that rather than you taking personal action against an offender, the legal system takes action on your behalf to obtain retribution for you. Yet *inverted self-regard* may be counterproductive for innocent individuals who have been harmed by the oppressive social body since the same system that has abused them or allowed them to be abused controls the process and can therefore ignore, censor or disallow complaints and refuse to give or allow redress. The person can feel as helpless when betrayed by the court system as when he was a child being circumcised against his will.

ASSERTIONS

From *When Healing Becomes A Crime* by Kenny Ausubel:[18]

> In a brief twenty years, the AMA came to dominate medical practice through brute financial force, political manipulation, and professional authority enhanced by rising public favor with "scientific" medicine. The AMA emerged as the supreme arbiter of medical practice, making binding pronouncements regulating even the most picayune details. American medicine surged forward as a profit-driven enterprise of matchless scope. By the time Dr. Morris Fishbein assumed the mantle of Dr. Simmons, who had himself started out as a homeopath, the AMA was at the helm of a strapping new industry flying the allopathic flag. The code word for competition was "quackery".

To be an acceptable member of a group, a person needs to conform to certain codes of conduct (cohort codes) that make him acceptable. In this, the social organization adopts *official positions*. Circumcision of healthy infant genital tissue is justified through the manipulative self-justificatory *advice* from self-proclaimed medical authority figures. The advice to circumcise comes from selfish impulses, for in America, circumcision represents a medical risk with an approximate and at the very minimum a four percent complication rate.[19] Add to that figure the 9-10% meatal stenosis rate that occurs only to circumcised boys and the figure rises to a 14% complication rate — far higher than any benefit claimed for the practice.

BLOOD & POWER

Morality is a doctrine or system that define proper and improper conduct. Social morality modifies individual behavior and empowers the social body through its authority. Genital rituals are a form of socialized sexual immorality through psychosexual power relations and are highly responsible for their

No, no, I'm anything but kind. In fact, I have a professional obligation to be malicious.
The Pitbull
Babe: Pig in the City

If anything is sacred, the human body is sacred.
Walt Whitman

It makes a big impact on their lives. The residents get that one-on-one personal socialization.
Amy Smith

historical imprint as memes.[20] Chris Knight in *Blood Relations* relates where females may have instituted social sexual morality:[21]

> It is nonetheless they who were the immediate agents of religious ideology's segregating action... Menstruating women, "are set apart from," and, in many ways, set above the rest of mankind. Earliest women established sexual morality by periodically repulsing men... History or cultural change, in this view, is basically an evolution of memes.

Menstruation in matriarchal societies is a blessed event for women. The menstrual hut allowed women to separate themselves from men at this important time of the month. This separation may have originated so women could be alone and away from pesky men. When patriarchy overcame matriarchy, menstruation came to be thought of as a curse, and menstrual blood an impurity — and the hut became a male-enforced prison of sorts, used to put down and dominate women. The separation that had given power to women now was used over them. Regarding power relations, Harriet Rubin in *The Princessa* states:[22]

> Her first order of business: She must change the battlefield first, neutralize the opponent's bid for control. Then take power... Powerful women of history coveted the power of separatedness.

Examples of the masculine attempt to reclaim power relations include:

1. Mayan penis bleeding to feed and serve their Great Mother Earth goddess established feminine blood primacy.

2. Australian Aborigines evolved subincision as a form of male menstruation to usurp the power of the feminine.

3. Female circumcision may have arisen because of fear and envy of some women to other women with a genetically larger clitoris and labia — along with the fear of men towards these women. Either way, the tribal hope is that group unity will be successful against nature, other tribes, and even themselves.

POWER ENVY

Psychosexual dominance inspires envy and resentment within those who are oppressed. *Power envy* gives rise to actions that are not designed to overthrow the system but rather to restructure the internal dynamics of society.

Any woman who is comfortable with her sexuality may figure that the concept of Penis Envy comes from someone who is frustrated about their own sexuality. So in reaction to Freud's *penis envy*,[23] the frustration of feminist psychologists may have also led to their own theories of *womb envy*[24] and *clitoris envy*.[25]

However, just as *penis envy* or *prepuce envy* may apply to males who have anxiety about the penis, *clitoris envy* may apply to women who are concerned about the clitoris. Clitoral envy may have given rise to some types of female genital mutilation and even to the unnecessary surgical alterations that have been performed on children born with *Congenital Adrenal Hyperplasia* (CAH).

These "envy" theories genitalize the person and may include envy of perceived socialized and acculturated sexual advantages. Social advantages and the rights of the opposite sex in matriarchy or patriarchy, may create resentments and lead to rebellion. Rebellion may take the form of the violence of female and male circumcision. Cultural envy of perceived imbalance and domination of either matriarchy or patriarchy may be defined as follows:

MATRIENVY **1.** Resentment of the perceived imbalanced advantages held by females from privileged social conditions conferred via a matriarchy. **2.** A masculine envious feeling caused by a perceived psychosexual sense of betrayal from an emotional disfranchisement created through matriarchal privileges and prerogatives.

PATRIENVY **1.** Resentment of the perceived imbalanced advantages held by males from privileged social conditions conferred via a patriarchy. **2.** A feminine envious feeling caused by a perceived psychosexual sense of betrayal from an emotional disfranchisement created through patriarchal privileges an prerogatives.

GENOCIDAL "PURIFICATION"

Purification rituals of circumcision concern the sexual body in collective guilt.[26] One African myth says that if a child in childbirth is touched by a clitoris it will die... and a man touched by a clitoris will become impotent. Women who are not circumcised, it is feared, will be promiscuous and may even become prostitutes. These are powerfully persuasive arguments for circumcision in Africa. Dirty, ugly, impure, disease-ridden... when socialized, collective guilt is accepted and all must believe and participate.[27]

Power never concedes anything without a demand. It never has and it never will.
Frederick Douglass

I envy her happiness. I envy his happiness.
Laurie
Little Women

It was the duty of these teams to segregate the prisoners of war who were candidates for execution,... and to report to the office of the Gestapo.
K. Lindeau
Nuremberg Trials

We may laugh at the myths of "primitive" cultures, but the USA has been similarly sold our own myths based on what we perceive as "scientific" — even though 85% of the male citizens of the world have no problem with their healthy, intact prepuces. Popular arguments in the USA for circumcision in the USA include the litany that the genitals are "dirty, ugly, impure, disease-ridden". Circumcised genitalia are praised as "clean" and "cute". We are threatened with social ostracism in the locker room and even in the family if Junior's genitals don't match Dad's. The medical team will frown, argue and harass new parents repeatedly for their signature to give them permission to circumcise. There has been an all-out medical public relations war on intact genitals in the USA.

In his book *Nazi Doctors: Medical Killing and the Psychology of Genocide*, Robert Lifton states:[28]

> Genocide is a response to collective fear of pollution and defilement... Purification tends to be associated with sacrificial victims, whether in primitive or contemporary religious or secular terms. Genocide can be understood as a quest to make sacrificial victims out of an entire people... It becomes an all-or-none matter, equally absolute in its claim to truth and in its rejection of alternate claims.
>
> Medical materialism can overlay symbol systems that closely parallel those of primitive purification rituals... As it becomes total — the violent cure draws upon all facets of the perpetrators' culture... The Nazis tapped mythic relationships between healing and killing that have had ancient expression in shamanism, religious purification, and human sacrifice, and evoked all three in ways that reveal more about their psychological motivations... That genocidal threshold requires prior ideological imagery of imperative. One has to do this thing, see it through to the end, for the sake of utopian vision of national harmony, unity, wholeness.

When all the pieces of the puzzle are put together, it is clear that social assimilation via circumcision has been at the very least disingenuous and at the very worst dishonest: a criminal attack, a form of social genocide for the sake of psychosexual power, control and authority for domination through manipulation from selfishness.[29]

*I like being in control.
It's safer.*
Sheila
Exit to Eden

The chief source of man's humanity to man seems to be the tribal limits of his sense of obligation to other men.
Reinhold Niebuhr

Good intentions may do as much harm as malevolence, if they lack understanding.
Albert Camus

EDDIE BERNAYS

The Prince of Puff and Baron of Ballyhoo

The conscious and intelligent manipulation of the organized habits and opinions of the masses is an important element in democratic society. Those who manipulate this unseen mechanism of society constitute an invisible government which is the true ruling power of our country. We are governed, our minds are molded, our tastes formed, our ideas suggested, largely by men we have never heard of. This is a logical result of the way in which our democratic society is organized. — *E. Bernays*

Freud's double nephew, Edward Bernays, proudly applied his uncle's psychological discoveries to the minds of the masses as a military propaganda officer during World War I. In 1928 Bernays wrote *Propaganda*, the handbook used by Joseph Goebbels, the director of internal propaganda for the Hitler's government. It mattered not to Goebbels that the author of his favorite book on propaganda was Jewish.

Bernays considered the general population — "the herd" — inferior. He humbly dubbed himself the "father" of Public Relations and after the war, he used his propaganda skills to fool the public into accepting his clients' commercial, medical and political products. Called the *Prince of Puff* and the *Baron of Ballyhoo* Bernays coined the phrase *Big Think* for his shrewdly-veiled marketing practices which included publicity stunts, third-party authorities such as doctor endorsements, national surveys and product branding.

Bernays believed in "the intelligent few". He paid his chauffeur "Dumb Jack" twenty-five dollars a week. "Dumb Jack" worked from 5:00 AM until 9:00 PM with a half day off every two weeks. "Not a bad deal," said Bernays, "but that's before people got a social conscience."

THE BERNAYS EFFECT: the improper and successful manipulation of an individual, group or the general public for power, control, authority or financial gain.

THE LIE

Sir Walter Raleigh

Go, soul, the body's guest,
Upon a thankless arrant:
Fear not to touch the best;
The truth shall be thy warrant:
Go, since I needs must die,
And give the world the lie.

Say to the court, it glows
And shines like rotten wood;
Say to the church, it shows
What's good, and doth no good:
If church and court reply,
Then give them both the lie.

Tell potentates, they live
Acting by others' action,
Not loved unless they give,
Not strong but by a faction:
If potentates reply,
Give potentates the lie.

Tell men of high condition
That manage the estate,
Their purpose is ambition,
Their practice only hate:
And if they make reply,
Then give them all the lie.

Tell them that brave it most,
They beg for more by spending,
Who, in their greatest cost,
Seek nothing but commending:
And if they make reply,
Then give them all the lie.

Tell zeal it wants devotion;
Tell love it is but lust;
Tell time it is but motion;
Tell flesh it is but dust:
And wish them not reply,
For thou must give the lie.

Tell age it daily wasteth;
Tell honor how it alters;
Tell beauty how she blasteth;
Tell favor how she falters:
And as they shall reply,
Give every one the lie.

Tell wit how much it wrangles
In tickle points of niceness;
Tell wisdom she entangles
Herself in over-wiseness:
And when they do reply,
Straight give them both the lie.

Tell physic of her boldness;
Tell skill it is pretension;
Tell charity of coldness;
Tell law it is contention:
And as they do reply,
So give them still the lie.

Tell fortune of her blindness;
Tell nature of decay;
Tell friendship of unkindness;
Tell justice of delay:
And if they will reply,
Then give them all the lie.

Tell arts they have no soundness,
But vary by esteeming;
Tell schools they want profoundness,
And stand too much on seeming:
If arts and school reply,
Give arts and school the lie.

Tell faith it fled the city;
Tell how the country erreth;
Tell manhood shakes off pity;
Tell virtue least preferreth:
And if they do reply,
Spare not to give the lie.

So when thou hast, as I
Commanded thee, done blabbing, - -
Although to give the lie
Deserves no less than stabbing, - -
Stab at thee, he that will,
No stab the soul can kill.

MANIPULATION

Lie to me, lie to me; tell me what I want to hear

How were we convinced to allow our children or ourselves to be genitally mutilated? What did it take to make us close our eyes and ears and look the other way, while someone in cut our children's healthy genitals? What kind of mental, emotional programming has made us blind to the practice of genital mutilation in the modern world – especially in a modern, industrialized country such as the United States?   It is through Power Relations.[1]

If I didn't mutilate the innocent, how could I make the guilty fear me?
Ugandan sub-chief of Karabenga
Tales of the African Frontier

SUGGESTIBILITY

Suggestibility is defined as: *responsiveness to suggestion*. Those who initiate, perpetrate and maintain ritual rely on suggestibility.[2-8] The two types of suggestion are *direct* and *indirect*. People respond to both, but are generally predisposed to one or the other. The physically-inclined respond more to *direct suggestion*. The emotionally-inclined respond more to *indirect suggestion*.

Suggestibility is fostered by three factors:

1. Extension — Bystanders get caught up in a movement.
2. Intensification — Individuals observe the opinion shared by the crowd.
3. Predisposition — Universal sympathy to the opinion makes a similar response easier the next time.

These three reactions are reinforced by an authority figure's perceived superior power, which leads to control due to awe or fear. The power may come from an individual — a parent, religious leader, physician, or a tribal elder — or society itself may act as the superior power. Due to the influence of this "power," people feel they must follow suit and maintain the precedence previously set of fixed ideas, manias, phobias and prejudices — the established cultural identity. This requires internal dissociation. The individual

Men have always liked to believe in their influence and direction in the course of time, these claims, however, sometimes conceal the truth.
Henry Hobhouse

mind blocks out the humanity of a sacrificial victim and transforms the victim into an object. Suggestion is reinforced by:

- repetition
- duration of acts
- prestige of the idea

So you lie to yourself
to be happy?
Teddy
Memento

Those who are more open to suggestion are the young, women, people who identify with a culture, and the criminally inclined. Suggestion may lead to a *Shared Psychotic Disorder* and other psychological conditions that could lead to a *Culture-Bound Syndrome*.

THE GENITAL BLOOD RITUAL SUGGESTION

Arguments promoting genital blood ritual are subtle, hidden, and protected by claims of religious demand or professional expertise. Because religious and medical rationalizations for circumcision cannot withstand genuine, unbiased, objective inquiry, the impetus behind the ritual requires hard-hitting emotional appeals that bypass the rational intellect. Marking the body and cutting the genitals have evolved from pagan rituals and are signs of tribal identification. Tribal body-marking practices evolved into primitive religious ritual and were eventually adopted into the secular scientific, medical format. How did that happen? This chapter will explore how belief systems are formed and maintained.

What luck for rulers
that men do not think.
Adolf Hitler

In primitive tribes, the group trumps the individual, ritual trumps individualism. The purpose of ritual is to make all members of the tribe subservient to the social norm and create a culture of conformity. Tribal programming structures and compartmentalizes thought. In the tribal structure this becomes an "us versus them" mentality. Tribes are formed and maintained by fear.

We join with the tribe and separate from not only other tribes, strangers, but we disconnect from ourselves as individuals, our own inner wisdom, our own feelings and integrity.

An idea, to be
suggestive, must come
to an individual with
the force of
revelation.
William James

Group cohesion could be thought of as acculturated codependence. Groupthink is valued over personal wisdom and discernment. Within a tribe that is worried about its survival, conforming to a tribal identification and its cultural and spiritual belief system is how loyalty is measured.

Anyone who strikes out on his or her own is cursed to be lost in a danger-filled jungle, to die of thirst out on a vast, dry desert, or to languish lonely in a land where he doesn't speak the language or understand the customs and may be killed by strangers. The biggest enemy of tribal rituals is courageous, clear thinking outside the box.

Standing outside and looking in, both religious and medical claims for genital blood ritual appear to be based on dubious "facts" and therefore, demand for the genital blood ritual may prove to closely align with symptoms of Munchausen by Proxy including Proxy's Malignant Hero Syndrome. And on a larger, social level: Munchausen in Collective Transmission. Bell states:[9]

> Ritual practices are themselves the very production and negotiation of power relations...
>
> Ritualization sees the qualities of the new person who should emerge; it does not see the schemes of privileged opposition, heirarchalization, and circular deferment by which ritualized agents produce ritualized agents empowered or disempowered by strategic schemes of practice. Ritualization sees the evocation of consensus...
>
> Ritual practices never define anything except in terms of expedient relationships that ritualization itself establishes among things, thereby manipulating the meaning of things by manipulating their relationships.

CODEPENDENT THINKING

Robert Burney wrote *Codependence: The Dance of Wounded Souls*. In it he listed nine modes of thinking that lead to and are involved in, dysfunctional relationships.[10] These follow, with this author's comments:

1) *BLACK AND WHITE THINKING* is any negative thing that happens gets turned into a sweeping generality.

This is the hallmark of a purification ritual. The genitals are inherently dirty and therefore all must be excised.

2) *NEGATIVE FOCUS* is always thinking a glass is half empty, not half full. The other extreme is focusing on the positive to deny feelings.

This is denial in ritual.

3) *MAGICAL THINKING* is often used in theology and religion to replace reality, and a way of creating self-fulfilling prophesy.

This is deflection in ritual. It eliminates personal responsibility by using God as the author of action.

The vision that you glorify in your mind, the ideal that you enthrone in your heart, this you will build your life by. This you will become.
James Allen

You are bewitched by reason.
Masbath
No, I'm beaten down by it.
Ichabod Crane

There is no 'If.'
Nyah
Devil Girl from Mars

4)   *STARRING IN THE SOAP OPERA* involves blowing things out of proportion. Users become the King or Queen of Tragedy. They are *trauma dramas*. Excitement and intensity of dramatic scenes in conflict are common themes. Individual overindulgence predominates.

Ritual participation through the *imago vivendi* is used as an expression of self glorification, and used in medical scare tactics.

5)   *SELF-DISCOUNT* includes the inability to receive, or to admit to our own positive qualities.

Allowing oneself to be demeaned in ritual, and maintaining successive generational ritualization of like-kind.

6)   *EMOTIONAL REASONING* is reasoning from feeling by believing that what we feel is who we are, without separating the inner child's feelings and adult feeling in the present.

Fear is a major use in initiating and maintaining genital blood ritual.

7)   *SHOULDS*, *musts* and *have tos*, come from authority figures. Adults don't have shoulds - adults have choices.

Ritual deferral to authority figures as adults abdicate responsibility

8)   *SELF-LABELING* identifies our perceived shortcomings and imperfections by not accepting one's humanity.

Accepting self-mortification in ritual.

9)   *PERSONALIZING THE BLAME* is blaming oneself as personally and totally responsible for happenstance, and how someone else feels. Conversely, it is blaming other people, or fate, to one's own attitudes and behavior that may have contributed to a problem.

Socially, this is explained by Original Sin and inherent fault.

LOGICAL FALLACIES

How do humans justify cutting healthy genitals? How are they railroaded into allowing it to be done to their children? Examples follow of logical fallacies and a few words about how each is used to rationalize genital cutting.[11]

1)   *AD MISERICORDIAM* is an appeal to pity for sympathy and compassion. It is most often used by children and charities. Charities attempt to

You lied to me.
Evelyn
I lie to everyone. What makes you so special?
Jonathan
The Mummy

Man can certainly keep on lying, and does so, but he cannot make truth falsehood.
Karl Barth

'The lie is the specific 'evil' that the human race has 'introduced into nature.'
Peters paraphrasing Burber

impart guilt in not helping with their implied desperate circumstances.

It is used in false claims for funding circumcision campaigns.

2)   *SPECIAL PLEADING* is akin to pity. This is an appeal to give special circumstance to one case, while such consideration does not apply to all others. Special Pleading is used by groups who base their argument on things as past abuses and assert the need for special treatment to make up for them. Affirmative Actions are based on Special Pleading.

The Female Genital Mutilation Act does not protect males.

3)   *AD VERECUNDIAM* is an appeal to authority. From childhood people are taught not to dispute the authority of parents and elders. This carries into adulthood by transferring to the employer, government and health care provider. In criminal trials both the prosecution and defense may have expert witnesses extolling the situation they are putting forth. Commercials often advocate: "More doctors prescribe...", "More hospitals use...;" and, "four out of five dentists recommend..." They rely on the expert's professional reputation, qualifications, and credentials.

Religious circumcisers use their authority as representatives of God. Medicine uses its authority in advocating circumcision through opinions, where all have been proven false, misleading, or clinically insignificant.

4)   *APPEAL TO SECRECY* is the adage that knowledge is power. Having knowledge that others do not possess imparts even greater power. It is an attractive tool which people may use to their benefit, and often to the detriment of others. Secrecy is an essential element for abuse, misuse of power, crime, and lies.

Circumcision discussion is socially taboo disallowing knowledge.

5)   *APPEAL TO PARTIALITY* is the one-sided proposition and similar to the appeal to pity. This argument puts forth one's cause while denying that the opposition has any justification. It is often used in agenda driven political speeches to sway voters.

This also applies to the FGM bill, and circumcision being required for feminine safety because of indiscriminate sexual practices of both partners.

6)   *AD BACULUM* appeals through fear, threat and force. No truth or falsity is involved, but whether or not one complies with the demand and the consequences of non compliance are real. This form of argument is used often

Your national security advisor has just been executed. He's a very good negotiator. He bought you another half hour.
Egor
Air Force One

A politician wouldn't dream of being allowed to call a columnist the things a columnist is allowed to call a politician.
Max Lerner

If 50 million people say a foolish thing, it's still foolish.
Vincent Bugliosi

in advertising for home alarm systems and pepper sprays to protect oneself against attackers.

After a circumcision in Australia, the physician said she would cut off more if her teen-age patient continued masturbating.[4]

7)   *AD HOMINEM* argues against the person with personal attacks to destroy the credibility of another person. If successful, then any valid viewpoint of the attacked person will be inherently discredited. Instead of direct attacks, this is often accomplished by snide remarks and derogatory adjectives about to the person being attacked. Arguments against a person are used in politics along with malicious and raunchy humor.

Circumcision involves body genitalization in an attempt to discredit a person. By destroying the person as a whole, then all of the parts are equally discredited. Then the physical attack is a matter of course.

8)   *GUILT BY ASSOCIATION* attacks by linking an unworthy or unpopular position, or a person of ill repute, by transferring the negative quality to the person being attacked. An example is: "You sound like your mother."

This is often used by mothers who have their sons circumcised in revenge against a father. The father is too powerful to attack.

9)   *TU QUOQUE* is the "You too," "Practice what you preach;" and, "If you can do it, so can I" argument. This is related to the Ad Hominem and Guilt by Association. In politics it is used as a mirror when one's opponent is being attacked for misbehavior by stating the other person's candidates have done the same.

It was quickly adopted by medicine in the 1800's in response to the religious movements advocating circumcision.

10) *AD POPULUM* appeals to the masses. This feeds the person's need to socially belong and be accepted. The thought is that if everyone is doing it, it must be correct. This argument is used in conjunction with the Tu Quoque for socialization. The practice then becomes what everyone expects. Following this is tribalization where one group is included and all others are considered outsiders. Then it becomes an unspoken premise. Propaganda, mob rule, and hate groups use this argument.

Medicine used this argument, in conjunction with Special Pleading, during the initiation of circumcision in the England speaking countries.[5]

11) *APPEAL TO TRADITION* is the Sacred Cow. This is close to the Ad Populum argument. It is structured toward respect for the social principles of loyalty, patriotism, and assumed rights. When challenging the Sacred Cow it is perceived as an attack to what society holds sacred.

Nothing is more sacred than an established religious tradition.

12) *APPEAL TO PRECEDENT* states that if something has been done before, it should continue to be done. And, to the contrary, if something has not been done in the past, it should not be done now. Legal precedent relies heavily on this argument.

There is no theological or religious precedent for Christian circumcision. Also, there is no precedent for full prepuce amputation of the male penis for Judaism or Islam because the covenant of Abraham only removed the prepuce's tip. On inspection such a demand was improperly added. And, there is no Testamental evidence in any of the three Jerusalemic religions for Female Genital Mutilation.

13) *AD IGNORANTIAM* is the argument of ignorance. If something cannot be proven wrong, it must be right. Also, the contrary is used where if something cannot be proven correct, it must be wrong.

Medicine relies heavily on past opinion. Once medicine takes a position, all too often they have had to be proven wrong over and over.

14) *COMPOSITION* argues that what is true for the part must then be true for the whole.

Some in medicine use this argument by stating that if circumcision cures or prevents a certain disease in one person, then everyone must be circumcised. This is a genocidal argument.

15) *DIVISION* is the opposite of Composition. Division argues that what is true for the whole must be true for the part. An example is if America has a high standard of living, then no one in America is poor.

This is used to attack a male by attacking his penis in the genitalization of the body. It is also a genocidal argument.

16) *IGNORATIO ELENCHI* is the Red Herring argument. Red Herrings are side issues added to discussion to confuse issues, or they are improper connections. A Red Herring is an irrelevant conclusion to the issue being discussed.

An expert is a person who avoids the small errors while sweeping on to the Grand Fallacy.
Benjamin Stolberg

I admire liars, but surely not clumsy they cannot fool even themselves.
Mencken

There are three kinds of lies – damned lies and statistics.
Benjamin Disraeli

According to Frederick Hodges "the prepuce is an organ waiting for a disease". Reasons to cut are concocted and publicized, but they are eventually and inevitably disproved. Then another excuse arises.

17) *SECUNDUM QUID* is the Hasty Generalization. This argument applies generalizations from too little evidence. Generalization is the basis for most stereotypical thinking. If the first five people one sees in a town are women, then one would conclude all the people in the town are women.

This applies to urinary tract infections that have a slightly higher incidence in uncircumcised infant males. All these boys have a prepuce, so the prepuce must be the cause. But, urine is sterile and the prepuce has immunological functions. What is overlooked is forcible premature prepuce retraction. Similarity is observable in people who clean their navels with a Q-tip and get a rash from doing it.

18) *REDUCTIO AD ABSURDUM* is taking an argument to an extreme. This is the Black and White argument with no areas of Grey allowed.

This study may be perceived as an example of taking an argument to the extreme. But, it is necessitated to briefly answer the extreme amount of excuses, causes and affects of socializing genital blood ritual.

19) *POST HOC ERGO PROPTER HOC* is the False Cause argument. If one event follows another, it is presumed the first event caused the second.

Some people argue that the prepuce is a major cause of AIDS. This does not necessarily follow because AIDS is too common in circumcising America. Venereal diseases must be looked at as a behavioral issue.

20) *PEPITO PRINCIPII* is Begging the Question and a circular argument. It involves assuming what one is trying to prove. The conclusion is the premise. Thus, Pepito Principii is a self fulfilling prophecy.

The Pepito Principii is involved in most arguments presented here on BOTH sides with regard to circumcision. But we stand that circumcision is abusive.

21) *STATISTICS* often depend on interpretation. Statistics are also dependent on variables, as the population studied. These include age, sex, location, and time. Statistics are often improperly applied, no matter how well intentioned.

UTI statistics do not consider premature forcible prepuce retraction. In fact, many in medicine have recommended it.

There are a lot of people who won't let the facts get in the way of their personal beliefs.
Dr. Dean Edell

Let me explain something to you – this business requires a certain amount of finesse.
Jake Gittes
Chinatown

The gesture acquires meaning, reality, solely to the extent to which it repeats a primordial act.
Mircea Eliade
Myth of the Eternal Return

22) *MISDIRECTION* is another Red Herring. Though a premise may be true, it is used to obscure the major issue at hand. It has been used with smoking tobacco. Though it is true that the use of tobacco products cause's harm, its campaign is an alternate to fighting that which is overwhelming: illegal drugs, which has not been controllable.

> Genital mutilations are used as methods of appearing to solve and attenuate other overwhelming social behavioral concerns as AIDS.

23) *POLITICAL CORRECTNESS: BE SILENT and CONFORM or BE PUNISHED!* This argument is akin to the Ad Baculum appeal to fear, threat and force that is so often used by those who commit incest. Political correctness uses all types of arguments to maintain control.

> Political Correctness is a use of social convention over the rule of law.

PERSUASION

Persuading is urging, influencing, or convincing someone to do something. Persuasion stimulates the emotions, and emotions occur when people are interested. There is nothing more interesting than the genitals and the desire to manipulate them. Often good intentions are clothed in power, and there is nothing more powerful than the control over another's genitals which includes aspects of deprivation including circumcision. Many techniques are used in persuasion, thus making the process involved and complex. These techniques have specific patterns. Most of the following discussion is taken from Hugh Rank's *Persuasion Analysis*. Summarizing:[12-15]

> *PERSUASION* involves *intensifying* certain things and *downplaying* other things. We intensify thoughts about a subject by repetition of thought about that subject, then association of that perception to other things, and unifying the composition into a single pattern of connections. Downplaying involves omission of things contrary to the desired effect, diversions away from the subject, and introduction of confusion to keep focus away from the defects of the arguments used to entice desired actions of others.

INTENSIFYING

1) *REPETITION* makes one comfortable because the subject becomes familiar. This includes favorite stories and songs, chants, prayers, dances, and rituals. Repetition imprints on the memory, as a meme, for identification, recognition, and eventually a response.

A sale is made on every call you make. Either you sell the client some stock or he sells you a reason he can't.
Jim Young
Boiler Room

The best liar is he who makes the smallest amount of lying go the longest way.
Samuel Butler

The psychology of deception is first to deceive yourself.
Anonymous

2)   *ASSOCIATION* intensifies through linking something that is already loved or desired, or hated and feared, by those intensifying to the person being influenced. Association is accomplished by direct assertions, or indirectly through metaphors, allusions, backgrounds, and context. Association feeds human needs, wants, and desires eliciting certainty, belonging, intimacy, safe space, and the perception of personal growth.

3)   *COMPOSITION* increases the affects through sequence and proportions in adding the impact of the movements conveyed in words and the images elicited. Strategy for complex issues involves combining a set of small established impressions into one coherent context. Verbal composition, often called 'The Pitch,' is systematic. Nonverbal composition, often used in ritual, uses colors, shapes, dimensional relationships, and music.

DOWNPLAYING

1)   *OMISSION*: Communication is limited in time and necessitates conciseness. But, communication is often biased and can deliberately conceal a truth. Half truths are difficult to detect. Omissions include cover-ups, censorship, and managed news. The receiver can also omit by being close-minded or prejudiced.

2)   *DIVERSION*: This involves diverting attention away from key issues and important oppositions. Diversion usually intensifies side issues, unrelated topics, and trivial matters. Tactics include: hairsplitting, nitpicking, *red herrings*, and emotional attacks by using the *ad hominem* and *ad populum*. Diversion depletes one's energy to concentrate on pertinent issues.

3)   *CONFUSION* is induced by making issues complex and chaotic so people become overloaded, weary, and give up. Confusion creates an atmosphere in which people cannot understand thus it makes it impossible to make reasonable connections and decisions. Confusion could come from faulty logic, contradictions, multiple diversions, or inconsistencies that blur understanding.

All people are *benefit-seekers* desiring what is perceived good. In this they want: *acquisition* to obtain the good, *protection* to keep the good, *relief* by getting rid of the bad, and *prevention* in avoiding further bad. Yet, only some people are *benefit promisers* when they are acting to influence others by promising fulfillment to the *benefit seeker*. In this they intensify their own good and intensify the other's bad; as well as, downplay their own bad and downplay another's good.

BENEFIT SEEKERS

1) *ACQUISITION*'s intent is to make one discontent with what he already has, as well as, wanting more or something else. Intangible elements include fulfilling: hopes, wisdom, virtue, admiration, and a feeling of being loved.

2) *PROTECTION* often targets caretakers. Caretakers include parents, health care providers, and the religious. A negative aspect of the persuader is a scare-and-sell approach to obtain desired compliance from others.

3) *RELIEF* involves convincing others that they have it bad so the promiser will be assured of his desired effect. Relief involves a scare-and-sell technique stressing that a problem exists and they, the promiser, have the solution. This uses the association of a problem linked to their service.

4) *PREVENTION* also uses the scare-and-sell. Once convinced that something is bad, people will want to avoid possessing it or its occurrence. Prevention associates things as dangerous, unpleasant, or inconvenient, and proposes a remedy. Prevention uses the predictability of the human fears to death, destruction, and ill health.

BENEFIT PROMISERS

1) *INTENSIFYING ONE'S OWN GOOD* often involves glittering generalities. This praises, exalts, and glorifies the promiser's self and/or profession. Intensifying own good is used in ritual's ceremonial speeches at funerals, graduations, and dedications. This stresses the good in a person or thing the promiser wants emphasized.

2) *INTENSIFYING THE OTHERS' BAD* is used aggressively to attack, criticize, blame, denounce, defame, and malign other people who have a different viewpoint. It sometimes degrades into tirades with condemnation, insults, and vulgarities. It is also used to associate a general bad in another product or thing.

3) *DOWNPLAYING ONE'S OWN BAD* omits, conceals, suppresses, masks, and minimizes the benefit provider's bad qualities. Techniques include stonewalling, passing the buck, hiding weaknesses, and giving the runaround. A subtle different downplay of one's own bad is using a *concessive argument* that admits a minor flaw as an illusion of fairness but only to reaffirm the major point of their negotiation. This method's apogee is used during a reversal of a turning point against their argument with words such as "nevertheless," and "on the other hand."

They can't tell the truth, even to themselves.
Commoner
Rashomon

Let us never negotiate out of fear.
John F. Kennedy

The only treaties that ought to count are those which effect a settlement between ulterior motives.
Paul Valery
Greatness and Decadence of Europe

4) *DOWNPLAYING THE OTHERS' GOOD* is used when the benefit provider needs subtle aggressiveness to minimize the opposition. This is achieved by ignoring, belittling, undervaluing, and disparaging a counter-point. Downplaying the others' good uses sarcasm and mockery the action is often from envy. One successful aspect used is to revise history.

CAUSE GROUP rhetoric uses a four part *pep talk*. *Cause group* starts with a threat then requests bonding, for a common cause, for a united response. Cause groups usually tackle difficult issues. Importance is not use emotional and inflammatory rhetoric. Saying an action is child abuse, of course, touches the emotions. Emotions, as denial, will obviously occur but must not be allowed to obscure a proper decision of what is truthful or untruthful.

THE PEP TALK

1)   *THE THREAT* often intensifies the possibility of a future bad. The scenario initially warns about hidden dangers creating a desired sequence, with the bad perceived as a contamination. (Circumcisers currently advocate the possibility of cervical cancer, penile cancer, and HIV. Medically, cervical cancer is caused by a virus. Penile cancer rate is 1:100,000 and also may be due to the same viral cause. The true issue of these diseases is behavior. Because sexual behavior is next to impossible to control, controlling behavior is denied and circumcision is used in deferral.)

2)   *THE BONDING* stresses need for unity, loyalty, and quality. Specific actions required by the *benefit promiser* are: support, joining, help, and donating.

3)   *THE CAUSE* emphasizes duty, obligation, and mission. Participating in a cause implies defending, protecting, helping and serving others in need. Often these are groups like the poor, the children, the church, the nation, as well as the earth and animals.

4)   *THE RESPONSE* involves achieving a desired action. In this subject the Response is whether a parent should genitally alter their children, and society allowing desired action.

PEP TALK and PITCH: There are 5 elements to the Cause Group Rhetoric's Pep Talk. As a group it is called *The Pitch*. They are: 1) Attention Getting, 2) Confidence Building, 3) Desire Stimulating 4) Urgency Stressing; and, 5) Response Seeking.

THE PITCH

1) *ATTENTION GETTING*: attention usually resides in a slogan, brand name, logo or even the personality of the *benefit promiser*.

External attention getters include *stories* for justification. *Internal attention getters* include the *physical, emotional* and *cognitive*. The physical includes sight and sounds which are often used in the structural pomp of ritual with music, chants, and audible prayer. *Emotional attention getters* associate the *benefit seeker* with basic needs, certitude and approval of the task taken. *Cognitive attention getters* appeal to the intellect rather than the senses and include claims and promises. They may quote statistics. *Product centered claims* stress intrinsic values like quality, utility, and beauty. *Audience centered claims* involve sex, health, intimacy, nature, and family. Circumcision itself is a logo, brand name and symbol.

2) *CONFIDENCE BUILDING* means establishing trust.

Benefit seekers want certitude. Thus, benefit promisers must appear as friendly authoritative figures that convey credibility, sincerity and benevolence. Confidence implies: *you can trust me*. Words and phrases used include: absolutely safe, rest assured, certainly, dependable, integrity, knowledgeable, proven prudent, and wise. Benefit promisers nonverbally use smiles, calm voice, and reassuring gestures. Body language is a powerful communication tool. As with any product or organization the benefit promiser represents a corporate image to which the benefit seeker may associate.

3) *DESIRE STIMULATING* relies on the merit of the intended action or product bought. Benefits are usually intangible as: sex appeal, psychological benefits, popularity, and fantasies. Words imply meaning. Some are:

Word Meaning

really works — efficiency	greatest — quality
classic — stability	practical — utility
beautiful — beauty	

Standard Phrases

Benefit: Improve. Be better. Solve. Prevent. Avoid.
Directive: You need, You should get, You ought to.
Negative: Don't be sorry later. Don't worry. You need it.
Desire: Everything you dreamed of. Everything you desire.
Satisfaction: You'll enjoy, You'll be pleased.
Satisfaction by others: She'll be pleased. Show her you care.

Half the truth is often a great lie.
Benjamin Franklin

Every great reform which has been effected has consisted, not in doing something new, but in undoing something old.
Henry Thomas Buckle

You mean you didn't believe his story.
Romana
No
The Doctor
But he had such an honest face.
Romana
You can't be successful with a dishonest face, can you?
The Doctor
Doctor Who

4)   *URGENCY*: Stressing *urgency* creates immediate anxiety. The *hard sell* uses *command urgency*. The *soft sell* uses *conditioning* for later action. Both rely on emotional responses without the benefit seeker's careful thought. Soft selling occurs mostly with established products and services. (The history of circumcision in England and America illustrates the difference. When initiating the procedure, the medical field wrote journal articles to justify the procedure and the religious field focused on the masturbation taboo. Once established, circumcision was easily sold thereafter as the "standard". The *hard sell* reestablishes itself when existing medical proof is found incorrect; another disease becomes the new rationalization.

5)   *RESPONSE SEEKING*: Response is the intent of persuasion. If the previous four elements are successful then the desired response is elicited. If it is not forthcoming, it is a sign that the tactics were ineffective. Ineffectiveness implies the *benefit promiser* did not establish: a) the desired attitude at the level of conviction, b) the value system extolled or c) the beliefs and presuppositions.

RELIGIOUS PERSUASION

Religious persuasion presents unique qualities due to the nature of its control. Robert Lifton in *Thought Reform and the Psychology of Totalism* states there are eight psychological techniques used in mind control that are peculiar to cult manipulations. Each possess a totalistic quality that depends on philosophical assumptions. These techniques all apply to genital rituals:[16]

1)   *Milieu control*: control of the physical, environment and language
2)   *Mystical manipulation*: behavior control: ritual social cohesion
3)   *Loading the language*: control of thinking: willing sacrifice
4)   *Doctrine over person*: control the person: sacrificial community
5)   *The sacred science*: scientific, psychological, and moral trust.
6)   *The cult of confession*: original sin: submission to subjugation
7)   *The demand for purity*: physical and moral purity over evil
8)   *The dispensing of existence*: the living sacrifice

VISUAL RHETORIC

The adage *A picture is worth a thousand words* is a familiar reference to *visual rhetoric*. Visuals include cartoon characters promoting a product and political commentary. The circumcised penis is an example of visual rhetoric.

PROPAGANDA

Propaganda is closely associated with persuasion. Propaganda techniques are: 1) self-evident, 2) others require additional information; and, 3) other techniques will require study.[17,18] Keep in mind their connections with genital mutilation social negotiations.

SELF-EVIDENT TECHNIQUE

1)   *APPEAL to AUTHORITY* uses and cites authoritative people in support of an idea, position, argument, or course of action. Doctors and the religious present themselves in vestments of authority.

2)   *ASSERTION* uses positive statements presented as fact, true or not.

3)   *BANDWAGON* and *INEVITABLE VICTORY* is the "Everyone else is doing it" argument. It asks the person to join the winning side.

4)   *OBTAIN DISAPPROVAL* often attempts association of actions with groups that are hated, feared, or held in contempt. (This Mandated Report is an argument of disapproval of genital alteration of infants and children).

5)   *GLITTERING GENERALITIES* use highly emotional words associated to concepts of value. They must relate to current conditions to be effective.

6)   *VAGUENESS* is related to generalities. Vagueness does not allow analyzing validity, or the reasonableness of the action requested.

7)   *RATIONALIZATION* for questionable acts or beliefs is the object of generalities and vagueness, and relies on opinion.

8)   *SIMPLIFICATION* Generalities give simple answers to complex political, economic, and social problems. (Social purification requires all to participate.)

9)   *TRANSFER* projects positive or negative values of a person, individual, group, object or action to another usually to transfer blame when people are in conflict. (Genitalization of the body is transference.)

10) *LEAST of EVILS* acknowledges that a course of action is unfavorable, but the alternative would be worse. This technique is used to explain the necessity of sacrifices or harsh actions that are displeasing or restrict personal liberties. (See California medical ethicist in Medicine chapter).

Propaganda, only propaganda is needed.
Adolf Hitler

Either way a sale is made, the only question is who is gonna close? You or him? Now be relentless.
Jim Young
Boiler Room

The casualty when war comes is truth.
Hiram Johnson

11) *NAME CALLING, SUBSTITUTIONS of NAMES or MORAL LABELS*
seek to create prejudice. It can be direct or indirect through insinuation.

12) *PINPOINTING the ENEMY* can be a form of Simplification when
applied to groups, and sometimes produces prejudice.

13) *PLAIN FOLKS* or *COMMON MAN* attempts to equate the propagan-
dist with the target group and that his position reflects the general opinion,
or what the general opinion should be. Leaders use this to humanize
themselves.

14) *SOCIAL DISAPPROVAL is* similar to *#4 Obtain Disapproval*, but
concentrates on social forces that will ostracize the opposing group, and is a
form of peer pressure.

15) *VIRTUE WORDS* These words must relate to the target audience's
value systems. Euphemisms include "cleanliness" and "prevention".

16) *SLOGANS* are brief phrases that may include labeling and stereotyping.

TECHNIQUES REQUIRING ADDITIONAL INFORMATION

1)   *INCREDIBLE TRUTHS* are used when impressing that a catastrophic
event will certainly take place and affect the target that may be a person or
thing.

2)   *INSINUATION* creates suspicion against people, groups, or ideas.
Insinuation uses leading questions, humor, rumor, and guilt by association.

3)   *EXPLOITABLE VULNERABILITIES* creates division among target
audiences and includes:

- Political, economic, social, ethnic, racial and regional differences
- Historical animosities
- Powerlessness of the individual

4)   *CARD STACKING* or *SELECTIVE OMISSION* choose only to present
the information the perpetrator wants to let the target know. (This is observable in medicine when not giving full disclosure with informed consent for
surgical procedures.)

5)   *LYING* and *DISTORTION* — People in authority have the trust of others. This represents willful fraud. Assertions and reassurances may be lies or
distortions.

6)   *SIMPLIFICATION* is concise. It builds the ego of the target because he thinks he has knowledge beyond technological jargon and science.

TECHNIQUES REQUIRING STUDY

1)   *CHANGE of PACE* is a switching from hostile to friendly, persuasion to threat, and gloom to optimism, or vise versa. (In hospitals it is common for the informed consent form to be presented to the parent right after birth. If refused, then ominous details are presented of what might happen to the child if his penis is not circumcised – *ad hominem* of a body part.)

2)   *STALLING* deliberately withholds information until the time of its importance is past. It reduces the perpetrator's failure.

3)   *SHIFT of SCENE* changes the *field of battle*. The spotlight is taken off an unfavorable situation or condition, and forces the opponent to go on the defense. Historically this occurred when medicine took over as the circumcision specialized ritual agent when the procedure moved to hospitals.

4)   *REPETITION* in propaganda is similar to persuasion's use in intensifying the perpetrator's position. Repetition relies on humans as creatures of habit and their self-centeredness. Successful repetition produces automatic responses that, with continued use, reinforce opinion.

PUBLIC RELATIONS

Public Relations is the use of communication to give a positive image of a person, group of persons, social organization, business, profession and many other entities to the public and others. Public Relations is also used by religions, points of view and to make behavior acceptable. It is to make, in the hearts and minds of others by popularizing success or perceived success, downplays and ignores discrepancies, reporting failures, announcing changes and updates as well as many other activities. Public Relations conveys information, influence politics and legislation, and seek general favor. And with many social organizations Public Relations is used to enhance fund raising. Specialties include: crisis, reputation and issue management; investor and labor relations; and grassroot relations. Professional Public Relations has its origins in Freudian psychology combined with military propaganda.[19],[20]

Resistance is futile.
Dalek
Dr. Who

Resistance is futile.
Capt Jean-Luc Picard
Star Trek: First Contact

Dare to be true: nothing can need a lie. A fault, which needs it most, grows two thereby.
George Herbert

METHODS, TOOLS AND TACTICS

Public Relations is basically publicity which is spreading information.[21]

1)   *AUDIENCE TARGETING* addresses the demographic group the message is to appeal to and may vary from one person, segment of the population to the worldwide audience.

2)   *PRESS RELEASES* are written statements distributed to the media and include the: Who, What, When, Where, Why and the How.

3)   *OPTIMIZING THE INTERNET* is the Internet press release and if skillful may be ranked high on search web sites.

4)   *LOBBY GROUPS* influence governments, corporations and public opinion. They represent particular interests and often hide true intentions.

5)   *SPIN* is a term implying heavily biased explanations that favor or position and situation often used in a manipulating deceptive and disingenuous manner.

- Presenting selected facts
- Non-denial denial
- Phrasing unproven assumptions as truth
- Euphemisms to mislead from group intentions
- Ambiguous language
- Being indirect
- Rejecting opposition facts
- Appeal to precedent of its policies
- Proper timing of releasing good news as well as releasing bad news

6)   *OTHER* methods used in Public Relations and advertising include:

- Publicity events, publicity stunts and photo opportunities
- Talk show programs on radio, television and meetings
- Books, professional journal articles, fliers and other writings
- Direct communication with in person messages and e-mails
- Internet web sites
- Speeches and seminars

7)   *PROCESS* in public relations is first an analysis of the situation and determines the strengths, weaknesses, threats and opportunities. Process evaluates research, objectives, strategies, implementation and evaluation. Then a plane is made and acted on.

A lie will easily get you out of a scrape, and yet, strangely and beautifully, rapture possesses you when you have taken the scrape and left out the lie.
Montague

The most dangerous untruths are truths moderately distorted.
Lichtenberg

When a man lies, he murders some part of the world.
Rospo Pallenberg

POLITICS AND CIVIL SOCIETY

Politics and civil society are the fabrics woven to be worn by the gregarious human species as we make our way in life. Public Relations is used to make life easier as well as to achieve dominance.[22]

*This isn't about me.
It's about you.*
Barak Obama

1) *DEFINING THE OPPONENT* is a tactic used to achieve safety, security and dominance. The use of Public Relations is often to destroy a competing company or those who hold different opinions.

2) *MANAGING LANGUAGE* controls the conversation. creates suspicion against people, groups, or ideas. Insinuation uses leading questions, humor, rumor, and guilt by association.

3) *PLAYING UP WEAKNESS* often uses individuals who are celebrities and in the entertainment industry. Often making a weakness can be made into an 'image' which is to say create a persona of an individual, group or organization that then becomes acceptable to the populace.

*Laws control the
lesser man. Right
conduct controls the
greater one.*
Chinese proverb

4) *BRANCHING OUT* also uses individuals who are celebrities and in the entertainment industry. This involves the recreation of an image that has become passe or unfavorable by becoming involved in new projects.

5) *FRONT GROUPS* are organizations that give the impression of serving the populace but in reality serve, in concealment and obscurity, the interests of their clients and sponsors.

6) *LOCALIZATION OF PUBLIC RELATIONS* focus' on the target market whether it be a neighborhood or the worldwide population.

INDIVIDUALS

People involved in and affected by Public Relations include:[23]

1) *STAKEHOLDER* a stakeholder is a person, persons or business entity that has affect on a business's actions.

A) *Narrowly Categorized*

*Every job is a
self-portrait of the
person who does it.
Autograph your work
with excellence.*
Anonymous

- Owner
- Partners
- Investors
- Shareholders
- Employees
- Customers

Quality means doing it right when no one is looking.
Henry Ford

B) *Broadly Categorized*

- Suppliers
- Labor Unions
- Government regulatory agencies
- Industry trade unions
- Professional associations
- Advocacy groups
- Prospective employees
- Prospective customers
- Local communities
- National community
- World community
- Competitors

The least initial deviation from the truth is multiplied later a thousandfold.
Aristotle

2)   *CHIEF COMMUNICATIONS OFFICER* is the head of an organizations communications, public affairs and public relations department. His responsibility includes both the company's internal and external communications.

3)   *SPIN DOCTOR* is the person who actually develops and writes the material to be used in public relations and advertising.

MARKETING

Marketing is not advertising. Advertising is a part of the total aspect of marketing. Marketing is one of the most important aspects of business and is the discipline for understanding customer needs. Marketing attempts to fill a need and provide a service. Advertising is one form of communicating marketing.[24]

1)   *STRATEGIC MARKETING* establishes internally how an organization will compete to gain advantage and is direct customer focused marketing:

Character is higher than intellect.
Ralph Waldo Emerson

- Product
- Pricing
- Promotion
- Placement

2)   *SIVA* is a variation in the thinking of the *PPPP* is direct customer.

- *Solution - Produc*t: The appropriate solution to the problem at hand.
- *Information - Promotion*: To disseminate the information for the solution.
- *Value - Price*: To inform the benefits and necessary sacrifices to be made.
- *Access - Place*: To make available the solution to the target group.

3) *OPERATIONAL MANAGEMENT* is focused on the external elements involved with the execution of Marketing, Public Relations and advertising.

- *People* are those desired to contact.
- *Process* involves providing the product and controlling the people.
- *Physical evidence* involves developing the 'perception' in the people's minds that the product is beneficial before the product is experienced.

4) *ADDITIONAL 4 P's* concentrates on strategic and tactical aspects of using the previous #1 - #3 Models of Marketing.

- *Personalization* makes the person feel important.
- *Participation* to get the person or people active in the cause or product.
- *Peer-to-peer* establishes a sense of equality.
- *Predictive Modeling* is to convince the product will work.

5) *COGNITIVE BIAS* involves psychological effects to statistics, social views and memory errors and alters anecdotal and legal evidence and outcomes.   Bias comes from life's loyalties. Bias is used as intellectual shortcuts for accommodation and leads to false beliefs, opinions and consensus.

- *Hindsight*: occurs when a person says they already knew an event was evident.
- *Fundamental*: seeks to explain an error made was personally made, not influenced by a situational analysis,
- *Confirmation*: confirms due to pre-conceptions as is cognitive dissonance.
- *Self-serving*: occurs when person claims more responsibility concerning successful events usually accompanied with ambiguous information.

6) *RESOURCES* available make competing more successful and include:

- *Finances* cash, money reserves and financing.
- *Physical* includes equipment and plant facilities.
- *Human* resources includes knowledge and skill.
- *Legal* resources involve securing trademarks and patents.
- *Organizational* assets are policies, competencies and business model.
- *Informational* is knowing the customer as well as the competition.

7) *RELATIONSHIPS* as in life with living with others the same applies with companies, organizations and social groups that come together. The eventual outcomes involve the following:

- *Win-Win*
- *Win-Lose*
- *Lose-Lose*
- *Lose-Win*

Try not to become a man of success but rather try to become a man of value.
Albert Einstein

Those who think it is permissible to tell white lies soon grow color blind.
Austin O'Malley

The right to do something does not mean that doing it is right.
William Safire

8) *BUSINESS MODELS* with standardization of products and products becoming very similar the concentration of Marketing involves less stress on the product and more on stressing the qualities of the business or organization itself.

9) *PRODUCT FOCUS* stresses innovation and then the new product's production and marketing. Yet some companies are solely research and development in the creation of our ever-expanding science and technology.

9) *CUSTOMER FOCUS* is the concentration of customer demands.

- Customer-driven approach
- Identifying market changes
- Market-driven approach

10) *OTHER* avenues that may aid in Marketing involve:

- *Internal Marketing* involves the training and management to help employees.
- *Diffusion of Innovations* stresses the reasons why and how customers accept new products because the most sophisticated product may not be the most successful product.
- *Personalized Marketing* includes the concept of "Reality Marketing" by using, with their permission, ordinary individuals to endorse their product.

THE HERD MENTALITY

Edward Bernays believed the common person was a member of the *Herd* of human existence and are to be led, directed, controlled and used by the *Elite* people in the world of which he considered himself to be one.

CENSORSHIP

An instance of censorship occurred when Marilyn Milos and her non-profit organization, NOCIRC, requested a presentation booth at a La Leche League's international conference. Her group advocates that circumcision disrupts breast feeding. NOCIRC was initially granted a booth but within 24 hours she was informed that Jewish and Muslim women threatened to boycott the conference if NOCIRC was granted a booth.[25]

Like all valuable com-modities, truth is often counterfeited.
James Cardinal Gibbons

Respect for the truth is an acquired taste.
Mark Van Doren

If you have integrity, nothing else matters. If you don't have integrity, nothing else matters.
Alan Simpson

Whoever would overthrow the liberty of a nation must begin by subduing freeness of speech.
Benjamin Franklin

LEGAL

Mute sanction legalizes

In 1996, United States Representatives Patricia Schroeder and Barbara Collins spearheaded a bill making Female Genital Mutilation (FGM) of minors a crime with up to five years imprisonment and a fine.[1] Yet infant and child clitoridectomy, clitoroplasty and labioplasty continue under the guise of a social need for conformity, and so doctors surgically alter the genitals of children born with Congenital Adrenal Hyperplasia (CAH).

In addition, male minors are not protected by the FGM law though Section 1 of the 14th Amendment to the United States Constitution clearly states:[2]

> All persons born or naturalized in the United States, and subject to the jurisdiction thereof, are citizens of the United States and of the States wherein they reside. No state shall make or enforce any law which shall abridge the privileges or immunities of citizens of the United States; nor shall any State deprive any person of life, or property, without due process of law; nor deny to any person within its jurisdiction the equal protection of the laws.

The FGM bill deprives the male child of *equal rights,* the *right to privacy* and *due process*. According to the existing law, protection of the male cannot extend from the FGM bill; a separate bill is required.

DELIBERATE DIFFERENCE

Deliberate indifference originated from prison inmate suits detailing a lack of, denial of or delay in needed medical care.[3] The opposite of deliberate indifference is *deliberate difference* where there is either:

1. special consideration given to an individual or group of persons or

2. overt and unnecessary action which harms one person or group of persons while those outside that group are legally protected from harm.

Well, those are the boobs that make our laws. That's the democratic process.
Hornbeck
Inherit the Wind

Law is a reflection and a source of prejudice. It both enforces and suggests forms of bias.
Diane B. Schudler

By the gender-based separation of protection[4] created by the Schroeder and Collins bill, genital mutilation of male minors should be perceived as a *deliberate difference.*[5]

> DELIBERATE DIFFERENCE: setting apart of an individual or identifiable group, either expressly or by mute sanction, for different laws, equality, equity, actions, or inactions

SOCIALIZED SEXUAL HARASSMENT

Sexual harassment is conduct of a sexual nature, including: verbal, physical, and visual conduct that is unsolicited and unwelcome. Title VII of the 1964 Civil Rights Act is the law used for most sexual harassment claims. Genital rituals constitute a socially sanctioned form of sexual harassment. There are two types of sexual harassment. These are: *hostile environment,* and *quid pro quo.*

To file a sexual harassment claim one does not need to be the person harassed. All that is necessary is to show a *hostile environment* exists or a *quid pro quo* has occurred. An institution is liable whether it knew, aided, or did not know sexual harassment occurred. It is the institution's responsibility to protect.

HOSTILE ENVIRONMENT

Hostile environment sexual harassment, like other sexual crimes, is based on power. It is usually perpetrated by people in authority on those who are perceived to be powerless. In the case of male genital alteration, this includes members of medical and religious institutions. Dominant attitudes that facilitate sexual harassment include: feeling one person is superior, the other inferior; a bias against the difference; required submission; and preference for the status quo, the societal norm. In short, the child will be a social outcast if he is not circumcised. All this before he is even one day old. It appears obvious that a hostile environment exists regarding circumcision.

> HOSTILE ENVIRONMENT: An atmosphere characterized by unwelcome sexual conduct which is severe and pervasive, some of which are:

- • Stalking behavior

- • Touching, hugging, kissing, or patting

- • Restraining or blocking a person's movement

STALKING BEHAVIOR: Decision makers (usually parents) have long reported having been pressured by authority figures (doctors, nurses, relatives) who demand they circumcise their male children. Some parents are asked numerous times, during delivery and after, for permission to circumcise, when they have clearly stated that they wish no circumcision to be performed. Others have had their infants returned to them, circumcised, even when they explicitly asked for no circumcision. Some lawsuits of this nature have been settled out of court. Due to the cavalier attitude toward routine infant circumcision, parents' wishes are not always taken seriously.

TOUCHING OR PATTING. The standard preparation for a medical circumcision is a five-minute rub on the penis with a sterile liquid.

RESTRAINING MOVEMENT: The child is usually restrained by a relative in a religious ritual circumcision and by the Velcro straps of a formfitting plastic *Circumstraint* board during a medical *routine infant circumcision* (RIC).

In religious ceremonies it is taught that circumcision is required to fulfill a covenant with God – for what? To ensure fame, power, honor and to procure land. And to avoid a curse: *Any uncircumcised male, who has not been circumcised in the flesh, will be cut off from his people; he has broken my covenant.*

In the case of routine infant circumcision protective parents have been disowned, harangued and harassed by medical personnel, relatives and friends. In the United States, once parents agree to circumcision, they are no longer harassed. They have pledged their allegiance to a system based on genital blood ritual. Protective parents have been harassed and threatened in numerous ways:

- Scowls of disapproval from the medical staff
- Your son will be teased in the locker room
- He will not fit in
- He will not bond with his father
- He will get venereal disease
- He will smell bad
- He will not be attractive to members of the opposite sex

QUID PRO QUO

QUID PRO QUO comes from the Latin term meaning *this for that*. This type of sexual harassment implies advantages in return for sexual favors.

It is true that the law is different, vis-à-vis for a woman.
Bianca Jagger

If you sue nobody will believe you, if you don't sue, your wife won't.
Catherine Alvarez

We live in an age of equality
Joe Orton

The point of *quid pro quo* is an exchange of something of value for sexual access. Social threats, coercion and extortion are all part of the circumcision ritual. Whether religious, medical, or tribal, circumcision costs money. And there is always someone who charges a fee.

Sex can be a form of value. This is a social precedent shown in what is called the *oldest profession*, prostitution. In some parts of Africa and the Middle East it is taught that both male and female circumcision is required for marriage. In the Philippines and the United States most the women appear to demand its males to be circumcised. The *quid pro quo* of circumcision is a socialized sexual trade-off for sex whether through religion or the secular.

LEGAL TRIANGLE

The legal basis for settling disputes can be seen as a triangle. At the center is *value*.

JUSTICE (JUDGE) INJUSTICE

ADMINISTRATIVE   CONGRESSIONAL
MORALITY   ETHICS
                    VALUE

RIGHT (PLAINTIFF) WRONG < = > LEGAL (DEFENDANT) ILLEGAL

PROSECUTION

A consultation with an attorney must be made. There have been successful suits against circumcision. Most have resulted from botched surgery. Yet, there has been success just because a circumcision has taken place. Avenues to prosecution, of individuals and medical personnel, *may possibly* be brought through breaches resulting from:

AGENCY

An agent or representative is in a position of great trust and confidence.[6] When it comes to the genital alterations of a minor, the fiduciary relationship is to the child, not the parent or social organization. Social agency responsibility is exclusively to and for the child.

An agent's power, control, and authority are supposed to be of a supportive capacity, yet in performing a genital blood procedure a circumcising agent is not neutral because he also derives benefit — monetary gain, social standing, or both. Whether performed by a secular physician or a mohel (religious ritual circumciser), substantial financial compensation is involved for genital blood ritual. So we see that the pressure exerted in favor of the procedure may be due to something other than potential benefit to the child.

ASSAULT & BATTERY

Given that genital injury is non-Jerusalemic, it is unlawful in religious origin, and it is immune from any civil protection when claimed to be medicine. If it happened to an adult, it would be considered assault and battery. Infant circumcision is assault and battery.[7,8]

> ASSAULT: An attempt or threat, with unlawful force, to inflict bodily injury upon another, accompanied by the present ability to give effect to the attempt if not prevented. Threat, coupled with present ability may be an assault. As a tort, an assault may be found even where no actual intent to make one exists if an actor places the victim in reasonable fear. Because an assault need not result in a touching so as to constitute a *battery*, no physical injury need be proved to establish an assault. An assault is both a personal **tort** and a criminal offense and thus may be a basis for a civil *action* and/or a criminal *prosecution*.

> AGGRAVATED ASSAULT: an assault where "serious bodily injury" is inflicted on the person assaulted; a particularly fierce or reprehensible assault; an assault exhibiting peculiar depravity or atrocity — including assaults committed with dangerous or *deadly weapons*; an assault committed with further crime.

> BATTERY: "the unlawful application of force to the person of another," the least touching of another person *willfully*, or in anger; . . In *tort* law the legal protection of battery extends to any part of one's body or to "anything so closely attached thereto that it is customarily regarded as a part thereof.

Assault with Attempt to Disfigure also applies to genital alterations.[9] This occurs often when parents divorce and one parent alters the son's genitals to punish the other parent.[10,11] This is a specific intent.[12]

> ASSAULT is a general intent offense requiring only the general *mens rea* common to any offense; "assault with intent to *rape*" is a specific intent offense requiring in addition to the general *mens rea* for an assault a special *mens rea* consisting of intent to rape the victim. In tort law, intent refers to an actor's desire to cause the consequences of his act or signifies that he believes that the consequences are substantially certain to result from it.

The judge is condemned when the criminal is absolved.
Publilius Syrus

Any action for which there is no logical explanation will be deemed Company Policy.
Second Law of Corporation

When the President does it, that means that it is not illegal.
Richard Nixon

CAUSE

Cause is the reason and motive for an action. Cause and effect is the relationship between an action to its results.[13]

CAUSE: that which effects a result. In law "cause" is not a constant and agreed-upon term. The following is a list of some of the attempts to conceptualize "that which effects a result":

DIRECT CAUSE: the active, efficient cause that sets in motion a train of events that brings about a result without the intervention of any other independent source.

IMMEDIATE CAUSE: the nearest cause in point of time and space; it is not necessarily direct or proximate cause.

PROXIMATE CAUSE: that which in natural and continuous sequence unbroken by any new independent cause produces an event, and without which the injury would not have occurred,

REMOTE CAUSE: that which does not necessarily produce an event without which injury would not occur. Thus, a cause which is not considered to be "proximate" will be regarded as "remote."

COERCION

Coercion is the act of compelling by force of authority.[14] It is forced compliance. Coercion changes the nature and range of options in choice. Force may be physical, or mental as: pressure, harassment, threats or intimidation. *Cultural coercion* is the fear produced from being forced out of the community. In the coercion of circumcision, it is the Modus Operandi in the Con type of Approach essential to obtaining compliance.

COMPETENCE

One is not competent to decide on circumcision when lacking knowledge. This may, or may not, be from an institution's purposeful misleading or omission to reasonably inform. Some people may not be physically or psychologically able to make a proper decision even if facts are presented. In *Competence to Consent*, Becky White explained:[15]

The procedures for informed consent include assessing patient's competence... Once patients are determined to be competent, they are given the information and a chance to digest it, ask questions, and relate it to their own value structures.

No written law has ever been more binding than unwritten custom supported by popular opinion.
Carrie Chapman Catt

It isn't a trial; it's a coroner's inquest – a much simpler procedure.
William Halleck
Thinner

In giving rights to others which belong to them, we give rights to ourselves and to our country.
John F. Kennedy

Patients are competent for the task of giving a free and informed consent if they are generally informable and cognitively capable of making decisions...

The nine individual criteria for competence to consent were assembled under four broad categories: informability, cognitive and affective capability, ability to choose, and ability to recount one's decision-making process. Informability consists of the capacities to (1) receive information, (2) recognize relevant information as information, and (3) remember information. Cognitive and affective capability includes the capacities to (4) relate situations to oneself, (5) reason about alternatives, and (6) rank alternatives. Choosing incorporates the abilities to (7) select an option and (8) resign oneself to the choice. Recounting one's decision-making process, alone among the broad capabilities, is not a composite. The only ability here is (9) the ability to explain, by way of recognizable reasons, how one came to one's decision...

This recognition requires that HCP's (Health Care Professionals) (1) provide their patients with full information about the situation in which a choice must be made; (2) work to maximize the Patient's ability to understand that information; (3) take care not to coerce patients' choices; and (4) implement autonomously chosen therapies."

CONSENT

One does not have a right to sign an Informed Consent form for a procedure they do not have informed knowledge of. Consent forms given to the parent for genital alteration do not include information about the many possible complications. The following definitions are from Pozgar's text *Legal Aspects of Health Care Administration*:[16]

CONSENT: Simply stated, a voluntary act by which one person agrees to allow someone else to do something

IGNORANCE OF FACT AND UNINTENTIONAL WRONG: Ignorance of the law is not a defense; otherwise, the ignorant would be rewarded. The fact that a negligent act is unintentional is no defense. Otherwise, defendants could never be found guilty.

FAILURE TO DISCLOSE/INFORMED CONSENT: A physician may be held liable for malpractice if, in rendering treatment to a patient, he or she does not make a proper disclosure to the patient of the risks involved in a procedure... The facts that must be disclosed are those facts the physician knows or should know that a patient needs to be aware of in order to make an informed decision on the course that future medical care will take.

Never again will I allow our self-interest to deter us from doing what we know to be morally right.
President James Marshall
Air Force One

This wasn't the deal! This wasn't the deal!
White Rabbit
Manhunt

Rights are invariably abridged as despotism increases.
Tacitus

After World War II, it was common for doctors to circumcise without parental consent. Lawsuits have recently lessened this practice.[17] Still there is tremendous pressure by hospitals and Health Care Providers for the procedure. Gifis *Law Dictionary* explains *express* and *implied* consent:[18]

> EXPRESS: To make known explicitly and in declared terms. To set forth an actual *agreement* in words, written or spoken, which unambiguously signifies intent. As distinguished from IMPLIED the term is not left to implication or interference from conduct or circumstances. When parties show their *agreement* in words they create an express *contract* as contrasted to a contract implied by circumstances alone, or a quasi-contract, which is applied in law in order to obtain justice.

CRUEL & UNUSUAL PUNISHMENT

From anger, hate, envy, and resentments actions of genital alteration constitute unwarranted punishment whose origins reside in psychosexual power relations.[19] It does not matter if these acts are from the social, medical, religious, or parental. These violent acts violate the 8th Amendment of the United States Constitution:

> Excessive bail shall not be required, nor excessive fines imposed, nor cruel and unusual punishments inflicted.

DUTY & ITS BREACH

Duty[20] is first to children. Parents, physicians, the religious and society are involved and share responsibility.

> DUTY: obligatory conduct owed by a person to another person. In *tort* law, duty is a legally sanctioned obligation the *breach* of which results in the *liability* of the actor. Thus, under the law of *negligence*, if an individual owes to others a DUTY OF CARE, he must conduct himself so as to avoid negligent injury to them.

> BREACH OF DUTY: a failure to perform a duty owed to another or to society; a failure to exercise that care which a *reasonable man* would exercise under similar circumstances.

> BREACH OF PROMISE: failure to do what one promises, where he has promised it in order to induce action in another.

> BREACH OF TRUST: violation by a *trustee* of a *duty* which *equity* lays upon him, whether willful and *fraudulent*, or done through *negligence*, or arising

through mere oversight and forgetfulness.

BREACH OF TRUST WITH FRAUDULENT INTENT: a *larceny* after *trust*, which includes all of the elements of larceny except the unlawful taking in the beginning.

ENDANGERMENT, ABANDONMENT & MOLESTATION

Due to the vast amount of medical errors, as well as from religious non-clinical procedures, genital alterations constitute child endangerment where protection of the minor is abandoned. Genital alterations constitute a form of socialized child molestation.

EXTORTION AND EXACTION

Extortion takes something of value by threat of violence or by undue exercise of power anything that is not due them, or more than due them. Extortion creates a fear. Exaction is a forced compliance and obedience as paying dues and fees. Circumcision is a form of social dues.

FRAUD

Fraud is an intentional deception. Surgery is defined as: *a medical procedure involving an incision with instruments; performed to repair damage or arrest disease in a living body*. Circumcision is performed on healthy genital tissue. The tissue is so pristine that it is sold in the pharmaceutical industry. Circumcision is the only elective surgery offered to infants in the United States. And the patient himself is not allowed a voice in the matter. The burden of "choice" is put upon the parents. But the choice is a false choice, not a legitimate choice.

Parents of American female children are not pressured by medical or religious authorities to make a decision between genital mutilation and genital integrity. Parents of male children should be protected from the pressure to circumcise their sons.

With a little research, parents will find that under the guise of religious or medical necessity, circumcision is not required either by God or for good health and hygiene. In societies where genitals are not mutilated, there is no social demand for unnaturally altered genitals. The American rate of male circumcision is decreasing to 50%. So, there is no social benefit for cutting boys' genitals and soon may become a source of family angst.

To ease adherents' minds, in the case of religious genital blood ritual,

So long as the paperwork's clean, you boys can do as you like out there.
MacAfee
Mad Max

Injustice anywhere is a threat to justice everywhere.
Rev. Martin Luther King, Jr.

I was forging documents before your parents were born.
Arthur
Apt Pupil

parents should be informed that the "circumcision covenant" was added to the original history of the Jewish people (*The Book of J*), over a thousand years after Abraham's death. Jewish scholars say that the "circumcision covenant" was added by corrupt priests. What better way to mandate a new fashion than to say God commanded it? It is edifying to compare the version of the story of the rape of Dinah in the Old Testament Bible to the original version in *The Book of J*. Circumcision and mass slaughter was also added to that story at the time the "circumcision covenant" was added to the Abraham story.

To eliminate medical pressure to circumcise, the full history and complete facts about refuted health claims plus the current information from healthy non-circumcising cultures such as Europe, China, and Japan should be provided parents. It should clearly be explained to parents that the child does indeed feel pain and that it is possible he will remember the procedure; recall can recur symbolically in childhood nightmares or as conscious memory in adulthood. Full disclosure of the details of the procedure, from the five-minute benzocaine rub to the separation of prepuce from glans, skin amputation and resultant common problems such as skin bridges and meatal stenosis, loss of pleasure sensors, pain upon erection, adult sexual dysfunction, and the danger of glans amputation and/or death should be provided. If cutting is to be performed by a medical school student, the parents should be warned of that possibility. Neglecting to inform parents of the full truth of what is to happen to a child in their care constitutes fraud. Ignorance of the law is not a defense, so professional continuing education in this matter is imperative.[21]

FRAUD: Intentional deception resulting in *injury* to another. Elements of fraud are: a false and material misrepresentation made by one who either knows it is falsity or is ignorant of its truth; the maker's intent that the representation be relied on by the person and in a manner reasonably contemplated; the person's ignorance of the falsity of the representation; the person's rightful or justified reliance; and proximate injury to the person.

CONSTRUCTIVE [LEGAL] FRAUD: Comprises all acts, omissions, and concealments involving *breach* of *equitable* or *legal duty*, trust or confidence and resulting in damage to another, no *scienter* is required. Thus, the party who makes the misrepresentation need not know it is false.

EXTRINSIC [COLLATERAL] FRAUD: Fraud that prevents a party from knowing about his rights or *defenses* or from having a fair opportunity of presenting them at a trial, or from fully *litigating* at the trial all the rights or defenses

Peace isn't merely the absence of conflict, but the presence of justice.
President James Marshall
Air Force One

You'll write this up as a training accident.
Colonel Mekum
Soldier

Wrong must not win by technicalities.
Aeschylus

that he was entitled to assert.

FRAUD IN FACT [POSITIVE FRAUD]: Actual fraud. Deceit. Concealing something or making a false representation with an evil intent [scienter] when it causes injury to another. It is used in contrast to CONSTRUCTIVE FRAUD (above) which does not require an evil intent.

FRAUD IN LAW: Fraud that is presumed from circumstances, where the one who commits it need not have any evil intent to commit a fraud; it is a CONSTRUCTIVE FRAUD.

FRAUD IN THE FACTUM: Generally arises from a lack of identity or disparity between the *instrument*, executed and the one intended to be executed, or from circumstances which go to the question as to whether the instrument ever had any legal existence; as for example, when a blind or illiterate person executes a deed when it has been read falsely to him after he asked to have it read. Fraud in the factum provides a stronger basis for setting aside an instrument than FRAUD IN THE INDUCEMENT.

FRAUD IN THE INDUCEMENT: Fraud which is intended to and which does cause one to execute an *instrument*, or make an agreement, or render a *judgment*. The misrepresentation involved does not mislead one as to the paper he signs but rather misleads as to the true facts of the situation, and the false impression it causes is a basis of a decision to sign or render a judgment.

HEALTH CARE FRAUD: Whoever knowingly and willfully executes, or attempts to execute, a scheme or artifice -

(1) To defraud any health care benefit program; or

(2) To obtain, by means of false or fraudulent pretenses, representations, or promises, any of the money or property owned by, or under the custody or control of, any health care benefit program,

In connection with the delivery of or payment for health care benefits, items, or services, shall be fined under this title or imprisoned not more than 10 years, or both. If the violation results in serious bodily injury (as defined by section 1365 of this section), such person shall be fined under this title or imprisoned not more than 20 years, or both; and if the violation results in death, such person shall be fined under this title, or imprisoned for any term of years or for life, or both (Sec. 1365.3) The term "serious bodily injury" means bodily injury which involves

(A) A substantial risk of death

(B) Extreme pain

> *No man is above the law and no man is below it; nor do we ask man's permission when we require to obey it. Obedience to the law is demanded as a right; not asked for as a favor.*
> **Theodore Roosevelt**

> *That which is not just, is not law.*
> **Lloyd Garrison**

> *The law hath not been dead, though it hath slept.*
> **William Shakespeare**

(C) Protracted and obvious disfigurement; or

(D) Protracted loss or impairment of the function of a bodily member, organ, or mental faculty, and

(Sec. 1365.4) The term "bodily injury" means -

(A) A cut, abrasion, bruise, burn, or disfigurement;

(B) Physical pain;

(C) Illness;

(D) Impairment of the function of a bodily member, organ, or mental faculty;

(E) Any other injury to the body, no matter how temporary

HATE CRIME

Hate crimes are crimes of intolerance.[22]

A hate crime is a criminal offense committed against persons, property or society that is motivated, in whole or in part, by an offender's bias against an individual's or group's race, religion, ethnic/national origin, gender, age, disability or sexual orientation.

There are four categories of hate crimes: 1) thrill seeking, 2) reactive, 3) retaliatory and (4) mission.

There is *thrill* in ritual events. (1) The offender is motivated by a social or psychological thrill and by the approval of peers. (2) Generally there is no precipitating incident on the part of the victim. (3) The offender usually seeks out the victim in the victim's setting; and, (4) The victim is identified as a "different" member of a particular group.

Reaction genital mutilations arise from being the opposite sex or different religion. Then perpetration stems from the *imago vivendi*. (1) The hate crime is motivated by the perpetrator's perception that an "outsider" poses a threat to a way of life. (2) Occurrence is chiefly within the perpetrator's living space. (3) Intimidation often turns to physical violence.

Retaliation involves (1) motivation from prejudice and (2) may involve large group activity.

With the *Mission* type perpetrator: (1) All members of the despised group are targeted, (2) Offenders believe they are attacking an inferior group, (3) Often the perpetrator believes he is instructed by a "higher power," (4) There is a sense of urgency and (5) The perpetrator may suffer from mental illness.

Wherever Law ends, Tyranny begins
John Locke

He's only the key witness in the biggest health reform issue, maybe the biggest, most-expensive corporate malfeasance case in the U. S. history.
Lowell Bergman

Whereas each man claims his freedom as a matter of right, the freedom he accords to other men is a matter of toleration.
Walter

The mission may be hygienic from fear of penetration giving rise to a purification ritual justified through the *imago Vivendi*. Missions also glorify, be it a glorification of the sex not mutilated, or the social body in which the inhabitants live.

INTENT

Intent of the perpetrator, or perpetrators, is not considered in child abuse. To stop social abuses as unwarranted medical and religious genital alterations, the defense *for the good of the children* is inadmissible as a falsity in denial, deferral and deflection.[23]

> INTENT: a state of mind wherein the person knows and desires the consequences of his act which, for purposes of criminal *liability*, must exist at the time the offense is committed. The existence of this state of mind is often impossible to prove directly; consequently, it must be determined from reasonable deductions, such as the likelihood that the act in question would result in the consequent injury.

Two general classes of *intent* exist in the criminal law:

> GENERAL INTENT, which must exist in all crimes, and SPECIFIC INTENT, which is essential to certain crimes and which, must be proved beyond a reasonable doubt.

MAYHEM

Mayhem[24] is the taking of a body part, rendering the victim less functional. With circumcision this is the specific intent in the 13th Century literature of Rabbi Moses Maimonaides. This is also the psychological intent related by Dr. Frank Zimmerman in the Psychoanalytical Review regarding the feminine demand for circumcision.[25] These intents are still used today as well as being factors within the Munchausen Complex.

> MAYHEM the common law *felony* of maliciously *maiming* or dismembering or in any other way depriving another of the use of any part of his body so as to render him less able to fight in the king's army.

Some states have retained *mayhem* as a separate offense, although usually the specific intent to maim or disfigure rather than the general intent to act with malice, must be established. Many states simply treat the crime of *mayhem* as an *aggravated assault*.

If you study hate crimes… you find that they tend to be highly public, highly symbolic.
John Douglas
Mind Hunter

The Geneva Convention is void here. Amnesty International doesn't know we exist.
Walton
Face Off

The Rule of Law can be wiped out in one misguided, however well-intentioned, generation.
William T. Gossett

MENS REA

Mens rea is the psychological state, frame of mind of the person who commits a crime. This is to be considered in the perpetrator who acts, as well as the person who transfers the authority to act. The following connects: 1) FBI findings regarding sexual homicides to, 2) Mens rea:[26,27]

> FRAME OF MIND is a general descriptive term for a dominant emotional state that acts as a primary filter and interpreting mechanism regarding external events. The frame of mind of the offenders just before the crime revealed highly negative emotional states... These findings suggest that there is little emotion experienced by the killer that reflects any sense of vulnerability, thereby permitting the killer to interpret the behavior of the victim in the most negative manner. The frame of mind and mood states illustrate how the killer supports his negative cognitions and justification for the crime. There is no emotional reservoir to relate to vulnerability, pain, and fear of the victim."

> MENS REA: a guilty mind; the mental state accompanying a forbidden act. For an act to constitute a criminal offense, the act usually must be accompanied by a requisite mental state. Criminal offenses are usually defined within reference to one of four recognized criminal states of mind that accompanies the actor's conduct: (1) intentionally; (2) knowingly; (3) recklessly; and (4) grossly [criminally] negligent.

NEGLIGENCE

Negligence is in all phases of circumcision from initial medical consultation, omissions in consent forms, to *administrative negligence* through *deliberate difference* or failure to protect. There is a high incidence of complications in genital alterations.[28] Ten percent of circumcised boys will suffer from meatal stenosis. One hundred percent of circumcised boys will suffer loss of sexual sensation. Willful negligence occurs when information is withheld on purpose, regardless of intent.[29]

> NEGLIGENCE: failure to exercise that degree of care which a person of ordinary prudence (a *reasonable man* [*person*]) would exercise under the same circumstances. The term refers to conduct which falls below the standard established by law for the protection of others against unreasonable risk of harm.

> CONCURRENT NEGLIGENCE: the wrongful acts or *omissions* of two or more persons acting independently but causing the same injury. The independent actions do not have to occur at the same time, but must produce the same

result. The actors are all responsible for paying the damages, and can usually be sued together in one lawsuit or individually in separate lawsuits.

CRIMINAL [CULPABLE] NEGLIGENCE: such negligence as is necessary to incur criminal liability; in most jurisdictions, culpable [criminal] negligence is something more than the slight negligence necessary to support a civil action for damages. Thus, culpable negligence, "under criminal law", is recklessness and carelessness resulting in injury or death, as imports a thoughtless disregard of consequences or a heedless indifference to the safety and rights of others.

WANTON NEGLIGENCE: an intentional act of an unreasonable character in disregard of a risk known, or so obvious that it must have been known, and so great as to make it highly probable that harm would follow. The act is usually accompanied by a conscious indifference to the consequences amounting to willingness that they shall follow. The term "wanton" is used synonymously with WILLFUL, or RECKLESS

RACKETEERING

Racketeering is dishonest and fraudulent business dealings. The Rico Act was established in 1970 to combat *racketeering* in organized crime. Section 1964(c) allows civil claims. There are provisions that appear to apply to genital alterations from the actions of some social entities, health care organizations as medical societies, hospitals, and birthing centers; as well as, individuals. Two specific areas are: 1) extortion that involves making an individual willing to give something of value induced through violence, fear (as false health claims about disease consequences if a person is not circumcised), or under color of official right; and, 2) the sexual exploitation of children under sections 2251, 2251A, 2252, and 2260 of the Rico Act.[30]

RELIGIOUS CHILD ABUSE EXEMPTIONS

The myth of Abraham is questionable because the original history of the Jewish people was edited to include circumcision. Anything other than Abraham's origin, from whom precedence is claimed, is not in the construct of religious exemption. Religious procedures are not protected under statutes of Religious Exemptions to Child Abuse laws.[31] With Abraham's covenant of the circumcision, this means nothing more and nothing less. Any and all instances of presently practiced genital alterations on any person under the legal age of consent may, and must, be halted.[32] The Committee on Bioethics states:[33]

Well there's nothing like avoiding a little manslaughter charge to turn a man's life around.
Kirk
Thinner

The United States is a nation of laws; badly written and randomly enforced.
Frank Zappa

There are too many lawyers in Memphis. The place is infested with them... Do you know when you sold out?
Rudy

However, the constitutional guarantees of freedom of religion do not sanction harming another person in the practice of one's religion, and do not allow religion to be a legal defense when one harms another... The Committee on Bioethics asserts that (1) the opportunity to grow and develop safe from physical harm with the protection of our society is the right of every child.

RELIGIOUS FREEDOM

Jerusalemic circumcision is based on the mythic Abrahamic account. The severity of the circumcision cut was increased around 140 AD and again about 500 AD. At the time that circumcision was in fashion, they only made a mark in the foreskin; they did not perform full prepuce ablation. Further both Islam and Judaism, as well as most mutilating cultures have mutilated both sexes. The Schroeder-Collins Bill, no matter how well meaning, by omitting males is in essence a form of Congressional religious establishment.[34]

> Congress shall make no laws respecting an establishment of a religion, or prohibiting the free exercise thereof; or abridging the freedom of speech, or of the press, or the right of the people peaceably to assemble, and to petition the government for a redress of grievances.

STATUTE OF LIMITATIONS

California eliminated time limits in child abuse claims. Recently California has allowed males suing priests for sexual abuse decades before.

TORT

In creating the social breach by changing the circumcision of Abraham, from whom precedence is claimed, with its transference to medicine, both religion and medicine have misguided society's expectations of them.[35,36]

> TORT: a wrong; a private or *civil* wrong or injury resulting from a breach of legal duty that exists by virtue of society's expectations regarding interpersonal conduct, rather than by *contract* or other private relationship. The essential elements of a tort are the existence of a legal duty owed by a *defendant* to a *plaintiff, breach* of that duty, and a causal relation between defendant's conduct and the resulting damage to plaintiff.

OTHER

Other avenues for prosecution are: solicitation, damages, medical records and medical staff relationships because destruction of medical records has occurred during law suits.

ENDNOTES

Two legal standards means no legal standards

INTRODUCTION

1.   Monteleone, James A., *Recognition of Child Abuse for the Mandated Reporter*, G. W. Medical Publishing, Inc., St. Louis, MO, 1996, p. 1.

2.   Dawkins, Richard, *The Selfish Gene*, Oxford University Press, Oxford, 1976.

3.   Young. Hugh, *Circumcision as a Memeplex*. Presented at the 8th International Symposium on Circumcision and Human Rights, Padova, Italy, September 3, 2004.

4.   Author unknown, thanks to Dorothy Davis, *That's the Way it's Always Been: Legacy Systems — Fear by Osmosis*.

5.   Slater, Philip, *The Glory of Hera*, Princeton University Press, 1992, p. 78.

6.   Monteleone, James A., *Recognition of Child Abuse for the Mandated Reporter*, p. 34.

7.   Benis AM, "A theory of personality traits leads to a genetic model for borderline types and schizophrenia," *Speculations in Science & Technology* (1990) Vol. 13, No. 3, pp. 167-175, (24 August 2008).

8.   Vaknin, Shmuel (Sam), *Malignant Self Love: Narcissism Revisited*. (All following web pages last accessed 10 February 2007) http://samvac.tripod.com/; http://samvac.tripod.com/cv.html; http://malignantselflove.tripod.com; http://malignantselflove.tripod.com/journal1.html; http://malignantselflove.tripod.com/indexqa.html; http://malignantselflove.tripod.com/abuse.html; http://malignantselflove.tripod.com/abusefamily.html. Narcissism is an important factor in serial sexual predation both individually and socially. Ken Heilbrunn's biography of Sam Vaknin states: "Sam Vaknin is the author of *Malignant Self Love — Narcissism Revisited* and *After the Rain — How the West Lost the East*. He served as a columnist for *Global Politician, Central Europe Review, PopMatters, Bellaonline,* and *eBookWeb,* a United Press International (UPI) Senior Business Correspondent, and the editor of Mental Health and Central East European categories in *The Open Directory and Suite 101*."

9.   Summit, Roland, "The Child Sexual Abuse Accommodation Syndrome," *Child Abuse and Neglect*, 7: 177, 1983.

10.   Garrison, Arthur H., "Child Sexual Abuse Accommodation Syndrome: Issues of Admissibility in Criminal Trials," *IPT Journal*, vol. 10, 1998. (24 December 2006)

11.   Finkel MA and Giardino AP, *Medical Evaluation of Child Sexual Abuse: A Practical Guide*, Sage, 2001.

12.   Hodges, Fredrick, "The Ideal Prepuce in Ancient Greece an Rome: Male Genital Aesthetics and Their Relation to 'Lipodermos', Circumcision, Foreskin Restoration, and the 'Kynodesme'", *The Bulletin of the History of Medicine*, vol. 75: pp. 375-405, Fall 2001.

13.   Jezeck, Laura, *What the Bible Really Says About Routine Infant Circumcision,* www.stopcirc.com/, 2010.

14.   Monteleone, James A., *Recognition of Child Abuse for the Mandated Reporter*, p. 34.

MUNCHAUSEN

1.   Asher, Richard (1951). "Munchausen Syndrome," *The Lancet*, i: 339-41.

2.   American Psychiatric Association, *Quick Reference to the: Diagnostic Criteria From DSM-IV*, American Psychiatric Publishing, Washington, DC, 1994, pp. 227.

3.   Meadow, Roy, (1977). "Munchausen Syndrome by Proxy: The Hinterland of Child Abuse," *The Lancet*, ii: 342-5.

4.   American Psychiatric Association, *Quick Reference to the: Diagnostic Criteria From DSM-IV*, American Psychiatric Publishing, Washington, DC, 1994, p. 228.

5.   Libow JA, Schreier HA, (1986), "Three Forms of Factitious Illness in Children: When is it Munchausen Syndrome by Proxy?," *American Journal of Orthopsychiatry*, 56(4):602:11.

6.   Douglas, John with Olshaker, Mark, *Journey into Darkness*, Pocket Books, NY, p.75.

7.   Douglas, John with Olshaker, Mark, *Obsession*, Pocket Books, NY, p. 284.

8.   Tantum D, Whittaker J, "Personality Disorder and Self-wounding," *British Journal of Psychiatry*, 1992, 161, 451-464.

9.   Van der Kolk BA, "The Compulsion to Repeat Trauma: Re-enactment, Revictimization, and Masochism," *Psychiatric Clinics of North America*, Volume 12, Number 2, Pages 389-411, June 1989.

10.   Glucklich A, "Self and Sacrifice, A Phenomenological Psychology of Sacred Pain," *Harvard Theological Review*, October 1999.

11.   Ibid

12.   D'Emilio, Francis, "Pope Canonizes Opus Dei Founder," *WorldWide Religious News*, 06 October 2002.

13.   Krushelnycky, Askold, "Afghanistan: Shias Openly Celebrate Ashura For First Time In Six Years," *Radio Free Europe*.

14.   Hayden, Dorothy C., "*Masochism As A Spiritual Path*," Sextreatment.com, 2004

15.   Campbell, Joseph, *The Power of Myth*, Doubleday, New York, NY, 1988.

16.   Petricolas T, Tillis SI, Cross-Poline GN, "Oral and Perioral Piercing: A Unique Form of Self-Expression,"

The Journal of Contemporary Dental Practice, Vol. 1, No 3, Summer 2000.

17.   Editorial, "Ice Age Acupuncture?," *Acupuncture*, June 2000, Volume 01, Issue 06.

18.   *Today*, June 2000, Volume 01, Issue 06.

19.   "The Ancient Mummies of China," television video, *The History Channel*.

20.   Editorial, "Highlight of the Maha Kumbha Mela," *Yoga in Daily Life News*, 6th Edition / 03 — 2001. p. 52.

21.   Editorial, "Looking behind the Bushes," *Star Weekly*, July 27, 1999.

22.   Marcus, Francis, "Chinese find learning English a snip," *BBC News*, Asia-Pacific, 31 July 2002.

23.   Fastlicht, Samuel, *Tooth Mutilations and Dentistry in Pre-Columbian Mexico*, Barnes & Noble, New York, NY, pp. 35-39, 105, 89 and 110.

24.   deMause, Lloyd, *The Emotional Life of Nations*, The Other Press, New York, NY, pp. 238 and 314.

25.   Dowd M, "Liberties: Herd on the Street," *New York Times*, New York, NY, April 11, 2001.

GENITAL PLAY

1.   Hellsten SK, "Rationalising circumcision: from tradition to fashion, from public health to individual freedom — critical notes on cultural persistence of the practice of genital mutilation," *Journal of Medical Ethics* 2004; 30: 248-253.

2.   Im-em, Wassana and Siriratmongkhon, "Gender Pleasure: Exploration of Sex Gadgets, Penile Implants, and Related Beliefs in Thailand," Mahidol University, I*nstitute for Population and Social Research*, first draft, August 18, 2002.

3.   deMause, Lloyd, "The Universality of Incest," *The Journal of Psychohistory*, Fall 1991, Vol. 19, No. 2.

4.   Talmudic paraphrase reference: Patricia Robinett. For Talmudic Socratic style of debate see: 1) Sanhedrin 55b, 2) Kethuboth 11b, 3) Niddah, 5:4, 4) Yebamoth 60b, 5) Kethuboth 5-6, 7) Yebamoth 55b.

5.   deMause, Lloyd, "The Emotional Life of Nations," in Chapter 7 (Part 2) — 'Childhood and Cultural

Evolution.' Originally: *The Journal of Psychohistory*, v.26, N. 3, Winter 1999.

6. deMause, Lloyd, "The History of Child Abuse," *The Journal of Psychohistory* 25 (3) Winter 1998. (10 August 2006). Last portion from text: *The History of Childhood: The Untold Story of Child Abuse*, Jason Aronson, 1995.

7. King, Paul, "Western History of Male Infibulation: Piercing of the Foreskin," *The Point*, Issue 19, 2001.

8. Coe, Michael, *The Maya*, Thames and Hudson, London, 1997, pp. 12, 173 and 184.

9. Schele, Linda and Freidel, David, *A Forest of Kings: The Untold Story of the Ancient Maya*, pp. 89, 111, 149, 202, 233, 281, 286, 426 and 447.

10. Private conversation with Charles R. Brown.

11. Faulkner, Raymond, trans., (The Papyrus of Ani), *The Egyptian Book of the Dead: The Book of Going Forth by Day*.

12. Slater, Phillip, *The Glory of Hera: Greek Mythology and the Greek Family*, p. 7.

13. Glick, Leonard, *Marked in Your Flesh: Circumcision from Ancient Judea to Modern America*, Oxford University Press, 2005.

14. Hoffman, Lawrence, *Covenant of Blood: Circumcision and Gender in Rabbinic Judaism*.

15. Schaalje, Jacqueline, "Timna," *The Jewish Magazine*, October 2005.

16. Wallerstein, Edward, *Circumcision: An American Health Fallacy*.

17. Slater, Phillip E., *The Glory of Hera: Greek Mythology and the Greek Family*, pp. 97, and 79.

18. deMause, Lloyd, *The Emotional Life of Nations*, Chapter 7 (Part 2: 'Childhood and Cultural Evolution.' Originally in: "The Journal of Psychohistory," v. 26, N. 3, Winter 1999.

19. Ngcakani, Anelisa, "Ban circumcision schools — pastor. Ungodly practices are taking place at them, he says, including initiates eating their foreskins," *Dispatch*, 01 Sept. 2006.

20. deMause, Lloyd, "The Universality of Incest,"

The Journal of Psychohistory, Fall 1991,Vol. 19, NO. 2:123-64.

21. Dr. Pia Gallo, University of Padua, Padua, Italy.

22. Lichtarowicz, Ania, "Genital Mutilation Still Common: Female genital mutilation is still commonplace in Sudan, despite it being illegal, a new study has found," *BBC News*, 10 June 2003. (07 August 2006)

23. Heitman, Rhonda, *Female Genital Mutilation*, Wolvesdreams, 2006.

24. World Health Organization, *Female Genital Mutilation*.

25. Slater, Phillip E., *The Glory of Hera: Greek Mythology and the Greek Family*, Princeton University Press, Princeton, NJ, 1968, pp. 78-79.

26. World Health Organization, *Female Genital Mutilation*,

27. Klein, Hanny-Lightfoot, *A Woman's Odyssey into Africa: Tracks Across a Life,* Nunzio Press, Eugene, OR 2009.

28. World Health Organization, *Female Genital Mutilation*.

29. Klein, Hanny-Lightfoot, "Similarities in Attitudes and Misconceptions toward Infant Male Circumcision in North America and Ritual Female Genital Mutilation in Africa," *FGM Network*, 2006.

30. Bryan, Jenny, "Designer vaginas," *Health Magazine*, February, 2002.

31. Klein, Hanny-Lightfoot, "Similarities in Attitudes and Misconceptions toward Infant Male Circumcision in North America and Ritual Female Genital Mutilation in Africa," *FGM Network*, 2006.

32. Ibid.

33. Farah, Caesar, *Islam*, Barrons Educational Series, Great Neck, NY, 1994, p. 13.

34. Williams, John Alden, *The Word of Islam*, Texas University Press, Austin, 1994, p. 180.

35. Lee, Romeo B, "Filipino experience of ritual male circumcision: Knowledge and Insights for anti-circumcision advocacy," *Culture, Health & Sexuality*, May-June 2006; 8(3): 225-234.

36. Diaz A, "Dorsal Slit, A Circumcision Alternative," *Ob & Gyn*, 37: 619, 1971.

37. deMause, Lloyd, *The Universality of Incest.*

38. Canserver, Gocke, "Psychological Effects of Circumcision," *British Journal of Medicinal Psychology*, Vol. 38: pp. 321-331, December 1965.

39. McFayden, Anne, "Children have feelings too," *British Medical Journal*, vol. 316, page 1616, 23 May 1998.

40. Glover E, "The 'screening' function of traumatic memories," *International Journal of Psychoanalysis*, 1929; 10:90-93.

41. Kennedy and Hansi, "Trauma in Childhood: Signs and Sequelae as Seen in the Analysis of an Adolescent," *Psychoanalytic Study of the Child* (1986), Vol. 41: Pages 20-219.

42. Estes, Clarissa Pinkola, *Women Who Run With the Wolves, Myths and Stories of the Wild Woman Archetype*, p. 9.

43. Glick, Leonard, *Marked in Your Flesh.*

44. Christiane Amanpour, *CNN News.*

45. Batsheva, Bonne-Tamir and Avinoam, Adam, editors., *New Perspectives on Genetic Markers and Diseases among Jewish People,* Oxford University Press, Oxford, 1992.

46. Congenital Adrenal Hyperplasia Education and Support Network, www.congenitaladrenalhyperplasia. org/, 2010.

47. "Newborn," *State of Texas Department of Health*, 2007.

48. Colapinto, John, *As Nature Made Him: the boy who was raised as a girl,* Harper Perennial, NY, 2001.

49. Surgery Encyclopedia, "Sex-Reassignment-Surgery," *Surgeryencyclopedia.com*, 2007.

RITUAL

1. Campbell, Joseph, *Primitive Mythology: The Masks of God*, Penguin Arkana, NY, NY, 1959, pp. 283-297 and 319-322.

2. Bell, Catherine, *Ritual Theory, Ritual Practice,* Oxford University Press, 1992, p. 215.

3. Ibid, pp. 215, 102 and 197.

4. Ibid, Bell referencing Pierre Bourdieu's *Outline of a Theory of Practice,* Cambridge University Press, Cambridge, UK, 1977, pp. 120, 207 (and note 75), and 111 (quoting Claude Levi-Strauss *The Naked Man: Introduction to a Science of Mythology*, vol. 4, Harper and Row, NY, 1981, pp. 185 and 188).

5. Bell, Catherine, *Ritual Theory, Ritual Practice*, pp. 173-174.

6. Dr. Joyce Brothers, *Today*, 28 October 1996.

7. Bell, Catherine, *Ritual Theory, Ritual Practice*, p. 106.

8. Ibid, Bell referencing Steven Lukes, "Political Rituals and Social Integration," *Journal of the British Sociological Association*, 9, no.2, (1975), pp. 289-291, 300 and 305.

9. Ibid, p. 96.

10. United Kingdom, Ambrose, "Somali refugee follows in Fortuyn's footsteps with attacks on imams," *The Standard*, 12 January 2003. Filed: 11 January 2003.

11. Bell referencing JC Heesterman, *The Inner Conflict of Tradition*, University of Chicago Press, Chicago, Il, 1985.

12. Premi Mahendra K, Raju S, "Born to Die: Female Infanticide in Madyha Pradesh, India," *Search Bulletin*, July-Sept. 1998, 13(3) pp. 94-105.

13. Aravamudan, Gita, "Born to Die," *Rediff Special*, India, 24 October 2001.

14. Miles, Tom, "6000 Girls Reportedly Circumcised Every Day," *Reuters, London*, 8 March 2002.

15. El-Gibaly O, Ibrahim B, Mensch B, Clark W, "The decline of female circumcision in Egypt: evidence and interpretation," *Social Science & Medicine*, 54 (2002) 205-220.

16. Durant, W, *The Story of Civilization: Part II: The Life of Greece*, Simon and Schuster, NY, 1966, pp. 582-584.

17. Fishkoff, Sue "Female Mohels Increasing Presence," *JTA Wire Service*, 19 Jan. 2006.

18. Bell, Catherine, *Ritual Theory, Ritual Practice*, pp. 23,26.

19. R.J. Zwi Werblowski and G. Wignor, editors., *The Oxford Dictionary of the Jewish Religion*, Oxford University Press, Oxford, UK, 1997, p. 161.

20. Bigelow, Jim, *The Joy of Uncircumcising*, Hourglass Book Publishing, Aptos, CA, 1992.

21. Rank, Hugh, *Language and Public Policy*, Macmillan, NY, 1975.

22. Bell, Catherine, *Ritual Theory, Ritual Practice*, pp. 173 and 216.

23. Ibid, p. 215.

24. Maslow, Abraham, *Motivation and Personality*, Harper, NY, 1954.

25. Berne, Eric, *Games People Play*, Harper, NY, 1967, p. 24.

26. Ibid, pp. 29, 35-36, 36-37, 41, and 48.

27. FitzMaurice, Kevin E., *The Tripartite Nature of Ego*. www.kevinfitzmaurice.com/ego_three_part_nature. htm and kevinfitxmaurice.com/ego_3_part_structure. htm, 2005.

CRIMINOLOGY

1. Evans, Colin, *The Casebook of Forensic Detection: How Science Solved 100 of the World's Most Baffling Crimes*, John Wiley & Sons, NY, 1996, p. 17.

2. Reid WH, Myths About Violent Sexual Predators and All That Pesky Legislation, *J Pract Psychiatry and Behav Health*, July 1998, 4:246-248.

3. Fletcher, Connie, *What Cops Know*, Pocket, NY, 1996, pp. 118 and 130.

4. Private conversation with two female Correctional Officers, Solano County, CA.

5. Michaud, Stephen with Hazelwood, Roy, *The Evil That Men Do*, St. Martin's, New York, NY, 1998, pp. 138-9, 313.

6. Keppel RD, and Birnes WJ, *Signature Killers*, Pocket Books, NY, 1997, pp. xxi, 2-7.

7. Michaud, Stephen with Hazelwood, Roy, *The Evil That Men Do*, p. 139.

8. Ibid, p. 40.

9. Arnold, Tom, "Female perversions not uncommon: study," *National Post*, 03 Dec. 1999.

10. Douglas, John with Olshaker, Mark, *Mind Hunter: Inside the FBI's Elite Serial Crime Unit*, Pocket Books, NY, 1995, p. 252.

11. Sacks, Glenn J., *4 Feminist Myths about Domestic Violence*. Referring to a study by R. I McNeeley and Coramae Richey Mann, www.glennsacks.com/4_feminists_myths.htm, 2005.

12. Cullen, Robert, *Citizen X*, Ivy Books, New York, NY, 1992.

13. Frazer, James George, *The Belief in Immortality and the Worship of the Dead*, Macmillan, New York, NY, p. 254.

14. Graves, Robert, *The Greek Myths*, Complete Edition, Penguin, New York, NY, 1992, p. 119.

15. Douglas, John and Olshaker, Mark, *The Anatomy of Motive*, Pocket, New York, NY, 1999, pp. 279, 262, 289-313 and 367.

16. Michaud, Stephen with Hazelwood, Roy, *The Evil That Men Do*, pp. 164-165, and 84.

17. Douglas, John with Olshaker, Mark, *The Anatomy of Motive*, Pocket, New York, NY, 1999, p. 351.

18. Douglas, John with Olshaker, Mark, *Obsession*, Pocket, New York, NY, 1998, p. 96.

19. *Victim Characteristics*, US Department of Justice.

20. Douglas, John with Olshaker, Mark, *Obsession*, pp. 332-333.

21. *Stalking*, South Carolina Coalition Against Domestic Violence and Sexual Assault.

22. Douglas, John with Olshaker, Mark, *Obsession*, pp. 277-279.

23. Vaknin, Shmuel (Sam), *Malignant Self Love Narcissism Re-visited*, Narcissus Pub., Czech Republic, 2003.

24. Douglas, John with Olshaker, Mark, *Obsession*, pp. 109-112, 124 and 352.

25. Hazelwood, Robert R., "The Criminal Sexual Sadist," *Law Enforcement Bulletin*, (FBI), February

1992.

26. Douglas, John with Olshaker, Mark, *Journey into Darkness*, Pocket, NY, 1995, pp. 33-34, 43, 66 and 75.

27. Michaud, Stephen with Hazelwood, Roy pp. 81-98.

28. University of Dundee, United Kingdom, *Personality Profiling,* Forensic Medicine Course Lecture Notes.

29. Douglas with Olshaker, *Obsession*, p. 31.

30. Sean Wolf Hill, *Nurture-Born Killers: The Motivation and Personality Development of the Serial Killer*, Fall 1994. Title of Student's paper, Wright State University.

31. *Effects of Domestic Violence on Children and Adolescents: An Overview,* www.aaets.org/article8.htm

32. National Association of Counsel for Children, *Child Maltreatment*, Denver, Colorado.

33. Ibid.

34. Monteleone James A, *Recognition of Child Abuse for the Mandated Reporter*, Second Edition, GW Medical Publishing, St. Louis, MO, 1996, pp. 1 and 34.

35. deMause, Lloyd, "The Universality of Incest," *The Journal of Psychohistory*, Fall 1991, Vol. 19, No. 2:123-164.

36. Douglas, John with Olshaker, Mark, *Obsession*, p. 13.

37. Hazelwood, Robert R and Burgess, Ann W, *Practical Aspects of Rape Investigation: A Multi-Discipline Approach*, CRC Press, Boca Raton, FL, 1987.

38. Banning, Peter, *Typology of Child Molesters*, "Breaking the Cycle: A Fresh Look," Chapter 5 – Myths, Exlibris, Jersey, UK, 2000.

39. Morgan WKC, Rape of the Phallus, *JAMA*, vol. 173, July 2, 1960.

40. Douglas, John; Burgess, Ann, Burgess, Allen; Ressler, Robert, *Crime Classification Manual: A Standard System for Investigating and Classifying Violent Crimes*, Jossey-Bass, San Francisco, CA, 1997, pp. 191-246.

41. Michaud with Hazelwood, pp. 91-98 and 160.

42. Campbell, Joseph, *The Power of Myth*,

"sacrifice," video.

43. Kelleher M, and Kelleher C, *Murder Most Rare: The Female Serial Killer*, Dell, New York, NY, 1998.

44. Horrigan, Bonnie, *Red Moon Passage: The Power and Wisdom of Menopause*, Three Rivers Press, New York, NY, 1996.

45. Estes, Clarissa Pinkola, *Women Who Run With the Wolves*, Ballantine, New York, NY, 1995.

46. Douglas, John and Olshaker, Mark, *The Anatomy of Motive*, p. 276.

47. Durant, Will, *The Story of Civilization: Part II; The Life of Greece*, Simon and Schuster, NY, 1966.

48. Jung, Emma, *Animus and Anima*, Spring Publications, Woodstock, CT, 1985.

49. Blackwell, Tom, "Psychologists Suggest Bernardo and Homolka are Psychopaths," *Psynopsis*, Fall, 1995.

50. Belsky J, (1980), "Child maltreatment: An ecological integration," *American Psychologist*, 35(4), 320-335.

51. Dietrich D, Berkowitz L, Kadushin A, McGloin J, (1990), "Some factors influencing abusers' justification of their child abuse," *Child Abuse & Neglect*, 14, 337-345.

52. Tuckman AJ, "Psychiatry and the Law: Child Murder," *Synapse On Line*, 1998.

53. Derbyshire J, "Maternal Madness," *National Review*, 01 October 2001.

54. "Mothers and murder: Mental illness is often the backdrop for this most baffling of crimes," *U.S. News & World Report*, 18 March 2002.

55. Kaye Neil S., *Families, Murder, and Insanity: A Psychiatric Review of Parental Neonaticide*. www.courtpsychiatrist.com/neonaticide.html, 2007.

56. *Postpartum Period (Peurperum)*, www.gynob.com/postpar2.htm, 2007.

57. "The Ancient Mummies of China," *The History Channel*, television and video.

58. Personal conversation, Dr. Lynn Schiveley.

59. Tolson, Mike, "Researchers say 'filicide' not rare," *Houston Chronicle*, 22 June 2001.

60. Resnick, Phillip J, (1969), "Child murder by

parents: A psychiatric review of filicide," *American Journal of Psychiatry*, 126: 325-334.

61. Douglas J, Burgess A, Ressler R, *Crime Classification Manual: A Standard System for Investigating and Classifying Violent Crime*, Josey-Bass, San Francisco, CA, 1997.

62. Bandura A, Ross D, Ross SA, (1963), "Vicarious reinforcement and imitative learning," *Journal of Abnormal and Social Psychology*, 67, 601-607.

63. Axtman, Kris, "Searching for Justice: Why juries often spare mothers who kill," *The Christian Science Monitor*, 09 July 2002.

64. Castro, Rafaela G, *Chicano Folklore – A Guide to the Folktales, Traditions, Rituals and Religious Practices of Mexican Americans*, Oxford University Press, USA, 2001.

65. Douglas, John with Olshaker, Mark, *Obsession*, pp. 33-34.

VIOLENT INITIATION

1. Burgess AW, Holstrom LL, *Rape: Victims of Crisis*, Robert J. Brady, Bowir, MD, 1974.

2. *When Men are Raped*, Homesafe Rape Crisis Center,

3. *Rape Trauma Syndrome*, Open UVic Resource Sexual Assault Centre.

4. *Rape Trauma Syndrome*, Bozeman Help Center.

5. *Rape Trauma Syndrome*, United Against Sexual Assault of Sonoma County.

6. *The Sacramento Bee*, Sacramento, CA.

7. Driscol, Fran, *The Trauma of Rape*, California ProLife Council, Inc.

8. *Rape Trauma Syndrome*, Chicago Police Department.

9. *Society's Second Assaults*, Abuse Counseling and Treatment, Inc.

10. Anand KJS, Phil D, "Pain and its effects in the human neonate and fetus," *New England J of Med,* Vol. 317, No. 21, pp. 1321-29, 19 November 1987.

11. Fitzgerald M, "The birth of pain," *MRC News*, (London), Summer, 1998:20-23.

12. Goodrich, Terry Lee, "Doctors more mindful of babies' pain," *Star-Telegram*, Fort Worth, Texas, 05 April 2003.

13. Chamberlain DB, *Babies don't feel pain: A century of denial in medicine*, Presentation: Second International Symposium on Circumcision, San Francisco, CA, 2 May 1991.

14. Pratt KC, Nelson AK, Sun KH, "The Behavior of the Newborn Infant," Ohio State University Student Contrib., *Psychology*, (1930), no. 10.

15. Crudden C, "Reactions of Newborn Infants to Thermal Stimuli Under Constant Tactual Conditions," *Journal of Experimental Psychology*, 20:350-370.

16. Blanton MG, "The behavior of the human infant in the first 30 days of life," *Psychological Review*, (1917), 24:(6):456-483.

17. McGraw M, "Neural Maturation as Exemplified in the Changing Reactions of the Infant to Pin Prick," *Child Development*, (1941), 12 (1):31-42.

18. Rich EC, Marshall RE, Volpe JJ, "The Normal Neonatal Response to Pin-Prick," *Developmental Medicine & Child Neurology*, (1974), 16:432-434.

19. Anand KJS, Phil D, Hickey PR, "Pain and its effects in the human neonate and fetus," *New England J of Med*, Vol. 317, No. 21, pp. 1321-29, 19 November 1987.

20. Rhinehart J, "Neonatal Circumcision Reconsidered," *Transactional Analysis Journal*, Vol. 29, No 3, pp. 215-221.

21. Connelly D, et al., "Gastric rupture associated with prolonged crying in a newborn undergoing circumcision," *Clinical Pediatrics*, September 1992, 560-61.

22. Ochsner M, "Acute urinary retention: causes and treatment," *Postgrad Med*, 1982, 71: 221-26.

23. Richards MPM, Bernal JF, Brackbill Y, "Early Childhood Differences: Gender or Circumcision," *Dev Psy*, Vol. 9, No. 1, pp. 89-95, January 1976.

24. Emde RN, Harmon RJ, Metcalf D, et al., "Stress and Neonatal Sleep," *Psychosomatic Medicine*, Vol. 33, No 6, pp. 491-97, November-December 1971.

25. Anders TF, Chalemian RJ, "The Effects of Circumcision on Sleep-Wake States in Human Neonates," *Psychosomatic Medicine*, Vol. 36, No 2, pp. 174-179, March-April 1974.

26. Bell RQ, Costello N, "Three tests for sex differences in tactile sensitivity in the newborn," *Biologica Neonatorum*, 1964, 7: 335-247.

27. Wolff PH, *The natural history of crying and other vocalizations in early infancy*. In BM Foss (Ed.), 'Determinants of Infant Behavior,' Vol. IV, London, Metheum, pp. 81-109.

28. Lipsitt LP, Levy N, "Electrotactile threshold in the human neonate," *Child Dev*, 1959, 30: 547-554.

29. Engel R, Crowel D, Nishijima S, *Visual and auditory response latencies in neonates*, 1968. In: Felicitation Volume in Honour of C. C. de Silva, Ceylon: Kulartne & Co.

30. Nisbett R, Gurwitz S, "Weight, sex, and the eating behavior of human newborns," 1970, *J Comp Physiol Psychol*, 73: 245-253.

31. Bench J, "Some effects of audio-frequency stimulation on the crying baby," *J Auditory Res*, 9: 122-128.

32. Bench J, Collyer Y, Langford C, "A comparison between the neonatal sound-evoked startle response and the head-drop (moro) reflex," *Dev Med Child Neurol*, 14; 308-317.

33. Hutt SJ, Lenard HG, Prechtl HFR, "Psychophysiological studies in newborn infants," 1969. In L. P. Lipsitt and H. W. Reese (Editors.), *Advances in Child Development and Behavior*, Vol. 4, New York, Academic, pp. 127-172.

34. Pretchtl HFR, *Patterns of reflex behavior related to sleep in the human infant*. 1972. In C. D. Clemente, P. Purpura, and F. Mayer (Editors.), "Sleep and the Maturing Nervous System," Academic, New York, NY, pp. 297-301.

35. Desor JA, Maller O, Turner RA, "Taste in acceptance of sugars in human infants," *J Comp Physiol*, 84: 496-501.

36. Dubignon J, Campbell D, Curtis M, Parrington M, "The relation between laboratory measures of sucking, food intake, and perinatal factors during the newborn period," *Child Dev*, 40: 1107-1120.

37. Levine S, *An endocrine theory of infantile stimulation*, In: J. A. Ambrose (Editor), Stimulation in Early Infancy, Academic, New York, NY, pp. 45-55.

38. Hepper PG, "Fetal Memory: Does it exist? What does it do?," *Acta Pediatrica*, supplement, vol. 416: pp. 16-20, 1996.

39. Milos MF, Macris D, "Circumcision: A Medical or a Human Rights Issue?," *J of Nurse-Midwifery*, Vol. 37, No 2 (Supplement), March/April 1992.

40. Van der Kolk, Bessel, *The Body Keeps The Score: Memory and the evolving psychobiology of post traumatic stress*, www.trauma-pages.com/a/vanderk4.php

41. Taddio A, Goldbach M, Ipp M, Stevens B, "Effect of neonatal circumcision on pain responses during vaccination in boys," *The Lancet*, 1995; 345:291-292.

42. Taddio A, Katz J, Ilersich AL, et al., "Effect of neonatal circumcision on pain response during subsequent routine vaccination," *The Lancet*, 1997; 349 (9052): 599-603.

43. Chamberlain DB, "Babies Remember Pain," *Pre – and Peri-Natal Psychology*, Vol. 3, No. 4; pp. 297-310, Summer 1989.

44. *Circumcision: Echoes in the Body*. Within: 'Circumcision: The Cruelest Cut,' The Birth Scene, www.birthpsychology.com/birthscene/circ.html

45. Immerman RS, Mackey WC, "A Proposed Relationship Between Circumcision and Neural Reorganization," *J of Genetic Psychology*, Vol. 159, No. 3, pp. 367-378, September 1, 1998.

46. Cook SE, "Retention of primary preferences after secondary filial imprinting," *Animal Behavior*, 1993, 46:405-407.

47. Cusick CG, "Extensive cortical reorganization following sciatic nerve injury in adult rats versus restricted reorganization after neonatal injury: Implications for spatial and temporal limits on somatosensory plasty," *Progress in Brain Research*, 1996, 108:379-390.

48. Cusick CG, Wall JT, Whiting HH, Jr., Wiley RG, "Temporal progression of cortical reorganization following nerve injury," *Brain Research*, 1990, 537:355-358.

49. Florence SL, Kaas JH, "Large-scale reorganization at multiple levels of the somatosensory pathway follows therapeutic amputation of the hand in monkeys," *J of Neuroscience*, 1995, 15:8083-8095.

50. Garraghty PE, Hanes DP, Florence SL, Kaas JH, "Pattern of peripheral deafferentation predicts reorganizational limits in adult primate somatosensory cortex," *Somatosensory & Motor Research*, 1994, 11:109-117.

51. Garraghty PE, Kass JH, "Functional reorganization in adult monkey thalamus after peripheral nerve injury," *Neuroreport*, 1991, 2:747-750.

52. Kelahen AM, Doetsch GS, "Time dependent changes in the functional organization of somatosensory cerebral cortex following digit amputation in adult raccoons," *Somatosensory Research*, 1984, 2:49-81.

53. Kelahen AM, Ray RH, Carson LV, Massey CE, Doetsch GS, "Functional reorganization of adult raccoon somatosensory cerebral cortex following neonatal digit amputation," *Brain Research*, 1981, 223:151-159.

54. Pons TP, Garraghty PE, Ommaya AK, Kaas JH, Taub E, "Massive cortical reorganization after sensory deafferentation in adult macaques," *Science*, 1991, 252:1857-1860.

55. Rhoades RW, Wall JT, Chiala NL, Bennett-Clarke CA, Killackey PP, "Anatomical and functional changes in the organization of the cuneate nucleus of adult rats after fetal forelimb amputation," *Journal of Neuroscience*, 1993, 13:1106-1119.

56. Wall JT, Huerta MF, Kaas JH, "Changes in the cortical map of the hand following postnatal median nerve injury in monkeys: Modification of somatotopic aggregates," *Journal of Neuroscience*, 1992, 12:3445-3455.

57. Wall JT, Kaas HH, "Long-term cortical consequences of reinnervation errors after nerve regeneration in monkeys," *Brain Research*, 1986, 372:400-404.

58. Anand KJ and Scalzo FM, "Can adverse neonatal experiences alter brain development and subsequent behavior," *Biology of the Neonate*, vol. 77, No. 2: pp. 69-82, February 2000.

59. Goleman, Daniel, "Early Violence Leaves its mark on the Brain: Adolescent violence is traced to abuse and neglect in childhood, early violence Found to be Etched in the brain," *The New York Times*, New York, NY, Tuesday, October 3, 1995, Page C1.

60. Neergaard, Lauran, "Lasting Stress Effects: Stress Hormones Change Brain Chemicals in Mice for Weeks," *The Associated Press*, 17 January 2002.

61. Barichello, Lawrence, *The Sexual and Psychological Consequences of Infant Circumcision,* Intact.ca.

62. *Foreskin Curriculum: Anatomy — A new structure*, Doctors Opposing Circumcision.

63. Miller, Alice, *Banished Knowledge: Facing Childhood Injuries*.

64. Miller, Alice, *Breaking Down the Wall of Silence*, Doubleday, 1990, pp. 135-141.

65. Taylor JR, Lockwood AP, Taylor AJ, "The prepuce: specialized mucosa of the penis and its loss to circumcision," *Brit J of Urology*, 1996, 77:291-295.

66. Cromie, WJ, "Childhood abuse hurts the brain," *Harvard University Gazette*, May 22, 2003.

67. Kellogg JH, *Treatment for Self-Abuse and its Effects: Plain Facts for Old and Young.*, P. Segner & Co., Burlington, IA, 1888.

68. Peterek, Anne V, *Circumcision: The Root of Misogyny,* www.birthpsychology.com/birthscene/circ.html

69. Anand KJS, Phil D, Hickey, "Pain and its effects in the human neonate and fetus," *New England J of Med*, vol. 317, No. 21, pp. 1321-29.

70. Bigelow J, *The Joy of Uncircumcising*, Hourglass, Aptos, CA, 1995, pp. 21, 49-51, 107-108, 113, 114-117, 179.

71. Falk J, *Psychological impacts of male circumcision*. (26 September 2006) www.cirpnocir/library/pain/anand/

72. Chamberlain DB, "Birth and the Origins of Violence," *Pre- and Perinatal Psychology J*, 10(2), Winter 1995, pp. 57-74.

73. Van der Kolk B, McFarlane A, Weisaeth L, *Traumatic Stress: The Effects of Overwhelming Experience on Mind, Body, and Society*, Guilford, New York, NY, 1996, Preface.

74. Cromie, WJ.

75. Miller, Alice, *The Untouched Key: Tracing Childhood Trauma in Creativity and Destructiveness*, Anchor, Harpswell, ME, 1991.

76. Jacobson B, Eklund G, Hamberger L, Linnarsson Sedvall G, Valverius M, "Perinatal origin of adult self-destructive behavior," *Acta Psychiatr Scand*, vol. 76, No. 42:364-371, October 1987.

77. Jacobson B, "Obstetric care and proneness of offspring to suicide as adults: case-control study," *British Medical Journal*, 1998; 317: 1346-1349, 14 November.

78. Collins, Simon, "Schizophrenia linked to childhood sexual abuse," *The New Zealand Herald*, Auckland, NZ, 01 April 2002.

79. Rhinehart J, "Neonatal Circumcision Reconsidered," *Transactional Analysis Journal*, Vol. 29, No 3, pp. 215-221, July 1999.

80. *Somatic Redecision*: reference article:

81. Blackstone P, "Between the Lines: Evolution of redecision and impasse theory and practice," *Transactional Analysis Journal*, 1995, 25:343-346.

82. Goldman R, "The psychological impact of circumcision," *BJU International*, 1999; 83 Supplement, 1:93-103.

83. Landau Elaine, *An American Epidemic*, Julian Messner, New York, NY, 1990.

84. Lukes, Steven, "Political Ritual and Social Integration," *Journal of Sociological Association* 9, No 2, (1975): 289-350.

MEDICINE

1. William Sears, MD and Martha Sears RN, *Deciding Whether or Not to Circumcise Your Baby Boy*, www.AskDr.Sears.com, 2007.

2. Bell, Catherine in *Ritual Theory, Ritual Practice*, Oxford University Press, Oxford, 1992, referenced Bordieu, Pierre's book *Outline of a Theory of Practice*, Cambridge University Press, Cambridge, UK, 1977, pp. 184, 40-41, 207 and 98-108.

3. Sheesholtz, Mel, "Religion and child abuse, fundamentalism and politics*," Justice Sunday III and Pastor*

Latham, 17 January 2006.

4. Ephron JM., *Medicine and the German Jews: A History*, Yale University Press, New Haven, CT, 2001, pp. 222-233.

5. Schwartz, W., *Pediatric Primary Care: A Problem-solving Approach*, 2nd edition, Year Book Medical Publishers, Chicago, IL, 1990, p. 861.

6. Jacobi, A., "On masturbation and hysteria in young children," *American Journal of Obstetrics*, 1876: 595-606.

7. *America fights back against masturbation*. www.whitehouse.georgewbush.org/initiatives/purity/index.asp (parody), 2007.

8. Johnson, Athol A. W., "On An Injurious Habit Occasionally Met with in Infancy and Early Childhood," *The Lancet*, vol. 1 (7 April 1860): pp. 344-345.

9. Semmelweis, Ignatz, K. Codell Carter, trans., *The Etiology, Concept, and Prophylaxis of Childbed Fever*, University of Wisconsin Press, Madison, WI, 1983, pp. 5 and 7. Translator's Introduction.

10. Kellogg, John Harvey, *Treatment for Self-Abuse and Its Effects, Plain Facts for Old and Young*, Burlington, Iowa: P. Segar & Co., 1888, p. 295.

11. Shryock, Harold, *On Becoming a Woman: A book for teenage girls,* Revire and Herald, 1951.

12. McNamara, Jo Ann Kay, *Sisters in Arms: Catholic Nuns Through Two Millennia*, Harvard University Press, Cambridge, MA, 1996, pp. 600, 606, and 602.

13. Tinari, Paul, presented at The Ninth International Symposium on Circumcision, Genital Integrity and Human Rights in Seattle, WA, www.nocirc.org, August 25, 2006.

14. Mendelshon, Robert S., *Confessions of a Medical Heretic*, McGraw-Hill, 1990, pp. 58-59.

15. Mendelsohn, Robert S., *How to Raise a Healthy Child in Spite of Your Doctor*, Ballantine, New York, NY, 1987.

16. Mugenzi J, "Circumcision Stops Penile Cancer," *New Vision* (Kampala), 13 Jan. 2003.

17. Philo, trans. Yonge CD, *The Works of Philo*, Hendrickson Publishers, Inc, Peabody, MA, 1993, p. 534.

18. Preston, NE, "Whither the Foreskin: A Condition of Routine Neonatal Circumcision," *JAMA*, 1970, 213: 1853.

19. Cusack V, "Boy and the Hood," *Toronto Life*, August 2006.

20. Siegel, Judy, "Court ruling threatens traditional circumcision," *The Jerusalem Post*, 12 December 2000.

21. Disraeli, Benjamin, 1804-1881.

22. Hart G, Wellings K, "Sexual behavior and its medicalisation: in sickness and in health," *Brit Med J*, 2002;324:896-900 (12 April).

23. Jung, Carl G., *The Undiscovered Self*, A Mentor Book, Denver, CO, 1958, pp. 16-17.

24. Lifton, Robert Jay, *The Nazi Doctors: Medical Killing and the Psychology of Genocide*, Basic Books, New York, NY, 1986, See: genocide, purification, and Doubling, pp. 418, 422, 423, and 488.

25. *KFBK* radio, 1530 AM, Sacramento, CA.

26. Landers, Ann, "Doctor Adds Women's Concerns to List of Circumcision Benefits," *Contra Costa Times*, Monday, April 12, 1993, p. 5f.

27. White C., "Little evidence for effectiveness of scientific peer review," *BMJ*, 2003; 326:241 (1 February).

28. Bolande, RP, "Ritualistic Surgery: Circumcision and Tonsillectomy," *New England J. of Medicine*, 1969: 280: 591-596.

29. The Boston Women's Health Book Collective, *Our Bodies, Ourselves: A Book By and For Women*, Touchstone, New York, NY, 1998, pp. 384, 272, 347-8, 460, 643-4, and 731.

30. Internet mailing list, from a North Carolina physician.

31. "Midwives Performing Circumcisions," Pennsylvania. American College of Obstetrics & Gynecologists, *Section Newsletter*, June 1999.

32. Lehman. Betsy A. "The Age Old Question of Circumcision." *Boston Globe*, Boston, Massachusetts, 22 June 1987:41,43.

33. Lifton, Robert, *The Nazi Doctors*, p. 420-424 and 210.

34. "Private health care advocates praise B.C. surgery plan," *CBC News*, 12 June 2003.

35. Conner, Jarrett, "Baby Parts For Sale In Massachusetts: Abortion Industry's 'Dirty Little Secret,'" *Massachusetts News,* www.massnews.com/past_issues/2000/Culture/pbaparts.htm.

36. VanValkenburgh, Jaan, "Circumcision yielding skin for ulcerous feet," *The Commercial Appeal*, Memphis, TN, 07 May 1996.

37. Euringer, Amanda, "Foreskin Facecream: And it's not the only body part on the chopping block for vanity. Ethical?," *The Tyee*, 19 April 2007.

38. Private conversation with Clora Ricci.

39. Private conversation with Gordon Raynor.

40. Salvatore, Steve, "Circumcision study halted due to trauma," *CNN Health*, 23 December 1997.

41. Gloria Lemay, Midwifery Educator, Vancouver, BC Canada.

42. Sayer LL, "Circumcision for the cure of Enuresis," *JAMA*, Vol. 7, 1887, pp. 631-3.

43. Money A, *Treatment of Diseases in Children*, P. Blakiston, 1887, p. 421.

44. Fisher CE, *Circumcision: A Hand-Book On the Diseases of Children and Their Homeopathic Treatment*, Medical Century Co., 1895, p. 875.

45. Editorial, "Circumcisus," *Medical Record*, vol. 49 (1896): p. 430.

46. Medical News. Our London Paper, *Medical World*, (1900), vol. 77: pp. 707-8.

47. Naylor HGH, "A Plea for Early Circumcision," *Pediatrics*, vol. 12 (1901): p. 231.

48. Steele WG, "Importance of Circumcision," *Medical World*, Vol. 20 (1920): pp. 518-9.

49. Pratt EH, "Circumcision, Orificial Surgery: Its Philosophy, Application and Technique," (Within) Edited by B. E. Dawson, Newark: *Physicians Drug News Co.* (1912): pp. 396-8.

50. Wolbarst AL, "Universal Circumcision as a Sanitary Measure," *JAMA*, (1914), Vol. 62. pp. 92-7.

51. Wuesthoff LW, "Benefits of Circumcision,"

Medical World, (1915), Vol. 33, p. 434.

52. Editor, "Routine Circumcision at Birth," *JAMA*, vol. 91 (1928): p. 201.

53. Melendy, Mary R., MD, *The Ideal Women — For Maidens, Wives and Mothers*, 1903. Referenced in: Bigelow, Jim, "The Joy of Uncircumcising," p. 69.

54. Spach, DH, et al, "Lack of circumcision Increases Risk of Urinary Tract Infection in Young Men," *JAMA*, vol. 267, no. 5, 5 February 1992, 679-81.

55. Aldeeb, Sami, *Male and Female Circumcision: Among Jews, Christians and Muslims Religious*, Shangri-La, Pennsylvania, 2001.

56. See the Bibliography in Periodicals: Viral Cancer Agents.

57. Aldeeb, Sami, *Male and Female Circumcision.*

58. Nguyen TC, Volmer KE, Holcroft CJ, Domico SG, et al., "Prune Belly Syndrome Caused by Phimosis," *Society for Fetal Urology*, International Maternal/Fetal Organization, Winter 2001, Newsletter. Note: Prune Belly Syndrome is a congenital condition often with absence of abdominal muscles, undescended testicles and urinary abnormalities. The fetus in this case was induced and delivered nonviable. The title suggests the authors confused the cause and effect.

59. Wallerstein, Edward, *Circumcision: An American Health Fallacy*, Springer, New York, NY, 1980, pp. 1-28.

60. Dewan, PA, Tieu, HC, Chieng, BS, "Phimosis: Is circumcision necessary?," *Journal of Paediatrics and Child Health* (1996), Vol. 32, pp. 285-289.

61. Philo, *The Works of Philo.*

62. Zaheer, Kamil, "UN urges circumcision in AIDS-hit southern Africa," *Reuters Foundation*, 19 December 2006. Re: Dr. Peter Piot, UNAIDS.

63. *Circumcision and HIV.* www.circumstitions.com

64. Talbott JR, *Size Matters: The Number of Prostitutes and the Global HIV/AIDS Pandemic,* Africans Against Aids, Inc., New York.

65. Brewer DD, Pottrat JJ, Roberts JM, Jr., & Brody S, "Male and Female circumcision associated with prevalent HIV infection in virgins and adolescents in Kenya, Lesotho, and Tanzania," *Annals of Epidemology*, 17: 217-226.

66. Boynton, Petra, *More concerns raised about HIV Circumcision research, www.drpetra.co.uk/blog.*

67. *Report on Male Circumcision: an Arguable Method of Reducing the Risks of HIV Transmission*, Republic of France, The Counseil du SIDA, 24 May, 2007.

68. "Multiple partners fueling AIDS: Sexual networks in southern Africa aid the spread of HIV, researchers say," *Reuters,* 15 August 2006.

69. Halprin D, Epstein H, "Concurrent sexual partnerships help to explain Africa's high HIV prevalence: implications for prevention," *The Lancet*, Vol. 364, Issue 9428, pp. 4-6

70. Hyena, Hank, *"Dry sex" worsens AIDS numbers in southern Africa: Sub-Saharans' distain for vaginal wetness accelerates the plague, www.Salon.com*, 10 December 1999.

71. Shoofs, Mark, "Death and the Second Sex," *Village Voice*, 1-7 December 1999.

72. Altman, Lawrence K., "Washing After Sex May Raise H.I.V. Risk," *The New York Times*, 21 August 2007.

73. Baker Rl, (Rear Admiral USN ret., "Newborn male circumcision: Needless and dangerous," *Sexual Medicine Today*, Vol. 3, No. 11, pp. 35-36, November 1979.

74. Schwartz W, Charney E, et al., *Pediatric Primary Care: A Problem-solving Approach*, Year Book Medical Publishers, 1990, Chicago, pp. 861-862.

75. Johnston, Martin, "Leave the circumcising to us, surgeon tells GPs," *The New Zealand Herald*, 13 August 2002.

76. Cairns, Gus, "Shocking rates of adverse events seen with traditional, medical circumcision," *Africa Science News*, 12 September 2008.

77. Talarico RD, and Jasaitis JE, "Concealed Penis: A Complication of Neonatal Circumcision," *Journal of Urology*, 110 (1973): 732-733.

78. *Circumcision Gallery.* www.circumstitions.com/Botched.html

79. "Circumcision Botched; He's Now a She," *Los*

Angeles Times, 10/30/75.

80. "Child Awarded Damages," *Leader Post Regina*, SK, Canada, November 1975.

81. "Family gets $2.75 million in wrongful surgery suit," *Lake Charles American Press*, 28 May 1986.

82. "Sex change should give circumcision victim near normal life," *Atlanta Constitution*, 9/21/85.

83. "Circumcision Kills 200 Babies a Year," *National Inquirer*, 22 October 1985.

84. "$22.8 million awarded in botched circumcision," *Atlanta Constitution*, 12 March 1991.

85. "Five Minutes That Ended a Baby's Boy's Life," *The Independent*, 4/30/91.

86. "Infant bleeds to death after being circumcised," *Miami Herald*, 26 June 1993.

87. "Circumcision Kills Miami Baby, Costs Marin Baby Tip of Penis," *Bay Area Reporter*, 7/8/93.

88. "Circumcision doctor killed boy, 9, with heroin overdose," *The Independent*, 9 July 1994.

89. "Doctor freed despite conviction in 2 deaths," *Arkansas Democrat Gazette*, 1/28/95.

90. "Boy in coma most of his 6 years dies," *The State*, Columbia South Carolina, 7/10/95.

91. "Boy's death to be probed," *Houston Chronicle*, 7/28/95.

92. "Circumcision slammed as 'barbarism,'" www.iafrica.com, Capetown, South Africa, 15 August 2003.

93. Marshall FF, ed., *Urologic Complications, Medical and Surgical, Adult and Pediatric*, Chicago: Year Book Medical Publishers, 1986. See: Gearhart JP, 'Complications of Pediatric Circumcision,' pp. 387-96.

94. Kaplan GW, "Complications of Circumcision," *Urologic Clinics of North America*, 10 (1983): 543-9.

95. *Associated Press, Report*, "CDC Off on Infection Deaths: 103,000 Deaths Linked to Hospital Infections in 2000, 75 Percent Preventable, Newspaper Says." www.abcNEWS.com, Chicago, 20 July 2002.

96. Sussman SJ, Schiller RP, Shashikumaro VL, "Fournier's Syndrome: Report of Three Cases and Review of the Literature," *Amer J of Diseases of Children*, 132 (1978): 1189-91.

97. Altman H, "Osteomyelitis of femur (probably due to circumcision) in infant," *Bulletin of the Hospital for Joint Disease*, 1946; 7:109-113.

98. Arnon R, et al., "Unilateral leg cyanosis: an unusual complication of circumcision," *European J Pediatrics*, 1992: 151: 716.

99. Berens R, Pontus S, "A complication of circumcision and dorsal nerve block of the penis," *Reg Anesth*, 1990, 15: 309-10.

100. Eason J, et al., "Male ritual circumcision resulting in acute renal failure," *BMJ*, 1994, 309: 660-1.

101. Gosden M, "Tetanus following circumcision," *Trans R Soc Trop Med Hyg*, 1935, 28: 645-8.

102. Jee LD, Miller AJ, Ruptured bladder following circumcision using Plastic bell device, *Brit J of Urology*, 1990: 65: 216-7.

103. Evbuomwan J, Aliu A, "Acute gangrene of the scrotum in a one-month-old child," *Trop Geogr Med*, 1984, 36: 299-300.

104. Carlos A. Angel, MD, Associate Professor of Surgery and Pediatrics, *Meatal Stenosis*, Division of Pediatrics and Surgery/Urology, University of Texas Medical Branch at Galveston.

105. Patel H, "General Practice: The problem of routine infant circumcision," *Canadian Med Assoc J*, vol. 95, pp. 576581, 10 September 1966.

106. Persad R, Sharma S, et al., "Clinical Presentation and Pathophysiology of Meatal Stenosis Following Circumcision," *Brit J of Urol*, 75 (1995): 90-91.

107. Lackey JT, Mannion RA, Kerr JE, "Urethral Fistula Following Circumcision," *JAMA*, 1968, 206: 2318.

108. John Geisheker, legal counsel for Doctors Opposing Circumcision (DOC).

109. Huntley JS, Bourne MC, Munro FD, Wilson-Storey D (September 2003). "Troubles with the foreskin: one hundred consecutive referrals to paediatric surgeons," *J R Soc Med*, 96 (9): 449–51.

110. Stolinsky, David C., "Our Moral Compass Is Mislabeled, Not Broken," *NewsMax.com*, 25 April 2002.

111. Dotinga, Randy, "Doctors Ignore Infection Risk for Uncircumcised Babies," *Health Scout News Reporter*, 22 January 2002.

112. American Academy of Pediatrics, *Newborns: Care for the Uncircumcised Penis, Guidelines for Parents, AAP*.

113. Wayne, Eileen, "Understanding Urinary Tract Infections," *Inf Urol*, 8 (4), 111, 114-20.

114. Michael Glass, NOCIRC.

115. Private conversation with Patricia Robinett relating a conversation with a pediatrics employee.

116. Marlow, Dorothy, *Textbook of Pediatric Nursing*, W. B. Saunders, 1965, p. 96.

117. Foley, John M., M.D., "The unkindest cut of all." *Fact* 1966;3(4):2-9.

118. Denniston George, M.D. *An Epidemic of Circumcision*, Presented at The Third International Symposium on Circumcision, University of Maryland, College Park, Maryland, May 22-25, 1994.

119. Menage, Janet, "Professionals should not collude with abusive behavior," *British Medical Journal*, 311:1088-1089, 21 October 1995.

120. Adams, RW, "Board Fines Doctor for Mistake: Dr. Eva Salamon must pay $5,000 plus expenses, and perform community service," *The Ledger*, Lakeland FL, 06 February 2002.

121. Lewis, Van, "Cut the budget, not the babies," *Tallahassee Democrat*, 24 January 2002.

122. Prais D, Shoov-Furman R, & Amir J. "Is ritual circumcision a risk factor for neonatal urinary tract infections?," *Arch. Dis Child*, published online, 6 Oct. 2008.

123. Fleiss, Paul M., "The Case Against Circumcision," *Mothering: The Magazine of Natural Family Living*, Winter 1997, pp. 36-45.

124. Donovan B, "Male Circumcision and Common Sexually Transmissible Diseases in a Developed Nation Setting," *Genitourinary Med*, 70, (1994): 317-20.

125. Smith GL, Greenup R, "Circumcision as a Risk Factor for Urethritis in Racial Groups," *American Journal of Public Health*, 77 (1987): 452-454.

126. Cook LS, Koutsky LA, Holmes KK, "Clinical Presentation of Genital Warts Among Circumcised and Uncircumcised Heterosexual Men Attending an Urban STD Clinic," *Genitourinary Medicine*, 69, (1993): 262-264.

127. Bassett I, et al., "Herpes Simplex Virus Type 2 Infection of Heterosexual Men Attending a Sexual Health Centre," *Med J of Australia*, 160 (1994): 697-700.

128. Laumann EO, Masi EM, "Circumcision in the United States: Prevalence, Prophylactic Effects, and Sexual Practice," *JAMA*, 277 (1997): 1052-1057.

129. Farrell Warren, *Women Can't Hear What Men Don't Say: Destroying Myths, Creating Love*, Tarcher, 2000, Chapter 8.

130. Kirkpatrick BV, Eitzman DV, "Neonatal Septicemia after Circumcision," Clinical Pediatrics, *Medical Journal of Australia*, 13 (1974): 767-8.

131. Scurlock JM, Pemberton PJ, "Neonatal Meningitis and Circumcision," *Medical Journal of Australia*, 1 (1977): 332-4.

132. Annobil S, Al-Halif A, Kazie T, "Primary tuberculosis of the penis in an infant," *Tubercle*, 1990, 71:229-30.

133. Lewis EL, "Tuberculosis of the penis: a report of 5 new cases, and a complete review of the literature," *J of Urology*, 1946; 56: 737-45.

134. Dr. Dorothy Greenbaum. (23 March 2002) www.brisdoctor.com

135. Bernstein R, Bernstein M, *Honey, Mud, Maggots and other Medical Marvels: The Science Behind Folk Remedies and Old Wives Tales*, Houghton Mifflin, Chapter "Full Circle", 1998.

136. Bailey RC, Muga R, Poulusson R, Abricht H, "The acceptability of male circumcision to reduce HIV infections in Nyanza Province, Kenya," *AIDS Care*, 2002 Feb. 14(1): 27-40.

137. McQuaid, Joe, "I bet you can't tell which studies are real and which are made up," *The Union Leader*, New Hampshire, 15 April 2002.

138. Grady, Denise, "Male Circumcision Is Found to Reduce Cervical Cancer," *The New York Times*, 11 April

2002.

139. Terris M., et al., "Relation of Circumcision to Cancer of the Cervix," *Amer J of Obstet and Gynec*, 117 (1973): 1056-1065.

140. Cold CJ, et al., "Carcinoma in Situ of the Penis in a 76-Year-Old Circumcised Man," *J of Family Practice*, 44, (1997): 407-410.

141. The Pill, 'HPV and Cancer,' www.*CBSNews.com*, 26 March 2002.

142. Henning, Rainer C, "Is the African AIDS pandemic a bluff?," www.afrol.com - *The African News Agency*, 04 October 2006.

143. Fiala, Christian, *An analysis of the predictions and assumptions about the former epicenter of the AIDS epidemic. Implications for other African countries*, University of Texas conference.

144. Times, 29 December 2001, Mbeki Appeals for End to Child Rape, *The World*, Johannesburg, South Africa.

145. Warner, Jennifer, "Baby Boys With Micropenis Happier as Males," *WebMD Medical News*, Reviewed by Michael Smith, MD, 25 January 2002.

146. Robinett, Patricia, *The Rape of Innocence: FGM and Circumcision in the USA,* Nunzio Press, Eugene, OR, 2009.

147. Taylor JR, Lockwood AP, Taylor AJ, "The prepuce: Specialized mucosa of the penis and its loss to circumcision," *British Journal of Urology*, Volume 77, pp. 291-295, February 1996.

148. Winkelmann RK, "The Erogenous Zones: Their Nerve Supply and Significance," *Proceedings of the Staff Meetings of the Mayo Clinic*, Volume 34, Number 2: pp. 39-47, Rochester Minnesota, January 21, 1959.

149. Fleiss FM, Hodges FM, Van Howe RS, "Immunological functions of the human prepuce," *Sexually Transmitted Infections*, Vol. 74, No 5, pp. 364-367.

150. Laumann EO, Masi CM, Ezra WZ, "Circumcision in the United States: Prevalence, Prophylactic Effects, and Sexual Practice," *JAMA*, vol. 277, No. 13: 1052-57, 2 April 1997.

151. Diaz A, "Dorsal Slit, A Circumcision Alternative," *Ob & Gyn*, 37: 619, 1971.

152. Harryman, Gary, *The Lost List*. www.circumstitions.com/Lost.html, 2006.

153. LeGuerer, Annick, *Scent: The Essential and Mysterious Powers of Smell*, Kodansha, International, 1992.

154. LeVay, Simon, *The Sexual Brain*, A Bradford Book, The MIT Press, 1993.

155. Jonson, Seigler, and Winslade, *Clinical Ethics*, 3rd ed., Mc Graw-Hill, NY, 1984, p. 42.

156. Children's Hospital Boston, Center for Young Women's Health, *A Guide to Vaginal Agenesis in Teens*.

157. Bigelow, Jim, *The Joy of Uncircumcising*, pp. 188-211.

158. Ellsworth, Barry, *The Nurses of St. Vincent: Saying No to Circumcision*, documentary video, Fireball Films, 1994.

159. Millhollan, Michelle, "Patient for bypass sues over circumcision," *The Advocate*, Baton Rouge, LA, 10 April 2001. Re: Dr. Mary Jo Wright. Possibly not her first.

160. Baughm, Christopher, "Doctor Testifies Surgeon Secretly Circumcised Woman," *The Advocate*, Baton Rouge, LA, 30 October 1996.

161. Johnson, Seigler, Winslade, *Clinical Ethics*, p. 5.

162. Private conversation with Dr. Janet Menage.

163. Lifton, Robert Jay, *The Nazi Doctors*.

164. Hammond, Tim, *Whose Body, Whose Rights?: Examining the Ethics and the Human Rights of Infant Male Circumcision*, documentary video, Dillonwood Productions, 1995.

165. "Doctor before board over penis surgery," *State News*, UK, 4 February 2002.

166. Francescan, Christopher, "Serviceman Sues Over Doc's 'unkind' cut at birth," *New York Post*, 23 December 2001.

167. Johnson, Seigler, Winslade, *Clinical Ethics*, p. 39.

168. Langmuir, Irving, "Pathological Science," (1989) *Physics Today,* Volume 42, Issue 10, October 1989, pp.36-48.

169. Hodges FM, Svoboda JS, Van Howe RS, "Prophylactic interventions on children: balancing human rights with public health," *J Med Ethics*, 2002, Feb., 28(1): pp.

10-6.

170. *The Bioethics of the Circumcision of Male Children,* www.cirp.org/library/ethics/

171. Schoen EJ, "Ode to the Circumcised Male," [letter] *American J Diseases in Children*, 1987; vol. 141:128.

172. *Stedman's Medical Dictionary 21st Edition*, Williams & Wilkins, Baltimore, MD, 1966, p. 738.

173. Thomas WI, "The Relation of the Medicine Man to the Origin of the Profession," *Decennial Publications of the University of Chicago*, First Series, 4 (1903): 241-256.

174. Jung, Carl G., *Man and his Symbols*, Dell Laurel Edition, NY, 1964, pp. 292-3.

175. Exodus 4:25.

176. Coe, Michael D., *The Maya*, Thames & Hudson, London Ltd., UK, 1997. See: penis perforator.

TRANSGENERATION

1. Van der Kolk B, "The Compulsion to Repeat the Trauma: Re-enactment, Revictimization, and Masochism," *Psychiatric Clinics of North America*, Volume 12, Number 2, Pages 389-411, June 1989.

2. Goldman R, "The psychological impact of circumcision," *BJU International*, Volume 83 Supplement 1, Pages 93-102, January 1, 1999.

3. Menage, Janet, "Circumcision and Psychological Harm," *NORM-UK*.

4. Jacobson B, Eklund G, Hamberger L, Linnarsson D, Sedvall G, Valverius M, "Perinatal origin of adult self-destructive behavior," *Acta Psychiatr Scand*, Vol. 76, No 42, pp. 364-371, October 1987.

5. Neppe VM, Smith ME, "Culture, Psychopathology and Psi: A Clinical Relationship," *Parapsychological J of S.A.*, 1982, 3:1, 1-5, edited.

6. Fongay, Peter, "The transgenerational transmission of holocaust trauma," *Attachment & Human Development*, Vol. 1, No. 1, April 1999, pp. 92-114(23).

7. Crawford, Christina and Bradshaw, John, *No Safe Place: The Legacy of Family Violence*, Barrytown/

Station Hill Press, 1994.

8. Barnard GW and Kripel JJ, editors. *Crossing Boundaries: Essays on the Ethical Status of Mysticism*, Chatham House, London, UK, 2002.

9. Forward, Susan with Buck, Craig, *Toxic Parents: Overcoming Their Hurtful Legacy And Reclaiming Your Life*, Bantam, New York, NY, pp. 15, 16, 17, 19, 5, 6, 11, 5, 130, and 6.

10. Graglia, Carol, *Domestic Tranquility*, Spence, Dallas, TX, 1998.

11. Miller, Alice, *For Your Own Good: Hidden Cruelty in Child-rearing and the Roots of Violence*, Farrar, Straus and Giroux, New York, NY, 1990.

12. deMause, Lloyd, *The History of Childhood*, Jason Aronson, Northvale, NJ, 1995, pp. 51-54.

13. deMause, Lloyd, *The Emotional Life of Nations*, The Other Press, New York, NY, 2002.

14. deMause, Lloyd, "Childhood and Cultural Evolution," *The Journal of Psychohistory* v. 26, N. 3, Winter 1999.

15. Burney, Robert, *Codependence: The Dance of Wounded Souls*, Joy to You & Me Enterprises, Cambria, CA, 1995.

16. Little, Margaret, *Transference Neurosis & Transference Psychosis*, Jason Aronson, pp. 167-168.

17. Holmes RM, and Holmes ST, *Profiling Violent Crime: An Investigative Tool*, Sage, Thousand Oaks, CA, p. 113.

18. Leo J, "Pedophiles in the schools," *U.S. & World Report*, 11 October 1993.

19. The Awareness Center, theawarenesscenter.org, 2006.

20. Sami Awad Aldeeb Abu-Sahlieh, *Male and Female Circumcision: Among Jews, Christians & Muslims*, Shangri-La Publications, Pennsylvania, 2001.

21. Greenberg DM, Bradford J, and Curry S, (1995), "Infantophilia—a new subcategory of pedophilia?: a preliminary study." *Bulletin of the American Academy of Psychiatry and Law*, 23(1), 63-71. (To age 5).

22. Denniston GC, Gallo PG, Hodges FM, Milos MF,

Viviani F, *Bodily Integrity and the Politics of Circumcision*, Springer, NY, 2006.

23. Myss, Caroline, *Sacred Contracts: Awakening Your Divine Potential*, Three Rivers Press, New York, NY, 2003.

24. Bittles AH, *A Background Summary on Consanguineous Marriage*, Centre for Human Genetics, Edith Cowan, University Perth Australia WA 6027, May, 2001

25. Adams, Kenneth, *Silently Seduced: When Parents Make Their Children Partners: Understanding Covert Incest*, HCI, Deerfield Beach, FL, 1991.

26. Miller, RK, *Collection of Tears*, Nunzio Press, Eugene, OR, 2006.

27. deMause, Lloyd, "The Universality of Incest," *The Journal of Psychohistory*, Fall 1991, vol. 19, No2. Included is a reference to: Landes, David S, "The Wealth and Poverty of Nations: Why Some are Rich and Some are Poor," pp. 6-14.

28. Farah, Caesar E., *Islam*, Barrons Educational Series, Great Neck, NY, 1994.

29. Williams, John Alden, *The Word of Islam*, University of Texas Press, Austin, TX, 1994.

30. Kitahara, Michio, "A Cross-Cultural Test of the Freudian Theory of Circumcision," *International Journal of Psychoanalytic Psychotherapy*, 5(1976): 535-46.

31. deMause, Lloyd, "The Universality of Incest," *The Journal of Psychohistory*, Fall 1991, Vol. 19, No. 2. Italics are direct quotes.

32. deMause, Lloyd, The History of Child Abuse, *The Journal of Psychohistory*, 25 (Winter) 1998.

33. Burney, Robert, *Codependence: The Dance of Wounded Souls*, Joy to You & Me Enterprises, Cambria, CA,.1995.

34. Love, Patricia with Robinson, Jo, *The Emotional Incest Syndrome: What to Do When a Parent's Love Rules Your Life.*, Bantam, New York, NY, 1991.

35. Forward, Susan with Frazier, Donna, *Emotional Blackmail: When People in Your Life Use Fear, Obligation and Guilt to Manipulate You*, HarperCollins, New York, NY, 1997.

36. Burney, Robert, *Codependence*.

37. Love, Patricia, *The Emotional Incest Syndrome*, Bantam, New York, NY, p. 126.

38. deMause, Lloyd, The Institute for Psychohistory.

39. Sa'ah, Randy Joe, "Cameroon girls battle 'breast ironing'", *BBC News*, 23 June 2006.

40. Tetchiada, Sylvestre, "Rights-Cameroon: An Unwelcomed 'Gift of God,'" *Inter Press Service News Agency*, 13 June 2006.

41. deMause, Lloyd, "The Universality of Incest," *The Journal of Psychohistory*, Fall 1991, Vol. 19, No.2.

42. Lichtarowicz, Ania, "Genital Mutilation Still Common: Female genital mutilation is still commonplace in Sudan, despite it being illegal, a new study has found," *BBC News*, 10 June 2003.

43. Lifton, Robert J, *The Nazi Doctors*, Basic Books, 1986,

44. Gonza, Sam, "Kenyan Bishop Calls on Widows to Take Stand Against Wife Inheritance," *Christianity Today*, 28 August 2000.

45. deMause, Lloyd, "The Universality of Incest."

46. Goldstein, Melvyn, Ed., The Center for Research on Tibet, *Tibetan Studies Internet Newsletter*, Vol. 2, #1, February, 2002.

47. Wallace BJ, "Pagan Gadding Spouse Exchange," *Ethnology*, 8: 183-188.

48. Bolton R, (1973), "Tawanku: Intercouple Bonds in Qolla Village (Peru)," *Anthropos*, 68: 245-255.

SOCIALIZATION

1. Campbell, Joseph, *The Power of Myth*, Doubleday, New York, NY, 1988, p. 48.

2. King, Gail and Wright, Meghan, University of Alabama, Department of Anthropology, *Diffusionism and Acculturation*.

3. Mishra, Vinod, *Is Male Circumcision Protective of HIV?* Presented at the 16th International AIDS Conference (AIDS) 2006, Toronto, Canada.

4. Knight, Chris, *Blood Relations: Menstruation and the Origins of Culture*, Yale University Press, New Haven, CT, 1991.

5.   deMause, Lloyd, *Foundations of Psychohistory*, Creative Roots, 1982.

6.   Thomas WI, "The Relation of Sex to Primitive Social Control," *American Journal of Sociology*, 3, (1898): 754-76.

7.   Thomas, WI, *Sex and Society: Studies in the Social Psychology of Sex*, University of Chicago Press, Chicago, IL, 1907.

8.   Eliade, Mircea, *The Myth of the Eternal Return*, Princeton University Press, Princeton, NJ, 1954.

9.   deMause, Lloyd, "Why Cults Terrorize and Kill Children," *The Journal of Psychohistory*, 21 (4) 1994.

10.   deMause, Lloyd, *The Social Alter*, Presented at the 18th Annual Convention of the International Psychohistorical Association on June 7, 1995 in New York City.

11.   Gould, Catherine, "Denying Ritual Abuse of Children," *The Journal of Psychohistory*, 22 (3) 1995.

12.   Douglas, JD, General Editor, *The New Bible Dictionary*, "Baal-Berith," Eerdmans, 1962, p. 115.

13.   Emery, Paul E., "Trauma in Psychohistory," *The Journal of Psychohistory*, V. 26, N. 3, winter 1999.

14.   Forward, Susan with Buck, Craig, *Toxic Parents: Overcoming Their Hurtful Legacy And Reclaiming Your Life*, Bantam, New York, NY, p. 15.

15.   PsychNet-UK, *Social Psychology 1*.

16.   Flynt, Henry A., *Self-Justification in Human Relations*, 1998.

17.   George Herbert Mead, "The Social Self," *Journal of Philosophy, Psychology and Scientific Methods*, 10, (1913): 374-38.

18.   Ausubel, Kenny, *When Healing Becomes a Crime*, Healing Arts Press, p. 291.

19.   Schwartz W, Charney E, et al., *Pediatric Primary Care: A Problem-Solving Approach*, 2nd Ed., Year Book Medical Publishers, Chicago, IL, pp. 861-862.

20.   Thomas WI, "Sex in Primitive Morality," *American Journal of Sociology*, 4, (1899): 774-787./

21.   Knight, Chris, *Blood Relations: Menstruation and the Origins of Culture*, Yale University Press, New Haven, CT, 1991, p. 379.

22.   Rubin, Harriet, *The Princessa: Machiavelli for Women*, Doubleday, New York, NY, pp. 9 and 13.

23.   Freud, Sigmund, *Three Essays of the Theory of Sexuality*, Avon Books, New York, NY, 1962.

24.   Horney, Karen, *Feminine Psychology*, Norton, New York, NY, 1967.

25.   Shaalan M, "Clitoris Envy: A psychodynamic construct instrumental in female circumcision," *WHO/EMRO Technical Publications*; 1982.

26.   Marindany, Kurgat, "Circumcise All Men, Says MP," *The East African Standard*, 18 December 2001.

27.   Paddock, Richard C., "Purified in the name of Allah," *Los Angeles Times*, Los Angeles, CA, 13 March 2001.

28.   Lifton, Robert, *The Nazi Doctors: Medical Killing and the Psychology of Genocide*, Basic Books, New York, NY, pp. 482, 484, 470-471, 482-483 and 199.

29.   Paddock, Richard C., "Teen Relives 'Nightmare' as a Muslim Slave," *Los Angeles Times*, Los Angeles, CA, 14 March 2001.

MANIPULATION

1.   Bell, Catherine, *Ritual Theory, Ritual Practice*, Oxford University Press, Oxford, UK, 1992.

2.   Ross, Edward, *Social Psychology*, Macmillan, NY, 1919.

3.   Bernard, LL, *An Introduction to Social Psychology*, Holt and Company, NY, 1946.

4.   Johnson C, *Suggestibility*. www.mb-soft.com/public/suggest.html, 2005.

5.   Znaniecki, Florian, *The Laws of Social Psychology*, Warsaw-Kraków-Poznań, Warsaw, Poland, 1925.

6.   deMause, Lloyd, "The Universality of Incest," *The Journal of Psychohistory*, Fall 1991, Vol. 19, No. 2.

7.   Bigelow, Jim, *The Joy of Uncircumcising*, Hourglass, Aptos, CA, 1995.

8.   deMause, Lloyd, The History of Child Abuse, *The Journal of Psychohistory*, 25 (Winter) 1998.

9.   Bell, Catherine, *Ritual Theory, Ritual Practice*, Oxford University Press, pp. 98-108, 196.

10. Burney, Robert, *Codependence: The Dance of Wounded Souls.*, Joy to You & Me Enterprises, Cambria, CA, 1995.

11. White, J., *The Power of Words*, JHWhite Pubsco, 1996.

12. Rank, Hugh, *Persuasion Analysis*, Counter-Propaganda Press, Portland, OR, 1988.

13. Rank, Hugh, *Language and Public Policy*, Macmillan, NY, 1975.

14. Rank, Hugh, *Pep Talk: How to Analyze Political Language*, Counter-Propaganda Press, Portland, OR, 1984.

15. Rank, Hugh, *The Pitch*, Counter-Propaganda Press, Portland, OR, 1991.

16. Beel, Nathan Charles, *A Study of the Persuasion Techniques Used by Jehovah's Witnesses and the Watchtower*. A research report submitted to Tabor College, Adelaide, as the Directed Study Project component for the degree of Bachelor of Arts in Christian Counselling, November, 1997

17. *Department of the Army*, "Psychological Operations Field Manuel No. 33-1," Headquarters, Washington, DC, 1979.

18. Bernays, Edward and Miller, Mark, *Propaganda*, Ig Publishing, 2004.

19. Bernays, Edward, *Public Relations*, Bellmen Publishing Company, 1945.

20. Seitel, Fraser P, *Practice of Public Relations*, 11th Edition, Prentice Hall, 2010.

21. Bernays, Edward, and Cutler, Howard, *The Engineering of Consent*, University of Oklahoma Press, 1955.

22. Herman, Edward S. and Chomsky, Noam, *Manufacturing Consent: The Political Economy of the Mass Media*, Pantheon, 2002.

23. Post P, Preston L and Sachs S, *Redefining the Corporation: Stakeholder Management and Organizational Wealth*, Stanford Business Books, 2002.

24. Bernays, Edward, *Crystallizing Public Opinion*, Kessinger Publishing, 2004.

25. *NOCIRC Newsletter,* Fall, 2003, pp. 1-2.

LEGAL

1. Schroeder, Patricia & Collins, Barbara, *The Federal Prohibition of Female Circumcision Mutilation Act of 1993, (HR 3247)*.

2. Spaeth, HJ., & Smith, EC., *HarperCollins College Outline: The Constitution of the United States*, 13th edition, p. 211. Amendment IX, (1868)), Section 1, HarperCollins, New York, NY, 1991.

3. Kay, Susan, *The Constitutional Dimensions of an Inmate's Right to Health Care*, National Commission on Correctional Health Care, 1991, p. 5. "To be successful in an individual action, a prisoner generally must show that there was an intentional delay in care, or callous indifference to obvious medical needs... such deliberate indifference can be shown by a demonstration that the medical care clearly was inadequate or that an inmate was denied recommended treatment or access to a physician capable of diagnosing the ailment and providing treatment... Delay in necessary medical treatment also may constitute deliberate indifference."

4. *Medical Board of California*, (Press Release), "Medical Board of California Arrests Santa Clarita Resident for Unlicensed Practice of Medicine," Sacramento, CA, 23 December 2002.

5. *Feminist Daily News Wire*, "Deportation Stayed, African Immigrant Woman Avoids Possible Genital Mutilation," 06 January 2003.

6. Gifis, Steven H., *Law Dictionary*, 2nd edition, Barron's Educational Series, Hauppauge, NY, 1984, p. 16.

7. Ibid, p. 30.

8. Ibid, p. 43.

9. Harrison, James, "Benefit for burn victim scheduled," *The Ukiah Daily Journal*, Ukiah, CA, 16 October 2001.

10. Thevenot, Carri Geer, "Father fights to stop son's circumcision," *Las Vegas Review-Journal*, Las Vegas, NV, 15 January 2001.

11. Shoemaker, Crissa, "Parents Battling over Circumcision of Son to Discuss Settlement Today," *Courier News*, Somerset, New Jersey, 18 January 2001.

12. Gifis, SH, p. 240.

13.   Ibid, pp. 62-63.

14.   Ibid, p. 76

15.   White, Becky Cox, *Competence to Concent*, Georgetown University Press, Washington, DC, 1994. pp. 16, 27-28, 49 and 154.

16.   Pozgar, George D., *Legal Aspects of Health Care Administration*, Aspen, Rockville, MD, 1990, pp. 336, 264 and 66.

17.   Svoboda, Steven, "Doctor pays parents $23,000 for circumcision without consent," *NOCIRC press release*. (15 September 2006)

18.   Gifis, SH, p. 172.

19.   Millholland, Michael, "Patient for heart bypass sues over circumcision," *The Advocate*, Baton Rouge, LA.

20.   Gifis, SH, p. 148.

21.   Ibid, 194-196.

22.   *Hate Crime: The Violence of Intolerance*. (15 September 2006) usdoj.gov/crs/pubs/htecrm.htm

23.   Gifis, SH, p. 240.

24.   Gifis, SH, p. 288.

25.   Zimmerman F, "Origin and Significance of the Jewish Rite of Circumcision," *Psychoanalytic Review*, 38(2): 103-112, 1951.

26.   Douglas, J, Ressler, RK, et al., *Sexual Homicide: Patterns and Motives*, Jossey-Bass, San Francisco, CA, 1992, p. 48.

27.   Gifis, SH, p. 289.

28.   Cronin, Danielle, "Circumcision victim's bid to help others," *The Canberra Times*, Canberra, Australia, 31 March 2002.

29.   Gifis, SH, pp. 309-310.

30.   Grell, Jeff, *The Rico Act*. (15 September 2006) www.ricoact.com

31.   Convention on the Rights of the Child, *Document A/RES/44/25*, U.N. General Assembly, 12 December 1989.

32.   Committee on Bioethics, American Academy of Pediatrics, "Religious Objections to Medical Care," *Pediatrics*, vol. 99, No. 2, pp. 279-81, February 1997.

33.   Committee on Bioethics, American Academy of Pediatrics, "Religious Exemptions from Child Abuse Statutes," *Pediatrics*, vol. 81, No. 1, Jan. 1988.

34.   Gifis, SH, p. 532.

35.   Taunton, Dana G., "Tort Law Update," *Montgomery County Bar Association, Montgomery*, Alabama, 21 December 1999. Section A. Evidence. Evidence-Medical, #3. Ex parte Pfizer, 1999, WL 357415 (Ala. June, 1999). Re: 3/4 penis lost after circumcision complication. Point. Circumcision in itself is a Tort in that the prepuce is removed.

36.   Gifis, SH, p. 482-483.

BIBLIOGRAPHY

ANTHROPOLOGY

Bancroft, Anne, *Origins of the Sacred*, Arkana, 1987.

Barnard GW, Kripel JJ, editors., *Crossing Boundaries: Essays on the Ethical Status of Mysticism*, Chatham House, 2002.

Bernard, Luther, *An Introduction to Social Psychology*, Henry Holt and Co., 1926.

Coe, Michael, *The Maya*, Thames and Hudson, 1997.

Crawford, Christina and Bradford, John, *No Safe Place: The Legacy of Family Violence*, Barrytown/Station Hill Press, 1994.

Dawkins, Richard, *The Selfish Gene*, Oxford University Press, 1976.

Durant, Will, *The Story of Civilization: Part II: The Life of Greece*, Simon and Schuster, 1966.

Farrell, William, *Women Can't Hear What Men Don't Say: Destroying Myth, Creating Love*, Tarcher, 2000.

Fastlicht, Samuel, *Tooth Mutilations and Dentistry in Pre-Columbian Mexico*, Barnes & Noble, 1976.

Graglia, Carolyn, *Domestic Tranquility: A Brief Against Feminism*, Spence, 1998.

Hobbsbawn, Eric, et al., *The Invention of Tradition*, Cambridge University Press, 1982.

Hunter, John A and Mannix, Daniel P, *Tales of the African Frontier*, Harper & Brothers, NY, 1954.

Josephus, trans., Whiston W, *The Works of Josephus*, Hendrickson, 1987.

Koestler, Arthur, *The Act of Creation*, Penguin/Arkana, 1964.

Koestler, Arthur, *The Sleepwalkers: A History of Man's Vision of the Universe*, Arkana, 1990.

Magray, Mary, *The Transforming Power of the Nuns: Women, Religion, & Cultural Change in Ireland, 1750-1900*, Oxford University Press, 1998.

McNamara, Jo Ann, *Sisters in Arms: Catholic Nuns Through Two Millennia*, Harvard University Press, 1996.

Meyers, Carol, *Discovering Eve: Ancient Israelite Women in Context*, Oxford University Press, 1988.

Philo, trans. Yonge, *The Works of Philo*, Hendrickson, 1993.

Rappaport, Roy, and Hart, Keith, *Ritual and Religion in the Making of Humanity*, Cambridge University Press, 1999.

Ross, Edward, *Social Psychology: An outline and source book*, Macmillan, 1919.

Rousseau, Jean-Jacque, *The Social Contract*, Penguin Classics, 1968.

Rubin, Harriet, *The Princessa: Machiavelli for Women*, Doubleday, 1997.

Schele, Linda and Freidel, David, *A Forest of Kings: The Untold Story of the Ancient Maya*, Morrow, 1990.

Tannahill, Rhea, *Sex in History*, Stein and Day, 1982.

Znaniecki, Florian, *The Laws of Social Psychology*, University of Chicago Press, 1925.

BLOOD

Buckley, Thomas and Gottleib, Alma, *Blood Magic: The Anthology of Menstruation*, University of California Press, 1988.

Ehrenreich, Barbara, *Blood Rites: Origins and History of the Passions of War*, Metropolitan, 1997.

Hoffman, Lawrence, *Covenant of Blood: Circumcision and Gender in Rabbinic Judaism*, University of Chicago Press, 1996.

Horrigan, Bonnie, *Red Moon Passage: The Power and Wisdom of Menopause*, Three Rivers Press, 1996.

Knight, Chris, *Blood Relations: Menstruation and the Origins of Culture*, Yale University Press, 1991.

Laferriere-Rancour, Daniel, *Signs of the Flesh: An Essay on the Evolution of Hominid Sexuality*, Indiana University Press, 1985.

Marshall, Paul with Gilbert, Lela, *Their Blood Cries Out*, Word Publishing, 1997.

CRIMINOLOGY

Cullen, Robert, *Citizen X*, Ivy Books, 1992.

Banning, Peter, *Breaking the Cycle: A Fresh Look*, Xlibris, 2000.

Burgess AW, Holstrom LL, *Rape: Victims of Crisis*, Robert J. Brady, 1974.

De River, J Paul, *The Sexual Criminal: A Psychological Study*, Bloat, 2000.

Douglas, John; Burgess, Ann; Burgess, Allen; and Ressler, Robert, *Crime Classification Manual: A Standard System for Investigating and Classifying Violent Crimes*, Jossey-Bass, 1997.

Douglas, John with Olshaker, Mark, *Journey into Darkness*, Pocket, 1997.

Douglas, John with Olshaker, Mark, *Mind Hunter: Inside the FBI's Elite Serial Crime Unit*, Pocket, 1995.

Douglas, John with Olshaker, Mark, *Obsession*, Pocket, 1998.

Douglas, John with Olshaker, Mark, *The Anatomy of Motive*, Pocket, 1999.

Evans, Colin, *The Casebook of Forensic Detection: How Science Solved 100 of the Worlds Most Baffling Crimes*, John Wiley & Sons, 1996.

Fairstein, Linda, *Sexual Violence, Our War Against Rape*, Berkeley, 1995.

Fletcher, Connie, *What Cops Know*, Pocket, 1990.

Hazelwood, Robert Roy and Burgess Ann W, *Practical Aspects of Rape Investigation: A Multi-Disciplined Approach*, Elsevier, 1987.

Heldman, Mary, *When Words Hurt*, Ballentine, 1998.

Holmes RM and Holmes, *Profiling Violent Crime: An Investigative Tool*, Sage, 2002.

Kelleher M, and Kelleher C, *Murder Most Rare: The Female Serial Killer*, Dell, 1998.

Keppel, Robert with Birnes, William, *Signature Killers: Interpreting the Calling Cards of the Serial Murderer*, Pocket, 1997.

Landau, Elaine, *An American Epidemic*, Simon and Schuster, 1990.

Michaud, Stephen with Hazelwood, Roy, *The Evil That Men Do*, St. Martin's, 1998.

Ressler, Robert; Burgess, Ann; Douglas, John, *Sexual Homicide: Patterns and Motives*, The Free Press, 1988.

Ressler, Robert & Shachtman, T, *I Have Lived in the Monster*, St. Martin's, 1997.

Ressler, Robert & Shachtman, T, *Whoever Fights Monsters*, St. Martin's, 1992.

Rhodes, Richard, *Why They Kill*, Alfred A. Knopf, 1999.

Rosenthal AM, *Thirty-eight Witnesses: The Kitty Genovese Case*, University of California Press, 1999.

Spencer, Judith, *Suffer the Child*, Pocket, 1989.

DICTIONARY

Douglas JD, General Editor, The New Bible Dictionary, Eerdmans Publishing Co., 1962.

Werblowski RJZ, Wignor G, *The Oxford Dictionary of the Jewish Religion*, Oxford University Press, 1997.

LEGAL

Gifis, Steven, *Law Dictionary*, 2nd ed., Barron's Educational Series, 1984.

Johnson, Seigler and Winslade, *Clinical Ethics*, 3rd edition, McGraw Hill, 1984.

Kay, Susan, *The Constitutional Dimensions of an Inmate's Right to Health Care*, National Commission on Correctional Health Care by the Corrections and Sentencing Committee, Criminal Justice Section of the American Bar Association, 1991.

Myers, John EB, *Legal Issues in Child Abuse and Neglect Practice*, SAGE Publications, Interpersonal Violence: The Practice Series, Second Edition, 1998.

Pozgar, George, *Legal Aspects of Health Care Administration*, Aspen, 1990.

Schroeder, Patricia and Collins, Barbara, *The Federal Prohibition of Female Genital Mutilation Act of 1993. (HR 3247)*. NOCIRC, Spring 1994, vol. 8, no. 1.

Spaeth, Harold & Smith, Edward, *The Constitution of the United States*, 13th edition, Harper Collins, 1991.

White, Becky, *Competence To Consent*, Georgetown University Press, 1994.

LITERATURE

Kurth, Peter, *Isadora: A Sensational Life*, Back Day Books, 2002.

Lamb, Charles, *The Works of Charles Lamb*, Volume IV., V., A. C. Armstrong and Son, 1881.

Majdalany, Fred, *The Monastery*, Corgi, 1957.

Paine, Thomas, *Common Sense*, Penguin Classics, 1986.

Shakespeare, William, *William Shakespeare: The Complete Works*, Barnes & Noble, 1994.

MEDICINE

Ambrose A, *Stimulation in Early Infancy*, New York Academic Press, 1969.

Ausubel, Kenny, *When Healing Becomes a Crime: The Amazing Story of Hoxey Cancer Clinics and the Return of Alternative Therapies*, Healing Arts Press, 2000.

Bernstein, Robert and Bernstein, Michelle-Root, *Honey, Mud, Maggots and other Medical Marvels: The Science Behind Folk Remedies and Old Wives Tales*, Houghton Mifflin, 1997.

Boston's Women's Health Book Collective, *Our Bodies, Ourselves*, Touchstone, 1998.

Boston's Women's Health Book Collective, *Ourselves and Our Children*, Touchstone, 1996.

Chamberlain, David, *Babies Remember Birth: Extraordinary Scientific Discoveries about the Mind and Personality of Your Newborn*, Ballentine, 1988.

Clemente CD, Purpura DP, Mayer F, editors., *Sleep and the Maturing Nervous System*, New York Academic Press, 1972.

Ephron, John M., *Medicine and the German Jews: A History*, Yale University Press, 2001.

Finkel, Martin A. and Giardino, Angelo P., *Medical Evaluation of Child Sexual Abuse: A Practical Guide*, Sage, 2001.

Foss BM, *Determinants of Infant Behavior*, John Wiley & Sons, 1961.

LeGuerer, Annick, trans., R. Miller, Sce*nt: The Essential and Mysterious Powers of Smells*, Kodansha, International, 1992.

LeVay, Simon, *The Sexual Brain*, A Bradford Book, The MIT Press, 1993.

Lieber, Arnold, *How the Moon Affects You*, Hastings House, 1996.

Lipsitt LP, Reese HW, editors., *Advances in Child Development and Behavior*, Vol. 4, New York Academic Press, 1980.

Marlow DR and Sellew G, *Textbook of Pediatric Nursing*, W. B. Saunders, 1965.

Marshall FF, editor., *Urologic Complications, Medical and Surgical, Adult and Pediatric*, Chicago,: Year Book Medical Publishers, 1986.

McCracken, Thomas, *New Atlas of Human Anatomy*, MetroBooks, Friedman/Fairfax, 2001.

Mendelshon, Robert, *Confessions of a Medical Heretic*, McGraw-Hill, 1990.

Mendelshon, Robert, *How to Raise a Healthy Child in Spite of Your Doctor*, Ballentine, 1987.

Monteleone, James, *Recognition of Child Abuse for the Mandated Reporter*, GW Medical Publishing, 1996.

Remindo P, *History of Circumcision*, 1st Edition, Philadelphia, PA, F. A. Davis, Co., 1891.

Schwartz WM, Charney EB, Curry TA, Ludwig S., *Pediatric Primary Care: A Problem-Oriented Approach*, 2nd edition, Year Book Medical Publishers, 1990.

Semmelweis, Ignatz, *The Etiology, Concept, and Prophylaxis of Childbed Fever*, University of Wisconsin Press, 1983.

van der Kolk B, McFarlane A, Weiseth L, *Traumatic Stress: The Effects of Overwhelming Experience on Mind, Body, and Society*, Guilford, 1996.

Zur Hausen H., *Advances in Viral Oncology: Papillomavirus as Carcinomaviruses*, (Klein G. Ed.), Vol. 8, N.Y., Raven Press, 1988.

MILITARY
duPicq, Ardant, *Battle Studies*, AMS Press, Inc., 1991.

Keegan, John, *The Face of Battle*, The Viking Press, 1976.

Patton, Gen. George S., *War As I knew It*, Bantam, 1989.

Tzu, Sun, *The Art of War*, trans. Samuel B. Griffin, Oxford University Press, 1971.

Weir, William, *Fatal Victories*, Archon Books, 1993.

MUTILATION
Abu-Sahleih, Dr. Sami Aldeeb, *Male & Female Circumcision: Among Jews, Christians & Muslims*, Shangri-La, 2001.

Abu-Sahleih, Dr. Sami Aldeeb, *To Mutilate in the Name of Jehova or Allah: Legitimization of Male and Female Circumcision*, St. SulpiceVD/Suisse, 14.

Batsheva, Bonne-Tamir and Avinoam, Adam, *New Perspectives on Genetic Markers and Diseases among Jewish People*, Oxford University Press, 1992.

Bigelow, Jim, *The Joy of Uncircumcising*, Hourglass, 1995.

Colapinto, John, *As Nature Made Him: the boy who was raised as a girl*, Harper Perennial, 2001.

Denniston, George C., Milos, Marilyn Fayre, *Sexual Mutilations: A Human Tragedy*, Plenum Press, 1997.

Fastlicht, Samuel, *Tooth Mutilations and Dentistry in Pre-Columbian Mexico*, Barnes & Noble, 1976.

Glick, Leonard, *Marked in Your Flesh: Circumcision from Ancient Judea to Modern America*, Oxford University Press, 2005.

Kellogg, John Harvey, *Treatment for Self-Abuse and Its Effects, Plain Facts for Old and Young*, P. Segner & Co., 1888.

Klein, Hanny-Lightfoot, *A Woman's Odyssey into Africa, Tracks Across a Life*, Nunzio Press, 2009.

Klein, Hanny-Lightfoot, *Children's Genitals Under the Knife: Social Imperatives, Secrecy and Shame*, Nunzio Press, 2009.

Klein, Hanny-Lightfoot, *Prisoners of Ritual, An Odyssey into Female Genital Circumcision in Africa*, Nunzio

Press, 2009.
Lewis J, *In the Name of Humanity*, New York, Eugenics, 1949.
Robinett, Patricia, *The Rape of Innocence: FGM & Circumcision in the U.S.A.*, Nunzio Press, 2009.
Wallerstein, Edward, *Circumcision: An American Health Fallacy*, Springer, 1980.

MYTHOLOGY

Campbell, Joseph, *Primitive Mythology: The Masks of God*, Penguin, 1991.
Campbell, Joseph, *The Mystic Image*, Princeton University Press, 1990.
Campbell, Joseph, *The Power of Myth*, Anchor/Doubleday, 1988.
Eliade, Mircea, *The Myth of the Eternal Return*, Princeton University Press, 1954.
Faulkner, Raymond, trans., (The Papyrus of Ani): *The Egyptian Book of the Dead: The Book of Going Forth by Day*, Chronicle Books, 1994.
Frazier, James George, *The Belief in Immortality and the Worship of the Dead*, Macmillan, 1913.
Graves, Robert, *The Greek Myths*, Complete Edition, Penguin, 1992.
Levi-Strauss, Claude, trans. Weidenfeld and Nicolson, *The Naked Man: An Introduction to the Science of Mythology*, Harper and Row, 1981.
Murray, Margaret, *The God of the Witches*, Oxford University Press, 1970.
Neumann, Erich, *The Great Mother*, Princeton University Press, 1991.
Pope, Alexander, *The Iliad of Homer*, The Heritage Press, 1943.
Pope, Alexander, *The Odyssey of Homer*, The Heritage Press, 1942.
Slater, Philip, *The Glory of Hera, Greek Mythology and Greek Family*, Princeton University Press, 1992.

NEGOTIATION - BUSINESS

Bernays, Edward, *Crystallization Public Opinion*, Kessinger Publishing, 2004.
Bernays, Edward and Miller, Mark, *Propaganda*, Ig Publications, 2004.
Bernays, Edward, *Public Relations*, Bellmen Publishing Company, 1945.
Bernays, Edward and Cutler, Howard, *The Engineering of Consent*, University of Oklahoma Press, 1955.
Burney, Robert, *Codependence: The Dance of Wounded Souls*, Joy to You & Me Enterprises, 1995.
Herman, Edward S. And Chomsky, Noam, *Manufacturing Consent: The Political Economy of the Mass Media*, Pantheon, 2002.
Post J, Preston L and Sachs S, *Redefining the Corporation: Stakeholder Management and Organizational Wealth*, Stanford Business Books, 2002.
Rank, Hugh, *Language and Public Policy*, MacMillan, 1975.
Rank, Hugh, *Pep Talk: How to Analyze Political Language*, Counter-Propaganda Press, 1984.
Rank, Hugh, *Persuasion Analysis: A Companion to Composition*, Counter-Propaganda Press, 1988.
Rank, Hugh, *The Pitch*, Counter-Propaganda Press, 1991.
Seitel, Fraser P, *Practice of Publish Relations*, 11th Edition, Prentice Hall, 2010.

PSYCHOLOGY

Adams, Kenneth, *Silently Seduced: When Parents Make Their Children Partners: Understanding Covert Incest*, HCI, 1991.
American Psychiatric Association, *Diagnostic and Statistical Manual of Mental Disorders, DSM-IV*, 4th edition, American Psychiatric Association, 1996.
American Psychiatric Association, *Quick Reference to the Diagnostic Criteria from DSM-IV*, American

Psychiatric Association, 1994.

Berne, Eric, *Games People Play*, Ballentine, 1964.

Bourdeaux, Pierre, *Outline of a Theory of Practice*, Cambridge University Press, 1977.

deMause, Lloyd, *Foundations of Psychohistory*, Creative Roots, 1982.

deMause, Lloyd, *The Emotional Life of Nations*, Other Press, 2002.

deMause, Lloyd, *The History of Childhood: The Untold Story of Child Abuse*, Jason Aronson, 1995.

Edinger, Edward, *Ego and Archetype: Individuation and the Religious Function of the Psyche*, Shambala, 1992.

Estes, Clarissa Pinkola, *Women Who Run With the Wolves, Myths and Stories of the Wild Woman Archetype*, Ballentine, 1995.

Favazza, Armando R., *Bodies Under Siege: Self-mutilation and Body Modification in Culture and Psychiatry*, The Johns Hopkins University Press, 1996.

Forward, Susan with Buck, Craig, *Toxic Parents: Overcoming their Hurtful Legacy and Reclaiming your Life*, Bantam, 1990.

Forward, Susan with Frazier, Donna, *Emotional Blackmail: When People in Your Life Use Fear, Obligation and Guilt to Manipulate You*, Harper Collins, 1997.

Freud, Sigmund, *Three Essays on the Theory of Sexuality*, Avon Books, 1962.

Harris, Thomas, *I'm OK – You're OK*, Avon Books, 1973.

Hobsbawn, Eric, et al., *The Invention of Tradition: Mass Producing Traditions: Europe, 1870-1914*, Cambridge University Press, 1983.

Horney, Karen, *Feminine Psychology*, Norton, 1967.

Lewis, Michael, *Shame: The Exposed Self*, The Free Press, 1995.

Jung, Carl, editor, *Man and his Symbols*, Dell Laurel Edition, 1964.

Jung, Carl, *The Undiscovered Self*, A Mentor Book, 1958.

Jung, Emma, *Animus and Anima*, Spring Publications, 1985.

Lifton, Robert, *The Nazi Doctors: Medical Killing and the Psychology of Genocide*, Basic Books, 1986.

Little, Margaret, *Transference Neurosis & Transference Psychosis*, Jason Aronson, 1993.

Love, Patricia with Robinson, Jo, *The Emotional Incest Syndrome*, Bantam, 1991.

Miller, Alice, *Banished Knowledge: Facing Childhood Injuries*, Anchor 1991.

Miller, Alice, *Breaking Down the Walls of Silence*, Doubleday, 1990.

Miller, Alice, *For Your Own Good: Hidden Cruelty in Child-rearing and the Roots of Violence*, The Noonday Press, 1990.

Miller, Alice, *The Untouched: Tracing Childhood Trauma in Creativity and Destructiveness*, Anchor, 1991.

Miller, Alice, *Thou Shalt Not Be Aware: Society's Betrayal of the Child*, Farrar, Straus and Giroux, 1998.

Miller, Robert K., *Collection of Tears*, Nunzio, Press, 2008.

Rutter, Virginia, *Woman Changing Woman*, Harper San Francisco, 1993.

Shay, Jonathan, *Achilles in Vietnam: Combat Trauma and the Undoing of Character*, Touchstone, 1994.

Thomas, WI, *Sex and Society: Studies in the Social Psychology of Sex*, University of Chicago Press, 1907.

Vaknin, Sam, *Malignant Self Love: Narcissism Revisited*, Narcissus Pub., 2003.

RITUAL

Bell, Catherine, *Ritual Theory, Ritual Practice*, Oxford University Press, 1992.

Bourdieu, Pierre, *Outline of a Theory of Practice*, Cambridge University Press, 1977.

Geertz, Clifford, *Negara: The Theatre State in Nineteenth Century Bali*, Princeton University Press, 1980.

Heesterman, J. C., *The Inner Conflict of Tradition*, University of Chicago Press, 1985.

Hobbsbawn, Eric, et al., The Invention of Tradition, University of Chicago Press, 1982.

Myss, Caroline, *Sacred Contracts: Awakening Your Divine Potential*, Three Rivers Press, 2003.

Rapport, Roy, and Hart, Keith, *Ritual and Religion in the Making of Humanity*, Cambridge University Press, 1999.

Sered, Susan, *Women as Ritual Experts: The Religious Lives of Elderly Jewish Women in Jerusalem*, Oxford University Press, 1992.

SCRIPTURAL

Alama, Sir Abdulla & Al-Mamum Al-Suhrawardybu-Sahleih, *The Sayings of Muhammad*, A Citadel Press Book, 1990.

Bloom, H., trans. David Rosenberg, *The Book of J*, Vintage, 1991.

Farah, Caesar, *Islam*, Barron's Educational Series, 1994.

Williams, John Alden, *The Word of Islam*, University of Texas Press, 1994.

PERIODICALS

ABUSE
(Child Abuse, Domestic Violence, Munchausen, Pedophilia, Incest, Infanticide, Filicide, Neonaticide)

Adams SR, with Freeman DR, "Women Who Are Violent: Attitudes and Beliefs of Professionals Working in the Field of Domestic Violence," *Military Medicine*, Vol. 167, No. 6, June 2002, 445-450.

Asher, Richard (1951). "Munchausen Syndrome," *Lancet*, i: 33-41.

Belinsky J, "Child Maltreatment: An ecological integration," *Amer Psychol*, 35 (40: 320-35).

Bools C, Neale BA, "Co-morbidity Associated with Fabricated Illness (Munchausen Syndrome by Proxy)," *Archives of Diseases in Childhood*, 67:77-79.

Bools C, Neale B, and Meadow R, "Munchausen syndrome by proxy: a study of psychopathology," *Child Abuse and Neglect*, vol. 18, no 9, pp. 773-88.

Boros SJ, Ophoven JP, et al., "Munchausen syndrome by proxy: a profile of medical child abuse," *Australian Family Physician*, vol. 24, no. 5, pp772-3; 768-69.

Crouse KA, (1992), "Munchausen Syndrome by Proxy: Recognizing the Victim," *Pediatric Nursing*, 18(3):249-52.

d'Orban P, "Women who kill their children," *Brit J Psychiat*, 1979; 134: 560-71.

deMause L, "The Universality of Incest," *The Journal of Psychohistory*, Fall 1991, Vol. 19, No. 2, 123-64.

deMause L, "Why Cults Terrorize and Kill Children," *The Journal of Psychohistory*, 21 (4) 1994.

Detrich D, Berkowitz L, Kadushin A & McGloin J, "Some factors influencing abusers' justification of their child abuse," *Child Abuse & Neglect*, 14, 337-345.

Devereaux G, "Mohave Indian Infanticide," *Psychoanal Rev*, 1948; 35:1236-39.

Garber C, "Eskimo Infanticide," *Scient Month*, 1947; 64:98-102.

Gould C, "Denying Ritual Abuse of Children," *The Journal of Psychohistory*, 22 (3) 1995.

Greenberg DM, Bradford J, and Curry S, "Infantophilia – a new subcategory of pedophilia?: a preliminary study." *Bulletin of the American Academy of Psychiatry and Law*, 23(1), 63-71.

Hanon KA, (1991), "Child Abuse: Munchausen Syndrome by Proxy," *FBI Law Enforcement Bulletin*, 60:8-11.

Harder T, "The Psychopathology of Infanticide," *Acta Psychiat Scand*, 1967; 43:196-245.

Jones JG, Butler HL, et al., (1986), "Munchausen Syndrome by Proxy," *Child Abuse and Neglect*, 10:33-40.

Kellum B, "Infanticide in England in the Latter Middle Ages," *History of Childhood Quarterly*, 1974,

1:367-88.

Laster K, "Infanticide: A Litmus Test for Feminist Criminological Theory," (1989) 22 *Aust & NZ J of Criminology*, 151-152.

Lewis CF, Baranoski MV, Buchannon J, Benedek EP, "Factors associated with weapon use in filicidal women," *J Forensic Sci*, 43(3): 613-618.

Lewis CF, Ednie KJ, "Koro and homicidal behavior," *Am J Psychiatry*, 154 (8): 1169.

Libow JA, Schreier HA, (1986), "Three Forms of Factitious Illness in Children: When is it Munchausen Syndrome by Proxy?," *Am J of Orthopsychiatry*, 56(4):602-11.

Marks MN, Kumar R, "Infanticide in England and Wales," *Medicine, Science and the Law*, 33: 329-339.

Marks MN, Kumar R, "Infanticide in Scotland," *Medicine, Science and the Law*, 36:299.

McCloskey LA, Walker M, "Posttraumatic Stress Disorder Common in Children Abused by Family Members," *J of the American Academy of Child & Adolescent Psychiatry*, 13 December 1999.

McKay M, "The link between domestic violence and child abuse: Assessment and treatment considerations," *Child Welfare League of America*, 73: 29-39.

Meadow, Roy, (1977). "Munchausen Syndrome by Proxy: The Hinterland of Child Abuse," *Lancet*, ii: 342-345.

Menage J, "Professionals should not collude with abusive systems," *BMJ*, 311:1088-1089, 21 October 1995.

Mercy JA, Saltzman LE, "Fatal violence among spouses in the United States, 1976-85," *Amer J of Public Health* 79(5): 595-9 May 1989.

Mire S, "Genital Mutilation By Any Other Name," *NOCIRC*, Fall, vol. 7, No. 2, p.1.

O'Leary KD, Barling J, Arias I, Rosenbaum A, Malone J, Tyree A, "Prevalence and stability of physical aggression between spouses: a longitudinal analysis," *J of Consulting & Clinical Psychology*, 57 (2): 263-8, April 1989.

Osborne J, "The Crime of Infanticide: Throwing Out the Baby with the Bathwater," (1987), 6, *Canadian J of Family Law*, 47-49.

Pitt SE, Bale EM, (1995), "Neonaticide, infanticide, and filicide: A review of the Literature," *Bulletin of the American Academy of Psychiatry and Law*, 23: 375-386.

Premi Mahendra K, Raju S, "Born to die: Female Infanticide in Madhya Pradesh," *Search Bulletin*, July-Sept 1998, 13(3): 94-105.

Reid WH, "Myths About Violent Sexual Predators and All That Pesky Legislation," *J Pract Psychiatry and Behav Health*, July 1998, 4:246-248.

Resnick PJ, "The Detection of Malingered Mental Illness," *Behav Sciences & the Law,* 2:21-38, 1984.

Resnick PJ, "The Detection of Malingered Psychosis," *Psych Clinics of North Amer*, 22:159-72, 1999.

Sadoff RL, (1995), "Mothers who kill their children," *Psychiatric Annals*, 25: 601-605.

Sakkuta T, Saito S, "A Socio-Medical Study of 71 Cases of Infanticide in Japan," *Keio J Med*, 1981; 30:155-168.

Scott PD, (973a), "Parents who kill their children," *Medicine, Science and the Law*, 13: 120-126.

Sheppard, "Double Jeopardy: the link between child abuse and maternal depression in child and family social work," *Child and Family Social Work*, 1997, vol. 2, pp. 91-107.

Sigal M, Gelkopf M, et al., "Munchausen Syndrome by Proxy: The Triad of Abuse, Self-Abuse, and Deception," *Comprehensive Psychiatry*, 30(6):527-33.

Simpson AIE, Stanton J, (2000), "Maternal Filicide: A reformulation of factors relevant to risk," *Criminal Behavior and Mental Health*, 10: 136-147.

Sosby D, "Altruistic Filicide: Bioethics or Criminology?," *Health Ethics Today*, vol. 12, No. 1, Fall/November

2001.

Sterck EHM, "Female dispersal, social organization, and infanticide in langurs: are they linked to human disturbance?," *Am J Primatol*, 44: 235-54.

Summit, Roland, "The Child Sexual Abuse Accommodation Syndrome," *Child Abuse and Neglect*, 7: 177, 1983.

Terr L, "Childhood trauma: An outline and overview," *Amer J of Psychiatry*, 148, 10-20.

U.S. Department of Health and Human Services, *The Third National Incidence Study of Child Abuse and Neglect (NIS-3)*.

Wilczynski A, (1997b), "Prior Agency contact and physical abuse in cases of child homicide," *British J of Social Work*, 27: 241-253.

Wilczynski A, Morris A, (1993), "Parents Who Kill their Children," (1993), *Criminal Law Review*, 31: 31-5.

Wilkey I, Petrie G, Nixon J, (1982), "Neonaticide, infanticide, and child homicide," *Medicine, Science and the Law*, 22: 31-34.

Wilkins A, "Attempted Infanticide," *British J of Psychiatry*, 1985; 146:206-208.

Yeo SS, "Munchausen syndrome by proxy: another form of child abuse," *Child Abuse Review*, vol. 5, pp. 170-80.

CANCER, VIRAL AGENTS

Amelar R, "Carcinoma of the penis due to trauma occurring in a male patient circumcised at birth," *J Urol*, 75: 728, (1956).

Baird PJ, "The Causation of Cervical Cancer, Part II: The Role of Human Papilloma and other Viruses," In: Singer A, editor, London, England: W. B. Saunders, Co., 1985. *Clinics in Obstetrics and Gynecology*, 1985: 12: 19-32.

Barrasso R, De Brux J, et al., "High prevalence of papillomavirus-associated penile intraepithelial neoplasia in sexual partners of women with cervical intraepithelial neoplasia," *New England J of Med*, Vol 317, No 15: 916-923, October 8, 1987.

Beckman A, Acker R, et al., "Human Papillomavirus Infection in Women with Multicentric Squamous-Cell Neoplasia," *Am J Obstet-Gynecol*, 165: 1431-1437, 1991.

Boczko S, Freed S, "Penile carcinoma in circumcised males," *NY State J Med*, 1979: 79(12): 1903-1904.

Brewer DD, Pottrat JJ, Roberts JM, Jr., & Brody S, "Male and female circumcision associated with prevalent HIV infection in virgins and adolescents in Kenya, Lesotho, and Tanzania," *Annals of Epidemiology*, 17:217-226.

Chao A, et al., "Risk factors associated with prevalent HIV-1 infection among pregnant women in Rwanda," *International J of Epidemiology*, (1994), vol. 23, pp. 371-380.

Cold CJ, et al., "Carcinoma of the Penis in a 76-&ear-Old Circumcised Man," *J of Family Practice*, 44 (1997): 407-410.

Cook LS, Koutsky LA, Holmes KK, "Clinical Presentation of Genital Warts Among Circumcised and Uncircumcised Heterosexual Men Attending an Urban STD Clinic," *Genitourinary Medicine*, Vol. 69, No. 4, pp. 262-64, August 1993.

Cupp MR, Malek RS, Goellner JR, Smith TF, Espy MJ, "The detection of human papillomavirus deoxyribonucleic acid in intraepithelial, in situ, verrucous and invasive carcinoma of the penis," *J of Urology*, Vol 154, No 3, pp. 1024-1029, September 1995.

Dean AL Jr., "Epithelioma of the penis in a Jew who was circumcised in infancy," *Tr Am A GU Surg*, 29: 493, (1936).

Donavan B, et al., "Male Circumcision and Common Sexually Transmissible Diseases in a Developed Nation Setting," *Genitourinary Medicine*, 70 (1994): 317-20.

Frisch M, Friis S, et al, "Falling Incidence of Penis Cancer in an Uncircumcised Population: Denmark 1943-1990," *British Medical Journal*, 311 (1995): 1471.

Gray RH, et al., "Probability of HIV-1 transmission per coital act in monogamous, heterosexual, HIV-1 discordant couples in Rakai, Uganda," *Lancet*, Vol. 357: pp. 1149-1153, 14 April 2001. "The risk of transmission was not significantly affected by the circumcision status of HIV-1 positive male partners."

Gupta J, Pilotti S, Rilke F, et al., "Association of Human Papillomavirus Type 16 With Neoplastic Lesions of the Vulva and Other Genital Sites by In-Situ Hybridization," *Am J Pathol*, 27: 206-215, 1987.

Kauffman RH, Adam E, "Herpes Simplex Virus and Human Papilloma Virus in the Development of Cervical Carcinoma," *Clin Ob Gynecol*, 1986: 29: 678-692.

Kessler II, "Etiological Concepts in Cervical Carcinogenesis," *Appl Pathol*, 1987: 5: 57-75.

Ledlie RC, Smithers DW, "Carcinoma of the penis in a man circumcised in infancy," *J Urol*, 75: 728 (1956).

Marshall VF, "Typical carcinoma of the penis in a male circumcised in infancy," *Cancer*, 1044, (1953).

McCance DJ, "Human Papillomavirus and Cancer," *Biochem, Biophys, Acta*, 1986, 823: 195-205.

McCance DJ, et al., "Human Papillomavirus types 16 and 18 in Carcinomas of the Penis from Brazil," *International J of Cancer*, Vol. 37, No. 1, 55-59, 15 January 1986.

Megafu U, "Cancer of the genital tract among the Ibo women in Nigeria," *Cancer*, vol 44, N0 5, Pages 1975-1878, November 1979.

Melmed EP, Payne, "Carcinoma of the penis in a Jew circumcised in infancy," *Brit J Surg*, 54: 729, (1967).

Nicoll A, "Routine male neonatal circumcision and risk of infection with HIV-1 and other sexually transmitted diseases," *Archives of Diseases in Childhood*, (U.K.), vol. 77: pages 194-195, September 1997.

Nuovo GJ, Hochman H, et al., "Detection of Human Papillomavirus DNA in Penile Lesions Histologically Negative for Condulomata. Analysis by In Situ Hybridization and the Polymerase Reaction," *Am J Surg Pathol*, 14: 829-836, 1990.

Paquin AJ, Jr., Pearce JM, "Carcinoma of the penis in a man in infancy," *J Urol*, 74: 626, (1955).

Reeves WC, Rawls WE, Brinton LA, "Epidemiology of genital papillomaviruses and cervical cancer," *Rev Infect Dis*, 1989; 11(3):426-39.

Reitman PH, "An unusual case of penile carcinoma," *J Urol*, 69: 547, (1953).

Sherman KJ, Daling JR, Chu J, et al., "Genital Warts, Other Sexually Transmitted Diseases, and Vulvar Cancer," *Epidemiology*, 2: 257-262, 1991.

Shingleton H, Heath CW Jr., "Letter to Peter Rappo, M.D.," *American Cancer Society*, Home Office, 16 February 1996.

Terris M, et al., "Relation of Circumcision to Cancer of the Cervix," *Amer J of Obstet and Gyn*, 117 (1973): 1056-1065.

Van Howe RS, "Circumcision and HIV infection: review of the literature and meta-analysis," *International J of STD & AIDS*, vol. 10, pp. 8-16, January 1999.

Van Howe RS, "Does Circumcision Influence Sexually Transmitted Diseases? A Literature Review," *British J of Urology International*, 83 Supplement 1 (1999): 52-62.

Warner, CD, "Neonatal circumcision does not protect against cancer," *British Medical Journal*, (London), vol. 312 no. 7033 (March 23, 1996), pp. 779-780.

Weaver MG, et al., "Detection and Localization of Human Papillomavirus in Penile Squamous Cell Carcinomas Using In Situ Hybridization With Biotinylated DNA Virus Probes," *Mod Pathol*, 2:

94-100, 1989.

Zur Hausen H, *Advances in Viral Oncology: Papillomaviruses as Carcinomaviruses*, (Klein G. Ed), Vol. 8, N. Y., Raven Press, 1988.

Zur Hausen H, "Genital Papillomavirus Infections," *Prog Med Virol*, 1985: 32: 15-21.

COMPLICATIONS - CIRCUMCISION SURGERY

Adams J, et al., "Fournier's gangrene in children," *Urology*, 35:439, 1990.

Adeyokunnu A, "Fournier's syndrome in infants: A review of cases from Ibadan, Nigeria," *Clin Pediatr Phila*, 1983, 22: 101-3.

Alter G, Horton C, "Buried penis as a contraindication for circumcision," *J Am Coll Surg*, 1994, 178: 487-90.

Altman H, "Osteomyelitis of femur (probably due to circumcision) in infant," *Bulletin of the Hospital for Joint Diseases*, 1946; 7:109-113.

Ameh EA, Sabo SY, Muhammad I, "Amputation of the penis during traditional circumcision," *Tropical Doctor*, 1997; 27: 117.

Anday E, Kobori J, "Staphylococcal scalded skin syndrome: a complication of circumcision," *Clin Pediatr*, Phila., 1982, 21: 420.

Annobil S, Al-Hilf A, Kazie T, "Primary tuberculosis of the penis in an infant," *Tubercle*, 1990, 71: 229-230.

Annunziato D, Goldblum L, "Staphylococcal scalded skin syndrome: A complication of circumcision," 132 *Am J Dis Child*, 1187-1188, 1978.

Arnon, R, et al., "Unilateral leg cyanosis: an unusual complication of circumcision," *Eur J Pediatr*, 1992: 151: 716.

Attalla M, Taweela M, "Pathogenesis of post-circumcision adhesions," *Pediatr Surg Int*, 1994, 9: 103-105.

Auerbach M, Scanlon J, "Recurrence of pneumothorax as a possible complication of elective circumcision," *Am J Obstet Gynecol*, 1978, 132: 583.

Baker RL, (RADM, USN, ret.), "Newborn male circumcision: needless and dangerous," *Sexual Medicine Today*, 1979, 3 (11): 35-36.

Berens R, Pontus S, "A complication of circumcision and dorsal nerve block of the penis," *Reg Anesth*, 1990, 15: 309-10.

Bergeson P, et al., "The Inconspicuous Penis," *Pediatrics*, 1993, 92: 794-9.

Berman W, "Urinary retention due to ritual circumcision," (Letter), *Pediatrics*, October 1975, 56: 621.

Bliss D, Healey J, Waldhausen J, "Necrotizing fasciitis after Plastibell circumcision," *J Pediatrics*, 1997, 131, 459-462.

Braun D, "Neonatal bacteremia and circumcision," *Pediatrics*, 1990, 85: 135-6.

Brennemann J, "The ulcerated meatus in the circumcised child," *Am J Dis Child*, 1921, 21: 38-47.

Breuer G, Walfisch S, "Circumcision complications and indications for ritual recircumcision – clinical experience and review of the literature," *Isr J Med Sci*, 1987, 23: 252-6.

Brimhall J, "Amputation of the penis following a unique method of preventing hemorrhage after circumcision," *St. Paul Med J*, 1902, 4: 490.

Brown MR, Cartwright PC, Snow BW, "Common office problems in pediatric urology and gynecology," *Pediatr Clin North Am*, 1997, Oct.: 44(5): 1091-115

Clayton M, et al., "Causes, presentation and survival of 57 patients with necrotizing fascitis of the male genitalia," *Surgery*, 170: 49-55, 1990.

Cleary DG, Kohl S, "Overwhelming infection with group B beta-hemolytic streptoccuc associated with circumcision," *Pediatrics*, Vol. 64, no 3, Sept. 1979: 301-303.

Cleary TG, Kohl S, "Circumcision Disasters," *Pediatrics*, 1980; 65:1053-4.

Cohen HA, Drucker MM, Vainer S, Ashkenasi A, et al., "Postcircumcision urinary tract infection," *Clinical Pediatrics*, 31(6):322-4, June 1992.

Connelly KP, Shropshire LC, Salzberg A, "Gastric rupture associated with prolonged crying in a newborn undergoing circumcision," *Clin Pediatr*, Sept. 1992, 560-561.

Craig J, et al., "Acute obstructive uropathy – a rare complication of circumcision," *Eur. J Pediatr*, 1994, 153: 369-71.

Curtis J, "Circumcision complicated by pulmonary embolism," *Nurse Mirror Midwives J*, 1971, 132: 28-30.

Datta N, Zinner N, "Complication from plastic bell circumcision ring," *Urology*, 1977, 9: 57-8.

Denton J, "Circumcision Complication Reaction to Treatment of Local Hemorrhage With Topical Epinephrine in High Concentration," *Clin Pedia*, 17: 285, 1978.

Dinari G, et al., "Umbilical arteritis and phlebitis with scrotal abscess and peritonitis," *J. Pediatr Surg*, 1971, 6: 176.

Du Toit D, Villet W, "Gangrene of the penis after circumcision: a report of 3 cases," *S Afr Med J*, 1979, 55: 521-2.

Eason J, et al., "Male ritual circumcision resulting in acute renal failure," *BMJ*, 1994, 309: 660-1.

Editor, "Hazards of circumcisions," *Practitioner*, 1967; 198:611.

Editorial, "The Case Against Neonatal Circumcision," *BMJ*, (BMJ), No 6172, pp. 1163-4, Saturday, 05 May 1979.

Editor/Banham, "Total denudation of the penis," *Urologic & Cutaneous Rev*, 1949; 53: 309.

El-Bahnasawy MS, El-Sherbiny MT, "Paediatric penile trauma," *BJU International*, Vol. 90:92; July 2002.

Eldin, Usama Saad, "Post-circumcision keloid - A Case Report," *Annals of Burns and Fire Disasters*, vol. XII, no. 3, September 1999.

Enzenauer R, et al., "Increased Incidence of Neonatal Staphylococcal Pyoderma in Males," *Military Medicine*, 1984: 47: 408.

Enzenauer R, et al., "Male Predominance in Persistent Staphylococcal Colonization and Infection of the Newborn," *Hawaii Med J*, 44 (10): 389-90, 392, 394-6, Oct. 1985.

Evbuomwan I, Aliu A, "Acute gangrene of the scrotum in a one month old child," *Trop Geogr Med*, 1984, 36: 299-300.

Feinberg AN, Balzek MA, "Mechanical complications of circumcision with a Gomco Clamp," *Amer J of Diseases of Children*, 1988; 142: 813-4.

Fergusson DM, "Neonatal Circumcision and Penile Problems: An 8 Year Longitudinal Study," *Pediatrics*, 81: 537-541, 1988.

Food and Drug Administration:

Editor, "Amputations with use of adult-size scissors-type circumcision clamps on infants," *Health Devices*, 1995; 24: 286-7.

Feigal, David W, (Director), Jr., "Potential for Injury from Circumcision Clamps," *Center for Devices and Radiological Health*, Food and Drug Administration, 29 August 2000.

FDA MedWatch Reports, July 1992 through January 2000.

"IPM Procedure: Circumcision Clamps," *Health Devices*, 2000 January; 29(1):22-3.

"Hazard: Routine inspection needed for scissors-type circumcision clamps," *Health Devices*, 1999 Mar.;

28(3):115-6.

"Hazard: Incompatibility of different brands of Gomco-Type circumcision clamps," *Health Devices*, 1997 Feb.; 26(2):76-7.

"Hazard: Amputations with use of adult scissors-type circumcision clamps on infants," *Health Devices*, 1995 July; 4(7):286-7.

"Hazard: Damaged Allied Healthcare Products Gomco circumcision clamp," *Health Devices*, 1993 Mar.; 22(3):154-5.

Frand M, et al, "Complication of ritual circumcision in Israel," *Pediatrics*, 1974, 54: 521.

Frank JD, et al., "Urethral strictures in childhood," *BJU*, 1988 Dec.; 62(6): 590-2.

Freud P, "The ulcerated urethral meatus in male children," *J Pediatr*, 1947, 31: 131-42.

Gearhart JP, *31/ Complications of Pediatric Circumcision*, Year Book Medical Publishers, Inc., 1986, Marshall F. F. editor, p. 387.

Gearhart JP, Rock JA, "Total Ablatment of the Penis After Circumcision With Electrosurgery: A Method of Management and Long-Term Follow-Up," *The Journal of Urology*, vol. 142, pp. 799-801, Sept. 1989.

Gee W, Ansell J, "Neonatal circumcision: A ten year overview. With comparison of the Gomco clamp and the plastibell device," *Pediatrics*, 58:824, 1976.

Gellis SS, "Circumcision," *Am J Dis Child*, 1978; 132:168.

Ginsburg C, et al., "Urinary tract infections in young infants," *Pediatrics*, 1982, 69: 409-12.

Gluckman GR, et al., "Newborn Penile Glans Amputation during Circumcision and Successful Reattachment," *J of Urology*, 153 (1995): 778.

Gold S, "Bleeding after circumcision," *Canadian Medical Journal*, 1940; 43: 473.

Goldman M, et al., "Urinary tract infection following ritual Jewish circumcision," *Israel J of Med Sci*, 1996, 32 (11): 1098-1102.

Gosden M, "Tetanus following circumcision," *Trans R Soc Trop Med Hyg*, 1935, 28: 645-8.

Gracely-Kilgore K, "Penile adhesions: the hidden complication of circumcision," *Nurse Pract*, 1984, 9: 22-4.

Graves J, "Pinpoint Meatus: Iatrogenic," *Pediatrics*, 41: 1013, 1968.

Griffiths D, Atwell J, Freeman F, "A perspective survey of the indications and morbidity of circumcision in children," *European Urol*, 1985, 11 (3): 184-87.

Hamm W, Kanthak, F, "Gangrene of the penis following circumcision with high frequency current," *South Med J*, 1949, 42: 657-9.

Hanukoglu, et al., "Serious complications of routine ritual circumcision in a neonate: hydro ureteronephrosis, amputation of glans penis, and hyponatraemia," *Eur. J Pediatr*, 1995, 154: 314-5.

Holman JR, Stuessi KA, "Adult Circumcision," *Am Family Physician*, p. 1514-20, March 15, 1999.

Horowitz J, et al., "Abdominal distention following ritual circumcision," (letter), *Pediatrics*, 1976, 57: 579.

Huntley JS, Bourne MC, Munro FD, Wilson-Storey D (September 2003). "Troubles with the foreskin: one hundred consecutive referrals to paediatric surgeons," *J R Soc Med*, 96 (9): 449–51.

Immerman RS, Mackey WC, "A Proposed Relationship Between Circumcision and Neural Reorganization," *J of Genetic Psychology*, Vol. 159, No. 3, 267-378, September 1, 1998.

Jee LD, Miller AJ, "Ruptured bladder following circumcision using Plasticbell device," *British Journal of Urology*, 1990; 65: 216-217.

Johansonbaugh RE, et al., "Complications of a Circumcision Performed With a Plastic Bell Clamp," *Am J Dis Child*, 118: 781, 1969.

Johnson S, "Persistent Urethral Fistula Following Circumcision," *US Naval Med Bull*, 49: 120-122, 1949.

Jonas G, "Retention of a Plastibell Circumcision Ring. Report of a Case," *Obstet Gynecol*, 23: 835, 1964.

Kanukoglu A, Danielli L, Katzir Z, Gorenstein A, Fried D, "Serious complications of routine ritual circumcision in a neonate: hydro-ureteroephrosis, amputation of the glans penis, and hyponatraemia," *European J of Pediatrics*, 1995; 154; 314-5.

Kaplan GW, "Complications of Circumcision," *Urol Clin N Am*, 1983: 10: 543-549.

Kendal DA, "Caution Against Routine Circumcision Male Infants," (Memorandum to physicians and surgeons of Saskatchewan). *Saskatoon: College of Physicians and Surgeons*, February 20, 2002.

Kirkpatrick BV, Eitaman DV, "Neonatal Septicemia After Circumcision," *Clinical Pediatrics*, 13: 767, 1974.

Klauber GT, Boyle J, "Preputial Skin-Bridging, Complication of Circumcision," *Urology*, 1974: 3: 722.

Kon M, "A rare complication following circumcision: the concealed penis," *J Urol*, 1983, 130: 573-4.

Kunz H, "Circumcision and Meatotomy," *Prim Care*, 1986, 13; 523-5.

Kural, S, "Iatrogenic penile gangrene: 10 year follow-up," *Plastic and Reconstructive Surgery*, 1995, 95: 210-1.

Lackey JJ, Mannion RA, Kerr JF, "Subglanular Urethral Fistula from Infant Circumcision," *Indiana State Med Assoc J*, 62: 1305-1306, 1969.

Lackey JT, "Urethral Fistula Following Circumcision," *JAMA*, 1968, 206: 2318.

Lau J, Ong G, "Subglanular urethral fistula following circumcision: repair by the advancement method," *J Urol*, 1981, 126: 702-703.

Lerner BL, "Amputation of the penis as a complication of circumcision," *Med Rec Ann*, 1952; 46: 229-31.

Levitt SB, et al., "Iatrogenic Microphallus Secondary to Circumcision," *Urology*, vol. 8, no. 5, November 1976, p. 473.

Lewis EL, "Tuberculosis of the penis: a report of 5 new cases, and a complete review of the literature," *J of Urology*, 1946; 56: 737-745.

Limaye R, Hancock, "Iatrogenic Microphallus Secondary to Circumcision," *J Pediatrics*, 1968, 72: 105.

Limaye RD, "Penile Urethral Fistula as a Complication of Circumcision," *J Pediatrics*, 1968: 72: 105-106.

Linshaw MA, "Circumcision and obstructive renal disease," *Pediatrics*, 1977; 59: 790.

MacKenzie AP, "Meatal Ulceration Following Neonatal Circumcision," *Obstet Gynecol*, 28: 221-223, 1966.

Malo T, Bonforte R, "Hazards of Plastibell Circumcision," *Obstet Gynecol*, 33: 869, 1969.

Mandel S, "Methemoglobinemia following neonatal circumcision," *JAMA*, 1989; 142: 799-801.

Marks M, "Preputal adhesions in the circumcised penis," *Arch Pediatr*, 1939, 56: 458-9.

Marsh, SK, Archer TJ, "Bipolar diathermy haemostasis during circumcision," *British J of Surgery*, 1995; 82: 533.

Mastin W, "Infantile circumcision a cause of contraction of the external urethral meatus," *Ann Anatomy Surg*, 1881, 4; 123-4.

McGowan AJ, "A Complication of Circumcision," *JAMA*, 207: 2104-2105, 1969.

Michelowski R, "Silica granuloma at the site of circumcision for phimosis; a case report," *Dermatologica*, 1983, 166: 261-3.

Miya PA, "Botched circumcisions," *Amer J of Nursing*, 1994; 94:56.

Money J, "Ablatio Penis: Normal Male Infant Sex Reassigned as a Girl," *Archives of Sexual Behavior*, 1975.

Mor A, et al., "Tachycardia and heart failure after circumcision," *Arch Dis Child*, 1987, 62: 80-81.

Mueller E, Steinhardt G, "The incidence of genitourinary abnormalities in circumcised and uncircumcised boys presenting with an initial urinary tract infection by 6 months of age," *Pediatrics*, September 1997, Vol. 100, p. 580, (Supplement).

Neulander E, et al., "Amputation of distal penile glans during neonatal ritual circumcision–a rare complication," 77, *BJU*, 924-925, (1996).

Ngan J, Waldhausen J, Santucci, "I think this child has an infected penis after neonatal circumcision," *Online Pediatric Urology*, April 1996.

O'Hara K, O'Hara, J, "The effect of male circumcision on the sexual enjoyment of the female partner," *British Journal of Urology,* vol. 83, Supplement 1, 1999, 79-84.

Ochsner M, "Acute urinary retention: causes and treatment," *Postgrad Med*, 1982, 71: 221-6.

Owen E, Kitson J, "Plastibell circumcision," *Br J Clin Pract*, 1990, 44: 661.

Ozbek N, Sarikayalar F, "Toxic methaemoglobinaemia after circumcision," *European J of Pediatrics*, 1993; 152: 80.

Ozdemir E, "Significant increased complication risk with mass circumcisions," *BJU*, vol. 80, 136-139, August 1997.

Palmer JM, Link D, "Impotence following anesthesia for elective circumcision," *JAMA*, 1979; 241: 2635-6.

Patel HI, "The Problem of Routine Circumcision," *Canadian Medical Association Journal*, vol. 95, 1966, pp. 576-581.

Patel HI, Moriarity KP, Brisson PA, Feins NR, "Genitourinary injuries in the newborn," *Journal of Pediatric Surgery*, Jan.; 36 (1): 235-9.

Pearlman C, "Caution advised on electrocautery circumcisions," *Urology*, 1982, 19; 453.

Persad R, et al., "Clinical Presentation and Pathophysiology of Meatal Stenosis Following Circumcision," *British Journal of Urology*, BJU, 75, 1995.

Pertot S, "Sensitivity is the rising issue on circumcision," *Australian Doctor*, 25 Nov. 1994.

Pinkham E, Stevenson A, "Unusual reaction to local anesthesia: gangrene of the prepuce," *US Armed Forces Med J*, 1958, 9: 120-2.

Ponsky J, Ross J, Knipper N, et al., "A Natural History of Penile Adhesions after Circumcision." *(*Presentation: *1999 Amer Urol Assoc)*.

Prais D, Shoov-Furman R, & Amir J., "Is ritual circumcision a risk factor for neonatal urinary tract infections?" *Arch. Dis. Child.* Published online 6 Oct. 2008.

Redman J, "Postcircumcision phimosis and its management," *Clin Pediatr*, 1975, 14; 407-9.

Reuben M, "Tuberculosis Following Ritual Circumcision," *Arch Pediatr*, 34: 186, 1917.

Ritchy M, Bloom D, "Re: Skin bridge - a complication of paediatric circumcision," *Urology*, 1974, 3: 722-3.

Rosenfsky J, Jonathan B, "Glans Necrosis as a Complication of Circumcision," *Pediatrics*, 39: 774-776, (May) 1967.

Rosenstein JL, "Wound Diphtheria in the Newborn Infant Following Circumcision," *J Pediatric*, 18: 657, 1941.

Rubenstein M, Bason W, "Complication of Circumcision Done With A Plastic Bell Clamp," *Am J Dis Child*, 116: 381-382, 1968.

Ruff M, et al., "Myocardial injury following immediate postnatal circumcision," *Am. J Obstet Gynecol*, 1982, 144: 850-1.

Sara C, Lowery C, "A Complication of Circumcision and Dorsal Nerve Block of the Penis," *Anesth Intensive Care*, 13: 79-82, 1985.

Sathaye V, "Skin bridge - a complication of paediatric circumcision," *BJU*, 1990, 66: 214.

Sauer LW, "Fatal Staphylococcus Bronchopneumonia Following Ritual Circumcision," *Am J Ob & Gyn*, 46:

583, 1943.

Schlosberg C, "Thirty years of ritual circumcisions: Appraisal of personal experience, after-care and postcircumcision complications," *Clin Pediatr*, 1971; 10: 205-209.

Scurlock JM, Pemberton PJ, "Neonatal Meningitis and Circumcision," *Medical Journal of Australia*, 1 (1977): 332-334.

Sharpe JR, Finnet RP, "Electrocautery Circumcision," *Urology*, 19 (1982): 228.

Shiraki IW, "Congenital Megalourethra With Urethrocutaneous Fistula Following Circumcision. A Case Report," *J of Urology*, 109: 723, 1973.

Shulman, Ben-Hur, Neuman, "Surgical Complications of Circumcision," *American J of Diseases of Children*, vol. 107, Feb., 1964, pp. 149-154.

Smey P, "Re: Penile denudation injuries after circumcision," *J of Urol*, 1985, 134: 1220.

Smith D, et al., "An uncommon complication of circumcision," *BJU*, 1994, 73: 459-60. (Penile Ischemia).

Smith GL, Greenup R, Takafuji ET, "Circumcision As A Risk Factor for Urethritis in Racial Groups," *American Journal of Public Health*, 77: 452-454, 1987.

Snellman L, Stang H, "Prospective evaluation of complications of dorsal penile nerve block for neonatal circumcision," *Pediatrics*, 1995, 95: 705-8.

Sorensen S, Sorensen M, "Circumcision with the Plastibell device: A long-term follow-up," *Internat Urol Nephrol*, 1988, 20: 159-66.

Sotolongo JR, Huffman S, Gribetz ME, "Penile Denudation Injuries After Circumcision," *J Urol*, 133: 102-103, 1985.

Southby R, Myers N, "A case against circumcision," *Med J Austr*, 1965, 2; 393.

Sterenberg N, Golan J, Ben-Hur N, "Necrosis of the glans penis following neonatal circumcision," *Plast Reconstruct Surg*, 1981, 68: 237-9.

Stewart D, "The Toad in the hole circumcision – a surgical bugbear," *Boston Med Surg J*, 1924, 191: 1216-8.

Stinson J, "Impotence and adult circumcision," *J Nat Med Assoc*, 1973, 65: 161.

Stranko J, et al., "Impetigo in newborn infants associated with a plastic bell clamp circumcision," *Pediatr Infect Dis*, 1986, 5: 597-9.

Strimling BS, "Partial Amputation of Glans Penis during Mogen Clamp Circumcision," *Pediatrics*, 87 (1996); 906-907.

Sussman SJ, Schiller RP, Shashikumaro VL, "Fournier's syndrome: Report of three cases and review of the literature," 132, *Am J Dis Child*, 1189-1191, (1978).

Talarico R, Jasanitis J, "Concealed Penis: A Complication of Neonatal Circumcision," *J Urology*, 110: 732, 1973.

Taylor PK, "Herpes Genitalis and Circumcision," *British J Venereal Dis*, 51: 274-277, 1975.

The Royal Society of Medicine, "Unsafe healthcare 'drives spread of African HIV," 20 February 2003.

Thompson A, "Stricture of the external meatus," *Lancet*, 1935, 1: 1373-7.

Thompson RS, "Routine Circumcision in the Newborn: An Opposing View," *Journal of Family Practice*, 31 (1990): 189-96.

To T, Agha M, Dick PT, Feldman W, "A Cohort Study on Male Neonatal Circumcision and the Subsequent Risk of Urinary Tract Infection," *Paediatrics and Child Health*, Vol. 2, Supplement A: p. 55a, May/June 1997.

Trier W, Drach G, "Concealed Penis: Another Complication of Circumcision," *Amer J Dis Child*, 125: 276, 1973.

Uwyyed K, et al., "Scrotal abscess with bacteremia caused by Salmonella group D after ritual circumcision,"

Pediatr Infect Dis J, 1990, 9: 65-6.

Van Duyn J, Warr WS, "Excessive Penile Skin Loss From Circumcision," *J Med Assoc*, GA, 51: 394, 1962.

Van Howe RS, "Is Circumcision Healthy - No," *Priorities*, vol. 9, no 4, 1997.

Walfisch, et al., "Complications of ritual circumcision," *BJU*, 77, June 1996, 924.

Warwick DJ, Dickson WA, "Keloid of the penis after circumcision," *Postgraduate Medical Journal*, 1993; 69: 236-7.

Wayne, Eileen Wayne, "Understanding Urinary Tract Infections," *Infect Urol*, 8 (4), 111, 114-120, 1995.

Williams K, Kapila L, "Complications of Circumcision," *British Journal of Surgery*, vol. 80, pp. 1231-1236, Oct. 1993.

Wiswell T, et al., "Staphylococcus aureus after neonatal circumcision in relation to device used," *J Pediatr*, 1991, 119: 302-4.

Woodside J, "Circumcision Disasters," *Pediatrics*, (Springfield Illinois), vol. 65, no. 5, May 1980, 1053-4.

Woodside J, "Necrotizing fasciitis after neonatal circumcision," *Am J Dis Child*, 134:301, 1980.

CRIMINOLOGY

Bandura A, Ross D, Ross SA, "Vicarious reinforcement and imitative learning," *J of Abnormal and Social Psychology*, 67, 601-607.

Belsky J, (1980), "Child maltreatment: An ecological integration," *American Psychologist*, 35(4), 320-335.

Blackwell T, "Psychologists Suggest Bernardo and Homolka are Psychopaths," *Psynopsis*, Fall, 1995.

Bromberg W, and Coyle E, "Rape: A Compulsion to Destroy," *Medical Insight*, 1974, April, 21-22, 24-25.

"Crime Scene and Profile Characteristics of Organized an Disorganized Murderers," *FBI Law Enforcement Bulletin*, vol. 54, No. 8, August 1985, pp. 18-25.

Dietrich D, Berkowitz L, Kadushin A, McGloin J, (1990), "Some factors influencing abusers' justification of their child abuse," *Child Abuse & Neglect*, 14, 337-345.

Geberth VJ, "Psychological Profiling," *Law and Order*, 1981, pp. 46-49.

Harder T, (1967), "The psychopathology of infanticide," *Acta Psychiatrica Scandinavia*, 43: 196-245.

Hartman CR, Burgess AW, "The Genetic Roots of Child Sexual Abuse," *J of Psychotherapy and the Family*, 1986, 2 (2), 83-92.

Hazelwood, Robert R, "The Criminal Sexual Sadist," *Law Enforcement Bulletin*, (FBI), February 1992.

Holmes WC, Slap GB, "Sexual Abuse of Boys: Definition, Prevalence, Correlates, Sequelae, and Management," *JAMA*, 1998; 280:1855-1862.

Lanning, Kenneth V, "Child Molesters: A Behavioral Analysis," *National Organization for Missing and Exploited Children*, 1992.

Lewis CF, Stanley CR, "Women accused of sexual offenses," *Behav Sci Law*, 18 (1): 73-81.

MacCollough MJ, Snowden PR, Wood PJW, Mills HE, "Sadistic Fantasy: Sadistic Behaviors and Offending," *British Journal of Psychiatry*, 1983, 143: 20-29.

Marks MN, Kumar R, "Infanticide in England and Wales," *Medicine, Science and the Law*, 33: 329-339.

Marks MN, Kumar R, "Infanticide in Scotland," *Medicine, Science and the Law*, 36: 299.

Mendelsohn B, "The Origin of the Doctrine of Victimology," *Excerpta Criminologica*, 1963, 3:239-44.

Milner JS, Chilamkurti C, "Physical child abuse perpetrator characteristics: a review of the literature," *J of Interpersonal Violence*, vol. 6,:345-66.

Morgan W, "Penile plunder," *Australian Medical J*, 1967, 1: 1102-1103.

Pitt SE, Bale EM, (1995), "Neonaticide, infanticide, and filicide: A review of the literature," *Bulletin of the American Academy of Psychiatry and Law*, 23: 375-386.

Podilsky E, "Sexual Violence," *Medical Digest*, 1966, 34:60-63.

Pynoos RS, Eth S, "Developmental perspective on psychic trauma in childhood." In C. R. Figley, editor, *Trauma and its Wake*, Brunnel/Mazel Psychological Stress Series, 1985.

Resnick PJ, (1969), "Child murder by parents: A psychiatric review of filicide," *Amer J of Psychiatry*, 126: 325-334.

Resnick PJ, "Murder of the Newborn: A Psychiatric Review of Filicide," *Amer J of Psychiatry*, 126:58-64, 1970.

Roth S, Lebowitz L, "The Experience of Sexual Trauma," *Journal of Traumatic Stress*, 1988, Vol. 1:79-107.

Rothenberg MB, "Is there an Unconscious National Conspiracy Against Children in the United States," *Clin Pediatr*, 1980: 19: 10-24.

Sadoff RL, (1995), "Mothers who kill their children," *Psychiatric Annals*, 25: 601-605.

Scott PD, (1973a), "Parents who kill their children," *Medicine, Science and the Law*, 13: 120-126.

Simpson AIE, Stanton J, (2000), "Maternal filicide: A reformulation of factors relevant to risk," *Criminal Behavior and Mental Health*, 10: 136-147.

Sosby D, "Altruistic Filicide: Bioethics or Criminology," *Health Ethics Today*, Vol. 12, No 1, Fall/November, 2001.

US Department of Health and Human Services, "The Third National Incidence Study of Child Abuse and Neglect (NIS-3)," 1996.

Wilczynski A, (1997b), "Prior agency contact and physical abuse in cases of child homicide," *British J of Social Work*, 27: 241-253.

Wilczynski A, Morris A, (1993), "Parents who kill their children," *Criminal Law Review*, 793: 31-36.

Wilkey I, Petrie G, Nixon J, (1982), "Neonaticide, infanticide, and child homicide," *Medicine, Science and the Law*, 22: 31-34.

Wood DP, "Sexual Abuse during Childhood and Adolescence and its effects on the Physical and Emotional Quality of Life of the Survivor: A Review of the Literature," *Military Medicine*, Vol. 161, October 1996, pp. 582-587.

FEMALE GENITAL MUTILATION

Black J, "Female genital mutilation in Britain," *BMJ*, 1995;310:1590-92

Dirie MA, Lindmark G, "The risk of medical complications after female circumcision," *East African Med J*, 1992;69(9):479-482.

Duffy J, "Masturbation and Clitoridectomy," The Journal of The American Medical Association, (JAMA), Oct. 19, 1962, Vol. 186, pp. 246-248.

El-Giblay O, Ibrahim B, Mensch B, Clark W, "The decline of female circumcision in Egypt: evidence and interpretation," *Social Science & Medicine*, 54 (2002) 205-220.

Elliott ML, "Chronic Pelvic pain: The Psychological Considerations?," *Amer Pain Soc Bulletin*, January/February 1996, vol. 6, No. 1.

Fernandez-Aguilar S, Noel J-C, "Neuroma of the clitoris after female genital cutting," *Obstet Gynecol*, 2003;101:1053-4.

Grisaru N, et al., "Ritual Female Genital Surgery among Ethiopian Jews," *Archives of Sexual Behavior*, 1997, 26 (20: 1997.

Hamilton, J, "UN condemns female circumcision," *BMJ*, 1997;314:1145 (19 April).

Harney K, "The Flight from Womanhood," *International J of Psychoanalysis*, 12 (1926): 360-364.

Kouba L and Muasher J, "Female Circumcision in Africa: An Overview," *African Studies Review*, 28:95-110

McDonald CF, "Circumcision of the Female," *GP*, 1958; XVIII(3):98-99.

Meniru GI, Meniru MO, Ezh UO, "Female Genital Mutilation," *BMJ*, 1995;311:1088 (21 October).

Messing SD, "The Problem of Operations Based on Custom in Applied Anthropology: The Challenge of the Hosken Report on Genital and Sexual Mutilations of Females," *Human Organization*, 39:295-297.

Montague A, "Infibulation and Defibulation in the Old and New Worlds," *Am Anthropologist*, 47: 464-467, 1945.

Morrone A, "Female genital mutilation: a new-old problem," *Dermatological Experiences*, vol. 3, Number 4, October 2001; 413-430.

Pieters G, Lowenfels AB, "Infibulation in the Horn of Africa," *New York State J of Med*, Vol. 77, No 6, pp. 729-31, April 1977.

Rathman WG, "Female circumcision: Indications and a new technique," *GP*, 1959; XX(3):115-120.

Slack A, "Female Circumcision: A Critical Appraisal," *Human Rights Quart*, 10;437-486.

Toubia N, "Female Genital Mutilation and the Responsibility of Reproductive health Professionals," *International J Gynecology & Obstetrics*, 46, pp. 127-135, 1994.

Van Der Kwaak A, "Female Circumcision and Gender Identity: A questionable Alliance?," *Social Science and Medicine*, 35 (6):777-787.

HISTORICAL MIS-MEDICAL

Bailey RC, Muga R, et al., "The acceptability of male circumcision to reduce HIV infections in Nyanza Province, Kenya," *AIDS Care*, 2002 Feb.; 14(1):27-40.

Bergman N, "Report of a Few Cases of Circumcision," *Journal of Orificial Surgery*, vol. 7 (1898): pp. 249-51.

Blanton MG, "The behavior of the human infant in the first 30 days of life," *Psychological Review*, (1917), 24(6):456-483.

Bleustein CB, Eckholdt H, Arezzo JC, Melman A, "Effects of Circumcision on Male Penile Sensitivity," *American Urologic Association*, Bronx, NY, 2003.

Brown SGA, "A Plea for Circumcision," *Medical World*, vol. 15 (1897): pp. 124-5.

Cockshut RW, "Circumcision," *BMJ*, vol.2 (1935): 764.

Crossland JC, "The Hygiene of Circumcision," *NY Medical Journal*, vol. 53 (1891): pp. 484-485.

Crudden C, "Reactions of Newborn Infants to Thermal Stimuli Under Constant Tactual Conditions," *Journal of Experimental Psychology*, 20:350-370.

Dawson B, "Circumcision in the Female: It's a Necessity and How to Perform it," *American Journal of Clinical Medicine*, vol. 22, no. 6. pp. 520-523, June 1915.

Editor, "A Plea for Circumcision," *Medical News*, vol. 77 (1900): pp. 707-708.

Editor, "Circumscius," *Medical Record*, vol. 49 (1896): p. 430.

Editor, "Routine Circumcision at Birth," *JAMA*, vol. 91 (1928): p. 201.

Freeland EH, "Circumcision as a Preventive of Syphilis and Other Disorders," *Lancet*, vol. 2, (29 December 1900): 1869-1871.

Hucthinson J, "On Circumcision as Preventative of Masturbation," *Archives of Surgery*, vol. 2 (1891): pp.267-268.

Jacobi A, "On masturbation and hysteria in young children," *Am J of Obstetrics*, 1876: 8: 595-606.

Johnson AAW, "On An Injurious Habit Occasionally Met with in Infancy and Early Childhood," *Lancet*, vol. 1 (7 April 1860): pp. 344-345.

Mark EG, "Circumcision," *American Practitioner and News*, vol. 31 (1901): pp. 121-126.

McGraw M, "Neural Maturation as Exemplified in the Changing Reactions of the Infant to Pin Prick," *Child*

Development, (1941), 12(1):31-42.

Moses MJ, "The value of circumcision as a hygienic and therapeutic measure," *New York Medical Journal*, 1971: 14: 368-74.

Naylor HGH, "A Plea for Early Circumcision," *Pediatrics*, vol. 12 (1901): p. 231.

Pratt KC, Nelson AK, Sun KH, "The Behavior of the Newborn Infant," Ohio State University Student Contrib. *Psychology*, no. 10.

Rich EC, Marshall RE, Volpe JJ, "The Normal Neonatal Response to Pin-Prick," *Developmental Medicine & Child Neurology*, (1974), 16:432-434.

Robinson WJ, "Circumcision and Masturbation," *Medical World*, vol. 33 (1915): p. 390.

Sayer LL, "Circumcision for the Cure of Enuresis," *JAMA*, 7, 1887, pp. 631-633.

Schoen EJ, "Ignoring Evidence of Circumcision Benefits," *Pediatrics*, 2006; 118: 385-387.

Schoen EJ, Christopher JC, Ray GT, "Newborn Circumcision Decreases Incidence and Costs of Urinary Tract Infections during the First Year of Life," *Pediatrics*, 2000: 105: 789-793.

Solomons L, "For and Against Circumcision," *BMJ*, June 5, 1920, p. 768.

Spratling EJ, "Masturbation in the Adult," *Medical Record*, vol. 24 (1895): pp. 442-443.

Steele WG, "Importance of circumcision," *Medical World*, vol. 20 (1902): pp. 518-9.

Tait L, "Masturbation," *Med News*, 53: 1-3, 1888.

Talbot ES, "Inheritance of Circumcision Effects," *Medicine*, 1898.

Taylor AW, "Circumcision - Its Moral and Physical Necessities and Advantages," *Medical Record*, vol. 56 (1899): p. 174.

West DC, "Cliteroidectomy," *BMJ*, 2: 585, 1866.

Wolblast AL, "Circumcision and penile carcinoma," *Lancet*, 1:150, (1932).

Wolbarst AL, "Universal Circumcision as a Sanitary Measure," *JAMA*, (1914) Vol. 62. pp. 92-97.

Wuesthoff LW, "Benefits of Circumcision," *Medical World*, vol. 33, (1915): p. 434.

LEGAL

Aldeeb, Sami, "To Mutilate in the Name of Jehova or Allah: Legitimization of Male and Female Circumcision," *Med and Law*, Vol. 13, No. 7-8: pp. 575-622, July 1994.

American Academy of Pediatrics, Committee on Bioethics, "Female Genital Mutilation (RE9749)," *Pediatrics*, vol. 102, no 1, pp. 153-56, July 1998.

American Academy of Pediatrics, Committee on Bioethics, "Informed consent, parental permission, and assent in pediatric practice," 95, *Pediatrics*, 314-317, (1995).

American Academy of Pediatrics, Committee on Bioethics, "Religious Exemptions from Child Abuse Statutes," *Pediatrics*, Vol. 81, No. 1, pp. 169-71, Jan. 1988.

American Academy of Pediatrics, Committee on Bioethics, "Religious Objections to Medical Care," *Pediatrics*, Vol. 99, No. 2, pp. 279-81, February 1997.

American Academy of Pediatrics Committee on Bioethics, "Policy Statement," *Pediatrics*, 95, (1995), 314-317.

American Academy of Pediatrics, *Committee on Fetus and Newborn*, "Standards and Recommendation for Hospital Care of Newborn Infants," 1971.

American Academy of Pediatrics, Task Force on Circumcision, "Circumcision Policy Statement," 103, *Pediatrics*, 686-693, (1999).

Boyle GJ, Svoboda JS, Price CP, Turner JN, "Circumcision of Healthy Boys: Criminal Assault," 7, *J Law Med*, 301-10 (2000).

Brigman WE, "Circumcision as Child Abuse: The Legal and Constitutional Issues," *Journal of Family Law*, vol. 23 no 3, 1984-85, pp. 337-357.

Brown R, "The pediatrician and malpractice," *Pediatrics*, 1976, 57 (30: 392-401.

Canning DA, "Informed consent for neonatal circumcision: an ethical and legal conundrum," *J Urol*, 2002 Oct. 168(4 Pt1): pp. 1650-1.

Capron AM, "Right to refuse medical care," (In: *Encyclopedia of Bioethics*,) The Free Press, 1978, 1498-1507.

Chessler, A, "Justifying the Unjustifiable: Rite V. Wrong," 45, *Buffalo Law Rev*, 555, (1997).

Christensen-Szalanski J, "Circumcision and Informed Consent. Is More Information Always Better?," *Medical Care*, vol. 25, 198, pp. 856-866.

"Circumcision of Male Infants Research Paper," *Queensland Law Reform Commission*, Brisbane, 1993.

Convention on the Rights of the Child, "Document A/RES/44/25," U.N. General Assembly, 12 December 1989.

Denniston GC, "Circumcision and the Code of Ethics," *Humane Health Care International*, April, 1996; 12.

Denniston GC, "Circumcision Violates All Seven Principles of Medical Ethics," *AMA*, 1992.

Dwyer JG, "Parents' Religion and Children's Welfare: Debunking the Doctrine of Parents' Rights," 82, *Cal Law Rev*, 1371, (1994).

Dwyer JG, "The Children We Abandon: Religious exemption to child welfare and education laws as denials of equal protection to children of religious objectors," 74, *North Carolina Law Review*, 1321-1478, (June 1996).

Epstein LC, Lasagna L, "Obtaining Informed Consent: Form or Substance," *Arch Intern Med*, 1969, 123: 682.

Gianetti MR, "Circumcision and the American Academy of Pediatrics: Should Scientific Misconduct Result in Trade Association Liability?," *Iowa Law Review*, Volume 85, Number 4, Pages 1507-1568, May 2000.

Garrison, Arthur H., "Child Sexual Abuse Accommodation Syndrome: Issues of Admissibility in Criminal Trials," *IPT Journal*, vol. 10, 1998.

Hausmann R, et al., "The Forensic Value of the Immunological Detection of Oestrogen Receptors in Vaginal Epithelium," *International J of Legal Med*, 109 (1996): 10-30.

Herrera AJ, "Parental Information and Circumcision in Highly Motivated Couples with Higher Education," *Pediatrics*, vol. 71, no. 2, February 1983, pp. 233-234.

Herrera AJ, "The Role of Parental Information on the Incidence of Circumcision," *Pediatrics*, vol. 70, 1982, pp. 597-598.

Hodges F, Svoboda JS, Van Howe RS, "Prophylactic interventions on children: balancing human rights with public health," *J Med Ethics*, 2002 Feb. 28(1): pp. 10-16.

Holder A, "Law & medicine: circumcision," *JAMA*, vol. 218, no. 1, (Oct. 4, 1971): 149-50.

Hollander RD, "Changes in the Concept of Informed Consent In Medical Encounters," *J Med Educ*, 1984, 59: 783.

Katz, Howe, & McGrath, "Child Neglect Laws in America," 9, *Family L Q*, 1,3 (1975).

Kessler HW, "Pre-operative Education and the Informed Patient," *Legal Aspects of Medical Practice*, 1977, 46.

Kirby, "Informed Consent: What Does it Mean?," *J Med Ethics*, 1983, 9-69.

Lebit L, "Compelled Medical Procedures Involving Minors and Incompetents and Misapplication of the Substituted Judgement Doctrine," 7, *Journal of Law and Health*, 73, (1992).

Leikin S, "Minors' assent or dissent to medical treatment," *J Pediatr*, 1982, 102: 169-176.

Lidz C, et al., "Two models of implementing informed consent," *Arch. Inter Med*, 1988, 148: 1385-1389.

Mason C, "Exorcising Excision: medico-legal Issues Arising From Male and Female Genital Surgery in Australia," *Journal of Law and Medicine*, (Australia), Vol. 9, No 1: pp.58-67, August 2001.

Miller, Geoffrey, "Circumcision: Cultural-legal Analysis," *Virginia J of Social Policy & the Law,* Vol. 9: 497-585, spring 2002

Milos MF, Macris D, "Circumcision: A Medical or a Human Rights Issue?," *Journal of Nurse-Midwifery*, Vol. 37, No. 2 (Supplement.), March/April, 1992.

Morse H, "Law and medicine; ritual circumcision," *JAMA*, vol. 203, no. 12 (March 18, 1968): 257-8.

Office of the United Nations High Commissioner for Human Rights, "Other Human Rights Issues: Other Issues: Male Circumcision," (Steven Svoboda), Fifty-fourth Session, Item 6 (c) of the provisional agenda, 23 March 2002.

Povenmire R, "Do Parents have the Legal authority to consent to the surgical Amputation of Normal healthy Tissue From Their Infant children?: The Practice of Circumcision in the United States," 7, *J of Gender, Social Policy & the Law*, 87 (1998-1999).

Price C, "Male Circumcision: An Ethical and Legal Affront," *Bulletin of Medical Ethics*, 1997, 128: 13.

Reed CS, "The Effect of an Education Intervention on the Rate of Neonatal Circumcision," *Obstetrics & Gynecology*, 1983, 62: 62-68.

Reid WH, "Myths About Violent Sexual Predators and All That Pesky Legislation," *J Pract Psych and Behav Health*, July 1998:246-8.

Sidley P, "Eastern Cape tightens law on circumcision to stem casualties," (Johannesburg), *BMJ*, 2001; 323:1090 (10 November).

Skegg P, "Informed Consent to Medical Procedures," *Med Sci Law*, 1975: 15: 124.

Svoboda JS, Van Howe RS, Dwyer JG, "Informed consent for neonatal circumcision: an ethical conundrum," *J Cont Health Law Policy*, Winter 2000, vol. 17, (1): 60-134.

Taunton, Dana G., "Tort Law Update," *Montgomery County Bar Association*, Montgomery, Alabama, 21 December 1999.

Turner N, "Circumcised Boys May Sue," *Health Law Update*, Melbourne, Feb. 23. 1996.

Van Howe R, Svoboda JS, "Involuntary circumcision: the legal issues," *BJU International*, 1999, 83, Supplement, 1: 63-73.

Wallace LM, "Informed Consent to Elective Surgery: The 'Therapeutic' Value?," *Soc Sci Med*, 1986: 22-29.

Zitter J, "Liability for medical Malpractice in Connection with Performance of Circumcision," 4, *American Law Reports*, 710, (1975).

MEDICAL CORRECTING & CONSERVATIVE PREPUCE SURGERY

Ahmed S, et al., "Penile reconstruction following post-circumcision penile gangrene," *Pediatr Surg Int*, 1994, 9: 295-6.

Alter GH, Horton CE Jr., Horton CE, "Buried penis as a contraindication for circumcision," *J of American College of Surgeons*, 1994; 178:487-90.

Audry G, Buis J, Vazquez M, Gruner M, "Amputation of penis after circumcision – penoplasty using expand-able prosthesis," *Eur J Pediatr Surg*, 1994, 4: 44-45.

Azmy A, Boddy S, Ransley P, "Successful reconstruction following circumcision with diathermy," *BJU*, 1985, 57: 587-8.

Baskin L, Canning D, Snyder H, Duckett J, "Surgical Repair of urethral circumcision injuries," *Journal d'Urologie*, vol. 158 (6a): 2269-71, 1997.

Beauge M, "Traitement Medical du Phimosis Congenital de l'Adolescent," (Conservative Treatment of Primary Phimosis in Adolescents), trs. John P. Warren: Thesis for the University Diploma of Andrology, *Sainte-Antonie Univ*, Paris VI, 1990-1991.

Belkacem R, Amrani A, Benabdellah F, Outarahout O, "Reconstruction of the penis after necrosis due to circumcision," *Ann Urol Paris*, 1997; 31 (5): 322-5.

Brandes S, McAnich J, "Surgical methods of restoring the prepuce: a critical review," *BJU International*, 1999, 83, suppl, 1: 109-113.

Brown J, "Restoration of the entire skin of the penis," *Surg Gynecol Obstet*, 1937, 65: 362-5.

Brown JB, Fryer MP, "Surgical reconstruction of the penis," *GP*, 1958, 17: 104-7.

Byars LT, Trier WC, "Some Complications of Circumcision and Their Surgical Repair," *Arch Surg*, 76: 01477-482, 1968. Elsewhere referenced as 1958.

Cuckow PM, et al., "Preputial Plasty: A Good Alternative to Circumcision," *Journal of Pediatric Surgery*, vol. 29, no. 4, April 1994, pp. 561-563.

de Castella H, "Prepuceplasty: an alternative to circumcision," *Ann R Coll Surg Engl*, 1994, 76: 257-258.

DeVries CR, Miller AK, Packer MG, "Reduction of Paraphimosis with Hyauronidase," *Urology*, 48 (1996): 464-465.

Diamond M, Sigmundson K, "Sex reassignment at birth: long-term review and clinical implications," *Archives of Pediatrics and Adolescent Med*, 1997, 151: 298-304.

Diaz A, Kantor H, "Dorsal Slit: A Circumcision Alternative," *Ob & Gynecology*, 37: 619, 1971.

Donahoe P, Keating M, "Preputal unfurling to correct the buried penis," *J Pediatr Surg*, 1986, 21: 1055-57.

Dunn HP, "Non-surgical Management of Phimosis," *Australian and New Zealand Journal of Surgery*, Vol. 59: p. 963, Dec. 1989.

Emmett AJJ, "Z-Plasty Reconstruction for Preputial Stenosis - A Surgical Alternative to Circumcision," *Australian Ped J*, vol. 18, 1982, pp. 219-220.

Gilbert DA, Jordan GH, Devine CJ Jr, Winslow BH, "Phallic construction in prepubertal and adolescent boys," *Journal of Urology*, 1993; 149:1521-26.

Gluckman G, et al., "Newborn Penile Glans Amputation During Circumcision and Successful Reattachment," *J of Urol*, vol. 153, no. 3, Part 1, March 1995, 778-779.

Goodwin W, "Uncircumcision: A technique for Plastic Reconstruction of a prepuce after circumcision," *J Urol*, 1990, 144(5): 1203-1205.

Griffiths D, Frank JD, "Inappropriate Circumcision Referrals by G.P.'s," *Journal of the Royal Society of Medicine*, vol. 85, June 1992, pp. 324-325.

Hall, Robert G, "Epispasm: Circumcision in Reverse," *Bible Review*, August 1992: 52-57.

Hanash K, "Plastic reconstruction of partially amputated penis at circumcision," *Urology*, 1981, 18 (3): 291-3.

Hoffman S, et al., "A New Operation for Phimosis: Prepuce-saving Technique with Multiple Y-V Plasties," *British Journal of Urology*, (BJU), vol. 56, 1984, pp. 319-321.

Holmund DE, "Dorsal incision of the prepuce and skin closure with Dexon in patients with phimosis," *Scand J Urol Nephrol*, 1973; 7:97-99.

Horton C, Vorstman B, Teasley D, Winslow B, "Hidden penis release: adjunctive suprapubic lipectomy," *Ann Plast Surg*, 1987, 19: 131-4.

Izziden A, "Successful replantation of a traumatically amputated penis in a neonate," *Journal of Pediatric Surgery*, vol. 16, no. 2, 202-203, April 1981.

Jorgensen ET, Svensson A, "Problems with the Penis and Prepuce in Children: Lichen Sclerosus Should Be Treated with Corticosteroids to Reduce Need for Surgery," *BMJ*, 313: 692, 14 September 1996.

Kikiros CS, et al., "The Response of Phimosis to Local Steroid Application," *Pediatric Surgery International*, vol. 8, 1993, pp. 329-332.

Kural S, "Iatrogenic penile gangrene: 10-year follow-up," *Plastic and Reconstructive Surgery*, 1995; 95: 201-11.

Maizels M, "Surgical correction of the buried penis: description of a classification system and a technique to correct the disorder," *J Urol*, 1986, 136: 268-73.

Money J, "Ablato Penis: Normal Male Infant Sex-Reassigned As A Girl," *Archives of Sexual Behavior*, vol. 4, no. 1, January 1975, 65-71.

Ohjimi H, Ogata K, Ohjimi T, "A new method for the relief of adult phimosis," *J Urol*, 1995; 153-1607-1609.

Pearlman CK, "Reconstruction Following Iatrogenic Burn of the Penis," *Journal of Pediatric Surgery*, 11 (1976): 121-122.

Radhakrishnan J, Reyes H, "Penoplasty for buried penis secondary to "radical" circumcision," *J Pediatric Surg*, 1984, 19: 629-31.

Schultheiss D, et al., "Uncircumcision: A Historical Review of Preputial Restoration," *Plast Reconstr Surg*, (1998), 101: 1990.

Shapiro S, "Surgical treatment of the "buried" penis," *Urology*, 1987, 30: 554-9.

Sherman J, Borer J, Horowitz M, Glassberg K, "Circumcision: successful glanular reconstruction and survival following amputation," *J Urol*, 1996, 156: 842.

Shulman J, Ben-Hur N, Neuman Z, "Surgical complications of circumcision," *Am J Dis Child*, 1964, 107: 149-54.

Stefan H, "Reconstruction of the Penis Following Necrosis from Circumcision Used High Frequency Cutting Current," *Sbornik Vedeckych Practi Lekarske Fakulty Karlovy University*, vol. 35, no. 5 (Supplement), 1992, pp. 449-454.

Thorek P, "Reconstruction of the penis with split-thickness skin graft: a case of gangrene following circumcision for acute balanitis," *Plast Reconst Surg*, 1949, 4: 469-72.

Van Howe, RS, "Cost-effective Treatment of Phimosis," Pediatrics (Electronic Article), *Pediatrics*, Vol. 102 No. 4 October 1998, p. e43.

Wahlin N, ""Triple Incision Plasty.' A convenient Procedure for Preputial Relief," Scandinavian J of Urology and Nephrology, vol. 26, no. 2, 1992, pp. 107-110.

Wilson C, Wilson M, "Plastic repair of the denuded penis," *South Med J*, 1959, 52: 288-90.

Wright JE, "The Treatment of Childhood Phimosis With Topical Steroid," *The Australian and New Zealand Journal of Surgery*, vol. 64, no. 5, May 1994, 327-328.

Yilmaz A, Sarikaya S, Yildiz S, et al., "Rare complication of circumcision: penile amputation and reattachment," *European Urol*, (Basel), 1993, 23 (3): 423-4.

Ying H, Zhou X, "Balloon Dilation Treatment of Phimosis in Boys," *Chinese Medical Journal*, vol. 104, no. 6, 1991, pp. 491-493.

NERVE REORGANIZATION

Anand K, Scalzo F, "Can adverse neonatal experiences alter brain development and subsequent behavior?," *Biol Neonate*, 2000, Feb., 77(2): 69-82.

Cusick CG, "Extensive cortical regeneration following sciatic nerve injury in adult rats versus restricted reorganization after neonatal injury: Implications for spatial and temporal limits on somatosensory plasticity," *Progress in Brain Research*, 1996, 108:379-390.

Cusick CG, Wall JT, Whiting HH, Jr., Wiley RG, "Temporal progression of cortical reorganization following nerve injury," *Brain Research*, 1990, 537:355-358.

Florence SL, Kaas JH, "Large-scale reorganization at multiple levels of the somatosensory pathway follows therapeutic amputation of the hand in monkeys," *Somatosensory & Motor Research*, 1994: 11:10-117.

Garraghty PE, Hanes DP, Florence SL, Kaas JH, "Pattern of peripheral deafferentation predicts reorganizational limits in adult primate somatosensory cortex," *Somatosensory & Motor Research*, 1994, 11:109-117.

Garraghty PE, Kaas JH, "Functional reorganization in adult monkey thalamus after peripheral nerve injury," *Neuroreport*, 1991, 2:747-750.

Higgins TS, "The Elusive Mechanism of Phantom Limb Pain," *Journal of Young Investigators*, Undergraduate Peer-reviewed Science Journal, Issue 2, August 2001.

Immerman RS, Mackey WC, "A biological analysis of circumcision: a kinder gentler tumescence," *Sociobiology*, 1998, 44: 265-275.

Immerman RS, Mackey, WC, "A Proposed relationship between circumcision and neural reorganization," *J of Genetic Psychology*, 1998, 159 (3): 367-378.

Kelahen ER, Doetsch GS, "Time dependent changes in the functional organization of somatosensory cerebral cortex following digit amputation in adult raccoons," *Somatosensory Research*, 1984, 2: 49-81.

Kelahen AM, Ray RH, Carson LV, Massey CE, Doetsch GS, "Functional reorganization of adult raccoon somatosensory cerebral cortex following neonatal digit amputation," *Brain Research*, 1981, 223:151-159.

Pons TP, Garraghty PE, Ommaya AK, et al., "Massive cortical reorganization after sensory deafferentiation in adult macaques," *Science*, 1991, 252:1857-1860.

Rhoades RW, Wall JT, Chiala NL, Bennett-Clarke CA, Killackey PP, "Anatomical and functional changes in the organization of the cuneate nucleus of adult rats after fetal forelimb amputation," *J of Neuroscience*, 1993, 13:1106-1119.

Stein M, Koverola C, Hanna C, et al., "Hippocampal volume in women victimized by childhood abuse," *Psychol Med*, 1997, 27: 951-959.

Taddio A, Goldbach M, Ipp E, et al., "Effect of Neonatal Circumcision on Pain Response during vaccination in Boys," *Lancet*, 345 (1995): 291-292.

Taddio A, Katz J, et al., "Effect of neonatal circumcision on pain response during subsequent routine vaccination," *Lancet*, vol. 349, 599-603, March 1, 1997.

Wall JT, Huerta MF, Kaas JH, "Changes in the cortical map of the hand following postnatal median nerve injury in monkeys: Modification of somatotopic aggregates," *J of Neuroscience*, (1992), 12:3445-3455.

Wall JT, Kaas HH, "Long-term cortical consequences of reinnervation errors after nerve regeneration in monkeys," *Brain Research*, 1986, 372:400-404.

PAIN, STRESS, PSYCHOLOGICAL & BIOPHYSIOLOGY

Anand KJS, "Hormonal and Metabolic Functions of Neonates and Infants Undergoing Surgery," *Current Opinion in Cardiology*, 1:681-689.

Anand KJ, Hickey PR, "Pain and its effects in the human neonate and fetus," *New England J of Med*, 1987: 317: 1321-1329.

Anders T, "The Effects of Circumcision on Sleep-Wake States in Human Neonates," *Psychosomatic Medicine*, 36(2): 174-179, 1974.

Anders T, et al., "Behavorial state and plasma cortisol response in the human neonate," *Pediatrics*, 1970, 46 (4): 532-7.

Arons BS, "Self-mutilation: Clinical Examples and Reflexions," *Am J Psychotherapy*, 25:550-558.

Astbury J, Brown S, et al., "Birth events, birth experiences and social differences in postnatal depression," *Australian J of Public Health*, vol. 18, no. 2, pp. 176-184.

Bell RQ, Costello N, "Three tests for sex differences in tactile sensitivity in the newborn," *Biologica Neonatorum*, 7: 335-347.

Bench J, "Some effects of audio-frequency stimulation on the crying baby," *J. Auditory Res*, 1969, 9: 122-128

Bench J, Collyer Y, et al., "A comparison between the neonatal sound-evoked startle response and the head-drop (moro) reflex," *Dev Med Child Neurol*, 14: 362-372.

Berry FA, Gregory GA, "Do Premature Infants Require Anesthesia for Surgery?," *Anesthesiology*, 67(3):291-293.

Blackstone P, "Between the lines: Evolution of redecision and impasse theory and practice," *Transactional Analysis Journal*, 1995, 25:343-346.

Blanton MG, "The Behavior of the Human Infant in the First 30 Days of Life," *Psychological Review*, 1917, 24(6):456-483.

Blass EM, Hoffmeyer LB, "Sucrose as an analgesic for newborn infants," (sic), Abstract, *Pediatrics*, vol. 87, No 2, pp. 215-218, February 1991.

Block A, "Sexual Perversion in Female," *New Orleans Med Surg J*, 22: 1-7, 1894-5.

Bower B, "Exploring trauma's cerebral side," *Science News*, 1996; 149: 315.

Boyle GJ and Bensley GA, "Adverse Sexual and Psychological Effects of Male Infant circumcision," *Psychological Reports*, (Missoula), Volume 88, pp. 1105-6.

Boyle GJ, Goldman G, Svoboda JS, Fernandez E, "Male Circumcision: Pain, Trauma and Psychosexual Sequelae," *J of Health Psychology*, (An Interdisciplinary, International Journal), Men's Health, Vol. 7, Issue 3, 01 May 2002.

Bremner J, Randall P, et al., "Magnetic resonance based imaging-based measurement of hippocanthal volume in posttraumatic stress disorder related to childhood physical and sexual abuse - a preliminary report," *Biol Psych*, 1997, 41: 23-32.

Canvaser G, "Psychological effects of circumcision," 38, *Brit J Med Psych*, 321-331, (1965).

Chamberlain D, "Babies Don't Feel Pain: A Century of Denial in Medicine," Presented at The Second International Symposium on Circumcision, San Francisco, CA, 2 May 1991, *NOCIRC*.

Chamberlain D, "Babies Remember Pain," *Pre- and Peri-natal Psychology Journal*, (Summer), 1989.

Chamberlain D, "Birth and the Origins of Violence," *Pre- and Perinatal Psychology J*, (Winter), 1995, 10 (2),: 57-74.

Coleman L, "The psychological implications of tonsillectomy," *N Y State J Med*, 50: 75, 1950.

Coons PM, Ascher-Svanum H, Bellis K, "Self-amputation of the female breasts," *Psychosomatics*, 27:667-68, 1986.

Coons PM, Milstein V, "Self-mutilation associated with dissociative disorders," *Dissociation*, 3:81-87, 1990.

Cope D, "Neonatal Pain: the Evolution of an idea," *The Amer Assoc of Anesthesiologists Newsletter*, September 1998.

Cowling VR, McGorry, Hay DA, "Children of parents with psychotic disorder," *Med J of Australia*, vol. 163, pp. 119-20.

Crudden C, "Reactions of Newborn Infants to Thermal Stimuli Under Constant Tactual Conditions," *Journal of Experimental Psychology*, 20:350-370.

Cunningham N, "Ethical Perspectives on the Perception and Treatment of Neonatal Pain," *J of Perinatal &*

Neonatal Nursing, 4(1): 75-83.

Cunningham-Butler N, "Infants, Pain, and What Health Professionals should Want to Know Now: An Issue of Epistemology and Ethics," *Bioethics*, 3(3):181-209.

Daly, "The Psycho-biological Origins of Circumcision," 31, *International J Psychoanalysis*, 217, (1950).

Davis M, "Sex differences in neonatal stress reactivity," *Child Dev*, 1995, 66: 14-27.

Desor JA, Maller O, Turner RA, "Taste in acceptance of sugars in human infants," *J Comp Physiol Psychol*, 84: 496-501.

Deutsch H, "Some psychoanalytic observations in surgery," *Psychosom Med*, 4: 86, 1942.

Diamond M, "Sex reassignment at birth: a long term review and clinical implications," *Arch of Pediatr and Adoles Med*, 1997, 151: 298-304.

Dixon S, et al., "Behavioral effects of circumcision with and without anesthesia," *J Dev Behav Peds*, 1984, 5: 246-50.

Dubignon J, Campbell D, Curtis M, Parrington M, "The relation between laboratory measures of sucking, food intake, and perinatal factors during the newborn patient," *Child Dev*, 1973, 40: 1107-1120.

Eklund JB, Hamberger L, Linnarsson D, et al., "Perinatal origin of adult self-destructive behavior," *Acta Psychiar Scan*, vol 76, No 42, pp. 364-371, October 1987.

Emde RN, Harmon RJ, Metcalf D, et. al., "Stress and Neonatal Sleep," *Psychosomatic Medicine*, 33(6): 491-497, 1971.

Engel R, Crowel D, Nishijima S, "Visual and auditory response latencies in neonates," 1968. In: *Felicitations Volume in Honour of C. C. de Silva,* Ceylon: Kulartne & Co.

Fink KS, Carson CC, DeVallis RS, "Adult circumcision Outcomes Study: Effect on Erectile Function, Penile sensitivity, sexual Activity and Satisfaction," *J of Urology*, Vol. 167, No 5, pp. 2113-2116, May 2002.

Fisher C, Byrne J, Edwards A, Kahn E, "The psychophysiological studies of nightmares," *J Amer Psychoanal*, 1970, 18:747-782.

Fisher CM, "Phantom Erection after Amputation of Penis. Case Description and Review of the Relevant Literature on Phantoms," *Canadian J Neurological Sci*, 1999; 26: 53-56.

Fitzgerald M, "The birth of pain," *MRC News*, 1998, Summer; 20-3.

Fitzgerald RG, Parkes CM, "Coping With Loss: Blindness and loss of other sensory and cognitive functions," *BMJ*, 1998;316:1160-1163 (11 April).

Flaherty J, "Circumcision and Schizophrenia," *J Clin Psychiatry*, 1980, 41: 96-98.

Florence SL, Kaas JH, "Large scale reorganization at multiple levels of the somatosensory pathway follows therapeutic amputation of the hand in monkeys," *Journal of Neuroscience*, 15:8083-8095.

Fongay, Peter, "The transgenerational transmission of holocaust trauma," *Attachment & Human Development*, Vol. 1, No. 1, April 1999, pp. 92-114(23).

Freud, Anna, "The role of bodily illness in the mental life of children," 7, *Psychoanalytic Study of the Child*, 69-81, (1952).

Friedman S, "An empirical study of the castration and Oedipus complexes," *Genet Psych Monogr*, 1952: 46.

Garbarino J, "The human ecology of child maltreatment: a conceptual model for research," *J of Marriage and the Family*, vol. 139: 721-35.

Glover E, "The 'screening' function of traumatic memories," *Int J Psy*, 1929; 10:90-3.

Glucklich A, "Sacred Pain and the Phenomenal Self," *Harvard Theological Review*, 91 (1998) 389-412.

Glucklich A, "Self and Sacrifice: A Phenomenological Psychology of Sacred Pain," *Harvard Theological Review*, October 1999.

Goldman R, "The psychological impact of circumcision," 83, Supplement. 1, *BJU International*, 93-102 (1999).

Grimes DA, "Routine circumcision of the Newborn Infant: A Reappraisal," *Am J Obstet & Gynecol*, 124: 39, 1976.

Grimes DA, "Routine circumcision of the Newborn Infant: A Reappraisal," *Am J Obstet & Gynecol*, 130: 125-129, 1978.

Grunau RVE, Craig KD, "Pain Expression in Neonates: Facial Action and Cry," *Pain*, 28:395-410.

Gunnar M, et al., "Adrenocortical activity and behavioral distress in human newborns," *Dev Psychobiol*, 1988, 21: 297-310.

Gunnar M, et al., "Coping with adverse stimulation in the neonatal period: quiet sleep and plasma cortisol levels during recovery from circumcision," *Child Dev*, 1985, 56: 824-34.

Gunnar M, Porter F, "Neonatal stress recactivity: predictions to later emotional temperament," *Child Dev*, 1995, 66: 1-13.

Gunnar MR, Fisch RO, Korsvik S, Donhowe JM, "The effects of circumcision on serum cortisol and behavior," *Psychoneuroendocrinology*, 1981, 6: 269-75

Gunnar MR, et al., "The effects of a pacifying stimulus on behavioral and adrenocortical responses to circumcision in the newborn," *J Am Acad Child Psychiatry*, 1984, 23: 34-8.

Gunnar MR, Malone S, Vance G, et al., "Quiet Sleep and Levels of Plasma Cortisol During Recovery from Circumcision in Newborns," *Child Development*, 56:824-34.

Hepper P, "Fetal memory: does it exist? What does it do?," *Acta Paediatr Scand*, 1996, Supplement, 416: 16-20.

Holve R, et al., "Regional anesthesia during newborn circumcision. Effect on pain response," *Clin Pediatr*, (Phila), 1983, 22: 813-8.

Howard C, et al., "Acetaminophen analgesia in neonatal circumcision: the effect on pain," *Pediatrics*, 1994, 93: 641-6.

Hutt SJ, Lenard HG, Prechtl HFR, "Psychophysiological studies in newborn infants," 1969. In L. P. Lipsitt and H, W. Reese (Editors), *Advances in Child Development and Behavior*, Vol. 4, New York, Academic, pp. 127-72.

Jacobson B, Bygdeman M, "Obstetric care and proneness of offspring to suicide," *BMJ*, 1998, 317: 1346-49.

Jacobson B, Eklund G, Hamberger L, et al., "Perinatal origin of adult self-destructive behavior," *Acta Psychiatrica Scandinavia*, Vol 76, No 42: 364-371, October 1987.

Kennedy H, "Trauma in Childhood: signs and sequlea as seen in the analysis of an adolescent," *The Psychoanalytic Study of the Child,* 1986, 41: 209-219.

Kitahara, Michio, "A Cross-cultural Test of the Freudian Theory of Circumcision," *International J of Psychoanalytic Psychotherapy*, 5(1976): 535-46.

Koren G, "Effect of Neonatal Circumcision on Pain Responses," *Lancet*, 1995, 345:291-92.

Lander J, Brady-Freyer, Metcalf JB, et al., "Comparison of Ring Block, Dorsal Penile Nerve Block, and Topical Anesthesia for Neonatal Circumcision: A Randomized Controlled Trial," *JAMA*, Vol. 278, No. 24, pp. 2157-62, December 24/31, 1997.

Levine S, "An endocrine theory of infantile stimulation," In J. A. Ambrose (Editor.), *Stimulation in Early Infancy*. New York: Academic, pp. 45-55.

Levy D, "Psychic trauma of operations in children," *American Journal of Diseases of Children*, 1945, 69 (10): 7-25.

Lipsitt LP, Levy N, "Electrotactile threshold in the human neonate," *Child Dev*, 1959, 30: 547-554.

Lott DA, "Brain Development, Attachment and Impact on Psychic Vulnerability," *Psychiatric Times*, May 1998, Vol. XV, Issue 5.

Maguire P, Parkes CM, "Coping With Loss: Surgery and Loss of Body Parts," *BMJ*, Vol. 316, No. 7137, Saturday, 4 April 1998.

Malone S, et al., "Adrenocortical and behavioral responses to limb restraint in human neonates," *Dev Psychobiol*, 1985, 18: 435-46.

Marshall R, "Neonatal pain associated with caregiving procedures," *Pediatr Clin North Am*, 1989, 36: 885-903.

McFadyen A, *Children have feelings too*, BMJ, 1998, 316: 1616.

McGraw M, "Neural Maturation as Exemplified in the Changing Reactions of the Infant to Pin Prick," *Child Development*, (1941), 12(1):31-42.

Menage J, "Post-traumatic stress disorder in women who have undergone obstetric and/or gynaecological procedures: a consecutive series of 30 cases of PTSD," *J of Reproductive and Infant Psychology*, 1993, 11: 221-228.

Miller ML, "The traumatic effect of surgical operations in childhood on the integrative effects of the ego," *Psychol Quart*, 20: 57, 1951.

Neppe VM, Smith ME, "Culture Psychopathology and Psi: A Clinical Relationship," *Parapsychological J of S.A.*, 1982, #1, 1-5.

Neziroglu F, "Body Dysmorphic Disorder: A Common But Underdiagnosed Clinical Entity," *Psychiatric Times*, January 1998, vol XV, Issue 1.

Nisbett R, Gurwitz S, "Weight, sex, and the eating behavior of human behavior," *J Comp Physiol Psychol*, 73: 245-253.

Owens M, Todt E, "Pain in Infancy: Neonatal Reaction to Skin Lance," *Pain*, 20(1):77-86.

Ozturk O, "Ritual Circumcision and Castration Anxiety," *Psychiatry*, 36: 49-60, 1973.

Paige K, "The Ritual of Circumcision," *Human Nature*, May, 1978: 40.

Parkes CM, "Coping With Loss: Facing Loss," *BMJ*, 1998; 316:1521-1524 (16 May)

Patel D, "Factors Affecting the Practice of Circumcision," *American Journal of Diseases of Children*, 136(7):634.

Poland RL, Roberts RJ, Gutierrez-Mazorra JF, Fonkalsurd EW, "Neonatal Anesthesia," *Pediatrics*, 80(3):446.

Porter F, et al., "Neonatal pain cries: effect of circumcision on acoustic features and perceived urgency," *Child Dev*, 1986, 57: 790-802.

Porter F, et al., "Newborn Pain Cries and Vagal Tone: Parallel Changes in Response to Circumcision," *Child Development*, 1988, Vol. 59, pp. 495-505.

Porter F, et al., "Procedural pain in newborn in newborn infants: the influence of intensity and development," *Pediatrics*, 1999, 104:e13.

Prechtl HFR, *Patterns of reflex behavior related to sleep in the human infant*, 1972. In C. D. Clemente, D. P. Purpura, and F. Mayer (Editors.), 'Sleep and the Maturing Nervous System,' New York, Academic, pp. 297-301.

Prescott J, "Body pleasure and the origins of violence," *Bulletin of the Atomic Scientists*, 1975, November, 10-20.

Purcell-Jones G, Dormon F, Sumner E, "Pediatric Anesthetics Perceptions of Neonatal and Infant Pain," *Pain*, 33(2):181-187.

Rawlings D, et al., "The effect of circumcision on transcutaneous PO2 in term infants," *Am J Dis Child*, 1980, 134: 676-8.

Rhinehart J, "Neonatal circumcision reconsidered," *Transactional Analysis J*, 1999, July, vol. 29 (3): 215-221.

Rich EC, Marshall RE, Volpe JJ, "The Normal Neonatal Response to Pin-Prick," *Developmental Medicine & Child Neurology*, (1974), 16:432-434.

Richards MPM, Bernal JF, Brackbill Y, "Early Behavioral Differences: Gender or Circumcision?," *Develop Psychobiol*, 9(1): 89-95, 1976.

Roth, Susan and Lebowitz, Leslie, "The Experience of Sexual Trauma," *Journal of Traumatic Stress*, 1988, Vol. 1: 78-107.

Schoen, E, "Pain in neonatal circumcision," *Clin Pediatr*, (Phila), 1991, 30: 429-32.

Schwartzman, Richard & Schwartzman, Rebecca, "Circumcision From an Orgonomic Perspective," J*ournal of Orgonomy*, Vol. 31, no. 1.

Sherman M, Sherman I, "Sensori-motor Responses in Infants," *J of Comparative Psychology*, 1925, 5:53-68.

Skoyles JR, "Is there a genetic component to body schema?," *Trends in Neuroscience*, (1990), 13, 409.

Talbert L, et al., "Adrenal cortical response to circumcision in the neonate," *Obstet Gynecol*, 48: 208-10, Aug 1976.

Tantum D, Whittaker J, "Personality Disorder and Self-Wounding," *British J of Psychiatry*, 1992, 161, 451-464.

Taylor CG, Norman DK, Murphy JM, Jellinek M, Quinn D, Poitrast FG, Goshko M, "Diagnosed intellectual and emotional impairment among parents who seriously mistreat their children: prevalence, type, and outcome in a court sample," *Child Abuse and Neglect*, vol. 15, no. 4, pp. 389-401.

Tennes K, Carter D, "Plasma cortisol levels and behavioral states in early infancy," *Psychom Med*, 1973, 35: 121-128.

Tohill J, McMorrow O, "Pain Relief in Neonatal Intensive Care," *Lancet*, 336:569.

Van der Kolk B, "The compulsion to retreat the trauma: re-enactment, revictimization, and masochism," *Psychiatric Clinics of North America*, 1989, 12: 389-411.

Verit A, Aksoy S, Yeni E, Unal D, Ciftci H, "A Limited Study on the Perception and change in Attitude about Circumcision among Health Care Professionals and Their Male Family Members," *Urol International*, 2002; 69(4):302-5.

Viola JM, Ditzler TF, Batzer, WB, "Posttraumatic Stress Disorder: A Comment on the Value of 'Mixed Trauma' Treatment Groups," Manuscript accepted for publication: *Australian Psychiatry*, as of August 1996.

Walter G, Streimer J, "Genital self-mutilation: Attempted foreskin reconstruction," *Brit J Psych*, 156, Jan. 1990, 125-127.

Weisman S, et al., "Consequences of inadequate analgesia during painful procedures in children," *Arch Pediatr Adolescent Med*, 1998, 152: 147-9.

Williamson P, Williamson M, "Physiologic Stress Reduction by a Local Anesthetic During Newborn Circumcision," *Pediatrics*, 71,(1): 36-40.

Wolff PH, *The natural history of crying and other vocalizations in early infancy*. In BM Foss, (d.), 'Determinants of Infant Behavior,' Vol IV, Metheun, pp. 81-109.

Yorke C, "Reflections on the problem of psychic trauma," *Psychol Study of the Child*, 41: 221-236.

Zoske J, "Male Circumcision: a gender perspective," *The Journal of Men's Studies*, 1998, 6 (2): 189-208.

PARENTAL – DIAGNOSIS

Altschul MS, "The Circumcision Controversy," *APF*, vol. 41, No. 3, p. 817. American Academy of Family

Physicians.

Amato D, Garduno-Espinosa J, "Circumcision of the newborn male and the risk of urinary tract infection during the first year: A meta-analysis," *Bol Med Infant Mex*, Vol. 49, No. 10, Oct. 1992, 652-658.

American Academy of Family Physicians Commission on Clinical Policies and Research, "Position Paper on Neonatal Circumcision," Leawood, Kansas, *American Academy of Family Physicians*, 14 February 2002.

American Academy of Pediatrics, "*Breastfeeding and the Use of Human Milk (RE9729)*," *Pediatrics*, vol. 100, no 6, pp. 1035-1039, December 1997.

American Academy of Pediatrics, "Care of the Uncircumcised Penis: Guidelines for Parents."

American Academy of Pediatrics, "Circumcision Policy Statement," *Pediatrics*, Vol. 103, No. 3, pp 686-93, 01 March 1999.

American Medical Association, Report 10 of the Council on Scientific Affairs (I-99). Full Text, "Neonatal circumcision," December 1999.

Andrew G, Collin J, "Save the Normal Foreskin," *BMJ*, 1993, 306: 1-2.

Baker, "Newborn Male circumcision: Needless and Dangerous," *Sexual Medicine Today*, Nov. 1979, 35.

Birley H, et al., "Clinical features and management of recurrent balanitis; Association with atopy and genital washing," *Genitourinary Med*, 1993, 69: 400-403.

Boyce WT, "Care of the Foreskin," *Pediatr Rev*, 1983, 5: 26.

Brown MS, Brown CA, "Circumcision Decision: Prominence of Social Concerns," *Pediatrics*, vol. 80, No. 2, p. 215, 2 Aug. 1987.

Cadman D, "Newborn Circumcision: An Economic Perspective," *Canadian Medical Assoc J*, vol. 131, pp. 1353-1355, 1 Dec. 1984.

Chessare JB, "Circumcision: Is the Risk of UTI Really the Pivotal Issue?," *Clinical Pediatrics*, pp. 100-104, Feb. 1992.

Coppa G, et al., "Preliminary study of breastfeeding and bacterial adhesion to uroepithelial cells," *Lancet*, 335, (March 1990), 569-71.

Craig J, et al., "Effect of circumcision on incidence of urinary tract infection in preschool boys," *Dept of Nephrology*, Royale Alexandra Hospital for Children, Sydney, Australia.

Denniston G, "Unnecessary Circumcision," *The Female Patient*, vol. 17: 13, July 1992.

Dixon S, et al., "Behavioral effects of circumcision with and without anesthesia," *J. Dev Behav Peds*, 1984, 5: 246-50.

Dozer R, "Routine Neonatal Circumcision: Boundary of Ritual and Science," *AFP*, vol. 41, No. 3, p. 820, editorial.

Duffy LC, Faden H, Wasielewski R, Wolf J, et al., "Exclusive Breastfeeding Protects Against Bacterial Colonization and Day Care Exposure to Otitis Media," *Pediatrics*, vol. 100, no 4, p. e7, 04 October 1997.

Editor, "So that's what they do with it," *New Physician*, (May-June), 1989): 51.

Editorial: "The Case Against Neonatal Circumcision," *BMJ*, 1979: 1163-4.

Fetus and Newborn Committee, "Neonatal circumcision revisited," *Canadian Paediatric Society*, (CPS), Canadian Medical Journal, 1996; 154(6): 769-780.

Fleiss PM, Douglass J, "The case against neonatal circumcision," *BMJ*, 1979; 2: 554.

Foley J, "The Unkindest Cut of All," *Fact*, July-August, 1966, pp. 3-9.

Frisch M, Frios S, Kjear SK, Melbye M, "Falling incidence of penis cancer in an uncircumcised population (Denmark 1943-90)," *BMJ*, Vol. 311, No. 7018, p. 1471, 02 December 1995.

Goer, Henci, "The Assault on Normal Birth: The OB Disinformation Campaign," *Midwifery Today*, Issue 62,

Autumn 2002.

Gordon A, Collin J, "Save the normal foreskin," *BMJ*, 1993: 306: 1-2.

Griffiths D, Frank J, "Inappropriate circumcision referrals by GPs," *J R Soc Med*, 1992, 85: 324-5.

Groer MR, Davis MW, Hemphill J, "Postpartum stress: current concepts and the possible protective role of breastfeeding," *J of Obstetric, Gynecologic, and Neonatal Nursing*, 31 (4): 411-417, 2002.

Harris, Chandice, "Cultural Values and the Decision to Circumcise," *Image*, (Journal of Nursing Scholarship), vol. 18, 1986, pp. 98-104.

Hellsten SK, "Rationalising circumcision: from tradition to fashion, from public health to individual freedom – critical notes on cultural persistence of the practice of genital mutilation," *Journal of Medical Ethics*, 2004; 248-253.

Hepper PG, "Fetal Memory: Does it exist? What does it do?," *Acta Pediatrica Supplement*, Vol. 416, pp. 16-20, 1996.

Hofvander Y, "Circumcision in Boys: time for doctors to reconsider," *World Hosp Health Serv*, 2002; 38(2):15-17.

Hughs GK, "Circumcision - Another Look," *Ohio Medicine*, Vol. 86, No. 2, Feb 1990, p. 92.

Kikiros C, et al., "The response of phimosis to local topical steroid application," *Pediatr Surg Internat*, 8: 339-342.

Kitahara, "Social Contact Versus Bodily Contact: A Qualitative Difference Between Father and Mother for the Son's Masculine Identity," 10, *Behav Sci Research*, 1, (1975).

Klauber GT, "Circumcision and Phallic Fallacies, or the Case Against Routine Circumcision," *Connecticut Medicine*, vol. 37, no 9, 1973, p. 445-448.

Lane T, South L, "Lateral preputioplasty for phimosis," *J R Coll Edinb*, 1999, 44 (5): 310-2.

Lawler FH, Bisonni RS; Holtgrave DR, "Circumcision: A Decision Analysis of it's Medical Value," *Family Medicine*, vol 23, No. 8, p. 587, Nov-Dec. 1991.

Lee, Romeo, "Filipino experience of ritual male circumcision: Knowledge and Insights for anti-circumcision advocacy," *Culture, Health & Sexuality*, May-June 2006; 83): 225-234.

Leitch IO, "Circumcision - a continuing enigma," 6, *Aust. Paediatr J*, 59-65, (1970).

Loeb L, "The Blood Sacrifice Complex, Memoirs," *Am Anthropol Assoc*, #23, 1923.

Lovell JE, "Maternal Attitudes Toward Circumcision," *J Family Practice*, 1979: 9: 811-813.

MacKinlay GA, "Save the Prepuce. Painless separation of preputal adhesions in the outpatient clinic," *BMJ*, Vol. 297: pp. 590-591, 3 September 1988.

Mansfield CJ, Hueston WJ, Rudy M, "Neonatal circumcision: associated factors and length of hospital stay," *J of Family Practice*, 1996; 42(3): 307.

Marild S, "Breastfeeding and Urinary Tract Infections," *Lancet*, 336 (Oct. 1990) 942.

Marshall RE, Porter FL, Rogers AG, et al., "Circumcision II: Effects Upon Mother-Infant Interaction," *Early Human Development*, 1982: 7: 367-374.770

Marshall RE, Straighten WC, Moore JA, Boserman SB, "Circumcision I: Effects Upon Newborn Behavior," *Infant Behav Dev*, 1980; vol3: 1-14.

McCraken G, et al., "Options in antimicrobial management of urinary tract infections in infants and children," *Pediatr Infect Dis J*, 8 (8), Aug. 1989, 552-555.

Meyer H, "Meatal ulcer in the circumcised infant," *Med Times*, 1971, 99; 77-8.

Mueller E, et al., "The incidence of genitourinary abnormalities in circumcised and uncircumcised boys presenting with an initial urinary tract infection by 6 months of age," *Pediatrics*, September 1997, vol. 100, 580 (Supplement).

Nigel W, et al., "Why are children referred for circumcision?," *BMJ*, 1993, 306: 28.

Obstetrics & Gynecology, ACOG Committee Opinion Number 260, October 2001, "Circumcision," *Obstetrics & Gynecology*, Volume 98, Number 4: pp. 707-8, October 2001.

Oddy WH, Holt PG, Sly PD, et al., "Association Between breast feeding and asthma in 6 year old children: findings of a prospective birth cohort study," *BMJ*, 319:815-819, 25 September 1999.

Osborn LM, Metcalf, TJ, Mariani EM, "Hygienic Care in Uncircumcised Infants," *Pediatrics*, Vol. 67 No. 3, 3 March 1981, pp. 365-367.

Oster J, "Further Fate of the Foreskin," *Arch Dis Child*, 1968 : 48 : 200-3.

Perera CL, et al., "Safety and Efficacy of Nontherapeutic Male Circumcision: A Systemic Review," *Annals of Family Medicine*, 8:64-72 (2010).

Pisacane A, "Breastfeeding and urinary tract infection," *Lancet*, 1990, 336: 50.

Pisacane A, "Breast-feeding and urinary tract infection," *J Pediatr*, 1992, 120; 87–89.

Poland RL, "The Question of Routine Neonatal Circumcision," *The New England Journal of Medicine*, vol. 322, no. 18, pp. 1312-1314, May 3, 1990.

Pratt KC, Nelson AK, Sun KH, "The Behavior of the Newborn Infant," *Ohio State University Student Contrib. Psychology*, (1930), no. 10.

Preston EN, "Wither the Foreskin? A Condition of Routine Neonatal Circumcision," *JAMA*, 1970, 213: 1853.

Rickwood A, Walker J, "Is phimosis overdiagnosed in boys and are too many circumcisions performed in consequence," *Ann R Coll Surg England*, 1989, 71 (5): 275-7.

Robson WLM, Leung AKC, "The circumcision question," *Postgrad Med*, 1992;91:237-44.

Rockney R, "Newborn Circumcision," *AFP*, Oct. 1988, vol 38, No. 4, p. 151.

Russell PMG, "Vagitus Uterinus: Crying in Utero," *Lancet*, 1:137-138.

Schoen EJ, Christopher JC, Ray GT, "Newborn Circumcision Decreases Incidence and Costs of Urinary Tract Infections During the First Year of Life," *Pediatrics*, 2000; 105: 789-793.
    Peer Review Rebuttals: *Post-publication Peer Reviews to*:

Shaw RA, Robertson WO, "Routine Circumcision. A Problem for Medicine," *Am J Dis Child*, 106: 216, 1963.

Slater, Philip E, "On Social Regression," *American Sociological Review*, 28, June 1968, p. 349.

Storms, Michele R, "AAFP Fact Sheet on Neonatal Circumcision: A Need for Updating," 54, *Am Family Physician*. 1216-1217, (1999).

Strull WM, Lo B, Charles G, "Do Patients Want to Participate in Medical Decision Making," *JAMA*, 1984, 252: 2990.

Sugerman M, "Paranatal Influence on Mother-Infant Attachment," *American J of Orthopsychiatry*, vol 37, No. 3, pp. 407-421, 1977.

Thompson HC, King LR, Knox E, et al., "Report of the American Academy of Pediatrics Ad Hoc Task Force on Circumcision," *Pediatrics*, vol. 56, no. 4, October 1975, pp. 610-611.

Warren J, Bigelow J, "The case against circumcision," *Br J Sex Med*, 6-8, 1994, Sept/Oct.

Weil, Andrew, "Eleven Medical Practices to Avoid," East-West, National Health, Sept/Oct, 1992.

Whiting JWM, Landauer TK, Jones TM, "Infantile immunization and adult stature," *Child Dev*, 39:59-67.

Williams N, Chell J, Kapila L, "Why are children referred for circumcision?," *BMJ*, Vol. 306: p. 28, 2 January 1993.

Wright JE, "The Treatment of Childhood Phimosis with Topical Steroids," *Australian-New Zealand J of Surg*, 1994; 64:327-8.

Zimmer P, "Modern Ritualistic Surgery," *Clinical Pediatr*, 16(6): 503-506, June 1977.

PREPUCE - GLANS – IMMUNOLOGY

American Academy of Pediatrics, "Care of the Uncircumcised Penis," 2000.

Bassett I, et al., "Herpes Simplex Virus Type 2 Infection of Heterosexual Men Attending a Sexual Health Centre," *Medical Journal of Australian* 160 (1994): 697-700.

Bazett HC, et al., "Depth, Distribution and probable Identification in the Prepuce of Sensory End-organs Concerned in Sensations of Temperature and Touch; Thermometric Conductivity," *Arch of Neuol and Psychiatry*, 27 (1932): 489-517.

Berman B, Chen V, France D, et al., "Anatomical mapping of epidermal Langerhans cell densities in adults," *Brit J Derm*, 1983, 109: 553-558.

Birley H, Walker M, Luzzi G, "Clinical features and management of recurrent balanitis: association with recurrent washing," 69, *Genitourinary Med*, 400-403, (1993).

Chao A, et al., "Risk Factors associated with prevalent HIV-1 infection among pregnant women in Rwanda," *International J of Epidemiology*, (1994), vol. 23, pp. 371-380.

Cold C, Taylor J, "The Prepuce," *BJU International*, 83, Supplement. 1, (1999): 34-44.

Cook LS, Koutsky LA, Holmes KK, "Clinical Presentation of Genital Warts among Circumcised and Uncircumcised Heterosexual Men Attending an Urban STD Clinic," *Genitourinary Medicine*, 69 (1993): 262-264.

Davenport M, "Problems with the Penis and Prepuce: Natural History of the Foreskin," *British Medical Journal*, 312 (1996): 299-301. Re: 'Anatomy, Physiology, Innervation, Immunology, and Sexual Function,' BJU.

de Witte L, Nabatov A, Pion M et al., "Langerin is a natural barrier to HIV-1 transmission by Langerhans cells," *Nat Med*, 2007;3:367-371.

Deibert G, "The separation of the prepuce in the human prepuce," 57, *Anat Rec*, 387-399 (1933).

Edwards S, "Balanitis and balanoposthitis: a review," 72, *Genitourin Med*, 155-159, (1996).

Escala JM, Rickwood AMK, "Balanitis," 63, *Brit J Urol*, 196-197, (1989).

Fleiss, Paul, et al, "Immunological functions of the human prepuce," *Sex Trans Inf*, 74, 364-367, 1998.

Flower J, et al., "An Immunopathologic Study of the Bovine Prepuce." *Veterinary Pathology*, 20 (1983): 189-202.

Gomez J, et al., "Secondary megaprepuce," *BJU*, (1996), 78: 959-60.

Grosskurth H, Mosha F, Todd J, Senkoro K, et al., "A community trial of the impact of improved sexually transmitted disease treatment on the HIV epidemic in rural Tanzania: 2. Baseline survey results," *AIDS*, 1995; 9(8): 927-934.

Halata Z, Munger B, "The neuroanatomical basis for the protopathic sensibility of the human glans penis," *Brain Res*, 1986, 371: 205-30.

Hausemann R, et al., "The Forensic Value of the Immunohistochemical Detection of Oestrogen Receptors in Vaginal Epithelium," *International Journal of Legal Medicine*, 109 (1996): 10-30.

Hodges, Fredrick, "The Ideal Prepuce in Ancient Greece and Rome: Male Genital Aesthetics and Their Relation to 'Lipodermos,' Circumcision, Foreskin Restoration, and the 'Kynodesme'," *The Bulletin of the History of Medicine*, 75: pp. 375-405, Fall 2001.

Hyman AB, Brownstein MH, "Tyson's Glands: Ectopic Sebaceous Glands and Papillomatous Penis," *Archives of Dermatology*, 99 (1969): 31-37.

Jefferson G, Lond MS, (Eng.) Victoria BC, "The peripenic muscle; some observations on the anatomy of phimosis," *Surgery, Gynecology, and Obstetrics (Chicago)*, Vol. 23, No. 2: Pages 177-181, August 1916.

Keith A, Shellitoe A, "The preputal and odorferous glands of man," *Lancet*; I: 146.

Kitajima S, Fujiwara Y, Kato T, "Analysis of shape and retractability of the prepuce in 603 Japanese boys," 156 *J Urology* 1813-1815 (1996).

Lakshmanan S, Parkash S, "The human prepuce: some aspects of structure and function," *Ind J Surg*, 1980, 44: 134-137.

Laumann E, Masi C, Zuekerman E, et al., "Circumcision in the United States: Prevalence, Prophylactic Effects, and Sexual Practice," *JAMA*, 227(1997), 1052-1057.

Lee-Huang S, Huang PL, Sun Y, et al., "Lysozyme and Rnases as anti-HIV components in beta-core preparations of human gonadotropin," *Proceedings of the National Academy of Science (USA)*, vol. 96, no. 6: pages 2678-2681, 16 March 1999.

Maden C, Shertman KJ, Beckman AM, et al., "History of circumcision, medical conditions, and sexual activity and risk of penile cancer," *J of the National Cancer Institute*, vol. 85, no. 1, pages 19-24, 06 June 1993.

Modwing R, Valderrama E, "Immunohistochemical analysis of nerve distribution patterns within preputal tissues," *J Urol*, 1989. 141, Supplement. 1: 489A (Abstract).

Pertot S, "Sensitivity is the rising issue on circumcision," *Australian Doctor*, 25 Nov. 1994.

Prakash S, [*sic*, Parkash], Jeyakumar S, Subraman K, Chauldhuri S, "Human subpreputial collection: its nature and function," 110, *J Urol*, 211-212, (1973).

Prakash S, [*sic*, Parkash], Raghuram R, Venkatesan K, Ramakrishnan S, "Sub-preputial wetness - Its nature," 18 *Ann Nat Med Sci*, (India) 109-112, (1982).

Storms MR, "AAFP Fact Sheet on Neonatal Circumcision: A Need for Updating," *American Family Physician*, vol. 54, no 4, pages 1216-1217, 15 September 1996.

Tan HL, "Foreskin Fallacies and Phimosis," *Annals of the Academy of Med*, Singapore, 1985.

Taylor JR, Lockwood AP, Taylor AJ, "The Prepuce: Specialized Mucosa of the Penis and its Loss to Circumcision," *British Journal of Urology*, 77 (1996): 291-295.

Weiss GN, "The Distribution and Density of Langerhans Cells in the Human Prepuce: Site of a diminished Immune Response?," *Israel J of Med Sciences*, 29 (1993): 42-43.

Winkelmann RK, "The Cutaneous Innervation of Human Newborn Prepuce," *Journal of Investigative Dermatology*, 26 (1956): 53-67.

Winkelmann RK, "The Erogenous Zones: Their Nerve Supply and its Significance," *Proceedings of the Staff meetings of the Mayo Clinic*, 34 (1959): 39-47.

Winkelmann RK, "The mucocutaneous end-organ: the primary organized sensory ending in human skin," *AMA Arch Derm*, 1957, 76: 225-235.

Wright, Joyce, "How smegma serves the penis," *Sexology*, 1970, 37 (2): 50-53.

SOCIOLOGY-SOCIAL PSYCHOLOGY-PSYCHOHISTORY

Brown J, "A Cross-cultural study of female initiation rites," *Am Anthropol*, 65: 837-53, 1963.

Bandura A, Ross D, Ross A, (1963), "Vicarious reinforcement and imitative learning," *Journal of Abnormal and Social Psychology*, 67, 601-607.

Blackstone P, "Between the Lines: Evolution of redecision and impasse theory and practice," *Transactional Analysis Journal*, 1995, 25:343-346.

Bolande RP, "Ritualistic Surgery: Circumcision and Tonsilectomy," *New England Journal of Med*, 1969: 280: 591-596.

Bolton R, "Tawanku: Intercouple Bonds in Qolla Village (Peru)," (173), *Anthropos*, 68: 245-255.

deMause, L, "Childhood and Cultural Evolution," *The Journal of Psychohistory*, v. 26, N. 3, Winter 1999.

deMause L, "Restaging fetal traumas in war and social violence," *Pre- and Perinatal Psychology Journal*,

1996, 10 (4), 227-258.

deMause, L, "The History of Child Abuse," *The Journal of Psychohistory*, 25 (3) Winter 1998.

DeMeo J, "Desertification and the Origins of Armoring: The Saharasian Connection, Part V," *Journal of Orgonomy*, vol. 24, No. 1. re: MGM.

DeMeo J, "Desertification and the Origins of Armoring The Saharasian Connection, Part IV," *Journal of Orgonomy*, vol. 24, No. 2. re: FGM.

Dunsmir W, Gordon E, "The history of circumcision," *BJU International*, 1999, 83, Supplement. 1: 1-2.

Cook SE, "Retention of primary preferences after secondary filial imprinting," *Animal Behavior*, 1993, 46:405-407.

Emery PE, "Trauma in Psychohistory," *The Journal of Psychohistory*, V. 26, N. 3, Winter 1999.

Glucklich A, "Self and Sacrifice, A Phenomenological Psychology of Sacred Pain," *Harvard Theological Review*, October 1999.

Gollaher DL, "From Ritual to Science: The Medical Transformation of Circumcision in America," *Journal of Social History*, Vol. 28, No., 1, pp. 5-36, Fall 1994.

Halperin D, Epstein H, "Concurrent multiple partnerships help explain Africa's high HIV prevalence: implications for prevention," *The Lancet*, Vol. 364, Issue 9428, pp. 4-6.

Hart G, Wellings K, "Sexual behavior and its medicalisation: in sickness and in health," *BMJ*, 2002; 324:896-900 (13 April).

Hodges F, "The Ideal Prepuce in Ancient Greece and Rome: Male Genital Aesthetics and Their Relation to Lipodermos, Circumcision, Foreskin Restoration, and the Kynodesme," *Bulletin of the History of Med*, vol. 75, no. 3 (Fall 2001): pp. 375-405.

Hrdy, DB, "Cultural practices contributing to the transmission of human immunodeficiency virus in Africa," *Reviews of Infectious Diseases* (Chicago), Vol. 9, No. 6: pp. 1109-1119, November-December 1987.

King, Paul, "Western History of Male Infibulation – Piercing of the Foreskin," *The Point*, Issue 19, 2001.

Kirkpatrick LA, Waugh CE, Valencia A, Webster GD, "The functional domain-specifty of self-esteem and the differential prediction of aggression," *Journal of Personality and Social Psycho*logy, 82, 756-767.

Laumann E, Masi C, Zuckerman E, "Circumcision in the United States, Prevalence, Prophylactic Effects, and Sexual Practices," *JAMA*, 227 (13): 1052-7, 02 April 1997.

Loeb L, "The Blood Sacrifice Complex, Memoirs," *Am Anthropological Assoc*, #30, 1923.

Lukes, Steven, "Political Ritual and Social Integration," *Journal of Sociological Association*, 9, no. 2 (1975): 289-308.

Marck J, "Aspects of male circumcision in sub-equatorial Africa cultural history," *Health Transition Review*, 1997, 7 (Supplement): 337-359.

Mead, George Herbert, "The Social Self," *Journal of Philosophy, Psychology and Scientific Methods*, 10, (1913): 374-38.

Montague A, "Ritual Mutilation Among Primitive Peoples," *Cibia Symposium*, October 1946, pp. 421-436.

Moore J, "Population density, social pathology, and behavioral ecology," *Primates*, 40:5-26, 1999.

Neppe VM, Smith ME, "Culture, Psychopathology And Psi: A Clinical Relationship," *Parapsychological J. of S.A.*, 1982, 3:1, 1-5.

Peticolas T, Tillis T, et al., "Oral and Perioral Piercing: A Unique Form of Self-Expression," *The Journal of Contemporary Dental Practice*, Vol. 1, No. 3, Summer 2000.

Prescott JW, "Body Pleasure and the Origins of Violence," *The Bulletin of The Atomic Scientists*, November 1975, pp. 10-20.

Slater, Philip E, "On Social Regression," *Am Socio Review*, 28, June 1963, p. 349.

Southwold, Martin, "Religious Belief," *Man*, n.s. 14, no. 4 (1978): 628-644.

Stirling L, "Ritual Circumcision in Southern Tanganyika," *East African M J*, 18:81, 1941.

Szasz TS, "Remembering Masturbatory Insanity," *Ideas on Liberty,* 50: 35-36 (May), 2000. Pub: The foundation for Economic Education.

Thomas WI, "Sex in Primitive Morality," *American Journal of Sociology* 4, (1899): 774-787.

Thomas WI, "The Relation of Sex to Primitive Social Control," *American Journal of Sociology* 3, (1898): 754-76.

Thomas WI, "The Relation of the Medicine-Man to the Origin of the Professional Occupations," *Decennial Publications of the University of Chicago*, First Series, 4 (1903): 241-256.

Wallace BJ, "Pagan Gadding Spouse Exchange," *Ethnology*, 8: 183-188.

Wallerstein E, "Is Non Religious circumcision necessary?," *J Am Acad Child Psychiatry*, 1985, 24: (3): 364-5.

Zimmerman F, "Origin and Significance of the Jewish Rite of Circumcision," *Psychoanalytic Review*, 38(2): 103-112, 1951.

TISSUE RESPONSE – RESTORATION

Atilla MK, Dundaroz R, Odabas O, Oaturk H, Akin R, Gokcay E, "A non-surgical approach to the treatment of phimosis: local non-steroidal anti-inflammatory ointment application," *J Urol*, 1977; 158:196-197.

Austad ED, "The Origin of Tissue Expansion," *Clinics in Plastic Surgery*, vol. 14, no. 3, July 1987, p. 433.

Cohen M, Marschall M, "Tissue Expansion: An Alternative Technique in Reconstructive Surgery," 1990 *Surgical Annual, Chicago, University of Illinois College of Medicine*, vol. 22, pp. 347-348.

Dewan PA, Tieu HC, Cheing BS, "Phimosis: is circumcision necessary," *J Paediatr Child Health*, 1996; 32:285-289.

Golubovic Z, Milanovic D, Vukadinovic V, Rakic I, Perovic S, "The conservative treatment of phimosis in boys," *BJU*, 1996; 78:786-788.

Goodman T, et al., "Tissue Expansion: A New Modality in Reconstructive Surgery," *AORN Journal*, vol. 46, no. 2, Aug. 1987, p.198.

Goodwin WE, "Uncircumcision: A technique for plastic reconstruction of a prepuce after circumcision," *J Urol*, 144: 1203, 1990.

Greer DM, Mohl PC, "Foreskin reconstruction: A preliminary report," *Sexual Medicine Today*, 17 April 1982.

Hannafy, MN, Sadd, SM, Al-Ghorab, MM, "Ancient Egyptian Med," *Urol* 4, 114, 1974.

Jorgenson E, Svensson A, "The treatment of phimosis in boys, with a potent topical steroid (clobetasol propionate 0.05%) cream," *Acta Derm Venerol*, 1993; 73:55-56.

Kikiros CS, Beasley SW, Woodward AA, "The response of phimosis to local steroid application," *Pediatr Surg In*t, 1993; 8:329-332.

Lindhagen T, "Topical clobetasol propionate compared with placebo in the treatment of unretractable foreskin," *Eur J Surg*, 1996; 162:969-972.

Lynch MJ, Pryor JP, "Uncircumcision: A one-stage procedure," *BJU*, 72: 257, 1993.

Marcus J, et al., "Tissue Expansion: Past, Present, and Future," *Journal of the American Academy of Dermatology*, vol. 23, no. 5, pt. 1, Nov. 1990, p. 814.

Mohl P, et al., "Prepuce Restoration Seekers: Psychiatric Aspects," *Archives of Sexual Behavior*, vol. 10, no. 4, 1981, p. 383.

Olenius M, et al., "Mitotic Activity in Expanded Human Skin," *Plastic and Reconstructive Surgery*, vol. 91, no. 2, February 1993, p. 215.

Pasyk K, et al., "Quantitative Analysis of the Thickness of Human Skin and Subcutaneous Tissue Following Controlled Expansion with a Silicone Implant," *Plastic and Reconstructive Surgery*, vol. 81, no. 4, April 1988, p. 522.

Penn J, "Penile reform," *Br J Plast Surg*, 16: 287, 1963.

Rubin J, "Celsus' decircumcision operation," Urology, 16: 121, 1980.

Schneider T, "Circumcision and Uncircumcision," *S Afr Med J*, 50; 556, 1976.

Schulthesis, D, Truss, MC, Christian, GS, Udo, J, "Uncircumcision: A Historical Review of Preputal Restoration," *Plastic and Recon Surg*, 1998, Vol. 101, 1990-8.

Tushnet L, "Uncircumcision," *Medical Times*, 93; 588, 1965.

Wright J, "Treatment of childhood phimosis with topical steroid," *Australian and New Zealand J Surg*, 1994; 64:327-328.

ADDITIONAL

Acupuncture Today, "Ice Age Acupuncture?," June 2000, Volume 01, Issue 06.

Frisch M, Friis S, Kjear SK, Melbye M, "Falling incidence of penis cancer in an uncircumcised population (Denmark 1943-90)," *BMJ*, vol. 311, no. 7018: 1471, 02 December 1995.

Gairdner D, "The Fate of the Foreskin: A Study of Circumcision," *BMJ*, Dec. 24, 1949, 2: pp. 1433-1437.

Ganiatis TG, Humphrey BC, et al., "Routine Neonatal Circumcision: A Cost-Utility Analysis," *Medical Decision Making*, vol. 11, No. 4, p. 282, Oct-Dec. 1991.

Morgan WKC, "The Rape of the Phallus," *JAMA*, vol. 173: July 2, 1960.

Nguyen TC, Volmer KE, Holcroft CJ, Domico SG, et al., "Prune Belly Syndrome Caused by Phimosis," *Society for Fetal Urology, International Maternal/Fetal Organization*, Winter 2001 Newsletter. **Note**: Prune Belly Syndrome is an inherited condition. Phimosis may occur from Prune Belly Syndrome, but phimosis does not cause Prune Belly Syndrome.

Schoen EJ, "Ode to the Circumcised Male," [Letter], *American Journal of Diseases in Children*, Vol. 141; p. 128, February 1987.

White C, "Little evidence for effectiveness of scientific peer review," *BMJ*, 2003;326:241 (1 February).

Made in the USA
Charleston, SC
14 October 2010